AT THE FAIR.

"San Francisco at the Fair" by Edward Jump portrays one hundred fifty-eight prominent citizens at the Mechanics' Institute Industrial Fair in 1864. Among those mentioned in the *Call* by Clemens are the bearded Judge Shepheard (*second row from the top, two to the right of center*) and the Reverend Dr. Henry J. Bellows (just below and to the judge's left).

CLEMENS OF THE CALL

Samuel Clemens in the middle 1860's (*from a photo by Bradley and Rulofson, The Mark Twain Papers*).

CLEMENS OF THE Call

Mark Twain in San Francisco

Edited by Edgar M. Branch

UNIVERSITY OF CALIFORNIA PRESS

BERKELEY AND LOS ANGELES

1969

PS1302
.B7

item in a state of semi-con-
sciousness & entire absent-
mindedness & added my Ar-
abella's name to the list.
This sort of thing won't do,
you know. Some day, I'll
make a mistake & publish
her as arrested for arson
or manslaughter, or shop-
lifting, or infanticide, or
some other little eccentricity
of the kind, & she'll notify me
to inflict my company & my
extraordinary attentions
on somebody else. I'll go
& see her now! I'll go & fall
down on my knees & say "O,
my own —
        (Cries of Murder! without)
Thunder & blazes! here's an
item!"   [Exit.]

In the background of this page and the preceding page are the first two hand-
written pages of Twain's unfinished play "Brummel and Arabella," where a
young reporter scolds himself for letting his romance interfere with his work.

Grateful acknowledgment is made to Harper & Row,
Publishers, for permission to quote from pp. 254–257,
258–260, *Mark Twain in Eruption* by Mark Twain,
edited by Bernard De Voto (copyright 1922 by Harper
& Brothers, renewed 1940 by The Mark Twain Company), and from pp. 136–137, 138, 143–144, *Roughing
It* by Mark Twain.

UNIVERSITY OF CALIFORNIA PRESS, BERKELEY AND LOS ANGELES, CALIFORNIA
UNIVERSITY OF CALIFORNIA PRESS, LTD., LONDON, ENGLAND
PRINTED IN THE UNITED STATES OF AMERICA. DESIGN BY DAVID COMSTOCK

FOR MY MOTHER AND MY FATHER,
MARIAN MARQUESS BRANCH
AND
RAYMOND SYDNEY BRANCH

PREFACE

Samuel Clemens reported the city news for the San Francisco *Daily Morning Call* during approximately four months in 1864. This book examines the relationship between the reporter and his paper, and it presents a selection from those *Call* writings that I attribute to Clemens. The pieces reprinted here frequently are interesting for their style and for what they tell us of the author's attitudes and experience. Also they are a record of events in San Francisco during the summer and early fall prior to President Lincoln's reelection. They made good reading then, and by and large they still do today. When a writer as creative as Clemens takes a city like San Francisco for his daily beat, is it surprising that the sparkle remains even a century later?

In making my selections I used the *Call* files at the Bancroft Library in Berkeley, California, and at the Los Angeles Public Library. Most of my reading for this study was done in the Bancroft Library and in the nearby room housing the Mark Twain Papers, an ideal combination of resources for the job. The selections are grouped topically, but within each group chronology is observed except in two instances where closely related reports have been juxtaposed. Headnotes to individual items and prefaces to sections provide identifications and relevant background information.

A word about the topical organization. My original plan called for a chronological arrangement, which might facilitate future stylistic and biographical studies. But before long it appeared doubtful that the accidents of time, which determined what Clemens reported from day to day, also should determine the organization of this book. For one thing, two hundred diverse newspaper reports linked by chronology formed a disorganized mass of information, whereas, with some rearrangement genuine patterns within the *Call* writing began to emerge, especially those made by series of reports referring to one event or to a continuing situation. These items in series made full sense only when grouped together, and their juxtaposition sometimes brought to light additional evidence of their authenticity. Thus, strong considerations argued against strict chronology, at least to the extent of making bundles of related pieces that reported ongoing events such as the reassembly of the monitor *Camanche* or the ceremonies opening the new Ning Yeung temple.

Nearly all the selections, however, whether in series or not, tended to fall into groups defined by subject matter or categories of news coverage. Clemens had suggested as much in the discussion of his *Call* reporting in *Mark Twain in Eruption.* Even so, did not the utility to stylistic studies afforded by chronology still take precedence over the clarity resulting from topical grouping? Keeping this question in mind while taking another look at the *Call* reports, I observed once more the literary excellence of scattered pieces as well as the random evidence of Clemens' lively imagination and brilliant phrasing. I noted the growing intensity of his denunciations of incompetent officials and the increase in his satirical political reports as election day neared. But I saw little, if any, change in stylistic quality per se or in journalistic skill, excepting, perhaps, the more frequently jaded manner toward the end. The reasons for this seemed fairly obvious. Local news reports were not the ideal medium for developing literary effects, and four months was a relatively brief time for pronounced literary trends to show up in the work of a busy reporter. Moreover, Clemens was an old hand at local reporting, having developed approaches and routines in Virginia City that served him reliably in San Francisco. In short, a major justification for a chronological arrangement, namely, its usefulness in revealing stylistic change, did not materially apply to the *Call* reports, whereas a topical grouping offered the compelling advantages of clarity and greater meaningfulness.

To be sure, students of Mark Twain's literary development will find the *Call* reports valuable, but chiefly as a unique body of Twain's writing, having numerous relationships, including style, to his earlier and later productions. A chronological ordering of my selections would not have clarified these relationships. But it would have obscured the meaningful connections between the *Call* reports that prove illuminating when highlighted by topical arrangement.

Considered as biographical documents, the *Call* reports tell us much about the environment Clemens worked in and the variety of demands made upon him by his job. Their record of his attitudes and interests and of the subjects that claimed his attention opens a broad avenue into his mind. But it was apparent that a chronological arrangement of two hundred diverse pieces confronted the student with a difficult task of disentanglement. On the other hand, a topical organization preserving chronological arrangement within each group, suggested the relative importance of subjects and interests at the same time it revealed continuities or changes in attitude. It focused, for instance, upon Clemens' growing concern over the business practices of mining corporations, his attitude toward courtroom witnesses, his treatment of urban crime. Behind my preference for the topical over the chronological was the assumption that we experience in a fashion both cumulative and selective, partially shaping the meaning of each new event in terms of similar events remembered from the past, just as Clemens' experience of a succession of earthquakes over four months produced a snowballing of humorous speculation on causes and consequences. Clearly, a strictly chronological arrangement would fragment and obscure such subjective patterns. I concluded that because of the nature of the *Call* material, stylistic and biographical studies both would be served best by making my basic divisions topical.

In the *Call* pieces reprinted here I have changed a few slips in grammar and a few misspellings, although the alternate contemporary spellings *mattrasses, villany,* and *villanous* have been retained as possibly being those preferred by Clemens. The use of incorrect names and misspellings of proper names have not been corrected. I have, however, altered *Cathrine wheels* to *Catherine wheels,* in line with Clemens' spelling of the name Catherine elsewhere at this time; the *e* in *Cathrine* probably was dropped because of the line-end hyphenation of the name in the *Call* (Cath-rine). I have inserted hyphens (as in *twenty-five*) only when their use follows Clemens' known preference and not in such instances as the pun *lick-her ing* (liquoring) and the word *re porter* when it appears in a drunk's monologue. Most of my other changes, including the substitution of one punctuation mark for another, were called for, it would seem, because of printers' slips. *Call* typesetters often omitted the commas and the periods in figures expressing large sums of money, although they left spaces for them (as in $212 274 259 45). I have silently inserted the punctuation in those instances. Also I have silently regularized a very few capitalizations in the titles of items. Otherwise, all my emendations are listed below.

EMENDATIONS

Page	Line	Emended Form	Original Form
17	24	anointing	annointing
41	8	semi-monthly	semi monthly
57	16	unctuous	unctious
60	25	orders so that	orders that
61	4	patriots	partriots
65	32	was waiting	were waiting

Page	Line	Emended Form	Original Form
67	1	fitted	dtted
90	35	Catherine wheels	Cathrine wheels
92	28	b. stallion	b stallion
97	11	in attending	io attending
97	14	as much as any	as much an any
97	9	science, art	science art
100	42	extends	extend
106	25	pines. The	pines; The
108	30	hers	her's
110	14	twenty-five	twenty five
118	12	. Immediately	. immediately
145	2	Marsh	Masrh
151	12	strychnia, lately	strychnia; lately
158	13	stand,	stand;
163	19	green-backs	green backs
166	24	seventy-five	seventy-five
169	30	fifty-eight	fifty eight
176	4	non-committal	non committal
186	33	thirty-five	thirty five
192	7	forty-ninth	forty ninth
197	4	guard-house	guard house
213	44	others swore	other swore
215	14	corroborate	corrobborate
223	7	and it should	and should
227	17	found	founc
249	4	shells	shell
269	41	attendant	attendent
274	25	day, on	day; on
274	27	roost	roast
276	11	fratricidal	fraticidal
276	16	begun	began
276	23	Administration. We	Administration, We
277	13	irresistibly	irresistably

Finally, my frequent use of the name *Clemens* instead of *Mark Twain* is deliberate and goes to the heart of this book. Clemens, the anonymous local reporter tied to his routine, was not Mark Twain, the writer of sparkling humor and of fiction, despite their connections both public and subterranean. What the *Call* required of Clemens was not the expression in writing of Mark Twain's irrepressible genius. Nevertheless, what it did require afforded Clemens valuable new experience and also served as a creative irritant, a combination that had much to do with the full emergence of Mark Twain.

I wish to thank the staff of the Bancroft Library and especially Mr. John Barr Tompkins, the late Mrs. Helen Bretnor, Mr. Cecil Chase, Mr. James Kantnor, Mrs. Alma Compton, and Mr. Robert H. Becker, the Assistant Director, for their professional and courteous help during portions of three summers. Also, I wish to thank Mr. Frederick Anderson, Editor of the Mark Twain Papers, and Mr. Henry Nash Smith for numerous kindnesses and for making the resources in their custody available. To Mr. Anderson I am deeply grateful for his early reading of most of the *Call* pieces here reprinted and for his subsequent encouragement. Both Mr. Anderson and Mr. Tompkins generously answered my written appeals for help with difficult points. My thanks also go to Professor James D. Hart for his helpful suggestions.

I am grateful to the following persons who granted me access to other useful materials and who, in many instances, undertook investigations at my request: Mrs. Clara S. Beatty, Director, and Mrs. Marion Welliver, Nevada Historical Society, Reno; Mr. Robert J. Armstrong and Mr. Roger Tissier, University of Nevada Library, Reno; Mr. James de T. Abajian, California Historical Society Library, San Francisco; Mrs. Helen S. Giffen and Miss Dolores W. Bryant, Society of California Pioneers, San Francisco; Mr. Albert Harmon, San Francisco Maritime Museum; Mr. Roy Graves, Mr. Peter Tamony, and Miss Marjorie Anne Brown, all of San Francisco; Mr. Allan R. Ottley, California State Library, Sacramento; Miss Mary Isabel Fry, Huntington Library, San Marino; Mr. James E. Vale and Miss Yetive Applegate, Los Angeles Public Library; Mr. Kenneth Holmes, State Historical Society of Missouri, Columbia; Mr. Ralph Gregory, Mark Twain Birthplace Memorial Shrine, Florida, Missouri; Mr. Chester L. Davis, Mark Twain Research Foundation, Perry, Missouri; Miss Doris A. Foley, Public Library, Keokuk, Iowa; Mr. Felix Pollak, University of Wisconsin Memorial Library, Madison; Mrs. Elizabeth R. Martin, Ohio Historical Society, Columbus; Mr. Archie Green, University of Illinois Institute of Labor and Industrial Relations, Champaign; Miss Anne Freudenberg, Alderman Library, University of Virginia, Charlottesville; Mrs. Rae Korson, Library of Congress; Mrs. Lillian Tonkin, the Library Company of Philadelphia; Mrs. Lola L. Szladits of the Henry W. and Albert A. Berg Collection, Mr. Robert W. Hill, and Mr. Richard Jackson, New York Public Library; Miss Ellen Kenny, Buffalo and Erie County Public Library; Mrs. Christine D. Hathaway, Brown University Library, Providence; Mr. Donald

Gallup, Curator, Collection of American Literature, Mrs. Anne Whelpley, and Mr. Kenneth M. Nesheim, Beinecke Rare Book and Manuscript Library, Yale University, New Haven.

The library staff at Miami University has been helpful in many ways, and in particular I wish to thank Mr. Leland S. Dutton, Mr. John W. Weatherford, Mr. Peter Flinterman, Miss Mary D. Stanton, Mrs. Esther R. Crist, and Mr. Charles E. Irvin. To Mr. David Wykes, Mr. Larry Rosenthal, Miss Margaret Bonner, Miss Margaret Globig, Mr. Randall Mawer, and Mrs. Kathleen Herndon Harrick, all of whom worked long and cheerfully on the preparation of this book, I am especially indebted. I want to thank Mr. Phillip R. Shriver for directing me to useful information. The Miami University administration gave generous financial aid, as recommended by the University Senate Committee on Research. My grateful acknowledgment goes to both. Finally, to Mary Jo and Marian my thanks for lightening the toil and sharing the adventure that went into this book.

The Yale University Library has granted permission to quote from the Mark Twain Scrapbook in its Collection of American Literature, and the Bancroft Library at the University of California has granted permission to quote from materials in its custody. The Mark Twain Company has agreed to my quotation of other previously unpublished writings by Mark Twain. Harper and Row, Publishers, has permitted extensive quotation from *The Writings of Mark Twain,* Definitive Edition, and from *Mark Twain in Eruption,* edited by Bernard DeVoto. Various illustrations are used with the permission of the Bancroft Library, the Society of California Pioneers, the California Historical Society, the San Francisco Maritime Museum, The Mark Twain Company, Roy D. Graves, and Milton Meltzer. Nine of these illustrations have been redrawn by Steven Johnson. To all these institutions and persons I wish to express my gratitude.

Edgar M. Branch

CONTENTS

Contents *xv*

Part Two

CRIME AND COURT REPORTER/137

Part Three

CRITIC AND POLITICAL REPORTER/207

Contents

Appendices

INTRODUCTION

"THE WIDEST REPUTATION
AS A LOCAL EDITOR"

In his 1909 essay "The Turning-Point of My Life" Mark Twain singled out some links in the chain of circumstance that he believed had made him a writer. Circumstance, he explained, brought him to Nevada, where he wrote his Josh sketches, his earliest contributions to the Virginia City *Territorial Enterprise*. Because Joe Goodman, the editor of that newspaper, liked them, "the *Enterprise* . . . put me on its staff. And so I became a journalist—another link. By and by Circumstance and the Sacramento *Union* sent me to the Sandwich Islands for five or six months" [1]—he was on the direct road to *The Innocents Abroad,* and journalism had placed him there.

In such fashion Mark Twain briefly acknowledged the importance of western newspaper work to his career. But his statement skipped over the eighteen months he gave to San Francisco journalism, including the four months from June to October 1864 when he reported the local news for the *Morning Call*. Nowhere in the "Turning-Point" essay did he dignify his experience on the *Call* by designating it specifically as a link. Nor did he ever create a fictional character who was a big-city reporter, except in the early unfinished play "Brummell and Arabella" and fleetingly in *Roughing It*. Not until 1906, in fact, did he discuss the *Call* job in writing and did so only then, it appears, because he saw a picture of the *Morning Call* building reduced to its iron skeleton by the San Francisco earthquake. Moreover, the earthquake offered a first-rate opportunity to reflect on the ways of Providence. Simultaneously it awakened memories—hardly less convulsive than itself—of Bret Harte as Clemens the *Call* reporter had first known him in mid-1864. Giving in to this irresistible combination and wishing to explain his early relationship with Harte, Clemens for once freely dredged up memories of his work on the *Call:*

> About forty years ago—I was a reporter on the *Morning Call* of San
> Francisco. I was more than that—I was *the* reporter. There was no
> other. There was enough work for one and a little over, but not
> enough for two—according to Mr. Barnes's idea, and he was the
> proprietor . . .
>
> After having been hard at work from nine or ten in the morning
> until eleven at night scraping material together, I took the pen and
> spread this muck out in words and phrases and made it cover as much
> acreage as I could. It was fearful drudgery, soulless drudgery, and
> almost destitute of interest . . . I got to neglecting it . . . Mr.
> Barnes discharged me. It was the only time in my life that I have
> ever been discharged, and it hurts yet . . .[2]

Mark Twain's long silence on his days as a San Francisco local reporter
—or local editor, as the position sometimes was called—is understandable. The work had not satisfied him at the time; as early as 1869 he was
eager to lay the ghost of his semibohemian life in the West, and as late as
1906 the memory of his discharge still rankled.

Yet Clemens' work on the *Call* constituted the main link in his experience between the busy *Territorial Enterprise* office in Virginia City,
Nevada, and his friend Jim Gillis' isolated cabin at Jackass Hill, California, near where, in the course of his lazy visit, Clemens stumbled on a
literary bonanza in the jumping frog story.

Moreover, the *Call* kept Clemens professionally active. During the
four months of his employment, the *Call* published between five and six
thousand local items—a figure that includes brief squibs, fillers, and puffs
—many of which were his. This book presents a selection of two hundred
and six *Call* pieces, including the eight worked into my prefaces, that I
believe Clemens wrote. Other books have assembled his Western
sketches, and still others have collected his Nevada journalism. Notably
Mark Twain of the Enterprise and *Mark Twain: San Francisco Correspondent,* both edited by Henry Nash Smith and Frederick Anderson,
have included most of Mark Twain's extant correspondence—his out-of-
town "Letters"—to the *Territorial Enterprise*. Portions of other *Enterprise* letters picked up by the *Golden Era* may be found in Franklin
Walker's *The Washoe Giant in San Francisco*. This book includes no
newspaper correspondence. Rather, it brings together the local editor's
day-in-and-day-out reporting—a term that should be taken in a broad
and flexible sense. For, just as the self-advertising Mark Twain of the
Enterprise poured factual information, humorous chitchat, and fanciful
anecdotes into the mold of his letters, so the anonymous *Call* reporter
Sam Clemens went well beyond the factual itemizing of local events.

Clemens came to the *Call* an experienced local. He had joined the

Virginia City *Territorial Enterprise* on the strength of his humorous journalism, which Joe Goodman continued to encourage, but on that paper his primary duty was to handle the city news. He and Dan De Quille (whose real name was William Wright) divided the work and "often cruised in company," [3] as Clemens also did with reporters from rival papers. Probably local itemizing was a major responsibility, on and off, for about twelve of the twenty months he was with the *Enterprise*. At various times he took on other responsibilities that temporarily removed him from the routine of miscellaneous news gathering. Covering two sessions of the Territorial Legislature and a State Constitutional Convention in Carson City trained him in political reporting. Three visits to San Francisco and shorter stays at Lake Tahoe and Steamboat Springs permitted a more varied kind of out-of-town correspondence. Also, for an undetermined period of time Clemens acted as managing editor during Joe Goodman's two months' absence in the spring of 1864. Nevertheless, William C. Miller's estimate that Clemens published 1,500 to 3,000 local items in the *Enterprise* is not excessive.[4] For long periods Clemens was a legman for his paper. Dan De Quille wrote that they both were hard pressed to cover the news at the height of the boom times and especially after the big fire of August 1863, which led to overcrowding in the unburned sections of Virginia City. "Mark and I had our hands full, and no grass grew under our feet. There was a constant rush of startling events; they came tumbling over one another as though playing at leap-frog." [5] Under favorable and exciting conditions Clemens soon mastered the routine of daily reporting. In the summer of 1863 he wrote home in the assured tones of one who placed a high value on his professional status: "Ma, you have given my vanity a deadly thrust. Behold, I am prone to boast of having the widest reputation as a local editor of any man on the Pacific Coast." He did not agree with her opinion that "a place on a big San Francisco daily" would work to his advantage either "this side of the mountain or the other." [6]

Today we have fewer than fifty local items from the *Territorial Enterprise* presumably written by Clemens. These may be seen in the Moffett Scrapbooks, in rare copies of the *Enterprise* for 1862 to 1864, and in a few reprints preserved in other papers. Many of them were written early in 1863 when Dan De Quille was making a visit to his family in Iowa. Most are straightforward and factual. They speak of stock values, mining and mill yields, mine incorporations, fights, shootings, court cases, deaths, Indian activities, last night's concert, a meeting of the Library Association. In themselves they offer little evidence of Clemens' authorship. Other local items of the same period betray more distinctive handling. In some the telltale idiom flares out: a Washoe zephyr obscures the heavens with "vast clouds of dust all spangled over with lumber, and shingles, and dogs and things." [7] Others display familiar patterns of imagination, as in "Due Notice," where absurdly inflexible logic joins with fancied aggression. "Moralists and philosophers," the local proclaims, "have adjudged those who throw temptation in the way of the erring, equally guilty with those who are thereby led into evil." It follows that if his neighbor's "old gobbler," "suffered to run at large," should disappear, his neighbor is "as culpable as ourself," for "Turkey stuffed with oysters is our weakness . . . Wonder if those fresh oysters at Allmack's are all gone? We grow ravenous—pangs of hunger gnaw our vitals—if to-morrow's setting sun gleams on the living form of that turkey, we yield our reputation for strategy." [8] Here the impersonal report virtually disappears in the miniature personal essay. The humor of the ravenous belly and the murderous eye arouses the raucous laughter of "the boys" while the local comically exculpates the guilt of his ferocious greed. "Due Notice" is only a step away from Mark Twain's more elaborately fanciful aggressions against the Unreliable (Clement T. Rice) and Dan De Quille in the *Enterprise* columns.

Mark Twain wrote in *Roughing It* that as he worked into his *Enterprise* job he "ceased to require the aid of fancy to any large extent" and succeeded in filling his columns "without diverging noticeably from the domain of fact." [9] But it is very likely that at no time in his *Enterprise* reporting was he able for long to discard "fancy" for objectivity. Dan De Quille remembered that Clemens gave only "a lick and a promise" to the " 'cast-iron' items," those dealing with "figures, measurements and solid facts," but that he became "enthusiastic" in reports that suited him.[10] Early in 1864 a Virginia City journalist writing under the name of Meriden criticized Clemens' local reporting for its deviation from accepted norms:

> His satire tends to the amusement of his publishers only, when he ornaments a church item with such a remark as "dusty old Christian;" or when, in describing a public school, he rides to the humorous necessity of mentioning "an auburn-haired juvenile, who wiped his nose with his fingers in so audible a manner as to require due castigation from the teacher;" or, when he intermixes . . . numerous other familiarities equally contemptible in the literary sense, and equally scandalizing to the reportorial profession and public journalism.[11]

Meriden unerringly put his finger on other of his colleague's stylistic trademarks, including the expressions "so to speak," "as it were," and "infernal humbug."

Another anonymous writer, who asserted that he had worked with Clemens for a short time on the *Enterprise,* found the "freedom with which Sam Clemens sketched the 'news' "—precisely what Meriden disliked—to be breathtaking, a godsend that punctured "unto death the heavysides of brainless fact that in its narrowness becomes falsehood." As a local in Virginia City, Clemens aimed at "the poetic truth, and the jocular truth . . . He touched his matter with an edge as keen as the Damascus blade . . . He had a clear, buoyant, original brain, and was himself . . ." [12] Both Clemens' detractor and his partisan testify to the distinctive manner and freewheeling approach evident at times in his *Enterprise* reporting. When he went to the *Call* he could write with anonymous impersonality, but also he had developed a style that was "buoyant, original," and essentially "himself." That style appears in literally hundreds of his *Call* reports, sometimes incidentally, or briefly in a flashing phrase or two, and sometimes as a full-fledged strategy of humor or satire.

For some time scholars have known two of Clemens' 1864 *Call* writings: "A Small Piece of Spite" and "Due Warning." This book reprints those pieces and more than two hundred others that I attribute to Clemens. They fall under three heads: "The Local at Large," "Crime and Court Reporter," and "Critic and Political Reporter." The first group includes reports on the general run of local events, such as yesterday's earthquake, minor street accidents, human-interest tidbits, public meetings, developments in the business, labor, and Chinese communities, the latest at the theaters and the race track, civic events like the July Fourth celebration, and an occasional catastrophe like the explosion of the steamer *Washoe.* Also included here are a few virtuoso pieces brought together as "Five Sketches." The second group focuses on the local's crime and court reports: his inspection of the inmates of station house and jail, his regular Police Court notices and his less frequent write-ups of district and circuit court cases, and an occasional lead article on a murder or attempted "assassination." The final group shows off the *Call* local as critic-at-large and political reporter. Like a frustrated editorial writer, he often slipped in his say on the judicial process as he observed it. He castigated inefficient or irresponsible officials of various bureaus and boards. Writing in wartime, he reported military developments on the Coast and the political strife attending the Lincoln and McClellan campaigns.

Clemens' publications in the *Call* for 1864 make up the only sizeable body of his day-by-day local reporting that we have. They show him working under pressure and at the mercy of events, in contrast to the more controlled and favorable conditions he enjoyed as an out-of-town correspondent or as the owner-editor of the Buffalo *Express*. Some of them point ahead to later writings. They supply informative details for his biography for June through October 1864. From that period we have only six, or possibly seven, of his personal letters. Also relevant are a few of his written comments, ten pages in Paine's *Biography,* occasional references in contemporary publications, and reminiscences and letters of a small group of old-timers like George Barnes, Frank Soulé, and Joe Goodman. For such meager sources of information Clemens' daily *Call* writings provide a valuable context. They open a unique window on that brief stretch of his experience. If they do not provide a full view, they at least yield fascinating glimpses that help us to understand him better.

Unlike the Mississippi River and Clemens' boyhood Missouri, San Francisco never became a fantasy world for him, a home for great characters in his fiction. Village people, rather than city dwellers, usually flourished best in his imagination. Nevertheless, the insights he gained as an urban reporter were not inconsequential to his best creations. A comment he once made about his work for the *Territorial Enterprise* applies to his experience on the *Call:* "Reporting is the best school in the world to get a knowledge of human beings, human nature, and human ways. . . . Just think of the wide range of [a reporter's] acquaintanceship, his experience of life and society." Clemens' humorous substantiation of that statement drew on memories of his *Call* days:

> No other occupation brings a man into such familiar sociable relations with all grades and classes of people. The last thing at night—midnight—he goes browsing around after items among police and jailbirds, in the lock-up, questioning the prisoners, and making pleasant and lasting friendships with some of the worst people in the world. And the very next evening he gets himself up regardless of expense, puts on all the good clothes his friends have got—goes and takes dinner with the Governor, or the Commander-in-Chief of the District, the United States Senator, and some more of the upper crust of society. He is on good terms with all of them, and is present at every public gathering, and has easy access to every variety of people. Why I breakfasted almost every morning with the Governor, dined with the principal clergyman, and slept in the station house.[13]

No less than the lordly river pilot that he once was, the city reporter was exposed to the best and the worst in all kinds of people.

Moreover the decline from the boom days of '62 and '63 quickly accelerated while Clemens was with the *Call*. Financially he was hardly holding his own, and contact with members of "the upper crust of society" served to emphasize the real gulf between him and them. He was a "lokulitems"—the disparaging term for those whose main task was to grub for local news. His prospects for editorial advancement were not bright. Nor was his literary direction clear. In short, his life took on a new dimension of uncertainty and risk in the summer of 1864. Under such circumstances it would be surprising if the reporter's exceptional experience of "human beings, human nature, and human ways," including his daily awareness of the drifters and the dregs of society, had not proved especially meaningful to him then and later, as well, when he turned to fiction.

"THEY WANT ME TO CORRESPOND"

"These rotten, lop-eared, whopper-jawed, jack-legged . . . Californians . . . How I *hate* everything that looks, or tastes, or smells like California!"[14] For cause now unknown, the *Enterprise* reporter thus vented his rage in a letter home written from Nevada, probably early in 1863. Obviously California mattered greatly to him. San Francisco, especially, constantly drew him westward.

In February 1863 only the lack of a replacement kept him from taking "some comfort for a few days, in San Francisco,"[15] and by early April he had made the trip and was back at work. On 2 May he returned to "this Paradise" where he "lived like a lord"[16] for two months at the Lick House, and early in September he crossed over a third time. In "Those Blasted Children," written later in Nevada, he recorded his nostalgia for the city: "Ah me! Summer girls and summer dresses, and summer scenes at the 'Willows,' Seal Rock Point, and the grim sea-lions wallowing in the angry surf; glimpses through the haze of stately ships far away at sea, a dash along the smooth beach, and the exhilaration of watching the white waves come surging ashore . . . home again in a soft twilight, oppressed with the odor of flowers—home again to San Francisco, drunk, perhaps, but not disorderly."[17]

While he was in San Francisco during May and June 1863, he neglected his correspondence to the *Enterprise*—because "I have always got something more agreeable on hand"—and concluded later, "I believe they thought I wasn't coming back any more."[18] He was enjoying the "butterfly idleness"[19] that in *Roughing It* he assigned to a later period. "I suppose I know at least a thousand people here . . . and when I go down Montgomery street, shaking hands with Tom, Dick and Harry, it is just like being in Main street in Hannibal and meeting the old familiar faces."[20] Apparently he was a social success. He had two expensive suits made, and after a late breakfast he sometimes would not return to the Lick House until past midnight. He wrote home of excursions to the

Ocean House and Fort Point, of fun at the Willows and Hayes Park, and of trips to San Leandro, Benicia, Oakland, and Alameda. During his stay Miss Lotta and the Worrell Sisters played at Gilbert's Melodeon. Frank Mayo starred in *East Lynne, Othello,* and *Romeo and Juliet* at Maguire's Opera House. The American Theater presented a series of German plays, and the Metropolitan Theater booked an Italian opera troupe. But he preferred the San Francisco minstrels at the Eureka Minstrel Hall, featuring Billy Birch, Sam Wells, Ben Cotton, Rafaelle Abecco, George Coes, and Tommy Peel. "I *do hate* to go back to Washoe," [21] he wrote to his mother and sister on 1 June.

He had other reasons for staying. A letter to Orion dated 20 June shows that he had $1,200 in the bank, no debts, and a disposition to speculate in mining stock. Perhaps this was the period, mentioned by George Barnes, when Clemens "was accounted quite rich in this kind of property . . ." [22] By "visiting some of their haunts with those dissipated *Golden Era* fellows," [23] he smoothed the way for his first sketches in that paper. Also he arranged with the *Call* to do a series of letters from Nevada. About 20 May he wrote home: "They want me to correspond with one of the dailies here, & if they will pay me enough, I'll do it. (The pay is only a 'blind'—I'll correspond anyhow.)" [24] On 5 July, immediately after his return to Virginia City, he sent the first of his letters to the *Call.*

Like the other San Francisco papers, the *Call* publicized the Nevada mining boom in 1862 and 1863. It ran Washoe correspondence from "Argentoro" and "Observer," and it freely reprinted items from the *Enterprise* and other Nevada papers. Very likely, three of its *Enterprise* reprints of December 1862 were by Clemens, especially "Particulars of the Assassination of Jack Williams," the report of a desperado Mark Twain featured in *Roughing It* and recalled nostalgically in his old age.[25] The *Call* first mentioned Mark Twain by announcing his series of weekly letters that were to "set forth in his easy, readable style, the condition of matters and things in Silverland." [26] Ten chatty letters followed during the summer and fall of 1863. In addition, Mark Twain signed two brief telegrams and three "Dispatches by the State Line" in the 1863 *Call* (*see* Appendix B), which reported sensational events in Nevada, including two murders, the disastrous Virginia City fire of 28 August, and the Election Day turmoil less than a week later.[27] Mark Twain not only helped report the Nevada news in the *Call* but also helped make it. As his reputation grew, Argentoro sometimes recorded his doings, and Twain's controversy with James L. Laird of the Virginia *Union* rated unusual notice in the May 1864 *Call.*

Clemens spent six days at Steamboat Springs, Nevada, in August 1863,

trying to get over a bad cold. Soon after arriving, he wrote his eighth *Call*
letter, dated 20 August. It included "A Rich Decision," the effective first
version of the General Buncombe hoax later revised for Chapter 34 of
Roughing It. Possibly, this tale struck George Barnes and James Ayers of
the *Call* just right. Barnes recalled that "Mr. Clemens was at Steamboat
Springs, Nevada, for his health, when the letter was written offering him
a place on the CALL. He came down shortly after . . ." [28] No doubt his
coming down was made possible by Dan De Quille's return after almost
nine months' absence. Dan had arrived in San Francisco harbor 28
August, the day of the Virginia City fire. Learning by midnight that the
Enterprise office had escaped burning, he left for Nevada. Clemens, in
turn, left for San Francisco 6 September, probably for a vacation. A good
guess is that by then he had received Barnes's letter and planned to talk
with him, although he may have had no intention of changing jobs. He
had written home two weeks before: "Why, blast it, I was under the
impression that I could get such a situation as that [a place on a big San
Francisco daily] any time I asked for it. But I don't want it. No paper in
the United States can afford to pay me what my place on the 'Enterprise'
is worth." In part he was thinking of the mining stock sometimes given to
influential sagebrush reporters, and when he returned to Virginia City,
his September vacation over, presumably he still was "the most conceited
ass in the Territory." [29]

Nevertheless a lurking dissatisfaction with his life is suggested by
Pamela's comment in a letter the following spring: "My dear brother,
you talk of pursuing happiness, but never overtaking it." [30] Her remedy
—to turn to Christ Jesu—was not a specific for the "Washoe Christian"
who intimated three months later that the luxurious Occidental Hotel in
San Francisco was not only "Heaven on the half shell" but "Heaven on
the entire shell." [31] Washoe was a sorry contrast, no better than "a singed
cat" in appearance. It was a barren waste where the soul gets "caked with
a cement of alkali dust" and "the contrite heart finds joy and peace only
in Limberger cheese and lager beer." [32] Moreover, Fitzhugh Ludlow's
praise of Clemens' talents and Artemus Ward's urgent advice that he
"leave sage-brush obscurity" [33] for a wider audience were in his mind
early in 1864. On the *Enterprise,* to be sure, he was at least a cut above a
lokulitems, and much has been written about the freedom and the literary
opportunity that his position in Virginia City offered him. Yet Dan De
Quille was essentially right in observing that Mark Twain "wrote no long
stories or sketches for that paper." [34] There were the personalized reports,
the comic feuding, two hoaxes, a burlesque review, and the letters and
burlesque society columns written from San Francisco. But the closest he
came to writing developed sketches for the *Enterprise* may be seen in "Ye

Sentimental Law Student," "City Marshal Perry," and "Washoe—Information Wanted"; and it is unlikely that more ambitious efforts have been lost without a trace. On the other hand, in the late months of 1863 he published three lengthy sketches in the *Golden Era* ("How to Cure a Cold," "The Lick House Ball," and "The Great Prize Fight"), and early in 1864 two appeared in the New York *Sunday Mercury* ("Doings in Nevada" and "Those Blasted Children"). The busy local reporter perhaps had reason to believe that either New York or San Francisco would advance him as a literary comedian.

After almost two months in California, Joe Goodman returned to Virginia City 25 May 1864, at the very time Clemens was closing his "chapter of follies" [35] with James L. Laird, proprietor of the Virginia City *Daily Union,* and with the ladies of Carson City, the fiasco over Sanitary Fund contributions that precipitated his departure from Nevada. His irritation with Washoe and his need for a change are on record, and he may have planned a trip to New York to sell shares in a silver mine. [36] Apparently short of cash, he left with Steve Gillis on 29 May for San Francisco, intending to stay there a month and then go to the States. The Gold Hill *Evening News,* not without affection, called him an irreverent reprobate, "lost to society, lost," and John K. Lovejoy—Old Pi of the *Daily Old Piute*—lamented: "The world is blank—the universe worth but 57½, and we are childless. We shall miss Mark . . . to know was to love him . . . We can't dwell on this subject; we can only say—God bless you, Mark! be virtuous and happy." [37] Doing his best to be happy, Clemens registered at the Occidental Hotel on 8 June, about the time he took up his duties on the *Call.*

According to Bailey Millard, one of Clemens' successors as local editor of the *Call,* George Barnes said that Clemens appeared in Barnes's office and asked to be taken on as a reporter, telling "a hard-luck story about being out of money and out of work in a strange city. Mr. Barnes lent him five dollars, gave him a few assignments and after a while installed him as city editor." [38] The "strange city" does not ring true, but Barnes's recollection that Clemens "only wanted to remain long enough, he said, when he engaged to go to work, to make 'a stake,' "[39] fits with Clemens' intention to move on after a month. It also suggests a factual basis for the version in *Roughing It.*[40] There the Virginia City reporter, about to leave for San Francisco, fears that the coming change in Nevada from a territorial to a state government will destroy the flush times. He plans to cash in his stocks, hopefully on a rising market, and return to the East as a well-heeled prodigal. No doubt Mark Twain shaped the passage to suit his fiction. Yet Clemens' letter of 26 May to Orion shows that he still hoped to make something out of mining stock despite a spongy market:

"When I get to the Bay . . . I will fix the Hale and Norcross in a safe shape." [41] But the market, declining all year, broke sharply in midsummer. The sudden break, the need to pay assessments, even to keep what stocks he had, and the market's continuing weakness may explain why he stayed as long as four months on the *Call*, his purse, as Barnes noted, no heavier when he left in October than it had been in June. Unquestionably San Francisco had genuine attractions and opportunities for Clemens, but events and his own pride seem to have trapped him there for a longer time than he had hoped.

"IT WAS THE WASHERWOMAN'S PAPER"

The *Morning Call* was published every day but Monday. In June 1864 it was a compact paper of four eight-column pages, 18½ by 23½ inches in size. Priced at 12½ cents a week, it was the only "bit" paper in the city, substantially cheaper than its main competitors, the *Alta California* and the *Bulletin,* each a "four bit" paper, and, at two bits, the *Democratic Press* and the *American Flag.* During eight years of publication its subscription rate had not increased, but its physical size had tripled and its circulation had climbed steadily to about 10,000—the largest of any San Francisco daily. A few days before Clemens went to work, the *Call* began its sixteenth volume. The aim of "the cheapest paper in California," wrote the editor, was still "to afford to the masses a journal which would at once watch over their interests and convey to them as expeditiously as possible a knowledge of everything transpiring throughout the world." [42]

The *Call* had been born 1 December 1856 in a dingy room over the Blue Wing Saloon at 140 Montgomery Street. Five printers had pooled their resources to buy the stock of the dying San Francisco *Herald*. Calling themselves "An Association of Practical Printers," they gathered and wrote and edited the news and then set it in type. Even James J. Ayers, who had been the prime mover of the group and who handled most of the editing at first, put in time at the case. In February 1857 George Barnes bought into the paper. He and Ayers dominated the four-man partnership that came to be known as J. J. Ayers & Company. The paper's name was hit on by chance when the original founders noticed a poster advertising "A Morning Call," a one-act farce playing at the Metropolitan Theater and starring Charles Pope as Sir Edward Ardent and Mrs. Julia Dean Hayne as Mrs. Chillingtone.

In the face of stiff competition the cooperative venture began paying off after two years. But not until 1869 was the low-priced *Call* financially able to enter the telegraphic combine (controlled on the West Coast by the Sacramento *Union* and the *Alta California* and the *Bulletin* of San Francisco) and receive dispatches via the overland telegraph line that had been completed in 1861. In the meantime it fought gamely, pitting its ingenuity and a cocky spirit against the greater resources and impressive features of its rivals. Following a fire that burned it out of its quarters in November 1862, the *Call* before long moved into a new brick building at 612 Commercial Street. There in the third-floor editorial rooms Clemens was to write his items. The paper had a long and distinguished life. It kept its separate identity until 1929, when it merged with the *Bulletin*. In 1965, as the *News Call-Bulletin*, it was absorbed by the *Examiner*.

James J. Ayers, a primary founder of the Call (*redrawn from a contemporary portrait, Bancroft Library*).

Along with the other dailies, the 1864 *Call* printed city news that today often seems unusually trivial, but we must remember that in those days the only outlet for community news of a gossipy or sensational kind was the local column. Newspaper editors of the time rarely wrote about developments in industry, mining, railroads, farming, and real-estate operations. Then, as now perhaps, they were less sensitive to such matters than to political issues and to inflammatory social problems, which were the controversial questions debated on the editorial pages. In national politics the *Call* traditionally had supported the conservative Union-Democrats. But when war threatened and California seemed to teeter between staying with the Union and secession, the *Call* spoke out early for the Union. Its vigorous anti-Copperhead support of Lincoln in the 1864 presidential campaign is said to have temporarily cost it almost half its circulation. In local politics the *Call* was independent, and in 1864 it inclined to favor the Citizens' or Union party. It sharply criticized the powerful People's party, which had emerged in 1856 at the time of the second Vigilance Committee, for having become fat and corrupt. The paper charged it with supporting a gerrymandered redistricting bill and

George E. Barnes, Clemens' boss on the *Call*
(*redrawn from a contemporary portrait, Bancroft Library*).

with unnecessary proliferation of wasteful bureaus and boards, while it neglected the legitimate needs of the people. Moreover, asserted the *Call*, the People's party welcomed secessionist votes, and its elected officials, including Mayor Coon, sometimes acted like petty tyrants who were mainly interested in their "high salaries, prolonged terms of office, and profitable contracts." [43]

Somewhat in keeping with its reforming zeal in local politics, the *Call* often spoke up for the wage earner or the little man—so long as he was white. It stated the case for mistreated sailors and underpaid government workers. It took a special interest in the welfare of laborers or "mechanics." In 1864 it supported the right to strike as "the workingman's chief, if not his only barricade against the pressure of Capital's weighty column," [44] maintaining that the employer helped himself by paying a fair wage. It publicized the formation of a Trade Association Relief Fund in support of striking workers, and it argued for measures to improve safety on the job. In making its appeals, the *Call* was thinking of free Caucasian workers, for its labor policy rested partly but firmly on opposition to the labor contract system in state prisons and to Chinese immigration.

The *Call* regularly aired readers' complaints against the Chinese—about their alleged thievery, gambling, smuggling, and obstruction of the sidewalks. But basically the paper opposed the Chinese because "Coolie labor is ruining absolutely the business of many of our laboring men," and low-income laborers were a mainstay of the *Call's* subscription list. Chinese workers were "as unhealthy to the city as the small pox." They paid no taxes to speak of, owed no allegiance or military service, lied in court, and were "a nuisance as a neighborhood," the paper contended. From these premises the *Call* drew its historically ironic conclusion:

> Our sympathies are with our own race as against all others. Justice to all, but privileges, patronage, favors for our own people. While opposed to all oppression of the black or the yellow-skinned nations, our attachments are to those of our own blood, the pale faces. And we claim that in our legislation, so far as required, in this country the Caucasian should be considered superior to the Mongol, and should be protected at least, so far as treaties allow, against a ruinous competition in labor and trade.

Only in this way could a "civil war of the races" [45] be avoided.

At the same time that it urged restrictions for the Chinese, the *Call* supported Negro freedom—with qualifications. The Emancipation Proclamation was wise and just, and furthermore it was the duty of the white American "to atone for the huge wrong our Nation has done" to the Negro slaves. They were "worthy of freedom" because they had fought for it, said the *Call*. In 1864 San Francisco Negroes were seeking the freedoms to really exercise their suffrage, to testify with full rights in court, to ride unhindered in public conveyances, to march in the Fourth of July parade. The paternalistic *Call*, which had stated frankly that the real Negro question of the Coast was the Chinese question, urged gradual concessions to the city's Negro population. It did not believe the Negro to be equal "with the white race mentally," nor was it "prepared to say how far freedom, education, liberty, may, in the ages of the future, make him so." [46] As the *Call* management knew, Negroes did not pose the economic threat in their city that the Chinese did.

Clemens had known Negroes since his youth, and in Virginia City he had begun to understand the Chinese. He was more accustomed than most people to interracial fraternizing. In 1865 a contemporary observed him walking arm-in-arm with a San Francisco Negro journalist.[47] Because his freedom as a reporter and his attitude toward his job were to some degree affected by the *Call's* policy on Chinese-White relations, it may be appropriate to say a word here about James J. Ayers and George E. Barnes, the two men whose interests as proprietors led them to uphold that policy.

Ayers emigrated from Scotland in 1831 as a child, grew up in New York, and was trained in newspaper work on the St. Louis *Republican* before moving to California in 1849. There he began several papers, including the Calaveras *Chronicle,* before he helped establish the *Call.* He left the *Call* in 1866, briefly published the Hawaiian *Herald,* and eventually settled in Los Angeles, where he entered Democratic politics and continued to publish newspapers. Ayers had only a brief opportunity to get to know his new reporter in 1864, for he left on a long visit to the East on 22 June. Yet when the two men met in Hawaii in 1866, Clemens, only five years his junior, called him by his first name and ribbed him in his letters to the Sacramento *Union.* Ayers had followed Clemens' *Call* reporting with some uneasiness while he had been in the East, but he knew his former employee's worth as an entertaining writer and tried to get him to correspond for the *Herald.* Ayers noticed Clemens several times in the *Herald,* sometimes with irritation and sometimes with obvious respect; and in his book *Gold and Sunshine* he recorded his dissatisfaction with Clemens as a *Call* reporter and his relish for him as a man.

George Eustace Barnes was Clemens' boss on the *Call.* A large, handsome man, once called "the Adonis of the Press" [48] by a fellow journalist, he had gone as a boy from New Brunswick, Canada, to New York, where he became a printer on the *Tribune.* He drifted south and westward, and while on the *Call* he discovered his editorial ability. For a time in the mid-1860's he left journalism for mining, but soon he resumed editorial duties on the *Call* and began to take over the dramatic criticism. It was as drama critic that Barnes became well known later on the *Call* and, for a few years before his death in 1897, on the *Bulletin.* He was a kindly bachelor who led a proper, self-disciplined life, and not all his memories of his unpredictable reporter were sympathetic. Yet, in the main, Barnes and Clemens recalled each other with a sense of admiration and good fellowship, and Clemens understood the commercial need that led Barnes to support the restrictive racial policy of "the washerwoman's paper." [49]

"A REPORTER FOR A BRISK NEWSPAPER"

Very likely Clemens' first day on the job was Monday, 6 June.[50] Although it is known that Albert S. Evans (whose pseudonym was Fitz Smythe) had filled the position of local at the *Call* for several years before the early spring of 1864, when he joined the *Alta California,* Clemens' immediate predecessor is not known. Local reporters for other San Francisco dailies at the time included Frank W. Gross, Delos J. Howe, and R. M. McHenry. Clemens was an experienced journalist with a wider reputation than any of these. His hiring may have been part of a move to strengthen the paper, for a week earlier the management had stated that it wanted to provide "a more elaborate and satisfactory amount of local and general news." [51] Clemens' daily job entailed long and irregular hours. By midmorning he was checking Police Court records, beginning a day that might end only with the two o'clock deadline the following morning. He wrote in *Roughing It* that his weekly wage was thirty-five dollars, and later he was reported to have put the figure at fifteen dollars, but it probably was forty dollars.[52]

John McComb of the *Argus* observed that Clemens as local editor "had something else to do than sit at his desk," for, he continued, "Mark used generally to look out for the late police news, would report a lecture or anything that came to hand." [53] Clemens' account of his news-gathering specifically mentions only three regular beats: the Police Court, the higher courts, and the theaters. "During the rest of the day," he added, "we raked the town from end to end, gathering such material as we might . . ." [54] No doubt, bits of news sometimes were brought into the office, as "Mr. Bloke's Item" [55] was, but the "lazy" Clemens still had to range far and wide. Raking the town and reporting whatever came to hand in a city of San Francisco's size and character implies a responsibility for writing up a greater variety of events than his account indicates. The selections in this volume alone show that his job took him far beyond the courts and the theaters. In his run-of-the-mill items he reported occurrences as different as the latest earthquake, the races at Bay View Park, a meeting of hard-money advocates, the finding of an abandoned painting, and a strike of steamer employees. He attended and summarized meetings of the Board of Supervisors (the town council) and the Board of Education. He puffed local merchants and enterprises. He handled special continuing assignments like the Industrial Fair and covered some political gatherings. He wrote lead articles on important civic events and on sensational crimes and accidents. He contributed a few sketches and some articles pungently expressing his opinions on topics close to his heart. In fact, he was responsible for many pieces of considerable length and prominence.

When news was scarce, Clemens still had to produce his quota of words. He and the other reporters, he wrote, gathered "such material as we might, wherewith to fill our required columns—and if there were no fires to report we started some." [56] The exaggerated last comment is true to the spirit of many newspaper items of the time: the fillers, long on fluff and short on fact. The comment is doubly interesting because it may unconsciously reflect a memory of an event recorded in just such a *Call* filler published Friday 5 August 1864. President Lincoln had proclaimed the preceding Thursday a day of humiliation and of prayer for peace and forgiveness. On that day San Francisco churches held services, and public offices, schools, markets, banks, and many places of business closed down. But the Friday *Call* had to come out as usual—and it did, with this bit of padding:

> Almost an Item.—While "norating around" among the wharves yesterday, keeping the Fast, by reason of the last dime having been put into the collection-bag in the morning "for the benefit of the poor of the congregation," (of which we were one,) we discovered a speck of fire among broken up straw, which had communicated with the wharf timbers and promised fairly for an item. All this was at the corner of Clay and East streets. We took a position to watch the item growing, but alas! for human hopes; an energetic and public spirited young man who possessed an interest in a ready-made clothing store close by, conceived the wretched idea of squelching the item, which he accomplished with accelerated movements, by anointing the burning materials with a basin of water. The fire was doubtless the work of some careless smoker. We didn't mind the extinguishment, but the indignity of sousing our budding item with *dirty* water, provoked a profane utterance. [57]

Having expended his pious utterance in church, along with his last dime, the disappointed reporter turned to a more satisfying kind of prayer.

When speaking of his days on the *Call*, Clemens insisted that he was the paper's only local reporter while he worked full time. "There was enough work for one and a little over, but not enough for two—according to Mr. Barnes's idea . . ." [58] His letters of that period yield no hint that he shared his work with another *Call* reporter, and the fact that he had the paper sent home to his mother and sister suggests that he was at least a heavy contributor to its local columns, if not the only one. Moreover, the phrasing of most contemporary references to city reporters implies that the entire local staff of a given paper usually consisted of one man. On the other hand, John McComb of the *Argus* thought that Clemens worked with another *Call* reporter. Clemens seemed to say as much nine months after he had been fired. At that time he lightly criticized the *Call* local for taking some of his ideas to fill out an item, but then admitted: "I used to take little things from him occasionally when I reported with him on the *Call* . . ." [59]

The mystery is not entirely cleared up by George Barnes's enumeration of the *Call* editorial staff for the summer and fall of 1864. In reminiscing about Clemens, he wrote: "But they were pleasant days in the lang syne, if he was poor, when Soule, Ayers, Barnes, himself, and McGrew formed the whole staff of The Call in the cosy editorial rooms at 612 Commercial Street." [60] Ayers, as we have seen, left for the East soon after Clemens came on the job. Barnes's account makes clear that Frank Soulé,[61] a widely experienced journalist, took over some of the editorial work and proved particularly useful during the 1864 Presidential campaign. While Clemens raked in the city news, Soulé and Barnes must have written the editorials and the more weighty articles. Barnes went on to identify William K. McGrew, the fifth staff member, as a *Call* reporter. The 1865 city directory lists McGrew as the *Call's* local editor (probably the man Clemens criticized for borrowing his ideas) and also as a lawyer. The tail-end position of McGrew's name in Barnes's carefully ordered list suggests that the reporter was the lowliest member of the staff when Clemens was on it.[62]

During the summer and fall of 1864 McGrew may have had a specialized position on the *Call* staff that is not known today. Unless he worked full time, especially when Ayers was gone, the staff would have been small indeed. But the possibility also arises that William McGrew was the "hulking creature" that Mark Twain called Smiggy McGlural, the "good-natured, obliging, unintellectual" [63] person who assisted Clemens in his last month on the paper. Whether or not the inexperienced McGlural was McGrew, he was neither incompetent nor lazy. According to Mark Twain's later account, Smiggy worked with energy and enthusiasm, and as Clemens faded from the picture he took over increasingly. From late September on, in fact, the number of *Call* items suggesting Clemens' hand noticeably decreased, while at the same time a new and naïve spirit sometimes blew triumphantly through the local column. For example, having often been exposed to a chatty, irreverent tone in the city items, were *Call* readers startled by this description of the costume ball that closed the summer's Industrial Fair?

> Terpsichore and Apollo met at the Pavilion last night with their hosts of retainers. Orpheus was there with them; and with music and with dancing the hours wore away, until the time of night was represented by the small figures. There were about two thousand

persons present. . . . All the daughters of Flora were there—the stately Egyptian Lilly, cold and immaculate; the being of beauty and hauteur, the Rose, blushing at her own conquests . . . And then the male portion of the company were interesting, as presenting the different types of masculine beauty—shape and talent. Apollo, and old Charon himself, were industriously doing the agreeable. The affair passed off finely. There was no lack of enjoyment. . . .[64]

Because the item carries no hint of satire, one is tempted to lay it on Smiggy, who may have had his reasons for trying too hard. When Clemens read it, surely his fingers itched for a corrective pen.

In all likelihood, Smiggy McGlural was hired when Clemens arranged with Barnes to stop night work: someone had to handle the late news for the morning paper. The new arrangement, in effect by mid-September, permitted Clemens to enjoy shorter hours at reduced pay. He slept later, stopped work by 6:00 P.M., and still drew twenty-five dollars a week. Smiggy came on the job about the time Bret Harte began editing the *Californian,* with the 10 September number. Clemens believed that this journal was more "high-toned" [65] than the *Golden Era,* and before long he was using his leisure to write a weekly sketch for Harte at fifty dollars a month, direct evidence of his growing literary ambition. Also, he planned a book, encouraged by the praise of his friend the Rev. Dr. Henry W. Bellows, the president of the United States Sanitary Commission, who liked his *Call* writing. Frank Soulé recalled Clemens "scribbling" next to him in the *Call* editorial room with "grand aspirations," and George Barnes observed that Clemens was not by nature a bohemian but "was always looking to the end." [66] Clemens' wanderlust at the time—the thought of going to Asia and Mexico appealed to him—may have sparked his desire to improve his lot. Even more telling, he had put his cherished Hale & Norcross stock in Orion's name so that he might leave on a moment's notice without having to bother about it.[67]

Joe Goodman, William Wright, and John McComb all mentioned Clemens' dissatisfaction with the circumstances of his life in mid-1864. His discontent affected his *Call* writing, especially because the daily stint constantly teased his creativity without affording it a thoroughly satisfying release. Thus in his reporting he sometimes merely went through the motions, flippantly, disdainfully. Less than three weeks before he was fired, he wrote the brief "African Troubles":

No cause of complaint seems to be too insignificant to be brought before the Police Court. A negro, named Kane, appeared yesterday and set forth that he had a child boarding with a negro named Turner, and that for insignificant provocation, Turner set the child

down too roughly on a bench, or jammed him on it, or bounced him
on the floor. The case was dismissed.[68]

His boredom is evident. The comic-savage phrasing near the end of the
item signifies the stylist's reflex: Clemens' talent for language automati-
cally making at least a little out of nothing. Being subjected continually
to the event, often the trivial event, was irritating, an affront to his
constructive imagination. Describing the trial of Charles Lannigan for
robbery, he wearily observed: "Mr. Murphy proved that Lannigan's
character was good, because he had previously had opportunities of
stealing, but didn't steal, and Mr. Platt demonstrated that his character
was bad, because he had the opportunity of stealing, and did steal." [69]
Clemens wrote those words a few days before he and the *Call* parted
ways.

Mark Twain wrote no essay on local reporting, but he expressed
scattered opinions on the subject that sometimes implied a criticism of his
own news writing. In *Roughing It* he spoke of his scribbling "local
rubbish" and in "The Facts" he criticized items in San Francisco papers
for obscurity, pointlessness, and eccentric grammar. No doubt he liked to
think that his reports avoided those pitfalls, as they usually did, just as
he thought he used people's names skillfully to arouse the reader's interest. He recognized that newspaper policy often encouraged trivial and
sensational reporting. Nor were reporters above inventing items "to fill
out a local column," he commented in 1868. The "hurry of writing," he
continued, led to mistakes: "I know a good deal about that from experience." Was he again thinking of his reporting when he tried to teach
Buffalo *Express* reporters "to modify the adjectives, curtail their philo-
sophical reflections & leave out the slang"? About 1873 he mentioned
having published "vicious libels" in his newspaper writing. Later he
argued that a fundamental commandment for reporters was to avoid
"furtively venting their private spites through the columns of the paper"
and "trying to use the paper's power & influence for their private profit."
He knew something about those practices too.[70]

George Barnes recalled that Clemens was so slow in getting around his
news beat and so tortuously deliberate in writing the copy that he was the
most useless of local reporters. Because Clemens only "played at itemizing," Barnes wrote, "the paper was suffering in its local columns." [71] A
comparison of the local columns of the *Call,* the *Bulletin,* and the *Alta
California* indicates that Barnes had reason for dissatisfaction—although
today it is difficult to understand how one man, no matter how industrious, could have covered the local scene adequately. The local columns
of Albert Evans in the *Alta* usually are fuller than those in the *Call,* and

they show that Evans was more wound up in his work than Clemens was. Yet even Evans, whose reporting Barnes admired, made omissions and factual errors—even monumental bloopers.

James Ayers stated that Clemens' San Francisco items were deficient in "the plain, unvarnished truth," for in Virginia City Clemens had been encouraged "to give full play to his fertile imagination and dally with facts to suit his fancy . . ." [72] In speaking of "The Jumping Frog," Barnes, like Ayers, recognized Mark Twain's imaginative power: "His peculiar genius breathed upon inert material and gave it life and motion." [73] But Barnes and Ayers correctly felt that genius was somewhat miscast as a *Call* reporter, even though they may have valued the general appeal of Clemens' unorthodox journalism more than they ever admitted.

This book reprints some reports that are simply careless. A typical item that dallies playfully and intentionally with the facts—the sort of writing Ayers may have had in mind—is "Don't Bury Your Money in Oyster Cans" (reporters often supplied the heads to their items). Here it was not enough for the local to record the relevant details about the loss of a substantial sum of money buried in a can near a stable. He apparently felt compelled to add this sound but fanciful comment: "To bury money in a manure heap is a stupid way of disposing of it—all the manure on the Chinchas Islands will not make it grow. Better . . . to . . . invest in Government securities." [74] While reporting the ten-day sentence given to a wife-beater, he characterized the punishment as "a just and righteous equivalent for the enjoyment it must have afforded him to see his 'old woman' waltz around." [75] In San Francisco, as years before in Hannibal, stray dogs were a public nuisance, but they gave Clemens the opportunity to keep a good thing going. He injected the following aside into a sober write-up of the Board of Supervisors' regular meeting: "It is pleasant to know that during the month of August the Poundkeeper killed one hundred dogs, but that pleasure is greatly modified by the reflection that probably fifteen hundred were born during the same month." A week later in "The Pound-keeper Beheaded" he wrote: "The Board of Supervisors snatched the Pound-keeper out of office last night . . . Stray dogs will take notice, and demean themselves accordingly, with that recklessness of deportment warranted by their present freedom from consequences." Still later he slipped another message to the dogs: "Non-muzzled dogs will take notice that Joseph C. Gridley has been elected Poundkeeper, and will consequently refrain from skirmishing." [76]

Even in such brief and minor reports Clemens' fancy was active. Probably he often embroidered the facts merely to fill his columns or to vary the routine or just for fun. Sometimes he let his imagination soar when, in a savagely serious mood, he really needed the emotional release. At other times the mood he developed was more subtly mixed. For example, the sinking wharves fascinated him briefly. "The Old Nelson Restaurant," he wrote, "and the three or four buildings alongside, are canted out of the perpendicular, like a swell's hat, and the crazy stilts that still make a show of holding them up promise to throw up the contract shortly." Continuing a few days later, he coupled an alliterative, balanced style with a melancholy tone that carried a hint of mockery: "As sinks the aged man quietly into the grave, so silently settle the old wharves into the Bay, leaving a wretched wrecked aspect to remind us of the instability of earthly things. Fresh evidences of decay are daily exhibited among these old and uncertain structures. A new sink at the foot of Sacramento street repeats the story of time and the teredo." [77]

Evidence of an irrepressible imagination surprisingly often marks a *Call* report as his own. Like his fiction, his journalism often flares up and crackles with the fire of his personal style. His *Call* writing is potentially explosive. Even in the most routine items there can appear at any time the compelling phrase or the novel word combination that is exactly right —and beyond the reach of most reporters. Often the expression seems spontaneously original, like a reflex of sheer linguistic exuberance. Obviously his items drew on a vast reservoir of verbal raw material, a wealth of vernacular which included such special effects as the biblical style that laced through much of the writing. To be sure, he often used the straight treatment. He did his job as expected, by focusing neutrally on the event rather than bringing into play the idiosyncratic perception that transformed the event into a function of the vision. Moreover, when his subject was inherently dramatic and serious, he tended to keep in the background and to let the events speak for themselves in reporting that flowed easily. Sometimes when the subject touched him closely or spilled over into tabooed areas, he typically fell back on the pious, maudlin, or censorious clichés of polite rhetoric, unable to handle his topic otherwise. But by and large, a radical originality of style and personality—radical for local reporting, at least—makes itself felt. An indomitable quality— of funning, of criticism, of seeing things his own way—bubbles through his reports of frequently grubby and depressing human events.

The *Call* therefore was not simply a straitjacket that confined Clemens to writing pallid, neutral items—"the plain, unvarnished truth." As the selections in this book show, the newspaper permitted him leeway. Within limits that he stretched more than a little, he wrote much as he pleased and made numerous good hits. He was proud of some of his *Call* journalism. Yet as his later career demonstrates, the effervescence in his reporting gave evidence of a creativity that could not long remain bottled up, in important respects, as it had to be in what was supposed primarily to reflect the factual and the accidental. Even though he was not sure what direction to take in the autumn of 1864, by then he was ready to throw off the restraints on his writing that went with his job. Not long after leaving the daily routine of the *Call,* Clemens as though by instinct headed toward Tuolumne County for the freer life of pocket mining at Jackass Hill.

"THAT DEGRADED 'MORNING CALL'"

In 1906 Mark Twain reminisced about George Barnes's suppression of one of his local items, an event of considerable biographical interest. According to his account, after observing some street bullies abusing a peaceful Chinese, he wrote up the incident with warmth and indignation. "Usually I didn't want to read in the morning what I had written the night before; it had come from a torpid heart. But this item had come from a live one. . . . and so I sought for it in the paper next morning with eagerness. It wasn't there. . . . I went up to the composing room and found it tucked away among condemned matter on the standing galley. I asked about it. The foreman said Mr. Barnes had found it in a galley proof and ordered its extinction." [78] Barnes then informed him, Mark Twain wrote, that the paper could not afford to publish his piece because of its many Irish subscribers, who hated the Chinese. In his continuing account Twain made the censorship a key factor in his break with the paper.

During the early autumn of 1864, with "Smiggy McGlural looming doomfully in the near distance," Clemens knew himself to be, as he said, "a fading and perishing reporter." [79] The actual break came on or about 10 October. [80] George Barnes recalled the conversation that took place:

> . . . the managing editor observed one day, while he and Clemens were sitting in the editorial room:
> "Mark, do you know what I think about you as a local reporter?"
> "Well, what's your thought?"
> "That you are out of your element in the routine of the position, that you are capable of better things in literature."
> Mark looked up with a queer twinkle in his eye.
> "Oh, ya-a-s, I see. You mean to say I don't suit you."
> "Well, to be candid, that's about the size of it."
> "Ya-a-s. Well, I'm surprised you didn't find out five months ago."
> There was a hearty laugh. He was told his unfitness for the place was discovered soon after he entered on it . . .[81]

Clemens substantially agreed with Barnes's account when he wrote that he was tactfully "discharged" and that he "retired . . . by solicitation of the proprietor" and was "invited" or "advised" or given "an opportunity" to resign.[82]

To Rollin Daggett in 1878 Clemens wrote: "I always liked newspaper work; I would like it yet, but not as a steady diet." [83] A temperamental unfitness for his place on the *Call*, implied in his comment and affirmed by Ayers and Barnes, no doubt was basic to the dismissal. A quarter of a century later Rudyard Kipling listened to stories still going the rounds about Clemens' work habits: "In San Francisco the men of *The Call* told me many legends of Mark's apprenticeship in their paper five and twenty years ago; how he was a reporter delightfully incapable of reporting according to the needs of the day. He preferred, so they said, to coil himself into a heap and meditate until the last minute. Then he would produce copy bearing no sort of relationship to his legitimate work—copy that made the editor swear horribly and the readers of *The Call* ask for more." [84]

Clemens wrote that neglect of duty hastened his dismissal. The evidence does not suggest a spectacular failure in responsibility on a specific occasion, but a growing disinterest and a general lack of hustle. He indicated different reasons for neglecting his work. According to *Roughing It,* the lost opportunity for a big mine sale led to such "repinings and sighings and foolish regrets, that I neglected my duties and became about worthless, as a reporter for a brisk newspaper." [85] In the more plausible but still oversimplified version of 1906, he attributed the neglect to a loss of interest caused by the single instance of Barnes's censorship. The suppression of his piece was humiliating; moreover, "there was fire in it and I believed it was literature." [86] Clemens first wrote about the suppression of the item in the May 1870 *Galaxy:* "I was in the employ of a San Francisco journal at the time, and was not allowed to publish it because it might offend some of the peculiar element that subscribed for the paper." As he then reconstructed the attack, "Brannan street butchers set their dogs on a Chinaman who was quietly passing with a basket of clothes on his head; and while the dogs mutilated his flesh, a butcher increased the hilarity of the occasion by knocking some of the Chinaman's teeth down his throat with half a brick." [87] In 1906 he remembered the episode this way: "One Sunday afternoon I saw some hoodlums chasing and stoning a Chinaman who was heavily laden with the weekly wash of his Christian customers, and I noticed that a policeman was observing this performance with an amused interest—nothing more. He did not interfere." [88] The butcher had vanished, and a policeman had been added.

Writing to his good friend William Dean Howells in 1880, Clemens referred to "that degraded 'Morning Call,' whose mission from hell & politics was to lick the boots of the Irish & throw bold brave mud at the Chinamen." [89] Reports in the *Call* on the mistreatment of Chinese individuals by the Irish or others were, in fact, brief and infrequent.[90] A brutal attack on a Chinese which occurred Saturday, 3 September, received prominent notice in the city press that autumn, but the *Call* gave only one sentence to its initial report: "Andrew Benson, Wm. Silk and John Connors, were arrested yesterday on charges of assaults to kill, with deadly weapons; and another man was locked up, charged with having mashed a Chinaman's face into a jelly in a slaughter-house in Brannan street." [91] Within a week the *Call* printed two other items, equally brief, on the pre-trial examination of "the three men arrested for making hash of a Chinaman's head." [92] By contrast the initial report of the same attack in the *Alta California* was outspoken and detailed. The victim had been buying tripe from some butchers in a slaughterhouse. For making an impudent remark, he "was knocked down and disfigured for life, if not mortally injured, receiving one slash from a butcher knife across the forehead and through the nose, and another down the side of the head to the cheek bone, cutting through to the skull." The *Alta* reporter commented: "For the benefit of the future historian, we will add that this took place in the city and county of San Francisco, in A.D. 1864," and he suggested inviting "missionaries from India and China, to teach us a religion more honored [than is Christianity] through the practices of its believers." [93] The episode was made to order for arousing Clemens' holy wrath.

It is not possible to say, however, that the episode occasioned Clemens' vitriolic—and censored—item. At best we may observe that such a hypothetical piece about the "battered Chinaman" case fits nicely into the sequence of events leading to Clemens' dismissal. This censorship, which made his job less attractive than ever, would have come during the week of 4 September, about the time he stopped night work and began sharing his duties with Smiggy McGlural.

So long as Clemens lived in San Francisco, he must have remained acutely aware of the continual harassment of the Chinese. Two papers he worked on in 1865, the *Californian* and the *Dramatic Chronicle,* came to their defense that year. The *Californian* ironically recommended a children's game called "Hunt the Chinamen." Youngsters were advised to "procure a Chinaman" on any street corner. Then, "commence your game by pelting him with decayed oranges, which you may gradually exchange for pieces of coal, and eventually wind up with brick-bats." It was safest for "young beginners to commence with Chinamen carrying bundles . . ." Still, the game was not hazardous in any form, the paper said, because it was "protected by the police, who always interfere to shield any boy from an infuriated Chinaman."[94] Three months later, when Mark Twain was stepping up his campaign against the city police and their defender, Fitz Smythe of the *Alta*, the *Dramatic Chronicle* published "Our Active Police":

> The *Call* gives an account of an unoffending Chinese rag-picker being set upon by a gang of boys and nearly stoned to death. It concludes the paragraph thus: "He was carried to the City and County Hospital in an insensible condition, his head having been split open and his body badly bruised. The young ruffians scattered, and it is doubtful if any of them will be recognized and punished." If that unoffending man dies, and a murder has consequently been committed, it is doubtful whether his murderers will be recognized and punished, is it? And yet if a Chinaman steals a chicken he is sure to be recognized and punished, through the efforts of one of our active police force. If our active police force are not too busily engaged in putting a stop to petty thieving by Chinamen, and fraternizing with newspaper reporters, who hold up their wonderful deeds to the admiration of the community, let it be looked to that the boys who were guilty of this murderous assault on an industrious and unoffending man *are* recognized and punished. The *Call* says "some philanthropic gentlemen dispersed the miscreants;" these philanthropic gentlemen, if the police do their duty and arrest the culprits, can probably recognize them.[95]

Clemens was on the *Chronicle* staff when "Our Active Police" was published. Whoever wrote it, Clemens must have relished the combined attack on the *Call*, the police, and "fraternizing" reporters, three of his major targets at the time. In tone and phrasing the writing mildly anticipates his searing "What Have the Police Been Doing?"[96] written a month later, and his account of detective Rose's infallible nose for Chinese chicken thieves. Young hoodlums and indifferent policemen—not vicious butchers—here share the blame. The episode recorded in this piece may be the one that finally dominated in his memory.

Today it seems impossible to pinpoint with absolute certainty the incident that Clemens wrote up in his censored item. Mark Twain's later reconstructions of the attack and his fictional accounts of similar occurrences in "Disgraceful Persecution of a Boy" and "Goldsmith's Friend Abroad Again," both from 1870, seem to combine memories of several assaults on individual Chinese in the 1860's, some of which he had reported. As early as 1868 he had brought together the main images he associated with the harsh treatment of the Chinese in San Francisco:

[In San Francisco] a large part of the most interesting local news in the daily papers consists of gorgeous compliments to the "able and efficient" Officer This and That for arresting Ah Foo, or Ching Wang, or Song Hi for stealing a chicken; but when some white brute breaks an unoffending Chinaman's head with a brick, the paper does not compliment any officer for arresting the assaulter, for the simple reason that the officer does not make the arrest; the shedding of Chinese blood only makes him laugh; he considers it fun of the most entertaining description. I have seen dogs almost tear helpless China-men to pieces in broad daylight in San Francisco, and I have seen hod-carriers who help to make Presidents stand around and enjoy the sport. I have seen troops of boys assault a Chinaman with stones when he was walking quietly along about his business, and send him bruised and bleeding home. I have seen Chinamen abused and maltreated in all the mean, cowardly ways possible to the invention of a degraded nature, but I never saw a policeman interfere . . .[97]

We should remember, too, that in 1906 when he wrote about the suppression of his *Call* item, humanitarian feelings like those expressed above had been intensifying in Clemens for many years. Very possibly they colored his account.

Soon after Clemens was dismissed, Albert Evans noted, no doubt with some satisfaction, that Clemens was earning a living at writing "sundry literature," which Evans called "the grave of genius." [98] George Barnes remembered his ex-local's doing "all sorts of literary work whereby he could turn a cent. It was a terrible uphill business, and a less determined man than himself would have abandond the struggle and remained at the base." [99] From October to December 1864 Clemens continued to write for the *Californian* and tried unsuccessfully to make something out of his Hale and Norcross stock. Following his return from Jackass Hill in 1865, his fortunes gradually picked up. He still wrote for the *Californian,* eventually became a correspondent for the *Territorial Enterprise,* and joined the *Dramatic Chronicle* staff late in October. Eighteen hundred and sixty-five was the year he "investigated" spiritualism and began his attacks on the San Francisco police—possibly about the time he spent a night in jail for drunkenness and appeared the next morning before Justice of the Peace Alfred Barstow.

Probably about mid-1865 Clemens wrote the first part of an unfinished play,[100] a farce featuring John Brummel, a love-befuddled local reporter for a morning paper presumably published in San Francisco. Very likely he hoped to sell his play to a producer. He knew Charles H. Webb, "Manny" Noah, Charles Crocker, and Elizabeth C. Wright, city journalists whose plays had been staged, and he must have known that Thomas

Maguire had accepted scripts by other San Franciscans. While he had reported for the *Call,* that paper had reviewed plays by local writers.

Clemens' character Brummel, drunk or sober, is constantly on the alert for the latest "sensation item"—fire, riot, murder, or earthquake. Although the play is far from realistic, it suggests the nature of Brummel's work—and Clemens', while on the *Call*—and his attitude toward it. In his infatuation for Arabella, Brummel muses:

> I'm thinking about her all the time—and I don't care what I'm writing—whether the item's about pigs, or poultry, or conflagrations or steamboat disasters, I manage to get her mixed into it somehow or other. How humiliating it was last night when the chief editor looked over my proof and wanted to know what Arabella Webster it was who was going to fight the prize fight with Rough Scotty the Kentucky Infant. And the day before I had her in three financial notices and drat it, for a week past they haven't sent a pack of old blisters to the county jail for getting on a bender and breaking things but what I've written up the item in a state of semi-consciousness and entire absent-mindedness and added my Arabella's name to the list. This sort of thing won't do, you know. Some day I'll make a mistake and publish her as arrested for arson, or manslaughter, or shoplifting, or infanticide, or some other little eccentricity of the kind . . .

The topics of Brummel's items are typical of those in the *Call.* He is pictured in the play as a lackey to circumstance. He lives in "a cheap lodging room," cannot keep his mind on his work, is humiliated by the editor, gets in trouble, and thinks about suicide—all in a farcical context.

For a few months beginning in October 1865 Clemens, or someone who wrote very much as he did, picked at the *Call* through the columns of the fledgling *Dramatic Chronicle.* The *Chronicle* writer laughed at "the poor little *Squeak*" for its flat humor and its inaccurate reporting. "Be easy, citizens—calm yourselves, calm yourselves; there is no truth in the item; it was only a smoothly-written sensation paragraph." He ridiculed the editorial writer on "the profound perspicacious, logical little *Squeak*" for being overly solicitous toward rebels. He charged "the wicked little *Call*" with racial bias, for it talked "about 'obliterating' the black race as coolly as it would about scratching out an ink spot." In response to the *Call's* criticism of a local group, he wrote: "the little *Call* don't allow people to do as they 'darn please,' *unless they advertise in it.* Then it is all right." At other times he labeled the paper the "Cowardly Little 'Call'" and "the blood-thirsty little *Call*." A few days after Clemens took over as its drama critic, the *Chronicle* vigorously attacked the *Call's* critic—the theater was George Barnes's specialty—for venal inconsistency.[101] It should be said that these attacks were neither especially ill-tempered nor unusual. The *Chronicle* attacked other papers too and was attacked by them in turn—when they deigned to notice the upstart. Moreover, in January 1866 Clemens defended the right of the *Call* to look after "the little pet notions and partialities of its patrons"[102]—exactly what Barnes had done in censoring Clemens' item. Furthermore, Clemens seems to have been on good terms with Barnes the following August when he asked his advice about delivering a lecture and then, in the *Call* office, wrote the advertisement for his first speech in San Francisco about his trip to the Sandwich Islands, which was so successful that it led directly to his initial lecture tour.

As 1866 drew to a close, Clemens sailed from San Francisco, calling the city "my new home."[103] But he returned only once—in 1868, to secure full rights in his *Quaker City* travel letters published in the *Alta California*. And in the memories he recorded over the next forty years he returned only rarely to his days on the *Call*.

"A NEW HAND AT THE BELLOWS"

"The *Call* has secured the services of 'Mark Twain' as its local reporter. His items already give evidence of a new hand at the bellows."[104] Albert S. Evans, who made this comment in June 1864, apparently was impressed by a new presence making itself felt in the columns of the *Call*, and his remark implies that Clemens was the paper's only local reporter, precisely the dubious distinction later claimed by Mark Twain. City news items in the *Call* were of course not signed, and Clemens' authorship of any one of them during his employment must be conjectural when acceptable evidence is lacking. I believe, however, that the known facts tend to support Mark Twain's contention that he was *"the* reporter" for the *Call* until Smiggy McGlural arrived, and I agree with Evans' observation that the paper's local items during the period in question do yield indications of Clemens' authorship.

This collection partially measures the extent of my agreement with Mark Twain's contention and with Evans' awareness of a new, although unspecified, quality in the *Call's* local items. For I believe that Clemens wrote the selections reprinted here—as well as many others still in the files of the *Call*. This belief did not arise from a desire to substantiate the statements of either man (Evans' comment came to my attention relatively late), but from a general search for undiscovered early Twain writings. The more I looked into the *Call*, the more convinced I became that the paper was a mine of Clemens' daily journalism, some of which could be established as his. It became apparent that past studies of Mark Twain's writing, including my own, had relied too heavily on A. B. Paine's assertions that Clemens worked rather impersonally as "part of a news-machine" on the *Call,* and that "only one of the several severe articles he wrote criticizing officials and institutions seems to have appeared . . ." [105] Such a characterization of the paper and of Clemens' relationship to it suggested that his *Call* journalism was almost always innocuously routine and indistinguishable from the work of others. Albert Evans' recognition of "a new hand at the bellows" proved to be closer to the truth. And the small overworked staff responsible for the reading matter in the *Call* was far less a machine than a group of friendly men who enjoyed rather casual relations with each other on the job.

In the mid-1860's reporting the city news on San Francisco papers was still a notably personal activity. As we have seen, local reporters had their prescribed duties and responsibilities. Nevertheless, they enjoyed considerable leeway in selecting topics to write up, and they were relatively free to determine what they would say in reporting the news and how they would say it. For example, Albert S. Evans of the *Alta California* inserted many items involving an invented character, Armand Leonidas Stiggers,[106] and Clemens was disposed to gratuitously name—and pungently comment upon—former Washoe friends and antagonists in the columns of the *Call.*[107] All the reporters wrote objectively on occasion, but their preferences and idiosyncrasies often showed, too, frequently overshadowing the information imparted. For this reason alone it is not surprising that many *Call* reports for the summer of 1864 are less than objective. Instead, they are informal and strikingly individual in style, contrasting vividly, for instance, with the standardized formality of the usual *Call* editorial. They reflect a personality that had not been processed into anonymity by a "news-machine." [108] That personality was variously incisive, opinionated, humorous, sympathetic, indignant, mocking, cynical, and critical, and to read the *Call* before and after Clemens' period of employment is to experience its absence. For example, a standard subject for city locals to work up was the saga of the fallen woman. "Died in the Street" appeared in the *Call* while Albert S. Evans was the paper's local reporter:

> Every few weeks, for several years past, the prisoners' dock of the Police Court has been graced by the presence of a woman named Margaret Johns. She was generally presented for drunkenness, but sometimes she enlarged upon her offence and indulged in offensive and indelicate language. So frequent had she made her appearance,

and at such regular periods, that the prison-keepers used to ask the officers what had become of her if she failed to make her monthly visit. But she had gone before a higher court to answer for her misdeeds, and has made her appearance before Him who holds the universe in the palm of His hand. Yesterday morning she was found lying dead in an alley-way leading into Jackson street, between Dupont and Kearney. Her head was resting upon the door-step of a miserable Chinese hovel, and her emaciated hand was grasping a bottle partially filled with miserable whiskey. . . . A few years since she was moving in a respectable circle, and was the possessor of a neat little fortune . . . Afterwards she married a worthless wretch . . . And now at the close of her pilgrimage on earth she yields up her life, without one friend near her to receive her last words, and nothing to cover her but a few tattered rags and the broad canopy of Heaven, which, as if mourning for the event, had blackened its face with heavy clouds, and was weeping as a mother weeps when she sees her child, even though it is beyond the pale of christianity, struggling in the throes of dissolution.[109]

If the tearful reader will now turn to "Original Novelette" (Item 78), he can make his own comparisons. While Clemens was with the *Call,* he and Evans, then on the *Alta California,* often reported the same events in widely contrasting styles.

Compared with Evans, the reporter for the *Evening Bulletin* was unsentimental and concise. But his items also contrast with those in the *Call*. On 21 July he wrote: "John Dunn is confined in the City Prison on the charge of attempting to 'chaw the nose off' of John Hansen in a quarrel which occurred between them." [110] A more dramatic version of the event had appeared in the *Call* that morning:

Officers Ball and Glover arrested John Dunn yesterday evening, for taking a man's nose between his teeth and trying to bite it off; he came very near succeeding. After he was locked up in the station house, and as soon as the officers were gone, he got vicious and noisy, and abused the prison-keeper in language as strong and as obscene as he could make it. Captain Douglas came in and started with him to the dark cell, when he resisted furiously and tried his best to experiment on that officer's nose also. That fellow would rather bite a nose than a cream-puff or a banana, any time. The Captain choked him off, however, and shut him into the dark cell with his hands manacled behind him.[111]

The very next day this expert on John Dunn's vigorously pursued taste in soft foods wrote "The Police Court Besieged":

Yesterday at half-past two in the afternoon, applicants for position on the Police force, in numbers variously estimated at from two hundred to ten thousand, laid siege to the Police Court, where the Police Commissioners were entrenched to examine the qualifications of candidates for the twelve new places created at the last meeting of the Board of Supervisors, and the war went on from that time until five o'clock without flagging. They formed two long lines, Post-office fashion, and filed slowly in at one door and out at another, under a steady fire of jokes from the spectators, to which they replied with melancholy witticisms which would have been tolerated and even gravely admired at a well-regulated funeral. There were some stately, fine-looking men in the procession, and some that looked mighty "ornery;" some wore good clothes and were clean, and some were ragged, to some extent, and not stainless; some were cheerful, and some looked distressed and constitutionally out of luck. But what of it? The whole of that crowd, except, perhaps, twelve, were entirely out of luck yesterday—and it is something to have company in misfortune. The applicants had to write their names and addresses, to show the extent of their orthographic and calligraphic accomplishments; and they do say that some who write and spell well as a general thing, were so flustrated by excitement yesterday that they made hieroglyphics of so extravagant and shapeless a nature, that they could not recognize their own signatures in the list after the ink got cold.[112]

That evening the *Bulletin* soberly printed "The New Policemen":

The Police Court-room was crowded yesterday afternoon with applicants for positions on the police, under the recent ordinance appointing 12 more policemen; and the cry is "Still they come," for they are still applying to-day. To all such aspirants we will state that the appointments are already made, and will be announced in a few days. In the meantime the appointees are to go through a regular surgical examination, such as is given recruits in the United States army.[113]

The *Bulletin's* reporter conveyed more essential information than the *Call's* colloquial man, who splashed into his subject with outrageous exaggeration and then in a leisurely conclusion combined some minor details into a passage with overtones of mock-portentous mystery. With a typical imaginative flourish, the local of the *Call* also gratuitously intimated that he knew exactly what would be "gravely admired at a well-regulated funeral"—such as the expertise shown by Peter Wilks' gliding undertaker in *Huckleberry Finn*.

Certain general considerations thus increase the possibility that Clemens wrote a great many—perhaps most—of the *Call's* local items while he was employed on that paper. First, the information presented in this introduction supports Mark Twain's 1906 account of his position and duties on the *Call* staff. Second, a marked stylistic identity separates many *Call* items published between 7 June and 11 October 1864 from other contemporary newspaper pieces. It should be added that local items of that period were reprinted from the *Call* with unusual frequency in such out-of-town papers as the Placerville, California, *Daily News* and the Gold Hill, Nevada, *Daily News*. Presumably, those items had an unusual appeal, and in some instances the out-of-town editors actually ascribed them to Mark Twain.[114] Finally, clippings of twenty-six *Call* pieces are pasted in the Moffett Scrapbooks 4 and 5, which are family collections holding many of Clemens' Western writings. This group of items makes up a small but significant fraction of Clemens' reporting for the paper. Almost every piece was published during the three weeks ending 8 September, yet represented in the group are items long and short, ambitious and casual, routine and imaginative, humorous and factual, critical and informative—and the variety in subject matter is equally as impressive as the variety in kind.[115] Thus the family scrapbooks yield a group of *Call* items that appeared in a brief period and that represent a fair cross section of the *Call's* local reporting during the eighteen weeks of Clemens' employment. Although the general considerations above suggest the scope of Clemens' reporting for the *Call,* they are inconclusive evidence of his authorship of a given piece.

A good many *Call* items, however, can be claimed definitely for Clemens on evidence that is precise and conclusive. The manuscript of "Inexplicable News from San José" (Item 80) is in the Samuel C. Webster collection of the Clemens family materials. Clemens commented on "What a Sky-Rocket Did" (Item 79) in an unpublished letter, and in another his remarks on his friend Jerome Rice are only slightly less conclusive with respect to "Sad Accident" (Item 76), the emotionally written obituary of Rice. He identifies himself by name in "Due Warning" (Item 81). "How to Cure Him of It" (Item 18) recounts the incident with the howling dog that Paine mentioned in his biography.[116] "Charitable Contributions" (Item 75) refers to the steamboat explosion that took the life of his brother Henry, and other items refer less conclusively to episodes from his past experience. Many pieces, including Clemens' ambitious sketches of the new Chinese temple, are part of his journalistic duel with Albert S. Evans, who has identified several pieces as Clemens.' Other items fit nicely into Clemens' sustained attack on Prosecuting Attorney Davis Louderback, Jr. Some of Mark Twain's contemporary *Californian* and *Golden Era* sketches parallel topics and phrasing in several *Call* articles. A number of *Call* reports are rehearsals for portions of his later *Enterprise* correspondence or for passages in his fiction. An inconclusive but interesting consideration arises when we remember that local reporters customarily wrote the heads to their items. In choosing his titles the *Call's* man sometimes displayed a predilection for idioms ("The Boss Earthquake," Item 2) and entire phrases ("Moses in the Bulrushes Again," Item 16) that Mark Twain liked. These and other questions concerned with attribution are discussed further in the headnotes to sections and to individual items.

Various kinds of indications occasionally combine to increase the probability that Clemens wrote an article. Thus "Sad Accident" (Item 76), mentioned above, includes a passage germane to the episode in Chapter 32 of *Roughing It* about the horses that desert the snowbound travelers. An interlocking relationship between *Call* reports may also add validity to an ascription. Often two or more items report a newsworthy event or a protracted situation. Such related reports in series may continue over the entire summer's run of the *Call,* as do the many brief items on the reassembly of the monitor *Camanche.* Or they may appear almost daily for a week or a month, as they do for the two big summer fairs. Within these and similar series, continuities characteristically build up and internal references occur. Therefore, if evidence for Clemens' authorship is conclusive for one or more items in a well-knit group, the probability that he wrote the others is heightened. A study of the *Call* for the summer of 1864 reveals a network of different kinds of relationships among many of the local news reports and between them and Mark Twain's acknowledged writings.

As suggested earlier, one of these relationships is the reporter's writing style, a prominent feature of many of the following selections and one that is referred to from time to time in my commentary. Not infrequently, the style of a *Call* item is the sole indication of authorship. Doubtless, style alone, unaccompanied by external evidence, can support no more than conjectural attribution. Nevertheless, alone and unsupported it has more than sufficed to convince me that Clemens wrote many of the *Call* reports collected here. His prose often carried its own stamp of authenticity; even the "torpid heart" of lokulitems could not for long stifle the distinctive expression of his forceful imagination. Certain habits of punctuation, characteristic structural patterns of sentences and paragraphs, the use of favorite words and expressions, the gravitation to dramatic presentation, to the colloquial, to biblical phrasing and allusions, and not infrequently to brilliant imagery, the revelation of typical attitudes and familiar contours of a remarkable personality—these are some of the stylistic and personal qualities of the writing that shape a presence we can recognize. Precisely this susceptibility of Clemens' prose to self-revelation first caught my attention when I read through the *Call*. I have relied upon it heavily in making this book.

The *Call* building at 612 Commercial Street (*redrawn from the* Call, *19 December 1897, Bancroft Library*).

Part One

THE LOCAL AT LARGE

"THE SUPERNATURAL BOOT-JACK"

Clemens came to San Francisco about ten days after the season's first earthquake, one that the *Call* described as a series of "regular stunners." [1] Recurring at irregular intervals all summer long, the tremors never failed to call forth Clemens' rather nervously expressed humorous items. He did not know it at the time, but his earthquake reports were good practice for his more elaborate accounts of the big convulsion of 8 October 1865, which he wrote up in several excellent sketches and in *Roughing It*. On that day, referring to past quakes he had experienced, he commented: "I have tried a good many of them here, and of several varieties—some that came in the form of a universal shiver; others that gave us two or three sudden upward heaves from below; others that swayed grandly and deliberately from side to side; and still others that came rolling and undulating beneath our feet like a great wave of the sea." [2] But whatever the variety of the earth's motion, he seemed to feel that each quake was "freighted with urgent messages," as he wrote in the following item, "Another of Them." To Clemens the Unionist, the tremor of 7 September 1864 was meant "to shake up the Democratic State Convention" then being held in the city. But to Twain the irreverent teleologist, the big quake the following year was aimed at the pious: "What produced the great earthquake of the 8th October? What was the earthquake after? It was after the Methodist Conference"[3] which was then meeting in San Francisco.

"THEY ARE SHAKING HER UP FROM BELOW NOW"

**ANOTHER OF THEM
23 JUNE 1864**

At five minutes to nine o'clock last night, San Francisco was favored by another earthquake. There were three distinct shocks, two of which were very heavy, and appeared to have been done on purpose, but the third did not amount to much. Heretofore our earthquakes—as all old citizens experienced in this sort of thing will recollect—have been distinguished by a soothing kind of undulating motion, like the roll of waves on the sea, but we are happy to state that they are shaking her up from below now. The shocks last night came straight up from that direction; and it is sad to reflect, in these spiritual times, that they might possibly have been freighted with urgent messages from some of our departed friends. The suggestion is worthy a moment's serious reflection, at any rate.

**"UNCOMMON AND ALTOGETHER UNNECESSARY
ENERGY AND ENTHUSIASM"**

2

**THE BOSS EARTHQUAKE
22 JULY 1864**

On the evening of the boss earthquake of 1864 Fred Franks as Green Jones was playing opposite Annette Ince as May Edwards in Tom Taylor's "The Ticket-of-Leave Man" at the Metropolitan Theater on Montgomery Street. Just one month before, Mark Twain had paid Franks the ambiguous compliment of calling him his "favorite Washoe tragedian" and a man who possessed "the first virtue of a comedian, which is to do humorous things with grave decorum and without seeming to know that they are funny."[4]

When we contracted to report for this newspaper, the important matter of two earthquakes a month was not considered in the salary. There shall be no mistake of that kind in the next contract, though. Last night, at twenty minutes to eleven, the regular semi-monthly earthquake, due the night before, arrived twenty-four hours behind time, but it made up for the delay in uncommon and altogether unnecessary energy and enthusiasm. The first effort was so gentle as to move the inexperienced stranger to the expression of contempt and brave but very bad jokes; but the second was calculated to move him out of his boots, unless they fitted him neatly. Up in the third story of this building the sensation we experienced was as if we had been sent for and were mighty anxious to go. The house seemed to waltz from side to side with a quick motion, suggestive of sifting corn meal through a sieve; afterward it rocked grandly to and fro like a pro-digious cradle, and in the meantime several persons started downstairs to see if there were anybody in the street so timid as to be frightened at a mere earthquake. The third shock was not important, as compared with the stunner that had just preceded it. That second shock drove people out of the theatres by dozens. At the Metropolitan, we are told that Franks, the comedian, had just come on the stage, (they were playing the "Ticket-of-Leave Man,") and was about to express the unbounded faith he had in May; he paused until the jarring had subsided, and then improved and added force to the text by exclaiming, "It will take more than an earthquake to shake my faith in that woman!" And in that, Franks achieved a sublime triumph over the elements, for he "brought the house down," and the earthquake couldn't. From the time the shocks commenced last night, until the windows had stopped rattling, a minute and a half had elapsed.

"WHEN A COMMUNITY GET USED TO A THING, THEY SUFFER WHEN THEY HAVE TO GO WITHOUT IT"

**NO EARTHQUAKE
23 AUGUST 1864**

In consequence of the warm, close atmosphere which smothered the city at two o'clock yesterday afternoon, everybody expected to be shaken out of their boots by an earthquake before night, but up to the hour of our going to press the supernatural boot-jack had not arrived yet. That is just what makes it so unhealthy—the earthquakes are getting so irregular. When a community get used to a thing, they suffer when they have to go without it. However, the trouble cannot be remedied; we know of nothing that will answer as a substitute for one of those convulsions—to an unmarried man.

"NOTHING ACCUSTOMS ONE TO A THING SO READILY AS GETTING USED TO IT"

RAIN
23 AUGUST 1864

One of those singular freaks of Nature which, by reference to the dictionary, we find described as "the water or the descent of water that falls in drops from the clouds—a shower," occurred here yesterday, and kept the community in a state of pleasant astonishment for the space of several hours. They would not have been astonished at an earthquake, though. Thus it will be observed that nothing accustoms one to a thing so readily as getting used to it. You will always notice that, in America. We were thinking this refreshing rain would make everybody happy. Not so the cows. An agricultural sharp informs us that yesterday's rain was a misfortune to California—that it will kill the dry grass upon which the cattle now subsist, and also the young grass upon which they were calculating to subsist hereafter. We know nothing whatever about the matter, but we do know that if what this gentleman says is strictly true, the inevitable deduction is that the cattle are out of luck. We stand to that.

"IT WAS SENT EARLIER, TO SHAKE UP THE DEMOCRATIC STATE CONVENTION"

EARTHQUAKE
8 SEPTEMBER 1864

The Democratic State Convention, which Clemens reported for the *Call*, met at noon on 7 September in Turn-Verein Hall. Its business was to nominate representatives to Congress and Presidential electors to run on the McClellan-Pendleton ticket in the approaching November election.

The regular semi-monthly earthquake arrived at ten minutes to ten o'clock, yesterday morning. Thirty-six hours ahead of time. It is supposed it was sent earlier, to shake up the Democratic State Convention, but if this was the case, the calculation was awkwardly made, for it fell short by about two hours. The Convention did not meet until noon. Either the earthquake or the Convention, or both combined, made the atmosphere mighty dense and sulphurous all day. If it was the Democrats alone, they do not smell good, and it certainly cannot be healthy to have them around.

THE STREETS OF
SAN FRANCISCO

A. RUNAWAYS AND ACCIDENTS

A century ago San Franciscans were troubled by drag racers and by runaways down steep grades, even if their horse-drawn vehicles were not as lethal as automobiles. A writer for the *Californian* observed: "About one man in fifty knows how to drive, or has common sense and judgment sufficient to be trusted with women and children. And yet in San Francisco every other man drives a horse, and it is about an even thing, half the time, whether it is not a horse at one end and a jackass at the other" [1] —surely an ancestor of our jokes about accidents being caused by the nut *behind* the wheel, etc. Accident reports were routine for every city local, and the *Call's* man spiced his considerably, as though to relieve the repetition. It is interesting that he drew on memories of butcher-boy races in New York City and turned naturally to the vocabulary of the typecase.

The persons and firms named in these selections are listed in city directories for 1864 and 1865.

"THE FRANTIC HORSE DID NOT HASH UP A DOZEN OR TWO OF THEM IN HIS RECKLESS CAREER"

**RUNAWAY
14 JULY 1864**

Yesterday morning, a horse and cart were carelessly left unhitched and unwatched in Dupont street. The horse, being of the Spanish persuasion and not to be depended on, finally got tired standing idle, and ran away. He ran into Berry street, ran half a square and upset the cart, and fell, helplessly entangled in the harness. The vehicle was somewhat damaged, but two or three new wheels, some fresh sides, and a new bottom, will make it all right again. Considering the fact that little short narrow Berry street contains as many small children as all the balance of San Francisco put together, it is strange the frantic horse did not hash up a dozen or two of them in his reckless career. They all escaped, however, by the singular accident of being out of the way at the time, and they visited the wreck in countless swarms, after the disaster, and examined it with unspeakable satisfaction. The driver is a man of extraordinary intellect and mature judgment—he set his cart on its legs again as well as he could, and then whipped his horse until it was easy to see that the poor brute began to comprehend that something was up, though it is questionable whether he has yet cyphered out what that something was, or not. The driver, as we said before, was not in his wagon at the time of the accident, which accounts for the misfortune of his not being hurt in the least.

"CROSKY'S GROCERY WAGON . . . UNCEREMONIOUSLY KNOCKED INTO 'PI' "

**A GROSS OUTRAGE
16 JULY 1864**

Yesterday noon, Sansome street was witness of one of those feats so common to New York city, among the butcher boys, of racing through the public streets. The driver of Clark's furniture and Express wagon and some other Expressman, getting their mettle up as to the relative speed of their respective plugs, let out, both laying on the whip plentifully, until they overtook Crosky's grocery wagon, which Clark's vehicle (No. 2,859) unceremoniously knocked into "pi," landing driver, groceries and other sundries in the street. These outrages are becoming too frequent in our thickly-populated streets, and need the strict attention of our city authorities. Eye-witnesses to this race at full speed up the railroad track, freely expressed themselves that if any ladies or children had been unfortunate enough to be on the street at the time, nothing could have saved them from being ridden down.

"THE BUGGY WAS TAKING A GOOD DEAL OF INTEREST IN IT"

**COLLISION
10 AUGUST 1864**

A runaway buggy (at any rate the horse attached to it was running away and the buggy was taking a good deal of interest in it,) came into collision with a dray, yesterday, in Montgomery street, and the dray was not damaged any to speak of. The buggy was; the hub was mashed clear out of one wheel, and another wheel was turned inside out—so that it "dished" the wrong way. The crip-ple was entirely new, and belonged to Duff and Covert, California street. In meeting a dray, or a heavy truck-wagon, buggies should always turn out to one side, being safer than to go between it.

"THE MEN . . . WERE GOOD PROOF THAT THE LIQUOR WAS THERE"

SUNDRIES
13 AUGUST 1864

A pile of miscellaneous articles was found heaped up at a late hour last night away down somewhere in Harrison street, which attracted the notice of numbers of passers-by, and divers attempts were made to analyze the same without effect, for the reason that no one could tell where to begin, or which was on top. Two Special Policemen dropped in just then and solved the difficulty, showing a clean inventory of one horse, one buggy, two men and an indefinite amount of liquor. The liquor couldn't be got at to be gauged, consequently the proof of it couldn't be told; the men, though, were good proof that the liquor was there, for they were as drunk as Bacchus and his brother. A fight had been on hand somewhere, and one of the men had been close to it, for his face was painted up in various hues, sky-blue and crimson being prominent. The order of the buggy was inverted, and the horse beyond a realizing sense of his condition. The men went with some noise to the station-house, and the animal, with attachments, being set to rights, ambled off to a livery stable on Kearny street.

"'TIRED OF SICH D——D FOOLISHNESS'"

MAN RUN OVER
18 AUGUST 1864

A man fell off his own dray—or rather it was a large truck-wagon—in Davis street, yesterday, and the fore wheels passed over his body. A bystander stopped the horses and they backed the same wheels over the man's body a second time; after which he crawled out, jumped on the wagon, muttered something about being "tired of sich d——d foolishness," and drove off before a surgeon could arrive to amputate him!

B. "VAGRANT" HOUSES

A rash of house-moving broke out in San Francisco in the summer of 1864. Bulky frame structures, advancing sluggishly on rollers, clogged the traffic in busy downtown streets. The playful items below on these footloose and footer-free houses show that Clemens knew how to keep a good thing going from week to week. They also illustrate some of the similarities in style and tone displayed by scattered *Call* pieces on a single subject during the summer of 1864. These restless shanties drifting through the streets called forth a blend of sympathetic understanding, mild irritation, and respectful advice from the reporter, who saw them as rather forlorn and questionable females who should not have been out alone at night. He liked to use the river vocabulary to describe their lazy progress, and in denying that he was "stuck after" the listless vagrant of Commercial Street ("Trot Her Along"), he employed an uncommon variation of "stuck on" that proved to be a lifelong favorite.[2]

"HOUSES LOAFING AROUND THE PUBLIC STREETS"

11

HOUSE AT LARGE
1 JULY 1864

An old two-story, sheet-iron, pioneer, fire-proof house, got loose from her moorings last night, and drifted down Sutter street, toward Montgomery. We are not informed as to where she came from or where she was going to—she had halted near Montgomery street, and appeared to be studying about it. If one might judge from the expression that hung about her dilapidated front and desolate windows, she was thoroughly demoralized when she stopped there, and sorry she ever started. Is there no law against houses loafing around the public streets at midnight?

"STARING DEJECTEDLY TOWARDS MONTGOMERY STREET"

12

TROT HER ALONG
30 JULY 1864

For several days a vagrant two-story frame house has been wandering listlessly about Commercial street, above this office, and she has

"Number *2*" in this group of San Francisco newsmen is supposed to be Clemens (*from Mark Twain Himself by Milton Meltzer*).

The Occidental Hotel on Montgomery Street between Bush and Sutter. Clemens registered here on 8 June 1864 and later took many meals here (*Bancroft Library*).

Albert S. Evans ("Fitz Smythe"), city editor of the *Alta California* (*Bancroft Library*).

Russian Hill in 1865 (*from a photograph by T. E. Hecht, Bancroft Library*).

Pine and Montgomery streets in 1865 (*from a photograph by T. E. Hecht, Bancroft Library*).

The Russ House on Montgomery Street between Bush and Pine, 1865 (*Bancroft Library*).

finally stopped in the middle of the thoroughfare, and is staring dejectedly towards Montgomery street, as if she would like to go down there, but really don't feel equal to the exertion. We wish they would trot her along and leave the street open; she is an impassable obstruction and an intolerable nuisance where she stands now. If they set her up there to be looked at, it is all right; but we have looked at her as much as we want to, and are anxious for her to move along; we are not stuck after her any.

"PLAYING HERSELF FOR A HOTEL"

DISGUSTED AND GONE
31 JULY 1864

That melancholy old frame house that has been loafing around Commercial street for the past week, got disgusted at the notice we gave her in the last issue of the CALL, and drifted off into some other part of the city yesterday. It is pleasing to our vanity to imagine that if it had not been for our sagacity in divining her hellish designs, and our fearless exposure of them, she would have been down on Montgomery street to-day, playing herself for a hotel. As it is, she has folded her tents like the Arabs, and quietly stolen away, behind several yoke of oxen.

"WE MEET THESE DISSATISFIED SHANTIES EVERY DAY"

MYSTERIOUS
9 AUGUST 1864

If you have got a house, keep your eye on it, these times, for there is no knowing what moment it will go tramping around town. We meet these dissatisfied shanties every day marching boldly through the public streets on stilts and rollers, or standing thoughtfully in front of gin shops, or halting in quiet alleys and peering round corners, with a human curiosity, out of one eye, or one window if you please, upon the dizzy whirl and roar of commerce in the thoroughfare beyond. The houses have been taking something lately that is moving them a good deal. It is very mysterious, and past accounting for, but it cannot be helped. We have just been informed that an unknown house—two stories, with a kitchen—has stopped before Shark alley, in Merchant street, and seems to be calculating the chances of being able to scrouge through it into Washington street, and thus save the trouble of going around. We hardly think she can, and we had rather she would not try it; we should be sorry to see her get herself fast in that crevice, which is the newspaper reporter's shortest cut to the station-house and the courts. Without wishing to be meddlesome or officious, we would like to suggest that she would find it very comfortable and nice going round by Montgomery street, and plenty of room. Besides, there is nothing to be seen in Shark alley, if she is only on a little pleasure excursion.

"PROWLING AROUND MERCHANT STREET"

ASSAULT BY A HOUSE
9 AUGUST 1864

Shark Alley, Clemens' name for Dunbar Alley, ran behind City Hall. Persons arrested by the police—the sharks?—usually were brought through it, sometimes violently, on their way to the station house to await trial.

The vagrant house we have elsewhere alluded to as prowling around Merchant street, near Shark alley —we mean Dunbar alley—finally started to go around by Montgomery street, but at the first move fell over and mashed in some windows and broke down a new awning attached to the house adjoining the "Ivy Green" saloon.

C. "IN THE BY-PLACES AND UPON THE CORNERS"

On any given day the content of the local columns of the several San Francisco journals differed widely from paper to paper. Unusually important happenings were very likely to be recorded in all of them. Otherwise a city reporter's nose for news, his legwork, and his ability to crib from various sources helped determine what his paper printed. But his individual preferences for subjects also counted. Within limits he was free to "puff" what he liked, a painless way for him to fill his allotted space when news was scarce. The miscellaneous items below are about unimportant events on the city streets. They probably show Clemens selecting topics that pleased him and elaborating on them with some satisfaction.

**MOSES IN THE BULRUSHES AGAIN
16 JULY 1864**

Readers of *Huckleberry Finn* may recognize the above title, just as, a few pages back, they may have remarked the house at large "studying" where to go. Also, in the unsentimental, invigorating handling of infancy below, we sense Mark Twain's customary spirited concern at this time for the well-being of "Young America," whose unsquelchable, noisy vitality had echoed through his sketch "Those Blasted Children" earlier in the year.

The Catholic Orphan Asylum for girls only, where officers John R. Conway and Thomas King found the abandoned infant, was on Market Street near Kearny.

On Thursday evening, officers John Conway and King had their attention attracted by the crying of a child at the Catholic Orphan Asylum door; where, upon examination, they discovered an infant, apparently but a few days old, wrapped up in a shawl. It was delivered to the care of the benevolent Sisters at the Institution. It appeared to be a good-enough baby—nothing the matter with it—and it has been unaccountable to all who have heard of the circumstance, what the owner wanted to throw it away for.

**ANOTHER LAZARUS
31 JULY 1864**

A topic made to order for the *Call's* man was the famous dog Bummer and his changing retinue of dogs. Keenly aware of San Francisco's "characters"—animal as well as human—Clemens long since had discovered his ability to write animal sketches. He was especially good at portraying fawning or unprepossessing dogs. Bummer had come to the city in 1860 from a sheep farm. He quickly became known as a ratter and a cadger, and he called no man "master." Known throughout the city and publicized for years, he died 2 November 1865 after being kicked down-stairs by a drunk. Mark Twain wrote his obituary for the *Territorial Enterprise,* not failing to mention Bummer's latter-day "mean decep-tions" nor the "obsequious vassal" Lazarus, the dog that was Bummer's initial favorite.[3] At this time Clemens inclined toward reading mean human qualities into animals rather than romanticizing them—as he did Hans Oppert's dog in *The Mysterious Stranger*—in order to show how petty and cruel human beings could be.

The lamented Lazarus departed this life about a year ago, and from that time until recently poor Bum-mer has mourned the loss of his faithful friend in solitude, scorning the sympathy and companionship of his race with that stately reserve and exclusiveness which has always distinguished him since he became a citizen of San Francisco. But, for several weeks past, we have observed a vagrant black puppy has taken up with him, and attends him in his promenades, bums with him at the restaurants, and watches over his slumbers as unremittingly as did the sainted Lazarus of other days. Whether that puppy really feels an unselfish affection for Bummer, or whether he is actuated by unworthy motives, and goes with him merely to ring in on the eating houses through his popularity at such estab-lishments, or whether he is one of those fawning sycophants that fas-ten upon the world's heroes in order that they may be glorified by the reflected light of greatness, we can-not yet determine. We only know that he hangs around Bummer, and snarls at intruders upon his repose, and looks proud and happy when the old dog condescends to notice him. He ventures upon no puppyish levity in the presence of his prince, and es-says no unbecoming familiarity, but in all respects conducts himself with the respectful decorum which such a puppy so situated should display. Consequently, in time, he may grow into high favor.

"A PUPPY . . . WHICH IS INSIGNIFICANT AS TO SIZE, BUT FORMIDABLE AS TO YELP"

**HOW TO CURE HIM OF IT
27 AUGUST 1864**

Albert B. Paine (*MTB*, I, 256) mentions the howling dog of Minna Street. The 1864 and 1865 city directories list Clemens at 32 and 44 Minna Street, respectively.

More than two years after writing "How to Cure Him of It" the reporter, coming out in the open as Mark Twain, published in the *Call* a set of rules which, if followed, would invariably "render a dog insensible to bullet wounds." He commented: "The presence of the dog is often betrayed to the Policeman by his bark. Remove the bark from his system and your dog is safe. This may be done by mixing a spoonful of the soother called strychnine in his rations. It will be next to impossible to ever get that dog to bark any more." [4] Mark Twain's soothing syrup for dogs was equaled by his famous—permanent—cures for children's diseases.

In a court in Minna street, between First and Second, they keep a puppy tied up which is insignificant as to size, but formidable as to yelp. We are unable to sleep after nine o'clock in the morning on account of it. Sometimes the subject of these remarks begins at three in the morning and yowls straight ahead for a week. We have lain awake many mornings out of pure distress on account of that puppy—because we know that if he does not break himself of that habit it will kill him; it is bound to do it—we have known thousands and thousands of cases like it. But it is easily cured. Give the creature a double handful of strychnine, dissolved in a quart of Prussic acid, and it will soo——oothe him down and make him as quiet and docile as a dried herring. The remedy is not expensive, and is at least worthy of a trial, even for the novelty of the thing.

"AND STILL THE GENEROUS PROPOSITION GOETH UP FROM THE WANDERER'S LIPS"

"SHINER NO. 1"
31 AUGUST 1864

Clemens' interest in such San Francisco characters as the amiable lunatic Emperor Norton and the phrenologist Washington the Second (Uncle Freddy Coombs) extended to Shiner No. 1. That star bootblack, known to virtually all citizens, was a resourceful entrepreneur. In 1863 he had set up a telescope at Kearny and Washington Streets where for a fee anyone might have a look. Before he invested in a muscle-testing machine, he played a bit part in the racetrack scene of the play *Three Fast Women* at Maguire's Opera House.[5] In his condensed sketch of Shiner, Clemens worked for comic incongruity by splicing an Irish dialect to a biblical manner, two modes of expression that came easily to Clemens.

That industrious wild "Shiner" with his heavy brass machine for testing the strength of human muscles, is around again, in his original swallow-tail gray coat. That same wanderer, coat and machine, have been ceaselessly on the move throughout California and Washoe, for a year or more, and still they look none the worse for wear. And still the generous proposition goeth up from the wanderer's lips, in the by-places and upon the corners of the street: "Wan pull for a bit, jintlemen, an' anny man that pulls eighteen hundher' pounds can thry it over agin widout expinse." And still the wanderer seeketh the eighteen-hundred pounder up and down in the earth, and findeth him not; and still the public strive for that gratis pull, and still they are disappointed—still do they fall short of the terms by a matter of half a ton or so. Go your ways, and give the ubiquitous "Shiner" a chance to find the man upon whom it is his mission upon earth to confer the blessing of a second pull "widout expinse."

"IT IS LIKELY PROVIDENCE WASN'T NOTICING"

20

CRUELTY TO ANIMALS
18 SEPTEMBER 1864

Clemens' blast at the driver is strictly in character, and the sardonic comment closing the item is worthy of Philip Traum. The tone of the report fits in with other indications that Clemens was experiencing a difficult, unhappy period.

James R. Hardenbergh's and J. P. Dyer's Russ House, occupying an entire block from Pine to Bush on Montgomery Street, was a leading hotel.

Probably there is no law against it. A large truck wagon, with a load on it nearly as heavy as an ordinary church, came to a stand-still on the slippery cobble stones in front of the Russ House, yesterday, simply because the solitary horse attached to it found himself unable to keep up his regular gait with it. A street car and other vehicles were delayed some time by the blockade. It was natural to expect that a "streak" of lightning would come after the driver out of the cloudless sky, but it did not. It is likely Providence wasn't noticing.

"DURING THIS SANITARY DISPUTE,
THE SUBJECT HAD COME TO"

21

HAD A FIT
11 OCTOBER 1864

"Had a Fit" is the latest local item published in the *Call* that I ascribe to Clemens. It is my theory, unencumbered by the least shred of evidence, that the day George Barnes read this piece was the day he eased Clemens out of his job. The flippancy and the don't-give-a-damn attitude that sometimes rise to the surface in Clemens' reporting are readily seen here. The writing borders on the burlesque, and a general meaning that emerges is: What fools we are. One imagines that the item implies disrespect for the estate of journalism—or at least for lokulitem's role in it—as though he did not care whether he kept his job or not.

In speaking of the "salubrious" condition of the kindhearted drunk, the reporter sounds very much like Ballou in *Roughing It*.

A lad of some twelve years was seized with convulsions, while sitting in a buggy at the corner of Sacramento and Montgomery streets, yesterday afternoon. Restoratives were speedily brought in play, and in a short time the youth went on his way, viewing with astonishment the multitude that had collected, which was variously estimated at from one thousand to four thousand eight hundred and eighty. One kindhearted person, whose condition, unfortunately, bordered on the "salubrious," had his place close to the convulsed boy, and puffed smoke from a villanous cigar into his eyes with seeming industry, until gently remonstrated with by a Policeman, on whom he turned furiously, insisting upon tobacco smoke as an infallible remedy for fits, and that he would give the officer fits if he interfered further. However, during this sanitary dispute, the subject had come to and gone off; and the opportunity for determining fully the efficacy of burnt tobacco and whisky fumes in cases of fits, was unfortunately lost for the present.

"WE RAKED THE TOWN FROM END TO END"

Clemens' random itemizing was of course not restricted to the minor crises of the city streets. He reported other events as different from one another as a longshoremen's strike and the advent of quail for breakfast at the Occidental Hotel, where he boarded. Sometimes, as in the first two pieces below, he indulged himself by writing a miniature essay or a dramatized anecdote.

"ALKALI WATER TO THE INNOCENT MOUTHS OF CATTLE"

22

GOOD EFFECTS OF A HIGH TARIFF
22 JULY 1864

Late in June a *Call* item had noted that several leading citizens, among them a well known judge, had joined the Dashaways, the local temperance group. Like the chronicler of Tom Sawyer's and Huck Finn's adventures, the reporter was interested in the psychology of those who "took the pledge" or worked for abstention. One of the recruits, he recorded, had been moved less by considerations of morality than by the "recent high tariff imposed upon liquors." The new tax had caused the market to be flooded with a booze so inferior that the recruit "did not feel safe in drinking it" and needed all the support he could muster to "withstand the temptation." [1] Writing with high good humor, the reporter returned to this promising subject about three weeks later in the comically reflective piece that follows. The tolerant cynicism, the punning, the sustained military metaphor, the bold imagery, and the fusion of the colloquial with a more formal literary quality evident in the diction, the syntax, and the repetitions suggest a care in execution that may reflect Clemens' strong personal interest in the subject.

We are pleased to hear of the prosperous condition of the Dashaway Society. Their ranks, we are assured, are constantly filling up. The *draught* with them is working well, causing many to volunteer. The bounty they receive is sobriety, respect and health, and the blessings of families. We will not attribute all these new recruitings to the high tariff, and the difficulty of obtaining any decent whiskey. But some who join give this as their reason. They fear strychnine more than inebriation. They find it impossible to exhaust all the tarantula juice in the country, as they have been endeavoring to do for a long while, in hopes to get at some decent "rum" after all the tangle-leg should have been swallowed, and so conclude to save tariff on liquors and life by coming square up to the hydrant. Their return to original innocence and primitive bibations will be gladly welcomed. Water is a forgiving friend. After years of estrangement it meets the depraved taste with the same friendship as before. Water bears no enmity. But it must be a strange meeting—water pure and the tongues of some of our solid drinkers of Bourbon and its dishonest relations. Alkali water to the innocent mouths of cattle from the waters of the Mississippi could not seem stranger nor more disagreeable at first. But it will come around right at last. Success to the tariff and the Dashaways.

"HE WAS SMOKING THUS THOUGHTFULLY WHEN A CONTRABAND PASSED HIM"

A SCENE AT THE POLICE COURT—THE HOSTILITY OF COLOR 22 JULY 1864

The Board of Supervisors authorized the appointment of twelve new policemen on 18 July. Chief Martin J. Burke was then particularly concerned with the control of gambling in the city. The men selected from the 580 applicants were appointed within the week, bringing the regular force up to sixty-two. Clemens' report of these developments was his excuse for writing about Pat and the "contraband" at the Police Court. In form and dialect this expanded anecdote looks ahead to the brief sketch "Among the Fenians" in the 1867 volume *The Celebrated Jumping Frog of Calaveras County, and Other Sketches*. There Twain found his old friend Dennis McCarthy "solacing himself with a whiff at the national *dhudeen* or *caubeen* or whatever they call it—a clay pipe with no stem to speak of." [2]

A long file of applicants, perhaps seventy-five or eighty, passed in review before the Police Commissioners yesterday afternoon, anxious to be employed by the city in snatching drunks, burglars, petty larcenors, wife-whippers, and all offenders generally, under the authority of a star on the left breast. One of the candidates—a fine, burly specimen of an Emeralder—leaned negligently against the door-post, speculating on his chances of being "passed," and at the same time whiffing industriously at an old dhudeen, blackened by a thousand smokes. He was smoking thus thoughtfully when a contraband passed him, conveying a message to some official in the Court.

"There goes another applicant," said a wag at his elbow.

"What?" asked the smoker.

"A darkey looking for a sit on the Police," was the reply.

"An' do they give nagurs a chance on the Polis?"

"Of course."

"Then, be J——s," said Pat, knocking the ashes out of his pipe and stowing it away, "I'm out of the ring; I wouldn't demane mesilf padrowling o'nights with a nagur."

He gave one glance at the innocent and unsuspecting darkey, and left the place in disgust.

"FOR LANGUID, SLOW-MOVING, PRETENTIOUS, IMPRESSIVE, SOLEMN, AND EXCESSIVELY HIGH-TONED AND ARISTOCRATIC DANCING"

24

SOMBRE FESTIVITIES
2 AUGUST 1864

Clemens did not concede the artistry of the dancers in "Sombre Festivities," but took obvious pleasure in the dancing. The occasion celebrated the freeing of slaves in the British possessions some thirty years earlier. Probably he knew Hayes Park very well. Opened in 1860 by Thomas and Michael Hayes at Laguna and Grove Streets, it was a favorite public resort with a large pavilion and extensive fields. Its facilities, like those of the Willows and Woodward's Gardens, two other popular resorts of the period, accommodated circus and variety acts, concerts, balloon ascensions, and various sports.

All day yesterday the cars were carrying colored people of all shades and tints, and of all sizes and both sexes, out to Hayes' Park, to celebrate the anniversary of the emancipation of their race in England's West Indian possessions years ago. They rode the fiery untamed steeds that are kept for equestrian duty in the grounds; they practised pistol-shooting, but abstained from destroying the targets; they swung; they promenaded among the shrubbery; they filled themselves up with beer and sandwiches—all just as the thing is done there by white folks—and they essayed to dance, but the effort was not a brilliant success. It was interesting to look at, though. For languid, slow-moving, pretentious, impressive, solemn, and excessively high-toned and aristocratic dancing, commend us to the disenthralled North American negro, when there is no restraint upon his natural propensity to put on airs. White folks of the upper stratum of society pretend to walk through quadrilles, in a stately way, but these saddle-colored young ladies can discount them in the slow-movement evidence of high gentility. They don't know much about dancing, but they "let on" magnificently, as if the mazes of a quadrille were their native element, and they move serenely through it and tangle it hopelessly and inextricably, with an unctuous satisfaction that is surpassingly pleasant to witness. By the middle of the afternoon about two hundred darkies were assembled at the Park; or rather, to be precise, there was not much "darky" about it, either; for if the prevailing lightness of tint was worth anything as evidence, the noble miscegenationist had been skirmishing considerably among them in days gone by. It was expected that the colored race would come out strong in the matter of numbers (and otherwise) in the evening, when a grand ball was to be given and last all night.

"FOR ALL THE WORLD LIKE AN INFERNAL COUNCIL IN CONCLAVE"

25

ENTHUSIASTIC HARD-MONEY DEMONSTRATION 30 AUGUST 1864

The sedate gathering described below appealed to Clemens' sense of the ridiculous. Presumably it was part of California's answer to those persons who still may have wanted United States Treasury notes—greenbacks—to be recognized as legal tender under all circumstances.

In April 1863 the California legislature had passed the Specific Contract Act. Under its terms a borrower, at the time he signed a contract, was to specify whether he would repay his obligation in gold or in greenbacks. To the gratification of most Californians, who wanted to protect the stability of gold and silver coin, the United States Supreme Court had upheld the Specific Contract Act two weeks before Clemens wrote his piece. No doubt the court's decision and the record low price of greenbacks on the San Francisco market in August—they were quoted at 39¢—had removed the need for the hard-money dragons to breathe fire. But neither the reporter's satire nor his later publicizing of arguments favoring a paper currency indicated that *he* was willing to have *his* own salary in greenbacks. He demanded coin.[3]

The era of our prosperity is about to dawn on us. If it don't it had orter. The jingle of coin will still be heard in our pockets and tills. It's all right. The Hard Money Association held an adjourned meeting at the Police Court room last night, for the express purpose of considering dollars. The meeting was an adjourned one. It staid adjourned. It wasn't anything else. The room was dimly lighted. It looked like the Hall of Eolis. Silently sat some ten or a dozen of the galvanized protectors of our prosperity. They looked for all the world like an infernal council in conclave. They were dumb; but what great plans for the suppression of the green-backed dragon were born in that silence still remains hid in the arcana of the mysterious cabal. They said nothing, they did nothing. Like fixed statues they sat, all wrapped in contemplation of their mighty scheme. They didn't adjourn, for from the first it was an adjourned meeting, and it staid adjourned. Soon they all left—parted quietly, mysteriously, awfully. The lights were turned out, and—nothing more. Money is still hard.

"THEY . . . GOBBLED UP SHEETS,
SHIRTS AND PILLOW-CASES . . ."

THE COSMOPOLITAN HOTEL BESIEGED
1 SEPTEMBER 1864

The Cosmopolitan Hotel was a solid four-story building fronting on Bush and Sansom streets, which was known for its elegance and its elaborate fire protection system. Other observers of the hotel's opening "festivities" bore out Clemens' rather detailed account of the vandalism.[4] No doubt he was particularly interested in the occurrence, for he was a friend of John S. Henning, the hotel proprietor, who was widely known among Nevada men as an early settler in that territory. It was there that Clemens seems to have met him.[5]

As a proof that it is good policy to advertise, and that nothing that appears in a newspaper is left unread, we will state that the mere mention in yesterday's papers that the Cosmopolitan Hotel would be thrown open for public inspection, caused that place to be besieged at an early hour yesterday evening, by some thirty thousand men, women and children; and the chances are that more than as many more had read the invitation, but were obliged to forego the pleasure of accepting it. By eight o'clock, the broad halls and stairways of the building, from cellar to roof, were densely crowded, with people of all ages, sexes, characters, and conditions in life; and a similar army were collected in the street outside, unable to gain admission—there was no room for them. The lowest estimate we heard of the number of persons who passed into the Hotel was twenty thousand, and the highest sixty thousand; so we split the difference, and call it thirty thousand. And among this vast assemblage of refined gentlemen, elegant ladies, and tender children, was mixed a lot of thieves, ruffians, and vandals. They stole everything they could get their hands on—silverware from the dining room, handkerchiefs from gentlemen, veils and victorines from ladies, and even gobbled up sheets, shirts and pillow-cases in the laundry, and made off with them. They wantonly destroyed costly parlor ornaments, and pulled down and trampled under foot the handsome lace curtains of some of the windows. They "went through" Mr. Henning's room, and left him not even a sock or a boot. (We observed, a day or two ago, that he had a bushel and a half of the latter article stacked up at the foot of his bed.) The masses, wedged together in the halls and on the staircases, grew hot and angry, and smashed each other over the head with canes, and punched each other in the face with their fists, and to stop the thieving and save loss to helpless visitors, and get rid of the pickpockets, the gas had to be turned off in some parts of the house. At ten o'clock, when we were there, there was a constant stream of people passing out of the hotel, and other streams pouring towards it from every direction, to be disappointed in their hopes of seeing the wonders within it, for the proprietors having already suffered to the extent of several thousands of dollars in thefts and damages to furniture, were unwilling to admit decent people any longer, for fear of another invasion of rascals among them. Another grand rush was expected to follow the letting out of the theatres. The Cosmopolitan still stands, however, and to-day it opens for good, and for the accommodation of all of them that do eat and sleep, and have the wherewithal to pay for it.

"THOSE BOYS' LEGS AND ARMS HAVE BEEN DRILLED INTO A COMPREHENSION OF THOSE ORDERS"

**RINCON SCHOOL MILITIA
1 SEPTEMBER 1864**

This report of Rincon School's closing exercises once again demonstrates Clemens' delight in the stage performances of children. The unabashed sentimentality of R. S. Taylor's ballad "O Wrap the Flag Around Me Boys," which Clemens had called "a lugubrious ditty" two months earlier in the *Call*, never failed to astonish him, and already he was beginning that long struggle to comprehend German so vividly presented in "The Awful German Language" in 1880. Rincon School, on Harrison Street between Second and Third, enrolled 213 students in 1864. Its Professor of Calisthenics was Charles J. Robinson, and John C. Pelton was its outspoken and controversial principal. Pelton had been connected with the city's school system since 1849, when at his own expense he had opened a free school on Portsmouth Square. In 1864 the *Call* regularly championed him against the strictures of the Board of Education. Three weeks after Clemens' report appeared, Pelton was dismissed as principal and was forcibly ejected from his office following an adverse report on his activities by a committee of the board. The ensuing wrangle came to a climax with his election in May 1865 as Superintendent of Schools.[6] Many years later Pelton, an impoverished old man, wrote to " 'Mark Twain,' My well remembered and greatly respected Sir." He enclosed a "literary effort—this last of my life," and recalled the bygone times when Clemens, the San Francisco journalist, would have welcomed "compliment and congratulation." [7]

Before disbanding for a fortnight's furlough, the boys connected with Rincon School had a grand dress parade, yesterday. They are classed into regular military companies, and officered as follows, by boys chosen from their own ranks: Company A, Captain John Welch; B, Captain John Warren; C, Captain Henry Tucker; D, Captain William Thompson; E, Captain Robinson; F, Captain Charles Redman; G, Captain Cyrus Myers; H, Captain Henry Tabor. Companies I and J have no regularly elected officers, we are told. The drummers of the regiment are two youngsters named Douglas Williams and John Seaborn, and their talent for making a noise amounts almost to inspiration. Both are first-class drummers. The Rincon boys have been carefully drilled in military exercises for a year, now, and have acquired a proficiency which is astonishing. They go through with the most elaborate manoeuvres without hesitating and without making a mistake; to execute every order promptly and perfectly has become second nature to them, and requires no more reflection than it does to a practised boarder to go to dinner when he hears the gong ring. The word "drill" is the proper one—those boys' legs and arms have been drilled into a comprehension of those orders so that they execute them mechanically, even though the restless mind may be thinking of anything else in the world at the moment. Professor Robinson has been the military instructor of the Rincon Regiment for several months past. The School exercises, earlier in the day, were very interesting, and consisted of dialogues, declamations, vocal and

Portsmouth Square in 1865 (*redrawn from a photograph, Bancroft Library*).

instrumental music, calisthenics, etc. "The Humors of the Draft," a sort of comedy, illustrative of the shifts to which unwarlike patriots are put in order to compass exemption, was well played by a number of the School boys, and was received with shouts of laughter. Douglas Williams played, on his drum, a solo which would have been a happy accompaniment to one of our choicest earthquakes. A young girl sang that lugubrious ditty, "Wrap the Flag around me, Boys," and the extraordinary purity and sweetness of her voice actually made pleasant music of it, impossible as such a thing might seem to any one acquainted with that marvellous piece of composi-

tion. The Principal, Mr. Pelton's, heir, an American sovereign of eight Summers and no Winters at all, since his life has been passed here where it has pleased the Almighty to omit that season, gave a recitation in French, and one in German; and from the touching pathos and expression which he threw into the latter, and the liquid richness of his accent, we are satisfied the subject was a noble one and wrought in beautiful language, but we could not testify unqualifiedly, in this respect, without access to a translation. The Rincon School was mustered out of service, yesterday evening, for the term of two weeks.

"DISTRESSED LOOKING ABORTIONS DONE IN OIL . . . IN SUGAR, IN PLASTER, IN MARBLE, IN WAX"

**FINE PICTURE OF REV. MR. KING
1 SEPTEMBER 1864**

Clemens' friendship with the Rev. Dr. Henry W. Bellows lay behind "Fine Picture of Rev. Mr. King" and the later "Dedication of Bush Street School" (Item 30). Probably Bellows had shown Clemens Henrietta Molineux Gibson's portrait of Thomas Starr King, whose pulpit in the First Unitarian Church of San Francisco Bellows was filling. This drawing became Exhibit 597 in the art gallery of the Mechanics' Institute Industrial Fair that summer, and it brought $100 at auction. Mr. King, the venerated Unitarian clergyman and noted orator, had died six months earlier and was remembered warmly by most Californians. Clemens may have met him in Nevada through his brother Orion.[8]

California and Nevada Territory are flooded with distressed looking abortions done in oil, in water-colors, in crayon, in lithography, in photography, in sugar, in plaster, in marble, in wax, and in every sub-

stance that is malleable or chiselable, or that can be marked on, or scratched on, or painted on, or which by its nature can be compelled to lend itself to a relentless and unholy persecution and distortion of the features of the great and good man who is gone from our midst—Rev. Thomas Starr King. We do not believe these misguided artistic lunatics meant to confuse the lineaments, and finally destroy and drive out from our memories the cherished image of our lost orator, but just the contrary. We believe their motive was good, but we know their execution was atrocious. We look upon these blank, monotonous, over-fed and sleepy-looking pictures, and ask, with Dr. Bellows, "Where was the seat of this man's royalty?" But we ask in vain of these wretched counterfeits. There is no more life or expression in them than you may find in the soggy, upturned face of a pickled infant, dangling by the neck in a glass jar among the trophies of a doctor's back office, any day. But there is one perfect portrait of Mr.

King extant, with all the tenderness and goodness of his nature, and all the power and grandeur of his intellect drawn to the surface, as it were, and stamped upon the features with matchless skill. This picture is in the possession of Dr. Bellows, and is the only one we have seen in which we could discover no substantial ground for fault finding. It is a life size outline photograph, elaborately wrought out and finished in crayon by Mrs. Frances Molineux Gibson, of this city, and has been presented by her to Rev. Dr. Bellows, to be sold for the benefit of the Sanitary Commission. It will probably be exhibited for a while at the Mechanics' Fair, after which it will be disposed of, as above mentioned. Dr. Bellows desires to keep it, and will do so if bids for it do not take altogether too high a flight.

"THE BEST PAPER IN ITS PARTICULAR DEPARTMENT EVER ISSUED ON THIS COAST"

THE CALIFORNIAN
4 SEPTEMBER 1864

Less than a month after this announcement of a change in the top management of the *Californian,* that weekly paper began running Mark Twain's sketches. The reporter's puff for the new journal expressed his high regard for Bret Harte and Charles H. Webb, two friends who influenced his writing and whom he later turned against. It suggests that in early September 1864 he knew Webb, a fellow bohemian who also boarded at the Occidental Hotel, better than he knew Harte. Webb had come to San Francisco in April, and Clemens knew him first as a reporter for the *Evening Bulletin.* He wrote under the name "Inigo" for the *Golden Era* and the *Californian.* Captain Richard L. Ogden, like Webb a New Yorker, served in the Mexican War before moving to California, where he made money by manufacturing carriages. Ogden's pen name was Podgers. Later he repaid Clemens' compliment by writing to the *Alta*

California from New York: "Mark Twain's story in the Saturday Press of November 18th, called 'Jim Smiley and his Jumping Frog,' has set all New York in a roar . . . It is voted the best thing of the day. Cannot the Californian afford to keep Mark all to itself?" [9]

This sterling literary weekly has changed hands, both in the matter of proprietorship and editorial management. Mr. Webb has sold the paper to Captain Ogden, a gentleman of fine literary attainments, an able writer, and the possessor of a happy bank account—three qualifications which, in the lump, cannot fail to insure the continued success of the Californian. Mr. Frank Brett Hart will assume the editorship of the paper. Some of the most exquisite productions which have appeared in its pages emanated from his pen, and are worthy to take rank among even Dickens' best sketches. Taking all things in consideration, if the Californian dies now, it must be by the same process that resurrected Lazarus, which we are proud to be able to state was a miracle. After faithfully laboring night and day for about four months, and publishing fifteen numbers of the best paper in its particular department ever issued on this coast, Mr. Webb will now go and rest a while on the shores of Lake Tahoe. He has chosen to rest himself by fishing, and he is wise; for the fish in Lake Tahoe are not troublesome; they will let a man rest there till he rots, and never inflict upon him the fatigue of putting on a fresh bait. "Inigo" has our kindest wishes for his present and future happiness, though, rot or no rot.

"THE COLORS IN THE PICTURE ARE NOT GAUDY ENOUGH TO SUIT THE POPULAR TASTE, PERHAPS"

**A PROMISING ARTIST
6 SEPTEMBER 1864**

Five days after blasting the "artistic lunatics" who had distorted Starr King's features, the reporter-turned-critic spoke up again. Once more he showed his preference for paintings that "represent nature truthfully." He liked a realism of detail that would "tell the story."

William Mulligan, a native Missourian, studied art in Germany and France before moving to California in 1862 and settling on a large ranch near Healdsburg.

The large oil painting in the picture store under the Russ House, of the "Blind Fiddler," is the work of a very promising California artist, Mr. William Mulligan, of Healdsburg, formerly of St. Louis, Mo. In the main, both the conception and execution are good, but the latter is faulty in some of the minor details. Dr. Bellows has a smaller picture, however, by the same artist, which betrays the presence of genius of a high order in the hand that limned it. The subject is a dying drummer-boy, half sitting, half reclining, upon the battle field, with his body partly propped upon his broken drum, and his left arm hanging languidly over it. Near him lie his cap and his drum-sticks—unheeded, discarded, useless to him forever more. The dash of blood upon his shirt, the dreamy, away-at home look upon the features, the careless, resigned expression of the nerveless arm, tell the story. The colors in the picture are not gaudy enough to suit the popular taste, perhaps, but they represent nature truthfully, which is better. Mr. Mulligan has demonstrated in every work his hands have wrought, that he is an artist of more than common ability, and he deserves a generous encouragement. One or two of his pictures will probably be exhibited at the Mechanics' Fair now being held in this city.

"THERE WERE QUAILS FOR BREAKFAST AT THE OCCIDENTAL"

EXTRAORDINARY ENTERPRISE
16 SEPTEMBER 1864

It is said by those who ought to know, that the law against killing game only suspended operation at midnight on Wednesday, yet there were quails for breakfast at the Occidental at six o'clock the next morning. The man who brought those birds to town will wear himself out, some time or other, in getting up at such unseasonable hours of the night to take advantage of an outgoing law. It would be wrong to suspect him of having captured the quails the day before.

"GOOD AND CAPABLE MEN WOULD NOT WORK AT THE TERMS OFFERED"

STRIKE OF THE STEAMER EMPLOYÉS
22 SEPTEMBER 1864

The shipping strike that began on the evening of 20 September affected the Pacific Mail Steamship Company (S. S. *Golden City*) and the Central American Transit Company, usually known as the People's Opposition Line (S. S. *America*). Coal passers and firemen struck after having their wages reduced, and Clemens' sympathy is clearly with them, just as he felt for exploited teachers and underdog federal employees at this time. Contrary to his statement below, steamship officials agreed only in part to the strikers' demands, and presumably only the presence of the police prevented additional violence when the *Golden City* sailed the following day with a crew of strikebreakers as scores of sullen, idle men watched from the wharf. The wounded Captain of Detectives Isaiah W. Lees later became Chief of Police, climaxing a career of forty-four years on the force.

For two weeks after the initial clash, Clemens followed up the story in brief notices of further disturbances, arrests, and arraignments.[10] But coming when his days on the *Call* were numbered, his reports show a slipshod handling of the facts. Perhaps George Barnes had these very events in mind when he explained years later why the newspaper had needed a "more active man for reporter" than Clemens:

> "Mark," said the managing editor to him, one day, "there is a riot going on among the stevedores along the city front. Get the facts and make a column."
>
> "Ya-a-s," he responded, with his inimitable drawl; "but how can I get them. There's no street railroad down that way. You wouldn't want a fellow to walk a mile to see a couple of 'longshoremen in a fight, would you?" [11]

A large body of the strikers who have been employed on our ocean steamers, and who quit work because their wages were reduced below living rates, marched to Dall's shipping office, at the corner of Vallejo and Davis streets, yesterday morning, and afterwards proceeded to North Point, where the America was ready to set sail, but was waiting to ship a crew. Here they found men going aboard to take the vacant places at the reduced rates, and compelled them to take their kits ashore again, and give up the idea. Several men were knocked down and roughly handled in the melee which ensued, among them Captain Lees, of the Detective Police, who received a heavy blow on the head with a billet of wood. About noon the officers of the America acceded to the terms demanded by the workmen, and restored the former rate of wages, and a crew was then shipped without molestation. Wages on the Golden City will doubtless remain as they were before, also. The prices heretofore paid (and no increase was asked by the men,) were as follows: firemen, $70 a month; coal-passers, $50; sailors, $40, and waiters, $40; and they are little enough. Men who leave families ashore, could not support them on less, and it is anything but just to ask them to do it. The insignificant sum the steamship companies would make by the small reduction contemplated, would be lost again by the inferior capacity of the men employed, for good and capable men would not work at the terms offered.

"THIS PACIFIC COAST . . . WHERE
FORTY YEARS ENTITLED A MAN TO BE
CALLED VENERABLE"

33

DEDICATION OF BUSH STREET SCHOOL
23 SEPTEMBER 1864

Dr. Henry W. Bellows, a prominent Unitarian minister from New York City, was founder and president of the United States Sanitary Commission. An indefatigable and resounding orator—his name is amusingly appropriate—he vigorously raised funds for the commission during a five-month western campaign that began in early May and took him to California, Oregon, and Nevada. In San Francisco, where he was based, he often spoke on ceremonial occasions such as the one described below. He and Clemens soon were on familiar terms, and the local columns of the *Call* faithfully and admiringly tallied his activities.[12] Clemens' admiration for Bellows contrasts with his indifference toward the other dignitaries on the platform: Mayor Henry P. Coon, Superintendent of Schools George Tait, Principal James Denman, the Reverend G. J. Mingins of the First Presbyterian Church, and A. F. Sawyer, M.D.

Such preferential treatment is often found in Clemens' reporting. A comparison of his account below with its counterpart in the *Alta California*[13] shows that the *Alta* report more accurately reflected the structure of the occasion, that it was more balanced, more complete, more objective—and less interesting. Not only did the *Call's* man pass over other speakers in favor of Henry Bellows but he also ignored sections of Bellows' address. Here, as elsewhere, the writer's enthusiasm or pique, his way of seeing or imagining, strongly affected the tone and shape of his reporting.

The Bush Street Grammar School was a three-story box-like structure that cost approximately $65,000 to build.

The handsome and costly building lately erected on the corner of Bush and Taylor streets, was dedicated yesterday morning. The first part of the ceremonies consisted of some vocal and instrumental music.

Mayor Coon made a plain, sensible speech, pertinent to the occasion, and delivered the keys of the edifice into the hands of Mr. Tait, Superin-tendent of the Public Schools, who read a carefully prepared and rather interesting document relating to educational matters in the city and county of San Francisco. According to his estimate, there are about 29,000 persons among us under the age of eighteen years; of these, 18,000 were born in California; 6,000 attend the Public, and nearly

5,000 the Private Schools; 2,600 children, old enough to receive instruction, attend no School at all, and would not if they could; and there is a still larger number that would if they could, but are debarred by the want of School accommodations at present. The new Bush Street School contains twelve classes, numbering in the aggregate seven hundred and sixty pupils.

Mr. Denman, the Principal of the School, followed with a brief but interesting history of the rise and progress of the Public School system of San Francisco, and after a song by the girls, the Rev. Dr. Bellows delivered what was probably the ablest address that such an occasion ever called forth, either here or anywhere else. There were two things in his discourse which marked the profound thinker, and which had in them more of significance and matter for serious reflection than all the speeches and sermons we have heard in a year. He said California had been blessed beyond all other lands in her mild and salubrious climate, and she was proud of it and grateful for it—but let her look to it that this blessing be not turned into a curse. There was danger of it; there was unquestionably great and serious danger of it. There was room for profound apprehension for the future of a land that had no firesides! It was around the home fireside, in the midst of the sacred home circle, when the toils, and the vanities and the cares of the day were over, and the world, with its pomp and wretchedness, and its sin and show and folly, shut out and forgotten, that those sweet and holy influences were brought to bear that trained young hearts in the love of the good and the abhorrence of evil; first impressions that clung to them, and formed and

ennobled their characters, and fitted them to mould and purify society and advance the well being of the State in after life. He feared for the future happiness of a land without these fireside influences. In another division of his address the speaker dwelt upon the tremendous responsibilities resting upon those here in whose keeping was entrusted the moral, religious and educational training of the young, and said that in California those responsibilities were incalculably greater than in any other section of the Union, for upon them devolved the work of laying the foundations of a society and a government which, at the end of this generation, must be delivered into the hands of a community of young men and young women, with no old and experienced heads left among them to guide and watch over them with that sound wisdom and judgment which can only be gained by fighting the hard battle of life, and with few among their own numbers who have had an opportunity of getting even a theoretical idea of the worldly knowledge and wisdom that would have fallen to them in a land where old men and old women were numerous. He met only youths and maidens, comparatively speaking, in all the walks of life upon this Pacific Coast—a section of the world where forty years entitled a man to be called venerable. From his observation of the character, and habits, and domestic training of the new generation, full of life and activity, and impatient of restraint, which he saw growing up here, debarred from association with age and from wholesome instruction from the experienced, California had need to fear for her well-being when her few remaining veterans shall have passed away, and left this great and powerful State, with its mighty interests, in the keeping of a community who are men and women in age, but merely boys and girls in wisdom and experience. This was why he considered that the teachers of the youth on this coast were burthened with heavier responsibilities than those of any other land. The task before them is to raise up a great and good people, out of an army of youths and maidens springing up in a land where aged men and women are not, and firesides are unknown.

Dr. Bellows uttered many a great and original thought during his oration, but none seemed so new and startling, and withal so pregnant with significance as these two which we have attempted to set down here in outline. The spirit of prophecy was upon him. It will be well if California heeds the warning he has proclaimed to her.

SAWYER AND MINGINS

Dr. Bellows was followed by the Rev. Mr. Mingins and Dr. Sawyer. Their addresses contained nothing worth reporting, and only had the effect of postponing the calisthenic exercises of the school girls till two o'clock, thus disappointing many who had come on purpose to see them. Sawyer lauded the Board and the building, but he neglected to mention the salaries of the poor teachers. And he abused the newspapers for censuring the Board of Education—warned the people to disbelieve everything editors and reporters published against that spotless body of men.

An anti-Chinese riot at the Rope Walk in 1865 (*Bancroft Library*).

SAN FRANCISCO'S CHINESE

A. "THE CHINESE . . . ARE BECOMING CIVILIZED"

Clemens had known the Chinese quarter of Virginia City and had published at least one account of it in the *Territorial Enterprise,* the sketchlike "Chinatown" reprinted in *Roughing It.* Probably he wrote a good many other *Enterprise* items on the Chinese, especially about their troubles with the police. In the *Call,* at least, the local reporter's brief pieces about "John" or "Ah Chow" almost always referred to their arrest for some misdemeanor. Sometimes Clemens lightly sketched these law-breakers, but he never learned how to make a believable Chinese character in fiction. His understanding of the Chinese people deepened, though, and he had become a compassionate champion of their civil rights by the late 1860's. Still, it is difficult to say to what extent the selections below indicate that growth. Their comedy draws upon racial stereotypes and crudities, understandable in the context of that day even if not entirely excusable. In my opinion these crudities, so eloquent of insensitive attitudes, were intended primarily as "comic" strokes. In his *Call* writings he often placed Caucasians in a similar "comic" perspective, but by drawing upon national rather than racial stereotypes. His job as a police reporter was to notice infractions of the law by all kinds of persons—whites, Chinese, and Negroes. This he did, in rough proportion to their numbers in the city's population.

The reporter who speaks below also anticipates the writer of "Goldsmith's Friend Abroad Again," for he is beginning to see the Chinese as victims of an "enlightened" and "Christian" and "civilized" way of life. I feel, however, that Clemens' use of these terms in the selections below implies his growing acceptance of a new set of stereotypes, employed at that time as much for comic purposes as for the expression of social criticism or of a sense of compassion for the wronged.

"THE LATEST DODGE DETECTED WAS SAUSAGES, BOLOGNAS, AS IT WERE . . ."

34

**OPIUM SMUGGLERS
9 JULY 1864**

By 1864 the importation and smuggling of opium from China into San Francisco was big business. In January revenue officers seized a large consignment of the drug brought in on the *Derby,* a ship out of Hong Kong. Other seizures followed, but opium dens continued to flourish. On 5 July the *Derby* was back with a load of coolies. Custom House officials seized between two and three hundred artfully concealed boxes of opium, some, as Clemens noted, packed in Bologna sausages. In "Goldsmith's Friend Abroad Again," written six years later, Mark Twain probably was remembering such stratagems when he pictured customs inspectors seizing the opium sewed into Hong-Wo's queue—but his point of view had shifted to that of the smuggler's friend, Ah Song Hi.[1]

The ingenuity of the Chinese is beyond calculation. It is asserted that they have no words or expressions signifying abstract right or wrong. They appreciate "good" and "bad," but it is only in reference to business, to finance, to trade, etc. Whatever is successful is good; whatever fails is bad. So they are not conscience-bound in planning and perfecting ingenious contrivances for avoiding the tariff on opium, which is pretty heavy. The attempted swindles appear to have been mostly, or altogether, attempted by the Coolie passengers—the Chinese merchants, either from honorable motives or from policy, having dealt honestly with the Government. But the passengers have reached the brains of rascality itself, to find means for importing their delicious drug without paying the duties. To do this has called into action the inventive genius of brains equal in this respect to any that ever lodged on the top end of humanity. They have, doubtless, for years smuggled opium into this port continuously. The officers of Customs at length got on their track, and the traffic has become unprofitable to the Coolies, however well it has been paying the officials through the seizures made. The opium has been found concealed in double jars and brass eggs, as heretofore described, brought ashore in bands around the body, and by various other modes. The latest dodge detected was sausages, Bolognas, as it were, filled with opium; and yesterday we saw a tin can, with a false bottom about one third the distance from the base, the lower third of the can filled with opium, the rest with oil. John himself will have to be opened next—he is undoubtedly full of it.

"STOLEN AND BROUGHT FROM HONGKONG TO SAN FRANCISCO TO BE SOLD"

35

CHINESE SLAVES
12 JULY 1864

As this item indicates, kidnapped Chinese girls, imported for the brothels of Chinatown, were not as easily concealed aboard ship as a consignment of opium. Nevertheless, Chinese prostitution flourished and posed a serious problem for Police Chief Martin J. Burke. One of his solutions was that Chinese prostitutes be "driven to some locality where they may herd by themselves and not offend public decency." [2] Before he left office in 1866, he actually succeeded in closing most of the Chinese brothels, at least temporarily.

The Chinese Companies mentioned by Clemens were the six major associations of California Chinese, whose affiliation with one association or another depended upon their home district in China. The companies were formed between 1850 and 1854, and by 1862 all six were represented in a powerful coordinating council called The Chinese Consolidated Benevolent Association, known to Americans as the Chinese Six Companies. This central association kept in touch with the Imperial Manchu government, and it helped Chinese emigrate to California and return to China. Likewise, it promoted the interests of Chinese within America. It fought anti-Chinese legislation as well as the disruptive Tongs, it served as a Chinese Chamber of Commerce and arbitrated disputes among Chinese, and it provided educational, police, medical, and burial services to the Chinese community.

The policeman accompanying Captain William Y. Douglass aboard the *Clara Morse* was not named Hager, as Clemens had it, but Bernard Hagan.

Captain Douglass and Watchman Hager boarded the ship Clara Morse, on Sunday morning, the moment she arrived, and captured nineteen Chinese girls, who had been stolen and brought from Hongkong to San Francisco to be sold. They were a choice lot, and estimated to be worth from one hundred and fifty to four hundred dollars apiece in this market. They are shut up for safe-keeping for the present, and we went and took a look at them yesterday; some of them are almost good-looking, and none of them are pitted with small-pox—a circumstance which we have observed is very rare among China women. There were even small children among them—one or two not two years old, perhaps, but the ages of the majority ranged from fourteen to twenty. We would suggest, just here that the room where these unfortunates are confined is rather too close for good health—and besides, the more fresh air that blows on a Chinaman, the better he smells. The heads of the various Chinese Companies here have entered into a combination to break up this importation of Chinese prostitutes, and they are countenanced and supported in their work by Chief Burke and Judge Shepheard. Now-a-days, before a ship gets her cables out, the Police board her, seize the girls and shut them up, under guard, and they are sent back to China as soon as opportunity offers, at the expense of the Chinese Companies, who also send an agent along to hunt up the families from whom the poor creatures have been stolen, and restore to them their lost darlings again. Our Chinese fellow citizens seem to be acquiring a few good Christian instincts, at any rate.

"THESE TAEPINGS WERE CHARGED WITH TAPPINGS . . ."

"WON'T YOU WALK INTO MY PARLOR" 13 AUGUST 1864

Clemens' term *Taepings* referred to a contemporary rebellion in China led by Hung-siu-Tsuen, who aimed to establish the Tai-ping (Great Peace) native dynasty. The rebellion, which had begun in 1850, was finally put down by the forces of the Manchu dynasty, aided by the English and a few American officers.

A whole bevy of those funny-looking animals that totter through the street labelled "Chinese Women," had been invited to call upon Judge Shepheard yesterday morning, when they would hear something to their disadvantage. These Taepings were charged with tappings, and as they didn't appear, the Judge charged them for it, and much bail was forfeited. There were about a dozen cases. The offence is simply a conventional sign of invitation to persons passing, to walk in, and grows out of the characteristic hospitality of that class of persons.

**"PREPARING FOR A GRAND
RAILROAD DISASTER"**

37

**CHINESE RAILROAD OBSTRUCTIONS
30 AUGUST 1864**

The pioneer Sacramento Valley Railroad made its first trial run 17 August 1855 from Sacramento, where it began, to Folsom. Later it connected to San Francisco.

The Chinese in this State are becoming civilized to a fearful extent. One of them was arrested the other day, in the act of preparing for a grand railroad disaster on the Sacramento Valley Railroad. If these people continue to imbibe American ideas of progress, they will be turning their attention to highway robbery, and other enlightened pursuits. They are industrious.

"A STORY OF A CHINAMAN NAMED AH SIN"

38

**SUICIDE OUT OF PRINCIPLE
3 SEPTEMBER 1864**

Crimes of theft and of violence by Chinese were proof to Clemens in 1864 that the race could be civilized—even Americanized—but by 1870 he was less hopeful: "The Chinamen being smart, shrewd people, take to some few of our commercial customs and virtues, but somehow we can't make great headway in the matter of civilizing them. We can teach them to gamble a little, but somehow we can't make them get drunk. It is discouraging—because you can't regenerate a being that won't get drunk." [3] Ah Sin, of the 1877 play written by Bret Harte and Mark Twain, successfully made the transition to American shrewdness, unlike the earlier Ah Sin of this item, who definitively rejected the secure future offered him by officialdom. Clemens also came to realize, however, that the emotional needs of Americans promised a niche in our society for *all* Chinese, not excepting such stubborn individualists as the first Ah Sin, who even in death kept to the old Chinese ways. In 1870 Mark Twain advised his fellow countrymen: "You will find them ever so convenient, because when you get mad you can snatch a club and go out and take satisfaction out of a Chinaman. The native American negro is getting so insolent, now, that the patriot from Ireland cannot take a little recreation out of him without getting into trouble." [4]

The Grass Valley *National* was a well-established paper in Nevada County, California.

The Grass Valley National, of Tuesday evening, tells a story of a Chinaman named Ah Sin, who committed suicide in a very civilized way, impelled thereto by an enlightened motive. Ah Sin loved—to smoke opium. He had, it may be supposed, a quantity of his favorite drug, but lacked a pipe. In an evil hour, when suffering for the want of a smoke, he chanced upon a pipe "worth four bits or a dollar," and incontinently gobbled it up. At least that was the charge made against him by some other Chinamen, who were so angry with him for thus disgracing the national character for honesty, that they could not take time to starve the culprit to death in the usual manner, but undertook to beat him to death. A Policeman rescued him from the hands of the executioners, and for safety placed him in the calaboose. John called for his pipe and his opium bag, took a farewell smoke, and then taking his sash, a dirty silk one, from his waist, hung himself with it, with a great deal of difficulty and determination. The Policeman discovered him dead when he went in to give him his regular tea. He was in a kneeling position, from which it may be inferred that he died while saying his prayers to Josh.

"ONLY SO HOW—NOT TOO LITTY, NOT TOO MUCH!"

STABBED
21 SEPTEMBER 1864

Two Chinamen got into a dispute early yesterday morning in a butcher shop, in Washington Alley, when one of them seized a pork cleaver and aimed four murderous blows at the other's head; the latter removed his head from the line of attack, and received the blows on his arm, hand and side. His arm got two deep gashes, his side a slight scratch, and his right hand was cut nearly in half, the blade striking a straight line across it a little below the base of the fingers. At this point the wounded man seized a knife and plunged it into his assailant's side, and withdrew from the contest, leaving him dangerously scared and feeble, but not fatally injured. He considered that he withdrew from the contest with credit to his share in the transaction; he evidently prided himself upon the fine judgment and spirit of moderation he had shown under circumstances where the forgetting of such virtues for a moment or two might be naturally regarded as excusable. Holding a stick in his mutilated left hand, he designated upon it with his thumb nail a point two inches and a half from the end of the stick, saying, "Only so how—not too litty, not too much!" Only an elaborate experience and the spirit of the true artist could have enabled this bland Chinaman to cypher down to a fraction the just amount of stabbing necessary to square accounts with his adversary without overdoing the thing or falling short of it. Officer James Conway arrested the mathematical Chinaman and jammed him into the station-house.

40

AH SOW DISCHARGED
24 SEPTEMBER 1864

Ah Sow, the mathematical Chinaman, who stabbed Ah Wong "not too litty, not too much," but just exactly enough to make him uncomfortable, was discharged from custody yesterday, at the request of the grateful creature who was indebted for his life to his spirit of forbearance and the exercise of his extraordinary anatomical judgment.

"WHETHER A CHINAMAN'S WIFE IS HIS'N OR YOUR'N IF YOU WANT HER"

41

AN INTERESTING CORRESPONDENCE
6 OCTOBER 1864

A California statute of 1850 prohibited testimony of Negroes and Indians in court cases involving whites, and four years later this statute was interpreted to include Chinese as well. Clemens defined the problem in *Roughing It*: "Any white man can swear a Chinaman's life away in the courts, but no Chinaman can testify against a white man" [5]—just as Ah Sin, in the play by Twain and Harte, cannot testify against York. None of Clemens' write-ups of cases involving Chinese allude to this inequity, but surely he was aware of it. In 1868 Mark Twain wrote: "Formerly, in the police court, they swore Chinamen according to the usual form, and sometimes, where the magistrate was particularly anxious to come at the truth, a chicken was beheaded in open court and some yellow paper burned with awful solemnity while the oath was administered—but the Chinaman testified only against his own countrymen." [6]

In August 1864, when Clemens exhibited an acute interest in court reforms of all kinds, an anonymous *Call* contributor who wrote with a flair not unlike that of Clemens urged judges to make available a variety of oaths to the non-Christian "John" Chinaman on trial. "His is an accommodating conscience, and the oath is *equally* binding, let the form be breaking a saucer, decapitating a cock, burning a match, or kissing the Bible." The writer also urged the burning of yellow paper as the "most binding" of all forms to the Chinese. Flexibility in the courtroom was needed, he declared. He had once observed a Chinese prisoner who wished "to be sworn on thunder, but as the stock in possession of the Clerk was low at the time, the oath was declined." The unknown writer was an observer of trial procedure who was interested in exposing "the absurdities so often witnessed in the Court rooms of California." [7] Whether he was Clemens or another, the article is an additional indication that in 1864 Clemens was well aware of the legal inequities imposed on the Chinese.

Elisha Cook was the only attorney with that last name listed in the 1864 city directory. Charles T. Carvalho—not Carvalto—was a well known, accomplished court interpreter, a native of Batavia, Java, who read and spoke Chinese dialects with great facility. Scholars have noted Clemens' acquaintance with Bulwer Lytton's writings during the 1860's.[8] Possibly, literary friends in San Francisco had introduced him to the writings of the Marquise de Sévigné and those of Marguerite Power, the Countess of Blessington, whose *Conversations with Lord Byron* might have appealed to Clemens because of his interest in Byron at the time.

A case was brought before Judge Shepheard yesterday afternoon, on preliminary examination, which involved some nice points, and also enriched the polite literature of the country with what Mr. Cook, counsel for one of the parties, termed "foreign correspondence"—a number of epistolary communications, equal to the productions of Madame de Sevigne or the Countess of Blessington. One of the questions presented was, whether a Chinaman's wife is his'n or your'n if you want her. Ah Chung had a friend who had a wife; friend was in the mountains, wife in this city, and Ah Chung in Shasta. Ah Chung visited the city, and delivered to his friend's wife what purported to be a letter from her husband, directing her to pack up her trunks and go to him, the messenger to be her escort. She packed up, and Ah Chung took her to Shasta for his own use. She found herself betrayed, and in durance. A female friend of her own nation sympathized with her, and wrote a letter, informing a friend of the distressed captive in this city of Ah Chung's infamy— Bulwer Lytton couldn't have done it more eloquently—stating that the perfidious Ah Chung claimed the woman as his property, and asked two hundred dollars to redeem her. A correspondence on the subject followed, resulting in the liberation of the abducted victim; though without her baggage, which had been confiscated by the avaricious Ah Chung. The denouement was Ah Chung's being held yesterday, by Judge Shepheard, in the sum of twenty-five hundred dollars, to answer in the County Court to a charge of grand larceny. The letters, which were written, of course, in Chinese char- acters, were translated by Mr. Charles Carvalto, and afforded an interesting specimen of sentiment and condolence as expressed by they of the Flowery Kingdom.

B. "THE NEW JOSH HOUSE"

When Mark Twain wrote his "Around the World" letters and *Roughing It,* he recalled his visits in 1864 to the Ning Yeung Temple on Dupont Alley and may even have taken some of his facts from his *Call* sketches. Referring in *Roughing It* to the Chinese Six Companies, he wrote:

> The See Yup Company is held to be the largest of these. The Ning Yeong Company is next, and numbers eighteen thousand members on the coast. Its headquarters are at San Francisco, where it has a costly temple, several great officers (one of whom keeps regal state in seclusion and cannot be approached by common humanity), and a numerous priesthood. In it I was shown a register of its members, with the dead and the date of their shipment to China duly marked.[9]

The Ning Yeung Association, made up of Chinese from the Toyshan District, was formed in 1854 as an offshoot of the See Yup Society and became the largest association in The Chinese Consolidated Benevolent Association, or the Six Companies. Although sometimes unfriendly to the Chinese, the *Call* editors presumably believed that an event so important to this powerful association as the opening of its temple should be adequately noticed. Clemens seems to have kept in the good graces of the officers of the association, for a month later he was invited back to the temple for the company's banquet. At the feast were such notables as Police Chief Burke, Police Judge Shepheard, District Attorney Nathan Porter, Assistant Prosecuting Attorney Davis Louderback, Fire Chief David Scannell, Court Interpreter Carvalho, and Supervisors A. H. Titcomb and Dr. Isaac Rowell—the temple fathers knew whom to stuff with their birds' tongues and sharks' fins. Clemens reported that he worked up a "desolating appetite for the occasion," which was "a lavish display of barbarian magnificence." "The Chinese," he concluded, "have a princely way of getting up and conducting these affairs, that rather throw us Republicans into the shade." [10]

THE NEW CHINESE TEMPLE
19 AUGUST 1864

To-day the Ning-Yong Company will finish furnishing and decorating the new Josh house, or place of worship, built by them in Broadway, between Dupont and Kearny streets, and to-morrow they will begin their unchristian devotions in it. The building is a handsome brick edifice, two stories high on Broadway, and three on the alley in the rear; both fronts are of pressed brick. A small army of workmen were busily engaged yesterday, in putting on the finishing touches of the embellishments. The throne of the immortal Josh is at the head of the hall in the third story, within a sort of alcove of elaborately carved and gilded woodwork, representing human figures and birds and beasts of all degrees of hideousness. Josh himself is as ugly a monster as can be found outside of China. He is in a sitting posture, is of about middle stature, but excessively fat; his garments are flowing and ample, garnished with a few small circlets of looking-glass, to represent jewels, and streaked and striped, daubed from head to foot, with paints of the liveliest colors. A long strand of black horsehair sprouts from each corner of his upper lip, another from the centre of his chin, and one from just forward of each ear. He wears an open-work crown, which gleams with gold leaf. His rotund face is painted a glaring red, and the general expression of this fat and happy god is as if he had eaten too much rice and rats for dinner, and would like his belt loosened if he only had the energy to do it. In front of the throne hangs a chandelier of Chinese manufacture, with a wilderness of glass drops and curved candle supports about it; but it is not as elegant and graceful as the American article. Under it, in a heavy frame-work, a big church bell is hung, also of Chinese workmanship; it is carved and daubed with many-colored paint all over. In front of the bell, three long tables are ranged, the fronts of two of which display a perfect maze-work of carving. The principal one shows, behind a glass front, several hundred splendidly gilded figures of kings on thrones, and bowing and smirking attendants, and horses on the rampage. The figures in this huge carved picture stand out in bold relief from the background, but they are not stuck on. The whole concern is worked out of a single broad slab of timber, and only the cunning hand of

Chinatown, with the temple at Pacific and Dupont (now Grant) streets in the back, probably in the late 1860's (*Bancroft Library*).

a Chinaman could have wrought it. Over the forward table is suspended a sort of shield, of indescribable shape, whose face is marked in compartments like a coat of arms, and in each of these is another nightmare of burnished and distorted human figures. The ceiling of this room, and both sides of it, are adorned with great sign boards, (they look like that to a content Christian, at any rate,) bearing immense Chinese letters or characters, sometimes raised from the surface of the wood and sometimes cut into it, and sometimes these letters being painted a bright red or green, and the grand expanse of sign board blazing with gold-leaf, or *vice versa*. These signs are presents to the Church from other companies, and they bear the names of those corporations, and possibly some extravagant Chinese moral or other, though if the latter was the case we failed to prove it by Ah Wae, our urbane and intelligent interpreter. Up and down the room, on both sides, are ranged alternate chairs and tables, made of the same hard, close-grained black wood used in the carved tables abovementioned; devout pagans lean their elbows on these little side tables, and swill tea while they worship Josh. Now, humble and unpretending Christian as we are, there was something infinitely comfortable and touching to us in this gentle mingling together of piety and breakfast. They have a large painted drum, and a pig or two, in this temple. How would it strike you, now, to stand at one end of this room with ranks of repentant Chinamen extending down either side before you, sipping purifying tea, and all about and above them a gorgeous cloud of glaring colors and dazzling gold and tinsel, with the bell tolling, and the drums thundering,

and the gongs clanging, and portly, blushing old Josh in the distance, smiling upon it all, in his imbecile way, from out his splendid canopy? Nice, perhaps? In the second story there are more painted emblems and symbols than we could describe in a week. In the first story are six long white slats (in a sort of vault) split into one hundred and fifty divisions, each like the keys of a piano, and this affair is the death-register of the Ning-Yong Company. When a man dies, his name, age, his native place in China, and the place of his death in this country, are inscribed on one of these keys, and the record is always preserved. Ah Wae tells us that the Ning-Yong Company numbers eighteen or twenty thousand persons on this coast, now, and has numbered as high as twenty-eight thousand. Ah Wae speaks good English, and is the outside business man of the tribe—that is, he transacts matters with us barbarians. He will occupy rooms and offices in the temple, as will also the great Wy Gah, the ineffable High Priest of the temple, and Sing Song, or President of the Ning-Yong Company. The names of the temple, inscribed over its doors, are, "Ning Yong Chu Oh," and "Ning Yong Wae Quong;" both mean the same thing, but one is more refined and elegant, and is suited to a higher and more cultivated class of Chinese than the other —though to our notion they appear pretty much the same thing, as far as facility of comprehending them is concerned. To-morrow the temple will be opened, and all save Chinese will be excluded from it until about the 5th of September, when white folks will be free to visit it, due notice having first been given in the newspapers, and a general invitation extended to the public.

"THE OLD ORIGINAL JOSH . . . CAN COME ON EARTH, OR APPEAR ANYWHERE HE PLEASES"

43

THE CHINESE TEMPLE
21 AUGUST 1864

The New Chinese Temple in Broadway—the "Ning Yong Wae Quong" of the Ning Yong Company, was dedicated to the mighty Josh night before last, with a general looseness in the way of beating of drums, clanging of gongs and burning of yellow paper, commensurate with the high importance of the occasion. In the presence of the great idol, the other day, our cultivated friend, Ah Wae, informed us that the old original Josh (of whom the image was only an imitation, a substitute vested with power to act for the absent God, and bless Chinamen or damn them, according to the best of his judgment,) lived in ancient times on the Mountain of Wong Chu, was seventeen feet high, and wielded a club that weighed two tons; that he died two thousand five hundred years ago, but that he is all right yet in the Celestial Kingdom, and can come on earth, or appear anywhere he pleases, at a moment's notice, and that he could come down here and cave our head in with his club if he wanted to. We hope he don't want to. Ah Wae told us all that, and we deliver it to the public just as we got it, advising all to receive it with caution and not bet on its truthfulness until after mature reflection and deliberation. As far as we are concerned, we don't believe it, for all it sounds so plausible.

"WE . . . DROPPED A SYMPATHETIC TEAR IN A FRAGRANT RAT-PIE"

44

THE NEW CHINESE TEMPLE
23 AUGUST 1864

"Feuding" with other reporters was a staple of Nevada journalism that Clemens carried to the *Call.* In San Francisco he directed several darts at writers for the *Evening Bulletin,* but his main target in 1864 was Albert S. Evans, local reporter for the *Alta California.* As the novelty of writing up the new Chinese temple wore off, Clemens used this assignment for one of his more sustained attacks on Evans. The two men had begun trading insults through their local columns late in June, and they would carry it on with fair regularity through 1865 and into 1866, Clemens using the San Francisco *Dramatic Chronicle* and the *Territorial Enterprise* as his main outlets.

To other San Francisco journalists Evans was commonly known as Colonel Moustache, a nickname, and as Fitz Smythe, a comic pseudonym he seems to have chosen. "Amigo" and "Altamonte" were the names he signed to his correspondence to the Gold Hill *News* and the Chicago *Tribune,* respectively. Maybe he wrote too much too fast, to judge by the ease with which San Francisco's bohemian journalists ridiculed his writing. Clemens, Webb of the *Californian,* James F. Bowman of the *American Flag* and *Dramatic Chronicle,* Frank W. Gross of the *Bulletin,* R. M. McHenry of the *Democratic Press* and the *Examiner,* Tremenhere Lanyon Johns of *Puck,* and the "Town Crier" of the *News Letter and California Advertiser,* all joined in the kill. The beleaguered Evans was industrious and conscientious but pedestrian. His phrasing was often awkward and his humor flat. He had an unhappy knack for blundering. Outwardly he was unswervingly moral, easily shocked, usually naïve—a perfect target for irreverent bohemians, whom he genuinely disliked.

Evans became doubly vulnerable when he invented the satiric character Armand Leonidas Stiggers early in 1864. Stiggers, who was presented as Fitz Smythe's assistant on the *Alta,* was part dandy and part bohemian. He had "weak blue eyes, delicate pink hair," and "green spectacles," and he carried a "switch cane and maroon-colored gloves." [11] His predicaments were regularly aired in the paper's local columns, and his jokes were dismal.[12] Often in company with his flea-ridden dog Rienzi, he talked, ate, and drank too much. He was a thoroughly commonplace creation—a failure if he was meant as a parody of bohemians—and Clemens gleefully pounced on him. To gravel Evans even more, before long Clemens identified Stiggers with his creator. Six years after leaving the *Call,* Clemens must have had Stiggers in mind when he wrote to his publisher, Elisha Bliss of the American Publishing Company, about Evans: "A one-horse newspaper reporter who has been trying all his life to make a joke and never has and never *will* succeed. . . . And don't he hate *me?* I should *think* so. I used to trot him out in the papers lang syne." [13]

Being duly provided with passes, through the courtesy of our cultivated barbaric friend, Ah Wae, outside business-agent of the Ning-Yong Company, we visited the new Chinese Temple again yesterday, in company with several friends. After suffocating in the smoke of burning punk and josh lights, and the infernal odors of opium and all kinds of edibles cooked in an unchristian manner, until we were becoming imbued with Buddhism and beginning to lose our nationality, and imbibe, unasked, Chinese instincts, we finally found Ah Wae, who roused us from our lethargy and saved us to our religion and our country by merely breathing the old, touching words, so simple and yet so impressive, and withal so familiar to those whose blessed privilege it has been to be reared in the midst of a lofty and humanizing civilization: "How do, gentlemen—take a drink?" By the magic of that one phrase, our noble American instincts were spirited back to us again, in all their pristine beauty and glory. The polished cabinet of wines and liquors stood on a table in one of the gorgeous halls of the temple, and behold, an American, with those same noble instincts of his race, had been worshipping there before us—Mr. Stiggers, of the Alta. His photograph lay there, the countenance subdued by accustomed wine, and reposing upon it appeared that same old smile of serene and ineffable imbecility which has so endeared it to all whose happiness it has been to look upon it. That apparition filled us with forebodings. They proved to be well founded. A sad Chinaman—the sanctified bar-keeper of the temple—threw open the cabinet with a sigh, exposed the array of empty decanters, sighed again, murmured "Bymbye, Stiggins been here," and burst into tears. No one with any feeling would have tortured the poor pagan for further explanations when manifestly none were needed, and we turned away in silence, and dropped a sympathetic tear in a fragrant rat-pie which had just been brought in to be set before the great god Josh. The temple is thoroughly fitted up now, and is resplendent with tinsel and all descriptions of finery. The house and its embellishments cost about eighty thousand dollars. About the 5th of September it will be thrown open for public inspection, and will be well worth visiting. There is a band of tapestry extending around a council-room in the second story, which is beautifully embroidered in a variety of intricate designs wrought in bird's feathers, and gold and silver thread and silk fibres of all colors. It cost a hundred and fifty dollars a yard, and was made by hand. The temple was dedicated last Friday night, and since then priests and musicians have kept up the ceremonies with noisy and unflagging zeal. The priests march backward and forward, reciting prayers or something in a droning, sing-song way, varied by discordant screeches somewhat like the cawing of crows, and they kneel down, and get up and spin around, and march again, and still the infernal racket of gongs, drums and fiddles, goes on with its hideous accompaniment, and still the spectator grows more and more smothered and dizzy in the close atmosphere of punk-smoke and opium-fumes. On a divan in one hall, two priests, clad in royal robes of figured blue silk, and crimson skull-caps, lay smoking opium, and had kept it up until they looked as drunk and spongy as the photograph of the mild and beneficent Stiggers. One of them was a high aristocrat and a distinguished man among the Chinamen, being no less a personage than the chief priest of the temple, and "Sing-Song" or President of the great Ning-Yong Company. His finger-nails are actually longer than the fingers they adorn, and one of them is twisted in spirals like a corkscrew. There was one room half full of priests, all fine, dignified, intelligent looking men like Ah Wae, and all dressed in long blue silk robes, and blue and red topped skull caps, with broad brims turned up all round like wash-basins. The new temple is ablaze with gilded ornamentation, and those who are fond of that sort of thing would do well to stand ready to accept the forthcoming public invitation.

45

SUPERNATURAL IMPUDENCE
24 AUGUST 1864

All that Mr. Stiggers, of the *Alta,* has to say about his monstrous conduct in the Ning-Yong Temple, day before yesterday, in drinking up all the liquors in the establishment, and breaking the heart of the wretched Chinaman in whose charge they were placed—a crushing exposure of which we conceived it our duty to publish yesterday—is the following: "We found a general festival, a sort of Celestial free and easy, going on, on arrival, and were waited on in the most polite manner by Ah Wee, who, although a young man, is thoroughly well educated, very intelligent, and speaks English quite fluently. With him we took a glass of wine and a cigar before the high altar, and with a general shaking hands all around, our part of the ceremonies was concluded." That is the coolest piece of effrontery we have met with in many a day. He "concluded his part of the ceremonies by taking a glass of wine and a cigar." We should think a man who had acted as Mr. Stiggers did upon that occasion, would feel like keeping perfectly quiet about it. Such flippant gayety of language ill becomes him, under the circumstances. We are prepared, now, to look upon the most flagrant departures from propriety, on the part of that misguided young creature, without astonishment. We would not even be surprised if his unnatural instincts were to prompt him to come back at us this morning, and attempt to exonerate himself, in his feeble way, from the damning charge we have fastened upon him of gobbling up all the sacred whiskey belonging to those poor uneducated Chinamen, and otherwise strewing his path with destruction and devastation, and leaving nothing but tears and lamentation, and starvation and misery, behind him. We should not even be surprised if he were to say hard things about us, and expect people to believe them. He may possibly tremble and be silent, but it would not be like him, if he did.

TIME OFF

A. INDEPENDENCE DAY

Public entertainments and amusements were plentiful during the summer of 1864 in San Francisco. As always, there were the museums and the amusement parks, or "gardens," and in addition that year, Wilson's circus. By and large, the theaters had a busy season of minstrel shows, dramas, burlesques, and operas. A new racetrack was opened on the city's outskirts. Two big fairs put on by the Christian Commission and the Mechanics' Institute had successful runs. The reassembling of the monitor *Camanche* at Steamboat Point drew large numbers of onlookers. And, with the nation still torn by civil war and with a heated contest for the presidency in the offing, the Independence Day holiday seemed especially significant that year.

Late in the spring a committee which included Mayor Henry P. Coon, Coroner Benjamin A. Sheldon, and Sam Brannan, California's first millionaire and most versatile entrepreneur, had drawn up plans for the Fourth of July festivities. The city published a pamphlet, *Celebration of the Eighty-Eighth Anniversary of the National Independence of the United States,* giving the program for the day and listing all groups taking part in the big parade. The celebration was strongly Unionist and lasted the better part of twenty-four hours. At sunrise the First California Guard under Captain Bluxome fired the federal salute from Portsmouth Square, with city and harbor bells joining in. The Grand Procession, in eight major divisions, left Washington Square at 10:30 A.M. Winding forty blocks through the city as far north as Broadway and Powell streets and as far south as Folsom and Fourth, it officially ended before the Metropolitan Theater on Montgomery Street after a grand salute was fired in Union Square. The afternoon program at the Metropolitan Theater featured songs by the schoolchildren and an oration by Dr. Bellows. At dusk hundreds of persons jammed the large open square bounded by Fifth, Sixth, Harrison, and Bryant streets to see a fireworks display.

46

SCHOOLCHILDREN'S REHEARSAL
1 JULY 1864

Characteristically Clemens was drawn to the schoolchildren's part in the patriotic exercises, and again we see his particular interest in the pupils of Mr. Pelton's Rincon School. Washington Eliot, the chorus director, was professor of vocal music in the public schools. Among the honorary officers for the Independence Day ceremonies were the chaplain, the Reverend Abbott E. Kittredge of the Howard Street Presbyterian Church; the reader, W. H. L. Barnes, a vigorous orator and attorney; the poet, Clemens' friend James F. Bowman, assistant editor of the *American Flag;* and the orator, Dr. Bellows.

Almost a year later Mark Twain was still objecting to the prevalence of sentimental war ballads—"all the nauseating rebellion mush-and-milk about young fellows who have come home to die—just before the battle, mother." [1]

The pupils of the Public Schools assembled in strong force at the Metropolitan Theatre yesterday afternoon, to rehearse their portion of the Fourth of July ceremonies. The dress-circle was a swarming hive of small boys in an advanced state of holiday jollity, and the parquet was filled with young girls impatient for the performance to begin. There were but fourteen benches left vacant in the pit, and three in the dress circle. At the call to order by Mr. Elliott, a solemn silence succeeded the buzzing that had prevailed all over the house. He announced that one School was still absent, but it was too late to wait for its arrival. The pupils, led by the orchestra, then sang a beautiful chant—"The Lord's Prayer"—the girls doing the best service, the boys taking only a moderate amount of interest in it. However, the boys came out strong on the next chorus—"The Battle Cry of Freedom." Without prompting, the voices of the children broke forth with one accord the moment the orchestra had finished playing the symphony, which was pretty good proof that the pupils of all the Schools are accustomed to strict discipline. The next song—"The Union" —was sung with thrilling effect, and was entered into by both boys and girls, with a spirit which showed that it was a favorite with them. It deserved to be, for it had more music in it than any tune which had preceded it. "Oh, Wrap the Flag Around Me, Boys," was sung by the girls, and the boys joined in the chorus. It is a lugubrious ditty, and sadness oozed from its every pore. There was a pardonable lack of enthusiasm evinced in its execution. "America" (applause from the boys) was sung next, with extraordinary vim. The exercises were closed with this hymn, and the Schools then left the theatre and departed for home. Just as the rear rank was passing out at the door, the missing School—the lost tribe—came filing down the street, moved two abreast into the theatre without halting, and took possession of the stage. It proved to be the Rincon School, so distinguished for the numerous promotions from its ranks to the High School. The large stage was almost filled by the new comers, and had they arrived sooner there would not have been a vacant seat in the house. The lost tribe rehearsed the songs in regular order, just as their predecessors had done, and did it in an entirely creditable manner, after which they marched in procession up Montgomery to Market street. Even if everything else fails on the Fourth, we are satisfied that the Public Schools can be depended on to carry out their part of the programme faithfully and in the best possible style. The Schools will assemble at the Metropolitan Theatre about noon on the Fourth, where, in addition to their singing, the following exercises may be expected: Music, by the band; Prayer, by the Rev. Mr. Kittredge; Reading of the Declaration of Independence, by W. H. L. Barnes; Poem, by Mr. Bowman; Oration, by the Rev. H. W. Bellows.

"THAT INFAMOUS, ENDLESS, IRISH GIANT . . . STOOD EXACTLY IN FRONT OF US"

47

FOURTH OF JULY
6 JULY 1864

Clemens' report below is not as detailed and accurate as accounts in some other papers, for it omits mention of many sections of the parade and for one reason or another depends in part on hearsay. The "infamous, endless Irish Giant" of Gilbert's Market Street Museum who the reporter said had blocked his view was James Murphy, a growing boy more than eight feet tall and weighing nearly 300 pounds. To judge by later complaints in the newspapers, most of the spectators who went to see the fireworks also looked in vain for the colored lights, and as late as 11 August the *Call* reporter was referring dryly to "the confidential fireworks the committee gave us on the Fourth of July." [2]

The editor has deleted the following lists from "Fourth of July": names of military regiments, fire department companies, schools and their principals, and benevolent and protective associations, all taken by Clemens from the official program.

GRAND PROCESSION, FIREWORKS, ETC.—In point of magnificence, enthusiasm, crowds, noise, wind and dust, the Fourth was the most remarkable day San Francisco has ever seen. The National salute fired at daylight, by the California Guard, awoke the city, and by eight o'clock in the morning the sidewalks of all the principal streets were packed with men, women and children, and remained so until far into the afternoon. All able-bodied citizens were abroad, all cripples with one sound leg and a crutch and all invalids who were not ticketed for eternity on that particular day. The whole city was swathed in a waving drapery of flags—scarcely a house could be found which lacked this kind of decoration. The effect was exceedingly lively and beautiful. Of course Montgomery street excelled in this species of embellishment. To the spectator beholding it from any point above Pacific street, it was no longer a street of compactly built houses, but simply a quivering cloud of gaudy red and white stripes, which shut out from view almost everything but itself. Some houses were broken out all over with flags, like small-pox patients; among these were Brannan's Building, the Occidental Hotel and the Lick House, which displayed flags at every window.

THE PROCESSION.—The chief feature of the day was the great Procession, of course, and to the strategic ability and the tireless energy and industry of Grand Marshal Sheldon, San Francisco is indebted for the completeness and well ordered character of the splendid spectacle. He performed the great work assigned him in a manner which entitles him to the very highest credit.

Toward ten o'clock the streets began to be thronged with platoons, companies and regiments of schools, soldiers, benevolent associations, etc., swarming from every point of the compass, and marching with music and banners toward the gen-

eral rendezvous, like the gathering hosts of a mighty army. By eleven the Procession was formed and began to move, and in half an hour it was drifting past Portsmouth Square, rank after rank, and column after column, in seemingly countless numbers. Afterwards (on level ground) it was an hour and twenty minutes in passing a given point; coming down hill, through Washington street, the time was an hour and five minutes; therefore the Procession must have been two miles long at any rate, unless those composing it were remarkably slow walkers; many adjudged it to be over two and a half miles in length.

GRAND MARSHAL AND AIDS.—The Grand Marshal, in purple sash, studded with stars, led the van, attended by thirteen Aids, in white and gold. . . .

The military presented a fine appearance, with their handsome uniforms and brightly burnished arms. They were sufficiently numerous to occupy thirteen minutes in passing a given point.

A squad of twelve or fifteen little drummer boys, in uniform, accompanying the Sixth Regiment, attracted a good deal of attention.

In the military part of the procession, borne by the First Regiment, was a stained and ragged flag, pierced by nine bullet-holes and one bayonet-thrust, received at the bloody battle of Ball's Bluff. It was carried by Corporal Wise, who fought under it there.

CIVIL DEPARTMENT.—The civil department of the Procession was headed by carriages containing the President, Orator, Chaplain, Poet, and Reader of the Day, foreign Consuls, and foreign and domestic naval and military guests, in splendid uniforms, as a general thing. Following these came State, city and county officers, also in carriages.

The Society of California Pioneers and the Eureka Typographical Union were followed by a number of tradesmen's wagons, tastefully ornamented and bearing appropriate mottoes and devices.

The San Francisco Fire Department came next, headed by Chief Engineer Scannell and his Aids. . . .

The Butchers' Union Association came next, headed by a wagon containing a huge living buffalo, and followed by several gaily caparisoned fat cattle; following these was a soldierly platoon of infantry butchers, armed with cleavers, who were observed to obey the solitary command to "Shoulder arms!" with military precision and promptness. They were followed by about twenty open wagons, filled with members of the fraternity. One of these wagons bore the motto, "We Kill to Cure!"

After a glue factory wagon, bearing the motto, "We stick fast to the Union," came seven more butchers' wagons, followed by a fine array of mounted butchers, riding three abreast. The uniform of the fraternity was check shirts and black pantaloons, and it was distinguished in the civil department of the Procession for its exceeding neatness.

The Cartmen's Union Association, riding two abreast, in blue shirts and black pants—a stalwart, fine looking body of men, came next in the Procession, and rode with the Draymen and Teamsters' Associations. A fine regiment or so of cavalry might be constructed out of these materials.

SCHOOLS.—One of the most notable features of the great Procession was the public schools. The boys are all accustomed to military discipline, and they marched along with the order and decorum of old soldiers. Each school had its uniform, its own private music, and its multitude of flags and banners, and in the matter of numbers and general magnificence they did not fall much behind the Army of California at the other end of the Procession. There were twelve schools in the ranks . . .

Some of the mottoes inscribed upon the banners borne by the School children were as follows: "Knowledge is Power;" a globe, with the device, "We move the World;" "Children of the Union;" "We are Coming, Father Abraham;" "Our Public Schools, the Lever that moves the World—Give us more Leverage!" The Mason Street School carried silken banners, upon which were painted the arms of all the States. The boys of Rincon School, three hundred in number, were dressed in a sort of naval uniform, (two gold bands around their caps, and a gold stripe down the leg of their pants,) and each boy carried a flag. The girls of the Rincon School, numbering three hundred also, left the School in eight large furniture cars, but we saw only a few of these cars in the Procession. A pretty little girl in the first car was gorgeously costumed as the Goddess of Liberty. A beautiful banner, presented to the School early in the morning, was carried by the girls, and bore the suggestive inscription, "Our Country's Hope," (in case she becomes depopulated by the war, probably.)

BENEVOLENT SOCIETIES.—In uniform, and carrying flags and banners, were a long array of Benevolent and Protective Associations . . .

After these followed numberless

carriages, containing citizens, and in their wake came the rear guard of citizens on foot, which finished up the almost interminable Procession.

AT THE THEATRE.—After marching through the several streets marked down for it in the programme, the Procession filed down Montgomery street, and disbanded in the vicinity of the Metropolitan Theatre, where the concluding ceremonies of the celebration were to take place.

The Schools were admitted to the theatre first, and a sufficient number were taken from the multitude of citizens outside to fill up the room left vacant—which was not much, of course. The place was so densely packed that we could not find comfortable standing or breathing room, and left, taking it for granted that the following programme would be carried out all the same, and just as well as if we remained:

National Airs by the Bands.
Chant, the Lord's Prayer, by the Children of the Public Schools.
Prayer, by the Rev. Mr. Kittredge.
Reading of the Declaration of Independence, by W. H. L. Barnes, Esq.
"The Battle-Cry of Freedom," by the Children of the Public Schools.
Poem, by J. F. Bowman.
"The Union," by Children of the Public Schools.
Oration, by the Rev. H. W. Bellows.
"O wrap the flag around me, boys," by Children.
"America," by the Children.
Benediction.

THE FIREWORKS.—The huge framework for the pyrotechnic display was set up at the corner of Fifth and Harrison streets, and by the time the first rocket was discharged, every vacant foot of ground for many a square around was closely crowded with people. There could not have been less than fifteen thousand persons stretching their necks in that vicinity for a glimpse of the show, and certainly not more than thirteen thousand of them failed to see it. The spot was so well chosen, on such nice level ground, that if your stature were six feet one, a trifling dwarf with a plug hat on could step before you and shut you out from the exhibition, as if you were stricken with a sudden blindness. Carriages, which no man might hope to see through, were apt to drive along and stop just ahead of you, at the most interesting moment, and if you changed your position men would obstruct your vision by climbing on each others' shoulders. The grand discharges of rockets, however, and their bursting spray of many-colored sparks, were visible to all, after they had reached a tremendous altitude, and these gave pleasure and brought solace to many a sorrowing heart behind many an untransparent vehicle. Still we know that the fireworks on the night of the Fourth, mottoes, temples, stars, triangles, Catherine wheels, towers, pyramids, and, in fact, every department of the exhibition, formed by far the most magnificent spectacle of the kind ever witnessed on the Pacific coast. The reason why we know it is, that that infamous, endless, Irish giant, at Gilbert's Museum, stood exactly in front of us the whole evening, and he said so.

A number of balls and parties and a terrific cannonade of fire crackers, kept up all night long, finished the festivities of this memorable Fourth of July in San Francisco.

B. THE RACES AT BAY VIEW PARK

Clemens' friend James Anthony, proprietor of the Sacramento *Daily Union* in the 1860's, believed that "Mr. Twain . . . was the best reporter of a horse race that ever was made . . ." [3] In 1863 Clemens had reported races in Nevada, and in 1866 following his return from the Sandwich Islands, he wrote up the races of the California State Fair for Anthony's *Union*. [4] On the *Call* he enjoyed covering some of the races at the new Bay View Race Track at Hunter's Point, about six miles from City Hall. The two selections below report feature events during the World's Horse Fair, a trotting tournament held in early September at the Bay View Track. In them we see Clemens tuning up for the fine performance starring the "fifteen-minute nag" in "Jim Smiley and His Jumping Frog." For surely the accomplished but slabbering Sam, the winning horse in the item that follows, deserves to be sire of the mare who cavorts and wheezes her way to victory. And in the second item below, the trotter Kentucky Hunter also bears a family resemblance to Smiley's mare. He too comes from behind and wins consistently. [5]

*"WHAT IS NATURAL TALENT TO
CULTIVATION?"*

48

**THE HURDLE-RACE YESTERDAY
4 SEPTEMBER 1864**

The popular John Wilson was proprietor of the circus and hippodrome on Jackson Street, and his jumper, nicknamed Sam, was a white horse whose real name was Strideover.

The grand feature at the Bay View Park yesterday, was the hurdle race. There were three competitors, and the winner was Wilson's circus horse, "Sam." Sam has lain quiet through all the pacings and trottings and runnings, and consented to be counted out, but this hurdle business was just his strong suit, and he stepped forward promptly when it was proposed. There was a much faster horse (Conflict) in the list, but what is natural talent to cultivation? Sam was educated in a circus, and understood his business; Conflict would pass him under way, trip and turn a double summerset over the next hurdle, and while he was picking himself up, the accomplished Sam would sail gracefully over the hurdle and slabber past his adversary with the easy indifference of conscious superiority. Conflict made the fastest time, but he fooled away too many summersets on the hurdles. The proverb saith that he that jumpeth fences with ye circus horse will aye come to grief.

49

RACE FOR THE OCCIDENTAL HOTEL PREMIUM
10 SEPTEMBER 1864

Charles H. Shear, William Hendrickson, Harris R. Covey, George N. Ferguson, and Ben Fish were well known turfmen, the latter three also owners of livery and sale stables. Probably Clemens meant to indicate Wilson T. Grissim, on the executive committee of Bay View Park, when he wrote "Grissom." Wadsworth Porter, who presided over the crowd of "moral young men and cocktails," was the owner of a Kearny Street livery stable. According to C. H. Webb he was so fond of newspapermen he sometimes would give them carriages to ride in all night long. Lewis Leland, one of Clemens' character references to Jervis Langdon in 1868, was an owner of the Occidental Hotel and Clemens' favorite caterer for outdoor excursions. Dr. George F. Woodward was the surgeon and physician of the United States Pension Bureau. Among the horses referred to, Flora Temple and George M. Patchen, Jr., are remembered in the history of American horseracing.

The best trotting race of the season came off at Bay View Park yesterday afternoon, for the Occidental Hotel premium of three hundred dollars. The competitors for it were a stallion "Kentucky Hunter," entered by H. Fish; gr. stallion "Captain Hanford," entered by Charles H. Shear; and b. stallion "George M. Patchen, Jr.," entered by W. Hendrickson. These are set down in the bills as the three fastest stallions on this Coast. On the first heat "Hunter" came in a length ahead of "Patchen," and "Hanford" brought up the rear. Time, 2:38. The next heat was as closely contested as the first; "Patchen" was first, and "Hunter" and "Hanford" neck-and-neck to within two hundred yards of the Judges' stand, when "Hunter" roused himself and dashed up to the score a couple of lengths ahead of "Patchen." However, it was pronounced a dead heat, because "Hunter" had broken into a run once or twice in going around the track. Time, 2:41½. "Hanford" led for a considerable portion of the last half mile, and all thought he would win the heat. The second heat proper was a handsome race, and was won by "Hunter," again. Time, 2:43. "Hanford" came out third best. "Hunter" won the third heat also, leading "Patchen" about two lengths. Time, 2:40. The first premium, of two hundred and fifty dollars, was awarded to "Kentucky Hunter," and the second, of fifty dollars, to "George M. Patchen." There was a large crowd present, and the race created unusual interest; considerable money changed hands, but we did not bring any of it away. Previous to the Occidental contest, a tandem race came off for a purse of one hundred and twenty-five dollars, mile heats, best 3 in 5. "Spot" and "Latham," driven by Mr. Covey, and "Rainbow" and "Sorrell Charley," driven by Mr. Ferguson, ran. Before the first half mile post was reached, Ferguson's team ran away, and Covey's trotted around leisurely and won the purse. The runaways flew around the race-track three or four times, at break neck speed, and fears were entertained that some of this break-neck would finally fall to Ferguson's share, as his strength soon ebbed away, and he no longer attempted to hold his fiery untamed Menkens, but only did what he could to make them stay on the track, and keep them from climbing the fence. Every time they dashed by the excited crowd at the stand, a few frantic attempts would be made to grab them, but with indifferent success; it is no use to snatch at a cannon ball—a man must stand before it if he wants to stop it. One man seized the lead horse, and was whisked under the wheels in an instant. His head was split open a little, but Dr. Woodward stitched the wound together, and the sufferer was able to report for duty in half an hour. Mr. Ferguson's horses should be taught to economize their speed; they wasted enough of it in that one dash, yesterday, to win every race this season, if judiciously distributed among them. The only Christian way to go out to Bay View, is to travel in one of the Occidental coaches, behind four Flora Temples, and with their master-spirit, Porter, on the box, and a crowd inside and out, consisting of moral young men and cocktails. Mr. Leland should be along, to keep the portable hotel. The principal attraction at Bay View to-day will be a ten-mile race, single heat. Four entries have been made —"Fillmore," "Gentleman George," Grissom's mare, and another beast, whose name has escaped our memory. To-morrow the great equestrienne race, for the Russ House premium of silver service, valued at three hundred dollars, will come off. Thirteen ladies have already entered their names for the skirmish.

C. THE STAGE

Each weekday the *Call* printed a short column headed "The Theatres, Etc." that briefly noticed current performances of operas, plays, minstrel shows, and other amusements. The Sunday *Call* featured "Theatrical Record," a more detailed report of city entertainment and a summary of interior and Eastern theatrical news. Very possibly Frank Soulé or George Barnes, who later became a drama critic, helped draw up the ambitious Sunday column. Only occasionally, as in the excerpts below, can Clemens' distinctive voice be detected in either the daily or the weekly theater reports. The *Call* did not encourage extended reviews or critical commentary, and Clemens' claim that he often merely looked in on each performance as he made the rounds is convincing. But he sometimes stayed. The resulting snippets are not up to his pungent September 1863 review in the Virginia City *Territorial Enterprise* of the popular play *Mazeppa*. Still, their occasional subdued sparkle makes us regret the limits on his opportunity to speak out as a drama critic.[6] In San Francisco he seems to have especially disliked "sensational, snuffling dramatic bosh, and tragedy bosh" and to have especially enjoyed minstrel performances, skilled comedians like Dan Setchell, the versatile Lotta Crabtree as she danced and sang with the Worrell Sisters, and a very few opera stars, such as Caroline Richings whom the *Call* praised lavishly.[7]

"NOT THE DASH AND ABANDON OF THAT MANY-NAMED WOMAN"

50

**THE THEATRES, ETC.
25 AUGUST 1864**

After the summer of 1864 Clemens must have been something of an expert on Henry M. Milner's drama *Mazeppa,* adapted from Byron's poem of that name. During Clemens' visit to San Francisco in September, 1863, he saw the famous and buxom actress Adah Isaacs Menken—"many-named" by virtue of her many husbands—star in that play as the Tartar Prince Mazeppa. The most memorable scene of the production had Mazeppa, sensationally costumed in flesh-colored tights, strapped to the back of his enemy's "fiery untamed steed" to be borne into the savage wilderness. But as Mark Twain wrote for the *Enterprise,* in actuality it was "the Menken" clinging to a placid circus horse by digging her heels into his hams while the gentle nag cantered up a ramp hidden behind a painted cardboard mountain. Later Clemens probably saw others enact the role of the Tartar Prince. The popular Emily Jordan was the sixth actress to play the part in San Francisco, and in a few weeks Utie Clifford became the seventh. Mrs. Jordan, more modestly attired than Miss Menken but using the old original sluggish horse for her "run" up the mountain, opened before a boisterous house that demanded curtain calls of the horse. At Maguire's Opera House Mrs. Agnes Perry also was playing Mazeppa. On 28 August the *Call* plugged her performance this way:

Perry's Mazeppa.
One day on Lake Erie—you all know the story—
Brave Oliver Perry while fighting for glory,
The British fleet stripped; but playing for pelf,
Our Perry outdoes him by stripping herself.[8]

The stage manager of Mrs. Jordan's *Mazeppa* whom Clemens admonished was Alonzo R. Phelps.

METROPOLITAN.—"Mazeppa" was performed last evening, in the presence of about two thousand people. The personation of the Tartar Prince was assumed by the manageress herself—Mrs. Emily Jordan. The part involves some rather risky horsemanship, and, considering the sultriness of the weather, a refreshing scantiness of clothing, which, perhaps, had not the least to do with causing the presence of the crowd. We suppose, as Mrs. Malaprop says, "comparisons are odorous," but we must give Jordan the credit of doing the "runs" in better style than Menken. The general performance of the rôle had not the dash and abandon of that many-named woman, but the equestrian portion was decidedly superior; and it surprises us to learn that the actress, up to the time of consenting to play the part, had been entirely unfamiliar with equestrianism. We must, therefore, add to her merit of gracefulness, the quality of courage, moral and physical. It would make the spectacle more generally effective, if greater attention were paid to other parts of it than that assigned to Mazeppa. The scenery and appointments are very well indeed; but the cast is miserably defective. The people act with a hesitation and timidity that lead one to believe they expected the "wild" horse to break loose from his halterings behind the scenes, and distribute a few kicks among them, which, by the way, not a few of the supers richly deserve. Some of the combats were ridiculous, and were openly derided by the audience. Mr. Phelps, who deserves every credit for his untiring industry and ability as a stage manager, had better get those gay swordsmen together and drill them thoroughly. "Mazeppa" will be repeated to-night, and every night this week until further notice.

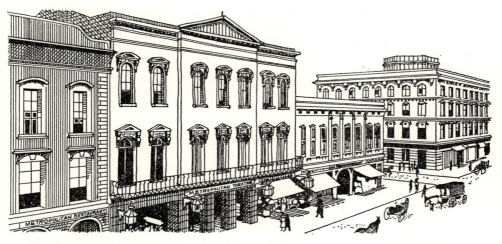

The Metropolitan Theatre in 1865 (*redrawn from a photograph, Society of California Pioneers*).

**"HE WILL DRIFT BEFORE HIS AUDIENCE,
SPREAD HIS SAIL TO THE POPULAR BREEZE"**

51

**THE THEATRES, ETC.
1 SEPTEMBER 1864**

Very likely, Clemens enjoyed Stephen Massett's potpourri entertainment "Drifting About," which reminded some critics of Artemus Ward's performances but was even more varied. On 1 September Massett's lecture, called "indescribable—serious, poetical, humorous, musical, original, always attractive, not at all tedious, now grave and anon gay," [9] included songs, recitations of poems, and imitations of Edwin Forrest, McKean Buchanan, and Madame Anna Bishop, all interspersed with anecdotes and narratives of adventure. Massett, known as Jeems Pipes, was a newspaperman, a world traveler, and an experienced trouper who first played San Francisco in 1849.

MR. MASSETT'S LECTURE—"DRIFT-ING ABOUT."—The printer having by mistake announced in the big bills the entertainment of Mr. Massett for last night, this is to say that to-night is the occasion when he will drift before his audience, spread his sail to the popular breeze, and make the waves ripple with prose, poetry, humor and song, imitation, incident and story. There is enough of variety to please the most exacting, fun enough for the most funny, humor for the gay, pathos for the serious, and whims for the eccentric. He will do a greater variety of things than any other man ever attempted before an audience in one night, and brevity will be united with the variety. As the entertainment is announced as for "one night only," those who would hear and see Massett, should go to-night.

**"THE TIME IS UNPROPITIOUS
FOR FILLING THE HOUSE"**

52

**THEATRICAL RECORD
18 SEPTEMBER 1864**

Charles R. Thorne, Jr., eventually became the leading man at the Union Square Theater in New York. Before sailing on a trip to Shanghai, he took his farewell benefit in San Francisco on 14 September in Tom Taylor's play *Ticket-of-leave Man*. Frank Mayo, who later starred in his own dramatization of *Pudd'nhead Wilson*, took his benefit 17 September as Marteau in the play *The Carpenter of Rouen*. Mayo and Mrs. Perry were the leads in W. Suter's *A Life's Revenge; or, Two Loves for One Heart*.

MAGUIRE'S OPERA HOUSE.—The past week has been devoted to benefits to the different leading members of the community; but the time is unpropitious for filling the house. Politics are surging; and our citizens find more amusement in attending their District Club meetings, mass meetings, and the rest, than in the theatre. To this cause as much as any other, perhaps, may be attributed the scant showing numbers present even when such popular actors as Charles R. Thorne and Frank Mayo made it a personal affair between themselves and the public.

Again, the Mechanics' Industrial Fair is under full headway, and possesses attractions for an evening promenade among its collections of the wonders of science, art and skilled industry which the ladies find hard to resist. The theatrical managers would—to use the language of one of them—"rather fight twenty shows than one Mechanics' Fair;" especially such a complete one as has been opened in this city. . . . Tonight, the drama of "A Life's Revenge" will be given; and next week James H. Warwick takes the stage.

"IT IS RATHER OVERWROUGHT IN THE MISERY LINE"

53

THE THEATRES, ETC.
20 SEPTEMBER 1864

James H. Warwick, an actor who had left the profession when elected to the state legislature, returned to the stage 19 September in Tom Taylor's *The Bottle; or, the Drunkard's Doom*, based upon George Cruikshank's temperance woodcuts. *His Last Legs* was by William Bayle Bernard, and *The Drunkard; or, the Fallen Sword*, which Clemens contrasted to *The Bottle*, was by William Henry Smith.

MAGUIRE'S OPERA HOUSE.—Mr. J. H. Warwick made his first appearance in an intensely sensational drama called "The Bottle." The play shows the unhappy results to a man of family which follow too close a devotion to the ardent, to the neglect of his regular business. Tableaux

occur in it illustrative of Cruickshank's celebrated pictures. It is rather overwrought in the misery line, and a man who sits it out will be inclined to neglect his favorite brandy and water for a week or more. It has no comforting wind-up, as in "The Drunkard," where the reformed inebriate sings "Home, Sweet Home," in the midst of a family group and with his arm about his wife's waist; but after a series of unrelieved wretchedness, the least of which is murder, the unfortunate man in "The Bottle" dies in delirium tremens. Warwick was impressive in the principal character, Richard Thornley; and Mrs. Perry made a good deal out of the suffering wife. The drama will be repeated this evening, together with the farce of "His Last Legs."

*"THE SUPERB BLACK HORSE OTHELLO . . .
EXECUTES HER BIDDING . . . 'LIKE A CHRISTIAN' "*

54

**THE THEATRES, ETC.
20 SEPTEMBER 1864**

John Wilson's circus opened 2 September at the Jackson Street pavilion. Star performers were the acrobatic Carlo family and the Zoyara troupe of riders. Ella Zoyara was really Omar Kingsley, whose skill at female impersonation kept the public guessing about his sex. Two camels, a novelty to San Franciscans, had appeared in Wilson's arena for the first time on 16 September.

WILSON-ZOYARA CIRCUS.—Some of the acrobatic feats at the pavilion excite the wonder of spectators. The most wonderful movements of the body are executed with a grace and precision that arouse unqualified admiration. Zoyara has the superb black horse Othello under the most perfect control, and he executes her bidding in the menage act with remarkable docility and accuracy— "like a Christian," as an enthusiastic horse man suggested. The camels are interesting; and altogether the show is very complete, and deserves to be visited by all.

D. THE LADIES' FAIR
OF THE CHRISTIAN COMMISSION

The Pacific Coast division of the United States Christian Commission was formed in 1864. By late July the Ladies' Auxiliary to the organization was planning a fund-raising fair in San Francisco. The money was to pay for supplies, aid, and spiritual comfort provided to sick and wounded soldiers in the field and in hospitals. When a puzzled reader of the *Call* asked how the Christian Commission differed from the Sanitary Commission, the editors replied: "The Sanitary Commission is not hampered in its operations by any sectarian considerations. Its coffers are supplied from every quarter; its benefactions embrace every suffering or needy man; while the Christian Commission prefers to receive (or did at its organization) contributions and support only from those who are members of what are called the Evangelical sects." [10] Amid a swirl of controversy over whether or not the Christian Commission discriminated against Catholics, Jews, Unitarians, Universalists, and liberals in general, some three hundred determined ladies persevered, gathered donations and exhibits (including the stuffed skin of the famed dog Lazarus), and opened their fair 24 August in Union Hall. Although the displays were criticized in the *Golden Era* as meager and uninteresting, the fair drew large crowds. According to the *Californian,* it cleared $26,000 over expenses before it closed 8 September. [11]

Clemens was familiar with the work of the Christian Commission before he arrived in San Francisco. In an 1863 letter to the *Call* from Virginia City, he had given publicity to his friend the Reverend Mr. Rising for collecting about $2,000 for the commission's charitable work. [12] His respect for the able ladies of San Francisco in the selections below is obvious. As the fair closed, he praised their enterprise, carried through with such "astonishing" success, "considering that the conservative male element was recklessly debarred from their counsels. In our private capacity we had a hankering to suggest things occasionally, but we did not consider it safe to do so . . ." [13] Maybe he remembered what had happened—the "miscegenation" imbroglio that he brought down upon himself—after he ran afoul of organized female virtue during his last days in Virginia City.

"A MOST EXTRAORDINARY OFFERING TO AN ARMY OF WOUNDED SOLDIERS"

THE LADIES' FAIR
25 AUGUST 1864

The fair's evening programs alternated between concerts and tableaux. The Presidio Band was the Ninth U.S. Infantry Union Band, and Charles Alpers—not Alper—led the Metropolitan Band. Mrs. Louisa Grotjan and Miss Louisa Tourney sang on opening night.

Clemens' "fragile young man" was the chairman of the fair. W. H. L. Barnes is the same who was the reader on the Fourth of July program.

The ministers mentioned were William C. Anderson of the First Presbyterian Church, Abbott E. Kittredge of the Howard Street Presbyterian Church, John D. Blain—not Blane—of the Howard Street Methodist Episcopal Church, and Charles Wadsworth of the Calvary Presbyterian Church (Emily Dickinson's friend and a man who, Mark Twain wrote, could "get off a firstrate joke" and was able to take one on himself too).[14] With all these ministers around, backed up by their female battalions, the *Call* reporter—who seems to have been thirsty at the fair—almost certainly had to make do, reluctantly, with the "Christian soda fountain." If only Jacob's Well had been spiked with "bay rum, or Jamaica rum" as he wished, the complacent duck in the grotto might have squawked from his shelf after all.

The great Union Hall, in Howard street, yesterday afternoon, was swarming with a busy hive of ladies and artisans, hurrying up the decorations and working against time in the effort to get all things in readiness for the great Fair in behalf of the Christian Commission, which was to begin in the evening. The chaos of flags, evergreens, framework, timbers, etc., was already beginning to take upon itself outlines of grace and forms of beauty, under the deft handling of the ladies and their assistants. A charming floral temple stands in the centre of the Hall; it is octagonal in shape, is composed of a cluster of evergreen arches which come together at the top like the rafters of a dome, and are surmounted by an eagle—not a live one. The bases upon which these arches rest, form counters, whereon are displayed baskets of fresh flowers for sale; one or two larger bouquets among them are perfect miracles of beauty. A succession of ample arches, swathed in evergreens and draped with flags and embellished with various designs, extends entirely around the sides of the hall; under these are miniature shops, in which the loveliest possible clerks will stand and dispose of all manner of wares at ruinously moderate prices, considering the object to which the profits are to be applied. There is one arch which bears this motto: "Santa Clara's Offering to the Soldiers," and under it were five handsome young ladies and two pretty glass work-baskets laden with fresh flowers—a most extraordinary offering to an army of wounded soldiers, it occurred to us. Over other alcoves were such mottoes as "God is Our Trust;" "M. E. Churches;" "In hoc signo vinces," surmounted by a stately cross; "Union is Strength," etc. No. 1 of these alcoves will be occupied by ladies from Oakland; No. 2, by Miss Baker and her School, of this city; No. 3, by members of Dr. Wadsworth's and Dr. Anderson's Churches, (Presbyterian;) No. 4 is erected by Methodists, Baptists and Presbyterians of Santa Clara; No. 5, by the United Methodists of San Francisco; No. 6, by the Congregationalists; No. 7, by the Episcopalians; No. 8, by members of Mr. Kittredge's congregation; Nos. 9 and 10, by the Baptists. At the left of the stage, under a splendor of silken flags, the smallest and fairest of hands will dispense some of the most useful and useless things to be found in the Fair—cigars and soap. (That sentence does not seem to sound right, somehow, but there is no time now to skirmish around it and find out what is the matter with it.) At the other corner of the stage is the Christian soda fountain. At the right of the entrance door they were building a "moss covered well" around an old oaken bucket which is to be filled with lemonade; (why not bay rum, or Jamaica rum, or something of that kind?) This is "Jacob's Well," and will be carried on exclusively by Rachel, in the costume of her day. On the left of the entrance is a cool, dripping grotto, built by some counterfeiter of Nature, out of pasteboard rocks; the effect is heightened by pendant sprays of Spanish moss, and a stuffed duck sitting placidly on a shelf in the grotto, renders the deception complete. No duck could look more complacent or more perfectly satisfied with his condition, or more natural, or more like a genuine stuffed duck than he does. It was hard to resist the temptation to squeeze his shelf, to see if he would squawk. One of the reception rooms was filled with fine oil paintings, loaned by the artists and picture dealers of the city.

THE OPENING.—By half-past eight in the evening, Union Hall was pretty well crowded with gentlemen and ladies, and the handsome decorations of the place showed to all the better advantage by contrast with the shifting panorama of life and light by which they were surrounded. The famous Presidio Band opened the ceremonies with superb music, after which the Rev. Mr. Blane, pastor of the Howard street Methodist Church, offered up a fervent prayer for the success of this effort in behalf of the Christian Commission. Mayor Coon was then introduced, and delivered an earnest and eloquent address in which he set forth the objects had in view by the Commission, and urged the importance of extending to it a generous aid and encouragement. W. H. L. Barnes, Esq., followed in a stirring speech of some length, which was well received. The several speakers labored under great disadvantage because of the immense space it was necessary to fill with their voices, and the noise and confusion consequent on such a vast gathering of people, but a fraction of whom were seated, and who were too impatient to stand still many minutes together. After a short interval, a fragile young man appeared suddenly in the centre of the stage, dazzled the audience for a single second, like a spark, and went out. Previous to going out, however, he whispered something, and immediately afterward the "Euterpeans," who have so often delighted our citizens with their music, stepped upon the stage and sang a beautiful quartette about The Flag. During the course of the evening, Mrs. Grotjan sang twice, as did also Mrs. Tourney. The singers found it as hard work to sing in such a place as the speakers did to talk. Great credit is due the Presidio Band, the Euterpeans and the two ladies, for volunteering their services last evening without compensation. To-night the grand feature will be a series of beautiful tableaux, in which the most lovely young ladies and gentlemen in the city will appear. Charles Alper's Band have volunteered for this evening, and there will doubtless be some fine vocal music in addition.

"THE COURT BETRAYED SURPRISE; AND SO WOULD THE ORIGINAL SOLOMON"

56

**THE FAIR
27 AUGUST 1864**

John Gregg was a member of the Richings' Opera Troupe, then playing at Maguire's Academy of Music. A Mrs. Shattuck—not Shattucx—sang Graben-Hoffmann's "The Brightest Angel." Clemens' handling of the bald, deaf stagehand who outshone the Queen of Sheba and King Solomon is similar to his more elaborate praise a few weeks later of "Signor Bellindo Alphonso Cellini, the accomplished basso-relievo furniture-scout and sofa-shifter" who stole the show in the opera *Crown Diamonds.* Cellini had placed a chair for the Queen of Portugal to sit in "and then leaned upon the back of it, resting his chin upon his hand, and in this position smiled a smile of transfigured sweetness upon the audience over the Queen of Portugal's head." [15]

The success of the Fair of the Christian Commission is no longer conjectural—it is a demonstrated fact. The receipts of the opening night were over eleven hundred dollars, those of the second, eighteen hundred dollars, and as there was a considerable larger crowd in attendance last evening than upon either of the former occasions, it is fair to presume that the receipts amounted to at least two thousand dollars—making a total, up to the present time, of about five thousand dollars. It is proposed to continue the Fair almost a fortnight longer, and inasmuch as its popularity is steadily increasing, it requires no gift of prophecy to enable one to pronounce it a grand success in advance. The prince of Bands—the Presidio—volunteered again last evening, and delighted the audience with its superb music. There was vocal music, also, of the highest degree of excellence. The first in order was a cavatina, by Mrs. Gleason; followed by a ballad, "Brightest Angel," by Mrs. Shattucx; grand aria from "Maritana," by Mr. John Gregg, of the Italian opera; "Who will care for Mother now?" ballad, by Miss Mowry; "Heart Bowed Down by Weight of Woe," from opera of "The Bohemian Girl," by John Gregg. These several musical gems were well received and highly appreciated. This evening the tableaux will be resumed, as follows: 1. Landing of the Pilgrims; 2. Crinoline Avenged; 3. Statuary; 4. Execution of Lady Jane Grey; 5. Winning the Gloves; 6. Statuary—Fair Rosamond and Queen Eleanor. The tableaux the other evening were gotten up in fine taste and gave great satisfaction, albeit while the one representing The Queen of Sheba at the Court of King Solomon, was before the house, the effect was unduly heightened by an assistant in citizen's dress rushing bald headed into Court, before he discovered that the curtain was still up. The Court betrayed surprise; and so would the original Solomon, if the same man, in the same modern costume, had ever appeared so unexpectedly before him. The intrusion was not premeditated; the gentleman was very deaf—so deaf, indeed, that he could not see that the curtain had not yet been lowered. We forbear to urge any one to go to the Fair, to-night, for the chances are that there will be people enough there to strain the sides of the building a little, anyhow.

"IT COSTS SOMETHING TO VOTE IN THAT WARD"

**CHRISTIAN FAIR
7 SEPTEMBER 1864**

Mrs. Alvord probably was the wife of William Alvord, importer and hardware dealer.

The Ladies' Fair of the Christian Commission will close positively to-morrow evening; to-night and to-morrow night there will be a sale or two at auction, but the ladies wish it distinctly understood that there will be no *general* auction of articles left on hand at the close of the Fair. They consider that when half a dollar may be the means of saving a soldier's life, they have no right to fritter away donations at a sacrifice. They have already reduced prices to cost, and in some instances even below cost, and if the articles cannot be sold at these rates, they will be retained and contributed to swell the resources of the Christian Commission in other portions of the State. They have a stove, a set of furs, several fine cakes, and a few other articles of value, which they are anxious to dispose of before the Fair closes; those who desire to purchase will please make a note of it. About the middle of the Hall, on the east side, Mrs. Alvord has, in a glass case, several bouquets, done in wax by Mrs. Selim Woodworth, wife of the commander of the U.S. ship Narragansett, which are to be given to the lady who polls the largest vote for them; it costs something to vote in that ward, and the money thus collected is to be forwarded directly to the wounded soldiers. The largest of these bouquets is an exquisite work of art and will bear the closest inspection. The silver vases containing the smaller bouquets, were donated by Mrs. Alvord. Near at hand, the last named lady has a rare set of books which she has contributed, and which are also to be voted for, and will be presented to the pastor who shall be in the majority. Pay your poll-tax and deposit your ballot. It has occurred to us just at this moment, that if any of the bare-footed Disciples, travelling according to their custom "without purse or scrip," should return to Earth, and happen into the Fair, they couldn't vote, could they? Consequently, it is risky, charging for votes, isn't it? Manifestly.

E. THE MECHANICS' INSTITUTE INDUSTRIAL FAIR

The fourth Industrial Fair of the Mechanics' Institute opened 3 September with a speech by Senator John Conness and fireworks at Geary and Stockton streets. It closed 3 October in a burst of cooperative benevolence. The last day's proceeds went to drought-stricken citizens of Santa Barbara County.

The Mechanics' Institute had not held a fair since 1860. The intervening years had brought remarkable growth in business, industry, and transportation. The Washoe silver mines had poured new wealth into the state, and those of Esmeralda, Reese River, Humboldt, and the Colorado region had been discovered. The time was right for a new display of the state's resources. By April 1864 the Committee of Arrangements had nearly $10,000 in hand for a spacious pavilion for the fair that soon began to rise in Union Square. An adjoining building, to house a gallery, was added so that Californians might see the work of their artists. The *Call's* reporter, browsing there two days before the official opening, described Butman's "Coast Scene on the Bay of Monterey" as having "a cool, stormy look about it, and a gradation of waves upon the flat beach 'shoaled up' so truly to Nature that any practised in reading the element that never lies, can tell the depth of the water anywhere inside the reef at a glance." [16] To cover the fair for the duration was an important assignment for Clemens.

The Mechanics' Institute was ten years old in 1864. Its rooms on California Street near Montgomery housed a library of 7,000 volumes. It collected mechanical apparatuses and works of art, with the intention of advancing technology and industrial prosperity. During a period of collapsing mining stocks, the fair was meant to shake up a sluggish economy or, as an official release put it, "to foster the Mechanic Arts, elevate the character of the workman, and stimulate ingenuity, invention, skill, and industry in all their branches, in the hope of exercising a wholesome influence upon the general prosperity of the country. Our Fairs bring together inventors, manufacturers, workmen, and the public . . ." [17]

The pavilion was a huge, one-story structure of thin redwood siding topped by a central dome over one hundred feet high. Directly underneath the dome in the center of the display hall was the Floral Fountain. Its jetting waters encircled a forty-foot lattice-work pyramid, or "pagoda," covered with flowers and approached by arched bridges spanning the basin of the fountain. Within the pagoda, fair-goers could view a special exhibit of two valuable donations—a silver brick from Nevada and a two-ton California cheese—by paying a small fee intended for the Sanitary Commission. Other unusual exhibits like the skating pond and the labyrinth garden were strategically placed among the machines and products on display. The hall was crowded, but its 55,000 square feet of floor space was roomy enough to hold almost everything from "quartz mashers and patent grindstones" to cordials labeled "Ladies' Tear Punch" and "The Soul's Consolation Syrup." [18]

Some of the *Call's* daily items on the fair were thoroughly routine. Into others the reporter injected fun and freshness, as though the dullness of his continuing assignment were a challenge. We notice him also in some typical moments. He rebuked the fair managers for not posting directions to the skating pond. He was fascinated by ingenious contrivances and by mechanical and biological marvels. He was sincerely behind the benevolent aims of the Sanitary Fund. He boosted California trade and enterprise, much as he encouraged them later in his Sandwich Island letters. The future lecturer who was to complain about verbatim newspaper accounts of his platform remarks because they gave away the punch lines he hoped to preserve for subsequent stage appearances, declined to quote the spirited discourse of a fair barker because it would not be "exactly fair to spoil its attractiveness in this way." Readers of *Huckleberry Finn* and *Tom Sawyer* will note the reporter's interest in such topics as the good King Herod, deaf mutes, English royalty, and the drowning of cats.

"FROM ART AND HORTICULTURAL TO HASH AND HOMINY!"

THE MECHANICS' FAIR
2 SEPTEMBER 1864

Clemens' "Mr. Beers" was really Henry Behre, who had the concession for the pavilion restaurant.

I have omitted a long list of exhibits accepted for display in the pavilion.

The stern, practical appearance which the great array of machinery and all manner of industrial implements has heretofore given to the Pavilion is being softened and relieved, now, by a pleasant sprinkling of fresh flowers and beautiful pictures; and by the time the Art halls are fully dressed with paintings, and the central tower with blooming plants, and the fountain below filled with limpid water, and the thousand lights a-blaze above a mass of people in ceaseless motion, the place will look as vivacious and charming as it now looks tumbled and shapeless. And while on this flight, it is proper to state that in the east wing of the Pavilion, Mr. Beers will have an ex-cellent and commodious restaurant, where visitors can obtain anything or everything they may choose to eat or drink, and in quantities to suit the capacities of all stomachs. How naturally doth the cultivated human mind ascend from art and horticultural to hash and hominy!

....

"PERFECT TREES, FROM ONE TO THREE INCHES HIGH"

59

**LABYRINTH GARDEN
3 SEPTEMBER 1864**

Frank Staeglich ran a landscaping and gardening service.

Visitors to the Mechanics' Fair, to-day, should examine carefully the pretty and ingenious Labyrinth Garden, in miniature, gotten up by Mr. Frank Staeglich, and situated near the Floral Tower. It is easy to see your way into it, and the paths are very straight, but to see your way out again is the impossible feature of the thing. Although this garden, with its endless complication of drives and avenues, is only about as large as an ordinary lunch table, the grass plats, flower-beds, and rows of microscopic trees, with which it is luxuriously embellished, are all alive and growing. There are within the garden one hundred and twenty-five perfect trees, from one to three inches high, belonging to many different species of California's lordliest forest monarchs, among which are the giant redwood and several kinds of pines. The long rows of lilliputian shrubs which inclose the garden are vigorous young cedar *trees*, and there are three thousand of them.

"LET CALIFORNIANS MAKE A NOTE OF IT, AND ACT UPON IT"

60

**DOMESTIC SILKS
4 SEPTEMBER 1864**

Louis Prevost, who exhibited his silkworms throughout the state, was widely known for his exotic gardens near San José. In December 1866 Clemens interviewed him there and wrote up his silk business in detail.[19] Prevost went bankrupt in 1882, still trying to promote the California silk industry.

California may branch out and become a great silk manufacturing State some day, when it becomes known that her facilities for doing so are much superior to those of most other lands. Mr. Louis Prevost, of San José, who has a lot of silk-worm eggs and cocoons on exhibition at the Mechanics' Fair, says that in Europe the greater portion of every crop of silkworms get diseased and die, but in this climate they all live and come to maturity—it is impossible for them to become diseased. He also says that here, it is but little trouble, and requires small care and attention to raise silkworms, and that in his department of labor, one man here can perform the work of eight in Europe, and do it with comparative ease. Mr. Pre-vost gets no opportunity to manufacture California silks, because the demand for his silkworm eggs is so great from foreign countries, and the prices paid him so liberal, that he finds it more profitable to lay the eggs and ship them off than to keep them and hatch them. As fast as the worms produce them, he sends them to Italy, and comes as near filling all orders from there as he can, at twelve dollars an ounce (containing forty thousand eggs.) He has an order from Mexico, now, for five hundred ounces, but he is unable to fill it. They say that a silkworm ranch is one of the few kinds of property in this world that never fail to pay. Let Californians make a note of it, and act upon it.

"A CAT AND A PILE OF KITTENS"

61

BEAUTIFUL WORK
8 SEPTEMBER 1864

The ladies should examine some of those rare specimens of embroidery on exhibition at the Mechanics' Fair. Among the finest is a tapestry picture of a royal party in a barge —names "unbeknowns" to us—by W. S. Canan, of Healdsburgh; a large portrait of G. Washington, by Mrs. Chapman Yates, of San José; and a cat and a pile of kittens, by Mrs. Juliana Bayer. We do not like the expression of the old cat's countenance, but the kittens are faultless —especially the blind brown one on the right. So perfectly true to nature are those young cats, that it is easy to see that every school-boy who comes along is seized with an earnest desire to drown them.

MRS. HALL'S SMELTING FURNACE
9 SEPTEMBER 1864

Mrs. E. J. Hall was a San Francisco physician. The influential *Mining & Scientific Press* favored her Volcanic Smelting Furnace over other types of furnaces because of its speed and economy in reducing ores. The machine had operated on Sutter Street since July.

We would call the attention of all persons interested in mines and mining machinery, to several bars of copper and galena, which are exposed to view on a table in front of the hot-air engine in the Mechanics' Fair. The bar modestly marked "galena," contains more silver than anything else, and was smelted from ordinary ore in Mrs. Hall's famous smelting furnace, by her daughter. The time occupied by the young lady in the production of this bar was only twenty minutes, and the materials used were a bushel of ore and a bushel of charcoal. By this process every particle of metal can be extracted from ore and saved, in less time and at smaller expense than the same ore could be roasted preparatory to crushing in a quartz mill. Copper ore can be reduced with the same facility and at the same slight expense. The furnace is a combination of principles long known to the votaries of science, but the "Condenser" attached to it is an entirely new invention, and the credit of originating it belongs to Mrs. Hall alone. It is a large drum, which sits upon the flue of the furnace, and into which all the smoke passes; a shower bath from above thoroughly washes this smoke, and the metallic particles which would otherwise float away upon the atmosphere are thus arrested and precipitated to the bottom of the drum. By this means, *all* the metal in the ore is saved, which is an achievement not hitherto compassed by any of our reduction machinery. Mrs. Hall's invention has been patented, and in a letter from the Department at Washington she was assured that there was no piece of mechanism gotten up for similar purposes, in the Patent Office, which could at all compete with this invention of hers. Let all who have the mining interest of California at heart, bestow upon Mrs. Hall's smelting apparatus the attention its importance deserves.

CURIOSITIES
10 SEPTEMBER 1864

I. H. Perry and J. H. Rines each had lost an arm while serving in the

Union Army. The great "Sanitary Cheese," manufactured and donated by Steele Brothers of Pescadero, weighed 3,930 pounds and measured almost six feet across. The silver bar, valued at $4,200, was a gift from employees of the Gould and Curry mill and mine at Virginia City.

The soldier boys, Perry and Rines, in charge of the Sanitary Cheese and Silver Bar, at the Mechanics' Fair, have been presented with several curiosities, which they have added to the greater attractions in their pagoda. One is an ancient teapot, two hundred, or two thousand years old, or along there, somewhere —at any rate, it is very old—which was given to the boys by a lady in whose family it had been preserved for several generations. Another is a wine-glass which was taken from one of the ships in Boston harbor just after our exasperated forefathers had thrown her cargo of tea overboard. The young lady who presented this relic, received it from her grandfather, who took it from the vessel with his own hands. And still another is an old half dollar, made in the second die ever cast in America. It was presented to Rines, and he has given it to the Sanitary Fund, and has it on exhibition. It is worth twenty-five cents to see the Sanitary cheese and the other curiosities, but it is worth double the money to hear the orator, Rines, deliver his spirited and entertaining discourse concerning them. The man who exhibits the lions and tigers in the menagerie isn't a circumstance to him. We could print an extract or so from his speech, but we do not think it would be exactly fair to spoil its attractiveness in this way. Go and hear it yourself. A lady gave a dollar, a day or two ago, for the privilege of lifting the silver bar, but she miscalculated her strength somewhat, and failed to carry out her design. The bar weighs nearly two hundred pounds, and her lifting capacity wouldn't reach. The privilege is still open, however, to others of the sex.

"DEPOSIT YOUR SPARE QUARTERS ON THE BIG CHEESE . . ."

64

**A PHILANTHROPIC NATION
10 SEPTEMBER 1864**

The Reverend Osgood Church Wheeler was a prominent Baptist minister and writer. Formerly a newspaper editor, an official of the State Agricultural Society, and Chief Clerk of the Assembly of California during its fifteenth session, in 1864 he lectured and worked tirelessly for the Sanitary Commission—sometimes being called the Reverend O. Coax'em Wheeler. Just one week before the following item appeared, Clemens had snappishly complained that Wheeler's office had refused to supply him with the names of contributors to the Sanitary Fund.[20]

Mr. O. C. Wheeler, Secretary of the California Branch of the U.S. Sanitary Commission, has furnished us a neat little volume entitled "The Philanthropic Results of the War in America," from which we learn that since the war began, the American people have not only paid for its prosecution by enormous taxes, but have voluntarily contributed, toward caring for the wounded, etc., the immense sum of $212,274,259.45! That was up to February, 1864; the figure must reach at least $250,000,000 by this time. This was not all given to the Sanitary Fund, of course, but to the hundred different departments of charity created by the war. How much of it came from California? The two hundredth part, say. Only that—and yet ours is one of the greatest States in the Union. Therefore, let her not complain, yet awhile, that the calls upon her in behalf of the Sanitary Fund are too heavy, but rather let her move steadily along, as she is now doing, in her aid to that charity, and continue to do it henceforward as cheerfully as she has done it heretofore. Deposit your spare quarters on the big cheese at the Mechanics' Fair. It is the contribution of two whole-hearted brothers, and it is worth twenty-five cents to look upon such a monument of kindly Christian charity. After that cheese has gone the rounds of the States and collected a quarter of a million for the Sanitary Fund, it will be cut up in New York and sold by the slice. What will California bid for the first slice?

"THIS ONE IS HANDSOME ENOUGH FOR A DRAWING ROOM"

65

AN INGENIOUS CONTRIVANCE
15 SEPTEMBER 1864

A. G. Dexter's sonorous door gong was a new invention operated by manual pressure upon a metal doorplate. Mrs. Nathaniel Holland was the wife of a city attorney.

There is nothing in the Mechanics' Fair more ingenious or pleasanter to look at than the Skating Pond, and neither is there anything about the Pavilion which is half so hard to find, unless it be the wretched school-boy who stealthily rings Dexter's excellent but distracting door gong, and then melts suddenly away under the neighboring billiard tables, and is seen no more in life. But the Skating Pond is really easy to find when you have intelligent directions by which to guide yourself. From the main entrance, you go straight to the floral tower, and glance off at an angle of forty-five degrees to the left and forwards; preserve the direction thus secured until you reach the wall of the building, and your object is attained. The Skating Pond sits on a table in a neat parlor, and if you would have one like it, you should line the inside of a wash-tub with mirrors, have the bottom peopled with male and female dolls in skating attitude, and arrange it so that it will turn around

The Reverend Dr. Henry W. Bellows, president of the United States Sanitary Commission (*California Historical Society*).

Scenes of Bay View Park Race Track at Hunter's Point (*from* California on Stone *by Harry T. Peters, Bancroft Library*).

Maguire's Opera House on Washington Street near Montgomery in the 1860's (*Society of California Pioneers*).

The pavilion of the Mechanics' Institute Industrial Fair in 1864 (*Bancroft Library*).

Telegraph Hill in 1865 (*from a photograph by T. E. Hecht, Bancroft Library*).

rapidly; you will observe that the little figures will be multiplied in the mirrors into countless multitudes of hurrying and skurrying skaters, growing smaller and smaller and more and more crowded together, as far as the eye can reach into the limitless distance; and if your dolls are dressed in as perfect good taste, and appropriate colors, and are arranged in as faultless skating postures as are these of which we are speaking, you cannot fail to be delighted with the liveliness, the unlimited variety and the magnificence of the scene, and if you are anything of a skater yourself, you must infallibly become inoculated with the dash and spirit and rushing excitement of it. Put your eyes down to the rim of the tub (this one is handsome enough for a drawing room,) and look far away into the mirrors, and you may see thousands and thousands of men and women swiftly passing and repassing each other, over a stretching sea of ice that apparently has no more limit than space itself. It is a beautiful work of art, and the more one looks at it the more he is pleased with it. Mrs. Nathaniel Holland, the lady who has charge of it, invented and constructed it herself, and the best artists in the city say that the grouping of her miniature figures, and the gracefulness and appropriateness of their carriage and costumes could not be improved upon. Two months of her time were given solely to its construction, and all the reward she asks for her labors is, that she may gather together, by exhibiting it, a thousand dollars for the Sanitary Fund. She will accomplish this, easily enough, and she might have already done so if placards to direct the public to her part of the Pavilion had been hung up here and there, where they would arrest attention. This will be looked to, directly. The Skating Pond was exhibited at the late Christian Commission Fair and netted fifteen hundred dollars in currency to that charity.

"A VOLUMINOUS AND VERY MUSTY OLD BOOK"

66

MORE DONATIONS
16 SEPTEMBER 1864

Presumably the musty old "Chronicle" Clemens found so intriguing was the fourth edition (1665) of Sir Richard Baker's *A Chronicle of the Kings of England,* which (on pages 616 and 617) names the commissioners who tried Charles I. Undoubtedly writing from memory, Clemens quoted inaccurately from page 619, leaving us an early example of Mark Twain's patented "antique English." The passage in Baker reads: "It is Observable in this first dayes Tryal, that while the Charge was reading, the head of the Kings staff fell off, which he wondring at, and perceiving no Body offer to take it up, stoop't for it himself, and put it in his pocket."

A Chinese merchant of this city has left a superb Chinese lantern at the Mechanics' Fair, to be sold for the benefit of the Sanitary Fund, and certain young ladies are in the pleasant habit of leaving handsome bouquets on the big cheese daily, to be disposed of for the same charity. By far the most interesting curiosity of all, however, has lately been added to the collection in the Floral Tower. It is a voluminous and very musty old book, printed in London two hundred years ago, in the reign of Charles II., and is rich with the quaint language, spelling, and typography of the olden time. It is a "Chronicle" of the Kings of England, and is carried down to the year 1664, the second of Charles' reign. The chapter which gives the names of the members of the High Commission before which Charles I. was tried and condemned to death, is racy with comments upon the bad character, the ignominious pursuits, and the former social obscurity of those gentlemen, and must have occasioned great discomfort to such of them as were still living at the time of its publication. During the trial of the friendless monarch, "his staff fell to the floor, and seeing that none moved to take it up, he put forth his hand and took it up himself." The chronicler seemed to feel that no comment was needed there to show the deep humiliation into which the poor King had fallen, and he made none. At another stage of the trial, the head of the King's staff fell off, and a sense of the dreadful omen flitted across the countenances of the superstitious multitude around him. The old book contains the genealogy of the reigning monarch and that of all the nobility of England.

"NO MORE THAN A SMALL POTATO"

67

QUEER FISH
22 SEPTEMBER 1864

At a case of pomological, ichthyological, mechanical, and a general variety of specimens, at the west side of the rotunda of the Mechanics' Fair building, is an unshapely looking animal, between a reptile and a fish, called the "Catfish Squid," preserved in alcohol. In size, the thing amounts to no more than a small potato, but the amount of physical force it is said to exert when not in liquor, and otherwise in good health, is somewhat enormous, being altogether disproportionate to its dimensions. A card appended to the jar that keeps the animal in spirits, informs the curious searcher after information that the squid can "take a man down and suck him to death." And if any is skeptical of the fact, he or she can just find out where there is one ready to perform, and try it on. This specimen was obtained near Oakland. Close by is another jar containing an odd looking individual of the lobster species, found on the islands. It lives in white sand, and is usually found in pairs.

**CHILDREN AT THE FAIR
24 SEPTEMBER 1864**

The children of the Public Schools come in droves and armies to the Fair now, every day, by invitation of the management. The children belonging to the Roman Catholic Orphan Asylum visited the Pavilion yesterday, and the pupils of the Mason Street Public School, to the number of eight or nine hundred, filed into the building during the afternoon. A strong force of Teachers and exhibitors has to be on hand on occasions like these, to keep Young America from getting ground up in the machinery.

69

**THE FAIR AT THE FAIR
25 SEPTEMBER 1864**

The Reverend and Mrs. S. S. Harmon operated the Pacific Female Seminary of Oakland, which was soon to be incorporated as the Female College of the Pacific.

About seventy of the handsomest young ladies in the State marched in double file into the Fair Pavilion yesterday morning, broke ranks, deployed as skirmishers, and effected a bloodless capture of the place, at five minutes to eleven o'clock. It was observed that they seemed to take a deeper interest in the pianos and pictures, and especially in the laces and hair-oil and furs, than in the quartz mashers and patent grindstones. It is because their tastes are not fully developed yet, perhaps. They made the only good music that has been extracted from the fine pianos in the Art Gallery since those instruments have been condemned to public persecution in that place; they played "Sweet Home," with tender expression, and thought of lively Oakland, where they came from, and sighed for the turmoil and excitement of its busy thoroughfares. This detachment of young ladies was from Mrs. Harmon's Pacific Female Seminary, one of the best schools in the State. It is situated about a mile from the city just named. Mr. McClure, Mr. Beldler, Miss Wills, Mrs. Harvey, Madame Parot, Miss Cameron, and perhaps other Teachers employed in the Seminary, accompanied Mrs. Harmon and her pupils to the Fair. We have ascertained that no young gentlemen pupils are wanted at present.

"ALWAYS LISTENING WITH THEIR
WATCHFUL, RESTLESS EYES"

70

THE DEAF MUTES AT THE FAIR
29 SEPTEMBER 1864

The pupils who went to the fair on 28 September were from Primary School No. 6 and from the State Deaf, Dumb, and Blind Association, situated at Mission and Fifteenth streets.

The inmates of the Deaf and Dumb Asylum, to the number of about three dozen, visited the Fair yesterday, in company with their Teachers, and kept up an unceasing and extraordinarily animated conversation about its wonders until their arms and fingers were utterly fagged out with talking. Poor fellows; we could not help thinking what a great advantage they have over ordinary people, for you might remove their tongues and break one of their arms, and they would go on talking with the other all the same. These pupils talk with incredible rapidity, and their hands, bodies, and the muscles of their expressive faces are never at rest. They are always listening with their watchful, restless eyes, and no movement escapes them. The pupils of the Public School at the corner of Fifth and Market streets also attended the Fair yesterday, in a crowd numbering between five and six hundred.

"IT WOULD HAVE WORRIED THE GOOD KING
HEROD"

71

MORE CHILDREN
30 SEPTEMBER 1864

It would have worried the good King Herod to see the army of school children that swarmed into the Fair yesterday, if he could have been there to suffer the discomfort of knowing he could not slaughter them under our eccentric system of government without getting himself into trouble. There were about eight hundred pupils of the Public Schools in the building at one time.

"CALIFORNIA IS A NOBLE OLD STATE"

**EVERYBODY WANTS TO HELP
2 OCTOBER 1864**

California is a noble old State. The echoes of the cry of distress jingle with the ring of dollars. Dr. Bellows says we're poor but don't know it, but generous, and can't help it, and Dr. Bellows knows. Almost every few minutes we receive a little note like this: "Mr. H. Behre, proprietor of the Pavilion Restaurant, will give all the profits from the receipts on Monday, day and evening, to the Santa Barbara sufferers." All the hands connected with the restaurant will also volunteer their services. Mr. Perkins drops in to say that the proceeds of his sale of fruits will be devoted to the same noble object; also the receipts of the Sanitary Cheese Exhibition.

The Golden Gate.

SUDDEN DEATH

In September Clemens wrote up two events that touched him closely: the death of his friend Jerome Rice and the explosion of the steamer *Washoe,* a public disaster that took over one hundred lives and awakened in him memories of the death of his brother Henry and of "poor flayed and mangled creatures" in a Memphis hospital. Consequently the writing carries emotional overtones of a sort not commonly found in his *Call* reporting.

"SHE TOOK A SHEER AND RAN ASHORE, HER BOW PROVIDENTIALLY TOUCHING A TREE"

73

TERRIBLE CALAMITY
7 SEPTEMBER 1864

Although Clemens drew on dispatches to the evening papers in writing his report, nevertheless we can see his characteristic attention to dramatic detail. His strong feelings take on validity deriving from his obvious knowledge of steamboats and river navigation. So far as I know, Clemens was the only San Francisco reporter at the time who could speak with authority on these matters.

The *Antelope, Chrysopolis,* and *Visalia* were three of six riverboats belonging to the California Steam Navigation Company that were based at the Broadway wharf. The Howard Benevolent Association was founded in 1857 and was supported mainly by San Franciscans. In the great floods of 1860 and 1861, referred to by Clemens in "Captain Kidd's Statement" (Item 74), it had aided hundreds of victims.

The editor has deleted a section of approximately 1,200 words from the middle of "Terrible Calamity." The portion omitted lists the dead and wounded and gives particulars about individual injuries.

EXPLOSION OF THE STEAMER WA-
SHOE'S BOILERS—SUPPOSED KILLED,
ONE HUNDRED—WOUNDED AND
MISSING, SEVENTY FIVE—SEVERAL
SAN FRANCISCANS AMONG THE
NUMBER—ATTENTION PAID BY THE
SACRAMENTANS TO THE WOUNDED
—THE CAUSE OF THE CALAMITY—
SCENES AND INCIDENTS—ETC., ETC.

We compile an account of this terrible disaster from dispatches published in the evening papers. The
explosion of the boilers of the
Washoe took place at ten o'clock, at a
point just above the Hog's Back,
about ten miles above Rio Vista, on
her up-trip on Monday night. One of
the boilers collapsed a flue, and, it is
said, made a clean sweep aft, going
overboard through the stern of the
boat. The cause of this dreadful calamity, according to D. M. Anderson, the engineer, (who died at the
Sacramento hospital just after he
made the statement,) was rotten
iron in the boiler. At the time of the
explosion there were one hundred
and twenty-five pounds pressure on
the boiler, with two cocks of solid
water. The engine was high pressure. The upper works of the boat
aft were completely shattered, some
portions of them, with the state-
rooms being blown overboard. The
boat had passed the Hog's Back
about four or five minutes before the
explosion. She was about twenty
yards off the left bank at the time,
and the whole steering gear being
destroyed, she took a sheer and ran
ashore, her bow providentially
touching a tree, to which those not
injured fastened the boat. Had she
not run ashore, almost everybody on
board would have been lost, as they
could not steer the wreck, and they
had no boats, the steamer sinking
gradually astern. The boat was set
on fire in three places, which added

to the horror of the scene. The fire,
however, was put out by the few who
were uninjured. The Chrysopolis
was a long way ahead, and knew
nothing of the matter. The Antelope
being behind, came up and took off
the wounded and a large number of
the dead, and brought the first news
of the sad affair to Sacramento.

MEASURES FOR RELIEF OF THE
WOUNDED, AND TAKING OFF THE
DEAD.

On the arrival of the Antelope at
Sacramento, about half-past five
o'clock yesterday morning, with the
terrible news, the alarm-bells of the
city were rung, and the Howard Association turned out to attend to the
wounded the steamer had brought
up. The scene for the three hours
that elapsed before the Antelope
reached the steamer Washoe is described as most horrible. All who
were alive had been taken ashore,
but there was no shelter for them.
Those of the wounded who were able
to move sought shelter in the sand
and brush, groaning and screaming
with pain. One man, who was
scalded from head to foot, got
ashore, and in a nude state stood and
screamed for help, but would not
allow any covering to be put on him.
A woman in a similar condition was
brought up on the Antelope. The
steamer carried only the wounded to
Sacramento. A large number of the
slightly wounded, who could walk or
ride, were taken to the rooms of the
Howard Association. The Association hired the Vernon House for a
hospital for the sufferers. On board
of the Antelope the scene was a most
dreadful one. Her entire upper
cabin, with the exception of the pas-
sage-ways, was covered with mattrasses, on which the injured were
lying, sixty-three in number. Others
were in the ladies' cabin, and still

others in the dining-room. Four are reported to have died on the way up, and at the time of landing others were gasping their last on the levee. At the Vernon House the Howard Association have a large number of members, who, with a large force of ladies, are doing all that can be done for the sufferers. The Association also has a committee out collecting, who have so far met with good success. Immediately on the arrival of the Antelope, the steamer Visalia fired up and went down to the wreck to bring the bodies of the dead left there by the A., and also such others as may be recovered while she is there.

. . . .

Flags were at half mast yesterday, on the Masonic Temple and most of the engine houses, and on a number of private buildings in Sacramento. The entire medical fraternity were in attendance on the sufferers, as well as the clergy of all denominations.

The opinion is now that the total dead will exceed ninety, if not one hundred.

Too much praise cannot be awarded the members of the Howard Association, who almost to a man were engaged in behalf of the sufferers after the arrival of the Antelope. A large number of ladies were in constant attendance also at the Vernon House, doing all that they could do to alleviate pain. The collections in Sacramento have been quite liberal. (See telegraph dispatches in another column.)

George W. Kidd, captain of the steamboat *Washoe* (*redrawn from a photograph, Bancroft Library*).

74

**CAPTAIN KIDD'S STATEMENT
8 SEPTEMBER 1864**

Captain George Washington Kidd had been a cabin boy and later a steward on a Mississippi steamer in the 1830's. Having moved to Sacramento in 1849, he made a fortune and built the steamship *Nevada* for the river trade. His ship sank in 1861, and its successor the *Washoe* took over as chief competition to the powerful California Steam Navigation Company. When the *Washoe* failed him, Captain Kidd turned to banking, a business that he may have felt was less likely to explode under him with no warning.

The *Washoe* was built at Henry Owens' shipyard on Hunter's Point in San Francisco and was launched 5 April 1864. Its boilers had been made at Goss and Lambard's—not Gass and Lombard's—Sacramento Iron Works. Although their construction had been supervised by Edward Foster, the *Washoe's* engineer, leaking flues necessitated an almost immediate overhauling at Sacramento. On July 1, a few days after operation had been resumed, the hard-luck ship was rammed by the steamer *Yosemite* at Benicia wharf. The public inclined to regard the collision as an infamous attempt by Captain Edward A. Poole of the *Yosemite* to sink his opposition, on orders from his superiors. The Government Inspectors of Boilers and Hulls later exonerated Captain Poole, but his reputation suffered again when the two ships collided once more on 29 August in a wide channel above Rio Vista. The *Call* reporter had this collision in mind when, in commenting on overzealous police action against a street urchin, he wrote: "It is a matter of wonder to some that a deliberate attempt to send an indefinite number of souls to Davy Jones' locker, by one who occupies a prominent position, escapes Judicial scrutiny, while the whole force conservatorial is hot foot in the chase after some little ragged shaver."[1] Patched up again, the *Washoe* was hardly back in business when the explosion came. The ship was raised and towed to Hathaway's wharf in San Francisco. There it was rebuilt and was sold to the Oakland Ferry and Railroad Company for ferry service across the bay.

Clemens' able defense of Captain Kidd combines a full paraphrase of the captain's words, considerable factual information, and emotional warmth.

Captain Kidd, of the ill-fated steamer Washoe, has been accused, according to telegraphic reports from Sacramento, of ungenerous and unfeeling conduct, in remaining with the wreck of his boat after the explosion, instead of accompanying the maimed and dying sufferers by the catastrophe to Sacramento. In defence of himself, he says he was satisfied that the wounded would be as well and kindly cared for on the Antelope as if he were present himself, and that he thought the most humane course for him to pursue would be to stay behind with some of his men and search among the ruins of his boat for helpless victims, and rescue them before they became submerged by the gradually sinking vessel; he believed some of the scalded and frantic victims had wandered into the woods, and he wished to find them also. He says that his course was prompted by no selfish or heartless motive, but he acted as his conscience told him was for the best. We heartily believe it, and we should be sorry to believe less of any man with a human soul in his body. His search resulted in the finding of five corpses after the Antelope left, and these he sent up on the small steamer which visited the wreck on the following day. However, he need not distress himself about the strictures of a few thoughtless men, for that class of people would have blamed him just as cordially no matter what course he had pursued. Whether one or more flues collapsed, or whether one or more boilers exploded, or whether the cause of the accident was that too much steam was being carried, or that the iron was defective or the workmanship bad, are all questions which must remain unsolved until the Washoe is raised. At present,

and so far as anything that is actually known about the matter goes, one of these conjectures is just as plausible as another. Captain Kidd thinks the cause lay in the inefficient workmanship of the boiler-makers. The surviving engineer says he looked at the steam-gauge scarcely two minutes before the explosion, and it indicated 114 pounds to the square inch (she was allowed to carry 140;) he tried the steam cocks at the same time, and found two of them full of water. The boat carried 120 to 125 pounds of steam from San Francisco to Benicia, and from here to where the accident occurred, it was customary to carry less, as the water grew shoaler, because, as every boatman knows, a steamer cannot make as good time, or steer as well, in shoal water with a full head of steam as she can with less; from Rio Vista to Freeport, it was customary to carry about 110, and above Freeport about 70 pounds of steam. The Chrysopolis was far ahead, and had not been seen for more than half an hour; and since the last collision Captain Kidd had given orders that the Washoe should be kept behind the line boats and out of danger; he was making no effort to gain upon the Chrysopolis, and had no expectation of seeing her again below Sacramento. Gass & Lombard, of Sacramento, contracted to build boilers for the Washoe which would stand a pressure of 225 pounds, and secure the inspector's permission to carry 150; Captain Kidd appointed Mr. Foster, one of the best engineers on the coast, to stay at the boiler works and personally superintend the work. The workmanship was bad; the boilers leaked in streams around the flues, and the Inspector would only allow a certificate for 113 pounds of steam. The boat made seven trips, but the leaks did not close up, as was expected. Gass & Lombard then contracted with boiler makers here to take out the flues and make the boilers over again, so that they would stand 140 pounds—Captain Kidd relinquishing 10 pounds from the original contract. It was done, at a cost of $7,000—about what a new set would have cost—and after a cold water test of 210 pounds, the Inspector cheerfully gave permission to carry 140. With a margin like this, the boilers could hardly have exploded under a pressure of 114 pounds unless the workmanship was in some sort defective, or the severe test applied by the Inspector had overstrained the boilers; or unless, perhaps, a rivet or so might have been started on some previous trip, under a heavier head of steam, and this source of weakness had increased in magnitude until it finally culminated in a general let-go under a smaller head of steam. The sinking of the boat is attributed to the breaking off of the feed pipes which supply the boilers with water, and which extend through the bottom of the boat; and as the wreck settled and careened, a larger volume of water poured in through the open ash ports forward of the fire doors. The boat sank very gradually, and had not settled entirely until nearly three hours had elapsed. But as we said in the first place, the real cause of this dreadful calamity cannot be ascertained until the wreck is raised and the machinery exposed to view. Captain Kidd leaves to-day with the necessary apparatus for raising his boat, and Mr. Owens, who built her, will accompany him and superintend the work. It will be several months, however, before the Washoe will be in a condition to resume her trips. Captain Kidd says he would raise the boat, anyhow, to satisfy himself as to the cause of the accident, even if he never meant to run her again. Capt. Kidd feels the late calamity as deeply as any one could, and as any one not utterly heartless, must. That his impulses are kind and generous all will acknowledge who remember that he kept his boat running night and day, in time of the flood, and brought to this city hundreds of sufferers by that misfortune, without one cent of charge for passage, beds or food.

"WE HAVE SEEN TWENTY THOUSAND DOLLARS COLLECTED IN . . . THE NOBLE LITTLE CITY OF MEMPHIS, TENNESSEE"

CHARITABLE CONTRIBUTIONS 9 SEPTEMBER 1864

Messrs. Barry & Patten collected over a hundred dollars yesterday, at their saloon in Montgomery street, for the sufferers by the explosion on the steamer Washoe. It will be forwarded to the officers of the Howard Association at Sacramento. An earnest and extended movement in this direction would produce enough money in a single day to secure to those poor flayed and mangled creatures every comfort and attention they may stand in need of, and it is proper that Sacramento should be liberally assisted in her humane work of ministering to their wants. Who will set the ball in motion? We have seen twenty thousand dollars collected in a short time in the noble little city of Memphis, Tennessee, for a similar purpose, years ago. If money is wanted by the unfortunates now suffering at Sacramento, San Francisco will respond promptly and with a will.

" 'ROANOKE,' AN OLD FAVORITE . . . WAS FOUND KEEPING FAITHFUL WATCH OVER HIS PROSTRATE MASTER"

76

SAD ACCIDENT—DEATH OF JEROME RICE 13 SEPTEMBER 1864

Jerome Rice was a leading auctioneer and real-estate dealer. It was Rice who ran up the bids on Ruel Gridley's famous Austin Sanitary Sack of Flour—which Gridley repeatedly auctioned off to raise money for the Sanitary Commission—when it reached San Francisco in late May 1864. During Clemens' stay at the Lick House in 1863, he and Rice had been billiard partners, and Clemens soon put him and other cronies into an early sketch.[2] At that time Rice's family had been stranded in Texas by the war. Two weeks after his friend died, Clemens wrote home about those earlier good times at the Lick House: "We always sat together at table. He used always to pledge his 'lost wife & babies' in his wine at dinner, & wonder whether they were living or dead & I used to stand security that he should live to see them again, poor fellow. He was one of the best men in the world. His wife went from the ship to the funeral—& afterwards lay in a swoon 36 hours." [3] Rowland B. Gardner, Rice's clerk, recovered rapidly from his injuries.

Clemens' account of Rice's ordeal is similar in tone to passages from his report on the *Hornet* disaster in 1866. Then he pictured shipwrecked men who "looked mutely into each other's faces, or turned their wistful eyes across the wild sea in search of the succoring sail that was never to come." [4] During this period of his life the adjectives were likely to surface in his writing when he confronted suffering and courage, especially if he felt close to the sufferers, as he did in these instances. To portray human nobility with restraint was not easy for him—calling to mind his late sentimental story "A Horse's Tale"—and the writing became maudlin where Rice's horse Roanoke shared the heroism. He was more successful in picturing men and animals in their moments of selfish weakness, from behind the shield of comedy.

Was he thinking of Roanoke when he wrote in *Roughing It* of the horses that deserted the narrator and his two companions who were hopelessly lost in a blizzard? Ollendorf, Ballou, and their friend "cursed the lying books that said horses would stay by their masters for protection and companionship in a distressful time . . ." [5]

On Wednesday evening last, while Jerome Rice, the well-known auctioneer, of this city, and Rowland B. Gardner, one of his clerks, were on their way to the Warm Springs, near Santa Clara, they lost their way in the hills north of Vallejo Mills, and the night being somewhat dark, they drove over an embankment twenty feet high. Mr. Rice fell upon his head, and the force of the concussion crushed in the base of his skull and fractured his collar bone, a fragment of which pierced one of his lungs. Mr. Gardner's left thigh was broken, and his body considerably bruised. Mr. Rice groaned in pain and muttered incoherent words at intervals, but was never conscious up to the hour of his death, which occurred at two o'clock yesterday morning, nearly three days and a half after the accident. All Wednesday night, and all Thursday and Thursday night, through the blistering sun, and the cold, benumbing air of evening, the two men lay side by side and suffered inconceivable tortures from hunger and burning thirst and the sharp pain of their stiffening wounds; and Gardner spent the lonely hours in calling for the help that never came, for himself and his insensible companion, until he could no longer speak for hoarseness and exhaustion. Think of the raging fires in a throat subjected to such exercise as this, when no water had moistened it for a day and two nights! On Friday morning Mr. Gardner began his terrible journey in search of assistance, and for two days and nights, without food or water, he crawled backwards, by the aid of his hands, in a half sitting, half reclining posture, and dragging his broken leg. Every movement must have caused him exquisite agony; the anguish of such a march cannot even be imagined. And the distance accomplished in those forty-eight hours of suffering was only *half a mile*. On Sunday morning he reached the vicinity of a field and attracted the attention of a man at work in it, and the two unfortunate men were soon conveyed to a neighboring house, and kindly cared for. When they went after Mr. Rice, one of the carriage horses had long since wandered away; but "Roanoke," an old favorite and the property of Mr. Rice, was found keeping faithful watch over his prostrate master, and gazing upon his face. The noble brute had never deserted his post for three days and a half—hunger and thirst had failed to drive him from his allegiance. If at any time, during the two days his comrade was absent from his side, the unfortunate man awoke from his delirium and realized that he was desolate and alone, and far from human help, it must have been some relief to his tortured mind, in that fleeting moment of consciousness—some balm to his aching wounds, some sense of friendly companionship to him in his loneliness—to see the eyes of his faithful horse looking down into his own, in mute sympathy for his distress. Mr. Rice's head, face and body were swollen in an extraordinary degree, and blackened and blistered by the fervent heat of the sun. After lingering in misery for so many hours, death at last put an end to his sufferings at two o'clock yesterday morning. His wife and family, who have been enduring for four years all the privations and misfortunes that war could entail upon them in a section of Texas desolated alternately by both contending parties, and whom he had not seen and scarcely ever heard from during that time, will arrive here from Boston, (to which port they lately escaped,) day after to-morrow, on the steamer Golden City. After the long separation and the hardships that have fallen to their life, it is cruel now to dash down the cup of happiness when it had almost touched their very lips. Who, among all the brave men that shall read this sad chapter of disasters, could carry, with firm nerve, the bitter tidings to the unsuspecting widow and her orphans, and uncoffin before them a mutilated corpse in place of the loving husband and father they are yearning to embrace? Mr. Gardner is at Centreville, under medical treatment, but the remains of Mr. Rice will be brought to the city and kept until the arrival of the steamer, so that the stricken family may have the sad consolation of looking upon them before they are consigned to the grave.

FIVE SKETCHES

Clemens occasionally inserted a brief sketch in the *Call*. The five that follow are uneven in quality, but each is lively and distinctive in tone. Perhaps the most remarkable feature they have in common, though, is simply the fact of their appearance in the *Call,* for that paper did not encourage frills or invite "literary" contributions. Its aim from the beginning had been to give the news, concise and unadorned. Its consistently cocky spirit had been no guarantee of verve in style. What, then, did its subscribers think about the witchery that enlivened its columns in the summer of 1864? And if George Barnes very quickly felt—as he claimed he did—that his local reporter was remiss in covering the news, why did he not fire him sooner? Obviously, Clemens was putting in time on humorous frills and literary copy that he might have spent in digging up news. Obviously too, the management permitted him a certain freedom: Mark Twain was not as hopelessly buried in lokulitems on the *Call* as Clemens later remembered. The questions above cannot be answered with certainty, but it is just possible that the shrewd Barnes who understood the *Call's* clientele knew they occasionally would relish some unadulterated Mark Twain.

"WILD FOWL SCREAM, AND SEA-LIONS GROWL AND BARK"

A TRIP TO THE CLIFF HOUSE
25 JUNE 1864

The Cliff House was a well known, isolated restaurant and bar overlooking the Pacific Ocean near Point Lobos and the Seal Rocks. To its south lay the long empty stretch of Ocean Beach. For merely thirty-five cents a *Call* subscriber in the city could reach the lonely shore via the street-railroad cars of the Central Railroad Company that connected with omnibuses at Lone Mountain. In August the *Call's* local reminded his readers that a sensible man would not "envy, in the pleasantness of his feelings and the economy of his cash, the fast young bloods who flash by him" in privately hired buggies. Once at the Cliff House, he advised, "you can saunter along the sandy beach, gratis, and feel, with Byron,

> There is a rapture on the lonely shore,
> There is society where none intrudes,
> By the deep sea, and music in its roar.

If the sea don't roar to please you, you can give ear to the seals on the neighboring rocks."[1] Clemens himself had played the fast young blood early one morning in June, if we are to believe his *Golden Era* sketch "Early Rising as Regards Excursions to the Cliff House."[2] From his buggy he damned the early hour, the bracing air, the suburban homes and gardens, the lonely road, the almost invisible seals, the fogbound beach. He decried Franklin's advice of "Early to bed, and early to rise" as pernicious nonsense. His sketch comes close to being a burlesque of such effusions as Lisle Lester's "Morning Rides."[3] The other side of the coin turns up in "A Trip to the Cliff House," an early and unusually "literary" sketch in the reporter's columns—and one with subversive thoughts carefully masked, perhaps with *Call* subscribers in mind.

On his way to the Cliff House the reporter rode over the new Mission Street Bridge, spanning Mission Bay, which was a half-moon cove in San Francisco Bay between Steamboat and Potrero Points. He drove through the Potrero, where most of the stockyards were. Perhaps Uncle Jim was James R. Willoughby, a wholesale butcher there. Farther on, the reporter passed between Lone Mountain and Calvary cemeteries on the partly macadamized Point Lobos Road. Dr. Isaac Rowell, then a city supervisor and president of the City Railroad Company, was a well known physician and professor of chemistry. He owned a tract of land between the Point Lobos Road and the United States Military Reserve. Ezekiel Wilson was a mining-stock broker who lived four miles out on the same road.

If one tire of the drudgeries and scenes of the city, and would breathe the fresh air of the sea, let him take the cars and omnibuses, or, better still, a buggy and pleasant steed, and, ere the sea breeze sets in, glide out to the Cliff House. We tried it a day or two since. Out along the railroad track, by the pleasant homes of our citizens, where architecture begins to put off its swaddling clothes, and assume form and style, grace and beauty, by the neat gardens with their green shrubbery and laughing flowers, out where were once sand hills and sand-valleys, now streets and homesteads. If you would doubly enjoy pure air, first pass along by Mission Street Bridge, the Golgotha of Butcherville, and wind along through the alleys where stand the whiskey mills and grunt the piggeries of "Uncle Jim." Breathe and inhale deeply ere you reach this castle of Udolpho, and then hold your breath as long as possible, for Arabia is a long way thence, and the balm of a thousand flowers is not for sale in that locality. Then away you go over paved, or planked, or Macadamized roads, out to the cities of the dead, pass between Lone Mountain and Calvary, and make a straight due west course for the ocean. Along the way are many things to please and entertain, especially if an intelligent chaperon accompany you. Your eye will travel over in every direction the vast territory which Swain, Weaver & Co. desire to fence in, the little homesteads by the way, Dr. Rowell's arena castle, and Zeke Wilson's Bleak House in the sand. Splendid road, ocean air that swells the lungs and strengthens the limbs. Then there's the Cliff House, perched on the very brink of the ocean, like a castle by the Rhine, with countless sea-lions rolling their unwieldy bulks on the rocks within rifle-shot, or plunging into and sculling about in the foaming waters. Steamers and sailing craft are passing, wild fowl scream, and sea-lions growl and bark, the waves roll into breakers, foam and spray, for five miles along the beach, beautiful and grand, and one feels as if at sea with no rolling motion nor sea-sickness, and the appetite is whetted by the drive and the breeze, the ocean's presence wins you into a happy frame, and you can eat one of the best dinners with the hungry relish of an ostrich. Go to the Cliff House. Go ere the winds get too fresh, and if you like, you may come back by Mountain Lake and the Presidio, overlook the Fort, and bow to the Stars and Stripes as you pass.

The Cliff House and Seal Rock, as they looked in Clemens' day (*redrawn from a photograph, Bancroft Library*).

78

ORIGINAL NOVELETTE
4 JULY 1864

The burlesque "Original Novelette" is a miniature condensed novel. Its main episode is the kind that local reporters sometimes served up as "human interest" news. If Albert S. Evans of the *Alta* had written the story, it is very likely he would have sauced it with a pious moralism. But Clemens preferred the informal idiom of his Nevada journalism.

The only drawback there is to the following original novelette, is, that it contains nothing but truth, and must, therefore, be void of interest for readers of sensational fiction. The gentleman who stated the case to us said there was a moral to it, but up to the present moment we have not been able to find it. There is nothing moral about it. Chapter I.—About a year ago, a German in the States sent his wife to California to prepare the way, and get things fixed up ready for him. Chapter II.—She did it. She fixed things up, considerably. She fell in with a German who had been sent out here by his wife to prepare the way for her. Chapter III.—These two fixed everything up in such a way for their partners at home, that they could not fail to find it interesting to them whenever they might choose to arrive. The man borrowed all the money the woman had, and went into business, and the two lived happily and sinfully together for a season. Chapter IV.—Grand Tableau. The man's wife arrived unexpectedly in the Golden Age, and busted out the whole arrangement. Chapter V.—Now at this day the fallen heroine of this history is stricken with grief and refuses to be comforted; she has been cruelly turned out of the house by the usurping, lawful wife, and set adrift upon the wide, wide world, without a rudder. But she doesn't mind that so much, because she never had any rudder, anyhow. The noble maiden does mind being adrift, though, rudder or no rudder, because she has never been used to it. And so, all the day sits she sadly in the highway, weeping and blowing her nose, and slinging the result on the startled passers-by, and careless whether she lives or dies, now that her bruised heart can never know aught but sorrow anymore. Last Chapter.—She cannot go to law to get her property back, because her sensitive nature revolts at the thought of giving publicity to her melancholy story. Neither can she return to her old home and fall at the feet of the husband of her early love, praying him to forgive, and bless and board her again, as he was wont to do in happier days; because when her destroyer shook her, behold he shook her without a cent. Now what is she to do? She wants to know. We have stated the case, and the thrilling original novelette is finished, and is not to be continued.

But as to the moral, a rare chance is here offered the public to sift around and find it. We failed, in consequence of the very immoral character of the whole proceeding. Perhaps the best moral would be for the woman to go to work with renewed energy, and fix things, and get ready over again for her husband.

"THE PEOPLE WHO LIVE IN MILTON PLACE ARE EXPECTING HIM, ALL THE TIME"

79

WHAT A SKY-ROCKET DID
12 AUGUST 1864

Clemens was proud of "What a Sky-Rocket Did." To Orion and Mollie in Nevada he wrote: "I have got Dr. Bellows stuck after my local items. He says he never fails to read them—said he went into 'convulsions of laughter' over the account of 'What a Sky-Rocket Did.' "[4] In this day and age the humor does not seem that good. The reason may be that the point of the sketch, which remains obscure to us, possibly depended on an in-group joke—now lost—among the city's leading Unitarians. Captain William Crawley Hinckley was an active and wealthy Unitarian—a fact that Dr. Bellows would not have overlooked in his fundraising—who had been close to his former minister Thomas Starr King and who became friendly with King's successor, Horatio Stebbins.

Even though the precise point eludes us, Clemens surely intended to ridicule Hinckley and possibly the city Board of Supervisors. Captain Hinckley (1809–1876) came from a Boston seafaring family and grew up in Milton, Massachusetts. He sailed as a "boy" on a three-year whaling voyage, entered the merchant marine, and in the 1840's engaged in West Coast and South Seas trade. In 1848 he converted his schooner into a storeship at Sacramento, and for a time he mined at Dry Diggings, Hangtown, and Placerville. He prospered, then settled for good in San Francisco where he made fortunate real-estate investments. In 1864 he lived at 1 Milton Place and remained there until he moved to Starr King's former house on Bush Street. From 1860 to July 1864 Hinckley was the supervisor representing the Seventh District. His loan of twenty dollars in 1864 to the De Young brothers, his tenants, was their stake to begin the *Dramatic Chronicle,* which became the San Francisco *Chronicle* on 1 September, 1868. Later he leased the land on which the California Theater was built, a project the De Youngs promoted as part of their determined journalistic effort to break the hold of autocratic Thomas Maguire, the prominent theater owner and producer, on San Francisco's theatrical world. Hinckley died a wealthy man and willed most of his estate to a trust fund to be used for charity and education.

No doubt, Clemens knew Hinckley as a supervisor, for the evidence shows that the *Call* reporter, like his fellow locals, attended the regular Monday evening meetings of the board. Hinckley did not talk much at these meetings, but occasionally he spoke up strongly—and conservatively. On 7 June the local of the *Bulletin* paraphrased Hinckley's argument against raising the salaries of deputy assessors: "Mr. Hinckley took occasion to denounce the poor economy of raising salaries and keeping down the police force. People, he said, are rushing crazily for office— willing to give half their pay to get it. If the salary is insufficient, let them resign." [5] To Clemens, who consistently favored higher wages for underpaid workers at this time, such an argument must have been obnoxious, particularly coming from one so well fixed. A few weeks later the *Call* reporter satirically quoted part of the captain's motion "to suspend the rules" in order to immediately take up a property owner's appeal to reduce an assessment.[6] Hinckley was on the Committee for Streets, Wharfs, and Public Buildings and was on the Board of Equalization, which corrected errors in assessments on personal property. As a member of these groups he seems to have spoken for property holders. Perhaps the nub of Clemens' sketch, therefore, is its suggestion that the wealthy landlord's "tenement" on Milton Place was unfit for people to live in. Probably the reporter especially enjoyed leveling that criticism if the frightened tenant happened to have been a friend of his, but there is no evidence to support such a supposition.

Night before last, a stick six or seven feet long, attached to an exploded rocket of large size came crashing down through the zinc roof of a tenement in Milton Place, Bush street, between Dupont and Kearny, passed through a cloth ceiling, and fetched up on the floor alongside of a gentleman's bed, with a smash like the disruption of a china shop. We have been told by a person with whom we are not acquainted, and of whose reliability we have now no opportunity of satisfying ourselves, as he has gone to his residence, which is situated on the San José road at some distance from the city, that when the rocket tore up the splinters around the bed, the gentleman got up. The person also said that he went out—adding after some deliberation, and with the air of a man

The top half of the front page of the August 12 *Call* (*opposite*) carries Clemens' story "What a Sky-Rocket Did" (*Bancroft Library*).

Daily Morning Call.

VOL. XVI.   SAN FRANCISCO, FRIDAY MORNING, AUGUST 12, 1864.   No. 63.

By the Overland Telegraph.

[From the Dispatches of the Associated Press.]

LATEST EASTERN NEWS.

Farragut's Success Against the Mobile Forts—Siege of Atlanta—Averill's Victory over the Raiders—The Raiders in Kentucky—Etc., Etc.

ACCOUNT OF FARRAGUT'S SUCCESS AT MOBILE FROM ENEMY SOURCES—FORT POWELL BLOWN UP AND FORT GAINES SURRENDERED.

MOBILE, August 8.—[Telegraphed to the Richmond Enquirer.] Lieutenant-Colonel Williams, commanding Fort Powell, evacuated and blew up the fort on Friday night. Yesterday and to-day the enemy's vessels are ready for the fray, and great confidence prevails. The people are satisfied with the conduct of Buchanan, Maury, and Burnett, of the navy.

MOBILE, August 9.—It is painfully humiliating to announce the shameful surrender of Fort Gaines, at half-past nine this morning, by Colonel Anderson, of the Twenty-first Kentucky Regiment, who was provisioned for six months, and had a garrison of six hundred men. He last night communicated with a large quantity of small arms, but is large. General Bradley Johnson was captured, with his colors and three of his staff, but subsequently made three of his purpose was, but received no reply. McClellan was pursued to the mountains.

THE VERY LATEST DISPATCHES.

THE RAIDERS IN KENTUCKY.

CINCINNATI, August 11.—The Gazette's special from Indianapolis says General Carrington has received information that Col. Adam Johnson is at Morganville, Kentucky, with one thousand men, heading throughout the adjoining counties, preparing to co-operate with Johnston. The river is very low and can be easily forded. Gunboats cannot operate. General Carrington has ordered the whole bank to be patroled.

NEW YORK, August 11.—The following dispatch from the army, dated Cumberland, the 8th, confirms the reported victory of Averill. Averill attacked McCausland's forces, capturing his artillery, over four hundred horses and equipments, three hundred and twenty prisoners, and the enemy killed in unknown.

THE TROPHIES OF AVERILL'S LATE VICTORY.

ENTHUSIASM IN FAVOR OF McCLELLAN BEING NOMINATED A COMMANDER.

NEW YORK, August 10.—The McClellan meeting to-night is the largest ever held in this city. The number present is roughly estimated at sixty thousand. Great enthusiasm is manifested.

GOLD QUOTATIONS.

Private dispatches from New York quote Gold, on the 10th, at 255; Sterling, 10s½.

WHAT A SKY-ROCKET DID.—Night before last, a stick six or seven feet long, attached to an exploded rocket of large size, came crashing down through the zinc roof of a tenement in Milton Place, Bush street, between Dupont and Kearny, passing through a cloth ceiling, and fetched up on the floor alongside of a gentleman's bed, with a smash like the disruption of a china shop. We have been told by a person with whom we are not acquainted, of whose reliability we have now no opportunity of satisfying ourselves, as he has gone to his residence, which is situated on the San José road at some distance from the city, that when the rocket tore up, the splinters around the house gave somewhat of the air of a battle, and that he went out—adding after some deliberation, but with the air of a man who has made up his mind that what he is about to say can be sustained if it necessary, that "he went out quick."

NEW YORK, August 10.—The statement that the Tecumseh was sunk while endeavoring to pass Fort Morgan, is disbelieved here.

FROM GRANT'S SCENE OF OPERATIONS.

NEW YORK, August 10.—Burnside and Meade each blame the other for the reverse at Petersburg. A misunderstanding as to who should superintend the attack occurred, and neither was present to take command. Convalescents were rejoining the army.

FROM SHERMAN'S ARMY—THE SIEGE OF ATLANTA.

The Herald's correspondent near Atlanta says operations around that city "are in style." We are

LETTER FROM SANTA CATALINA ISLAND.

[From our Regular Correspondent.]

SANTA CATALINA ISLAND, August 6, 1864.

EDITORS MORNING CALL:—I mentioned in a former letter to you that our island had been honored by a visit from Professor Silliman, who examined the mines, and took sampl s of ore from many of the ledges for assay. We have since received a report of the assay, as made under direction of Silliman, by Lockhart, of Los Angeles, and as it may be of public interest, I send you a correct copy of the same. The lodes first mentioned are located northwest of the Isthmus, producing mostly galena ore, from which the assay was made:

Description of Ore, and Name of Lode.	Per cent. of Lead.	Val. Silver per ton.	Val. Gold per ton.
GALENA.			
Silver Peak	41.70	$44 94	Trace.
Ditto, 2d sample	16.40	128 91	Trace.
Giant	43.70	58 66	
Mountain Chief	43.70	54 18	
Ditto, 2d sample	68.30	64 91	
Argentine	73.87	32 91	$9 37
Buckeye	58.30	35 77	
General Chief	50.90	38 72	
Vaughn	59.00	16 09	
Do. clay and small	4.00	2 47	
Morris	30.00	16 09	
Forry	36.50	19 90	
San Francisco	28.60	19 96	
Gould & Curry	30.30	82 83	
Orizoline	74.61	32 25	Trace.
Sunset	76.60	123 28	
Shamrock	33.50	24 72	Trace.

Manganite ore from the Guanajato yielded 33.11 per cent. of Manganese.

The following, mostly copper lodes, are located southwest of Isthmus:

	Per cent. Copper.	Per cent. Lead.	Value Silver per ton.	Value Gold per ton.
COPPER ORE.				
No Fun Ditto, No. 1.	7.10		$31 35	$17 51
No Galena, No. 2			21 65	
No Fun Ditto, No. 3.	11.70		1 09 72	
COPPER ORE.				
Yellow Jacket No.	22.50			Trace,
Bullion	3.50			9 75
Burlington	16.00		103 23	4 68
Kappa				
GALENA ORE.				
Occidental			9 73	Trace.
Castello			57.53	Trace.

The ' bove is a very good average, and rich enough in quality to pay well, provided the quantity highly probable. The expenses of the Professor's visit, and of the assays, etc., it is understood are paid by parties here. Engineers from the city, are interested in companies here, as well as owner of three

MOVEMENT OF THE KEARSARGE AND HER OFFICERS.

THE KEARSARGE ABOUT TO STEAM AFTER THE REBELS AGAIN.

[From Galignani's Messenger, July 6.]

Intelligence from Cherbourg states that the Kearsarge is to leave that port this day to cruise in the Channel, in order to watch the movements of Confederate vessels on the coasts of France and England.

THE DINNER TO CAPT. WINSLOW IN PARIS.

[From Galignani's Messenger, July 5.]

The Americans in Paris the evening before last invited Captain Winslow to a banquet at the Palais Royal, which he attended. The United States Minister, and the Secretaries of the Legation, were present. The Surgeon and the Paymaster of the Kearsarge were also among the guests.

At the close of the dinner, and on the proposition of one of the guests, a collection was made for erecting a monument to the Federal sailors who fell during the engagement. We have just learned that the amount was over three hundred dollars, which will be received in the action with the Alabama. The other two wounded men are going on favorably. The naval combat of the 19th June will, therefore, have cost the Kearsarge the loss of only one man.

ENTERTAINMENT TO THE KEARSARGE OFFICERS IN LONDON.

[From the London Star, July 5.]

Yesterday at two o'clock, the eighty-eighth anniversary of American independence, a number of Americans entertained at breakfast, in St. James' Hall, Captain Wheeler and Lieutenant Cushman of the Kearsarge. Many of the members of these officers in London are not known until late in the evening before, there was a considerable company present and much enthusiasm manifested. Among those present were: the Hon. Bradford R. Wood, United States Minister to Denmark; Captain Boyd, United States Marine Corps; C. E. Wilson, Secretary of Legation, London; Henry F. Baker, of Boston; A. E. Derby of New York; B. F. Brown, of Boston; R. Hunting, of New York; W. J. Valentine, of Maine; G. W. Belding; B. Moran, Henry B. Adams, C. F. Dennet, of Boston; A. G. Grant, of Ohio; M. D. Conway, of Boston, and others. When the excellent breakfast had been attended to, the Chairman, C. E. Wilson, Esq., proposed the health of the President. The Hon. Mr. Wood responded to this. He said the President was emphatically, an honest man. To a great extent unfamiliar with political life when he entered upon his present duties, and with a task of greater difficulty than is allotted to most men, he had advanced step by step, yet so far as was out partially done in 1776, [Applause] for by an unfortunate omission slavery was in that day still allowed to live by the very men who declared that ' all men were created free and equal.' It was only that cause slavery was permitted to import slaves—a few years longer that South Carolina accrued who has made up his mind that what he is about to say can be substantiated if necessary, that "he went out quick." This person also said that after the gentleman went out quick, he ran—and then with a great show of disinterestedness, he ventured upon the conjecture that he was running yet. He hastened to modify this rash conjecture, however, by observing that he had no particular reason for suspecting that the gentleman was running yet—it was only a notion of his, and just flashed on him, like. He then hitched up his team, which he observed parenthetically that he wished they belonged to him, but they didn't and immediately drove away in the direction of his country seat. The tenement is there yet, though, with the hole through the zinc roof. The tenement is the property of ex-Supervisor Hinckley, and some of the best educated men in the city consider that the hole is also, because it is on his premises. It is a very good hole. If it could be taken from the roof just in the shape it is now, it would be a nice thing to show at the Mechanics' Fair; any man who would make a pun under circumstances like these, and suggest that it be turned over to the Christian Commission Fair on account of its holy nature, might

think himself smart, but would the people—the plodding, thinking, intelligent masses—would *they* respect him? Far be it. Doubtless. What shadows we are, and what shadows we pursue. The foregoing facts are written to prepare the reader for the announcement that the stick, with the same exploded rocket attached, may be seen at the hall of the Board of Supervisors. It has remained there to this day. The man who set it off, and hung on to it, and went up with it, has not come down yet. The people who live in Milton Place are expecting him, all the time. They have moved their families, and got out of the way, so as to give him a good show when he drops. They have said, but without insisting on it, that if it would be all the same to him, they would rather he would fall in the alley. This would mash him up a good deal, likely, and scatter him around some, but they think they could scrape him up and hold an inquest on him, and inform his parents. The Board of Supervisors will probably pass an ordinance directing that missiles of the dangerous nature of rockets shall henceforth be fired in the direction of the Bay, so as to guard against accidents to life and property.

"SARROZAY'S BEAURIFUL PLACE. FLOWERS—OR MAYBE IT'S ME—SMELLS DELISHS"

80

**INEXPLICABLE NEWS FROM SAN JOSÉ
23 AUGUST 1864**

On Sunday, 14 August, Clemens and seven other newspapermen, escorted by the convivial Lewis Leland, made a pleasantly hazy all-day outing to the south, appropriately recorded in "Inexplicable News from San José." The party left the city at eight-thirty A.M. on the recently opened San Francisco and San José Railroad and were in San José by eleven. There they spent an hour rambling through shaded streets and gardens and quenching their thirst at George T. Bromley's well equipped Continental Hotel. Twelve miles by buggy brought them to Harrisburgh, popularly known as Warm Springs, where they hiked, swam, and dined. Back in San José well before dusk, they fortified themselves for the return trip and arrived in the city by nine P.M. Besides Leland, the only others who can be identified with any probability are Clemens' close friend Steve Gillis and Henry B. Livingston, law reporter for the *Alta California*. Michael N. Nolan was the accommodating morning conductor.[7]

Clemens' sketch as published in the *Call* consists largely of extracts purportedly from the "chatty letter" of an unnamed correspondent who drunkenly reported the San José excursion to his friend Mark Twain. It is evident that the *Call* version, given below, is closely related to a longer version which survives as an autograph manuscript that is not presently available for inspection except in a somewhat inaccurate, latter-day type-script in the Mark Twain Papers.[8] In the typescript the framework character Mark Twain supplies a few introductory remarks (addressed to the editors of the *Golden Era* to whom, it appears, he was submitting the manuscript) affirming that the report of the San José excursion was written by The Unreliable, Clemens' Nevada friend Clement T. Rice, the local reporter for the Virginia City *Daily Union*. It is not possible to say whether Clemens actually submitted the manuscript to the *Golden Era;* nor, if he did, when. It may be conjectured that the *Golden Era* rejected the sketch because the humor drew too exclusively on drunken dialect and that Clemens revised it for publication in the *Call*.

Whatever happened, at least we see that the sketch in all its versions is another assertion of Mark Twain's lifelong delight in satirizing Mrs. Felicia Hemans' poem "Casabianca" ("The boy stood on the burning deck . . ."). It happily lights up a single day's fun with "the f—f'ternity," to quote the typescript, and so suggests the kind of release from the daily grind that he must have needed from time to time. The appearance of "Inexplicable News" in the *Call* demonstrates once again that George Barnes did not prevent his local's occasionally advertising himself as Mark Twain.

We have before us a letter from an intelligent correspondent, dated "Sarrozay, (San José?) Last Sunday;" we had previously ordered this correspondent to drop us a line, in case anything unusual should happen in San José during the period of his sojourn there. Now that we have got his chatty letter, however, we prefer, for reasons of our own, to make extracts from it, instead of publishing it in full. Considering the expense we were at in sending a special correspondent so far, we are sorry to be obliged to entertain such a preference. The very first paragraph in this blurred and scrawling letter pictured our friend's condition, and filled us with humiliation. It was abhorrent to us to think that we, who had so well earned and so proudly borne the appellation of "M. T., The Moral Phenomenon," should live to have such a letter addressed to us. It begins thus:

"Mr. Mark Twain—Sir: Sarrozay's beauriful place. Flowers—or maybe it's me—smells delishs—like sp-sp-sp(ic!)irits turpentine. Hiccups again. Don' mind *them*—had 'em three days."

As we remarked before, it is very humiliating. So is the next paragraph:

"Full of newsper men—re porters. One from Alta, one from Flag, one from Bulletin, two from Morring Call, one from Sacramento Union, one from Carson Independent. And all drunk—all drunk but me. By Georshe! I'm stonished."

The next paragraph is still worse:

"Been out to Leland of the Occidental, and Livingston in the Warrum Springs, and Steve, with four buggies and a horse, which is a sp-splennid place—splennid place."

Here follow compliments to Nolan, Conductor of the morning train, for his kindness in allowing the writer to ride on the engine, where he could have "room to enjoy himself strong,

you know," and to the Engineer for his generosity in stopping at nearly every station to give people a "chance to come on board, you understand." Then his wandering thoughts turn again affectionately to "Sarrozay" and its wonders:

"Sarrozay's lovely place. Shade trees all down both sides street, and in the middle and elsewhere, and gardens—second street back of Connental Hotel. With a new church in a tall scaffolding—I watched her an hour, but can't understand it. I don' see how they got her in—I don' see how they goin' to get her out. Corralled for good, praps. Hic! Them hiccups again. Comes from s-sociating with drunken beasts."

Our special next indulges in some maudlin felicity over the prospect of riding back to the city in the night on the back of the fire-breathing locomotive, and this suggests to his mind a song which he remembers to have heard somewhere. That is all he remembers about it, though, for the finer details of its language appear to have caved into a sort of general chaos among his recollections.

The bawr stood on the burring dock,
Whence all but him had f-flowed—
    f-floored—f-fled—
The f-flumes that lit the rattle's
    back
Sh-shone round him o'er the shed—

"I dono what's the marrer withat song. It don't appear to have any sense in it, somehow—but she used to be abou the fines' f-fusion—"

Soothing slumber overtook the worn and weary pilgrim at this point, doubtless, and the world may never know what beautiful thought it met upon the threshold and drove back within the portals of his brain, to perish in forgetfulness. After this effort, we trust the public will bear

with us if we allow our special corre- | ing labors for a season—a long sea-
spondent to rest from his exhaust- | son—say a year or two.

**"SOMETHING OF A DRUG ON THE
MARKET, AS IT WERE"**

81

**DUE WARNING
18 SEPTEMBER 1864**

In "Due Warning" Clemens pulled an old, indelicate gag which looked back to his Washoe humor. The stolen hat—which came from Robert J. Tiffany's Eagle Hat Store on Washington Street—probably was not the same one he had lost at the Odd Fellows Ball in Gold Hill more than a year before,[9] but the "cutaneous diseases" were just as "virulent" in California as they had been in Nevada.

Some one carried away a costly and beautiful hat from the Occidental Hotel, (where it was doing duty as security for a board bill,) some ten days ago, to the great and increasing unhappiness of its owner. Its return to the place from whence it was ravished, or to this office, will be a kindness which we shall be only too glad to reciprocate if we ever get a precisely similar opportunity, and the victim shall insist upon it. The hat in question was of the "plug" species, and was made by Tiffany; upon its inner surface the name of "J. Smith" had once been inscribed, but could not easily be deciphered, latterly, on account of "Mark Twain" having been written over it. We do not know J. Smith personally, but we remember meeting him at a social party some time ago, and at that time a misfortune similar to the one of which we are now complaining happened to him. He had several virulent cutaneous diseases, poor fellow, and we have somehow acquired them, also. We do not consider that the hat had anything to do with the matter, but we mention the circumstance as being a curious coincidence. However, we do not desire to see the coincidence extend to the whole community, notwithstanding the fact that the contemplation of its progress could not do otherwise than excite a lively and entertaining solicitude on the part of the people, and therefore we hasten, after ten days' careful deliberation, to warn the public against the calamity by which they are threatened. And we will not disguise a selfish hope, at the same time, that these remarks may have the effect of weaning from our hat the spoiler's affections, and of inducing him to part with it with some degree of cheerfulness. We do not really want it, but it is a comfort to us in our sorrow to be able thus to make it (as a commodity of barter and sale to other parties,) something of a drug on the market, as it were.

Part Two

CRIME AND COURT
REPORTER

STATION HOUSE AND JAIL

A. "IN THE DIRECT LINE OF MISERY"

As a Virginia City reporter Clemens wrote up many brawls and fatal shootings—"a man for breakfast," the saying went—and in stories now lost with the burned files of the *Territorial Enterprise* he must have kept tabs on other ways people got into jail. But as a San Francisco reporter he seems to have found less gunplay but more varied and sophisticated brands of crime. After all, San Francisco was more civilized than Virginia

City. It was older, larger, farther from the frontier, and an active port. Of the two cities it had the more complex underworld and the more intricate social and economic structure. Therefore it offered its citizens more reasons to feel insecure and perhaps more ways to break the law. Its concentration of finance and industry provided unusual opportunity for high-level nonviolent finagling.

Very likely Clemens was more closely in touch with urban crime and misery while working for the *Call* than at any other time in his life. He used to visit the station house lockup and the city jail, where he observed or talked with the inmates—drunks, drifters, criminals, and the deranged. In this way he stored up details of human degradation for possible use in a sketch or a novel to be written years later. For example, he observed that "unconscious madness must be better than conscious mental distress"[1] to the religious John Fisher whose lunacy, somewhat like Father Peter's in *The Mysterious Stranger,* was brought on by misfortune and grief. In "The Story of the Bad Little Boy," Jim graduated to better things from the station house, having taken invaluable training there.[2] Huck's Pap, like Bad Boy Jim, was jailed for drinking. When he had the delirium tremens, snakes would crawl up his legs. The *Call* local made that association when he wrote: "An ancient patriot—Patrick Henry—turned up in the station house yesterday, with snakes in his boots. That is to say, the poor fellow was attacked with delirium tremens."[3] In New York City one summer night in 1867 Clemens himself was arrested for acting the peacemaker in a street fight. On his way to the lockup he must have had a good idea who would be there: "dilapidated old hags, and . . . ragged bummers, sorrowing and swearing," and a "negro man . . . with his head badly battered . . ."[4]

As we have noticed, the *Call's* local reporter understood very well the expediency that kept some San Franciscans on the wagon. He also knew that others could not keep "the pledge" under any circumstances. "From slight indulgences" they would run "into bad habits, and next into the lock up, and from there sometimes into worse, in the direct line of misery."[5] It seems that women drinkers really got to Clemens, for he seldom reported on the men. Maybe he took the male drunk for granted. Also the facts may explain why his "heifers" and "gin-barrels" made the news so frequently. At least John H. Titcomb, the clerk of the Police Court, believed that the supervisors should do something about the "large number of females who have . . . been arrested in a state of intoxication on the public streets, and who . . . cause citizens . . . to blush for humanity by their turbulent and obscene demonstrations and howlings in and about the City Prison."[6]

"MRS. ANN HOLLAND WAS THERE, VERY DRUNK, AND VERY MUSICAL"

**SWILL MUSIC
8 JULY 1864**

As a general thing, when we visit the City Prison late at night, we find one or two drunken vagabonds raving and cursing in the cells, and sending out a pestilent odor of bad whiskey with every execration. Last night the case was different. Mrs. Ann Holland was there, very drunk, and very musical; her gin was passing off in steaming gas, to the tune of "I'll hang my harp on a willow tree," and she appeared to be enjoying it considerably. The effect was very cheerful in a place so accustomed to powerful swearing and mute wretchedness. Mrs. Holland's music was touchingly plaintive and beautiful, too; but then it smelled bad.

"THE CRUEL WAR MUSIC WAS SO FUSED AND BLENDED WITH BLASPHEMY"

**CALABOOSE THEATRICALS
14 JULY 1864**

Anna Jakes is as unquenchable as the sociable "heifer" in *Roughing It* who will not let up on the other stagecoach passengers. Her specialty, "Weeping, Sad and Lonely; or, When This Cruel War Is Over," was an extremely popular ballad by Charles Sawyer and Henry Tucker.

Anna Jakes, drunk and disorderly, but excessively cheerful, made her first appearance in the City Prison last night, and made the dreary vaults ring with music. It was of the distorted, hifalutin kind, and she evidently considered herself an opera sharp of some consequence. Her idea was that "Whee-heeping sad and lo-honely" was not calculated to bring this cruel war to a close shortly, and she delivered herself of that idea under many difficulties; because, in the first place, Mary Kane, an old offender, was cursing like a trooper in a neighboring cell; and secondly, a man in another apartment who wanted to sleep, and who did not admire anybody's music, and especially Anna Jakes', kept inquiring, *"Will* you dry up that infernal yowling, you heifer?"—swinging a hefty oath at her occasionally—and so the cruel war music was so fused and blended with blasphemy in a higher key, and discouraging comments in a lower, that the pleasurable effect of it was destroyed, and the argument and the moral utterly lost. Anna finally fell to singing and dancing both, with a spirit that promised to last till morning, and Mary Kane and the weary man got disgusted and withdrew from the contest. Anna Jakes says she is a highly respectable young married lady, with a husband in the Boise country; that she has been sumptuously reared and expensively educated; that her impulses are good and her instincts refined; that she taught school a long time in the city of New York, and is an accomplished musician; and finally, that her sister got married last Sunday night, and she got drunk to do honor to the occasion—and with a persistency that is a credit to one of such small experience, she has been on a terrific bender ever since. She will probably let herself out on the cruel war for Judge Shepheard, in the Police Court, this morning.

"IMMENSELY COMFORTABLE IF ONE DIDN'T MIND THE IRKSOMENESS OF THE CONFINEMENT"

84

**THE COUNTY PRISON
17 JULY 1864**

The reader should not confuse the city jail with the county prison described below. The city jail was in the basement of City Hall, on Kearny Street at Portsmouth Plaza. It was a row of gloomy cells underneath the Police Station and the Police Courtroom. There prisoners would await trial for a day or a week. Then they were set free or were sent on to San Quentin or the county prison, or to one of various other places like the Stockton Insane Asylum or the Industrial School. The county prison was a two-story brick building on Broadway above Kearny Street. It provided far from ideal conditions for the prisoners. Three or four inmates often were crowded into one cell, five by twelve feet. Clemens' account below, coming not long before the building was enlarged, seems strangely benign.

Clemens' report tells us what we need to know about most of the stars of the "great Female Bummer Brigade," [7] although we should add that Mrs. O'Keefe really was Johanna Keefe and Mrs. McCarty, known as the Mother of Thieves, was named Julia. Almost any one of them, together with Gentle Julia Jennings, the finger biter of "Mayhem" (Item 89) could have sat for Mark Twain's portrait, in "Goldsmith's Friend Abroad Again," of the two drunken women who tormented Ah Song Hi in the San Francisco city jail. [8]

On 14 February James W. Rogers had fatally shot John Foster in the Plaza Exchange Saloon; he was sentenced on 30 July to five years in the state prison on a conviction of manslaughter. Henry L. Davis was Sheriff of the City and County of San Francisco, and Nathan Clark was the keeper of the county prison.

A visit to the County Prison, in Broadway above Kearny street, will satisfy almost any reasonable person that there are worse hardships in life than being immured in those walls. It is a substantial-looking place, but not a particularly dreary one, being as neat and clean as a parlor in its every department. There are two long rows of cells on the main floor—thirty-one, altogether —disposed on each side of an alley-way, built of the best quality of brick, imported from Boston, and laid in cement, which is so hard that a nail could not be driven into it; each cell has a thick iron door with a wicket in its centre for the admission of air and light, and a narrow aperture in the opposite wall for the same purpose; these cells are just about the size and have the general appearance of a gentleman's stateroom on a steamboat, but are rather more comfortable than those dens are sometimes; a two-story bunk, a slop-bucket and a sort of table are the principal furniture; the walls inside are white-washed, and the floors kept neat and clean by frequent scrubbing; on Wednesdays and Saturdays the prisoners are provided with buckets of water for general bathing and clothes-washing purposes, and they are required to keep themselves and their premises clean at all times; on Tuesdays and Fridays they clean up their cells and scrub the floors thereof. In one of these rows of cells it is pitch dark when the doors are shut, but in the other row it is very light when the wickets are open. From the number of books and newspapers lying on the bunks, it is easy to believe that a vast amount of reading is done in the County Prison; and smoking too, we presume, because, although the rules forbid the introduction of spirituous liquors, wine, or beer into the jail, nothing is said about tobacco. Most of the occupants of the light cells were lying on the bunks reading, and some of those in the dark ones were standing up at the wickets similarly employed. "Sick Jimmy," or James Rodgers, who was found guilty of manslaughter a day or two ago, in killing Foster, has been permitted by Sheriff Davis to occupy one of the light cells, on account of his ill health. He says his quarters would be immensely comfortable if one didn't mind the irksomeness of the confinement. We could hear the prisoners laughing and talking in the cells, but they are prohibited from making much noise or talking from one cell to another. There are three iron cells standing isolated in the yard, in which a batch of Chinamen wear the time away in smoking opium two hours a day and sleeping the other twenty-two. The kitchen department is roomy and neat, and the heavy tragedy work in it is done by "trusties," or prisoners detailed from time to time for that duty. Upstairs are the cells for women; two of these are dark, iron cells, for females confined for high crimes. The others are simply well lighted and ventilated wooden rooms, such as the better class of citizens over in Washoe used to occupy a few years ago, when the common people lived in tents. There is nothing gorgeous about these wooden cells, but plenty of light and whitewashing make them look altogether cheerful. Mesdames O'Keefe, McCarty, Mary Holt and "Gentle Julia," (Julia Jennings,) are the most noted ladies in this department. Prison-keeper Clark says the quiet, smiling, pious-looking Mrs. McCarty is just the boss thief of San Francisco, and the misnamed "Gentle Julia" is harder to manage, and gives him more trouble than all the balance of the tribe put together. She uses "awful" language, and a good deal of it, the same being against the rule. Mrs. McCarty dresses neatly, reclines languidly on a striped mattress, smiles sweetly at vacancy, and labors at her "crochet-work" with the serene indifference of a princess. The four ladies we have mentioned are unquestionably stuck after the County Prison; they reside there most of the time, coming out occasionally for a week to steal something, or get on a bender, and going back again as soon as they can prove that they have accomplished their mission. A lady warden will shortly be placed in charge of the women's department here, in accordance with an act of the last Legislature, and we feel able to predict that Gentle Julia will make it mighty warm for her. Most of the cells, above and below, are occupied, and it is proposed to put another story on the jail at no distant day. We have no suggestions to report concerning the County Jail. We are of the opinion that it is all right, and doing well.

"IT ORIGINATED IN WHISKEY"

85

AMAZONIAN PASTIMES
21 JULY 1864

Mollie Livingston and two friends of hers, Terese and Jessie, none of whom are of at all doubtful reputation, cast aside their superfluous clothing and engaged in a splendid triangular fist fight in Spofford Alley about seven o'clock yesterday evening. It was a shiftless row, however, without aim or object, and for this reason officers Evrard and McCormick broke it up and confined the parties to it in the City Prison. It originated in whiskey.

"THE TROUBLED SPIRIT AT PEACE AGAIN"

86

MRS. O'FARRELL
30 JULY 1864

This faded relic of gentility—or, rather, this washed-out relic, for every tint of that description is gone —was brought to the station-house yesterday, in the arms of Officers Marsh and Ball, in a state of beastly intoxication. She cursed the Union and lauded the Confederacy for half an hour, and then she cast up part of her dinner; during the succeeding half hour, or perhaps it might have been three-quarters, she continued to curse the Federal Union and belch fuming and offensive blessings upon the Southern Confederacy, and then she cast up the balance of her dinner. She seemed much relieved. She so expressed herself. She observed to the prison-keeper, and casually to such as were standing around, although strangers to her, that she didn't care a d—n. She said it in that tone of quiet cheerfulness and contentment, which marks the troubled spirit at peace again after its stormy season of unrest. So they tackled her once more, and jammed her into the "dark cell," and locked her up. To such of her friends as gentle love for her may inspire with agonized suspense on her account, we would say: Banish your foreboding fears, for she's safe.

"THIS COMPANY OF CHOICE SPIRITS (GIN)"

87

**ENLISTED FOR THE WAR
2 AUGUST 1864**

Elsewhere Clemens wrote that Ann Berry was "so soaked with gin that she would burn like a tar barrel if she should ever catch fire . . ."[9]

If ever you want to find Ellen Quinn, or Gentle Julia, or Mary Holt, or Haidee Leonard, or Annie Berry, please call at the County Jail, up stairs. Mary Holt has spent most of her time there for the past fourteen years, it is said, and the most inexperienced of this company of choice spirits (gin) has sojourned there chiefly for the last three years. Mary Holt has just enlisted again for the County Jail for fifty days, and next time she comes out she will probably enlist for the war. Following is the record of service of these old soldiers for the past twelve months: Out of the 365 days, Ellen Quinn spent 240 in the County Jail; Gentle Julia, 210 in the station house and County Jail together; Mary Holt, 190 in the County Jail alone; Haidee Leonard, 105 in the County Jail; Annie Berry, 111 in the County Jail. The balance of the year these fellows have spent in the stationhouse, for the most part, for they suffer arrest and confinement there three times, with about two days imprisonment for each arrest, before they can pass muster and get into the County Jail. The veteran Mary Holt commenced fighting the prisons in 1849 or '50.

88

**MARY KANE
20 AUGUST 1864**

This accomplished old gin-barrel came out of the County Jail early in the morning three days ago, and was promptly in the station-house, drunk as a loon, before the middle of the day. She got out the next day, but was in again before night. She got out the following morning, but yesterday noon she was back again, with her noble heart preserved in spirits, as usual. Having a full cargo aboard by this time, she will probably clear for her native land in the County Jail to-day.

89

**MAYHEM
31 AUGUST 1864**

"Gentle Julia," who spends eleven months of each year in the County Jail, on an average, bit a joint clear off one of the fingers of Joanna O'Hara, (an old offender—chicken thief,) in the "dark cell" in the station-house yesterday. The other women confined there say that is the way Gentle Julia always fights.

B. DERELICTS AND WAIFS

**"AMELIA . . . APPEALED FOR NO COMPASSION SAVE
IN THE PLEADING ELOQUENCE OF HER TEARS"**

90

**YOUNG OFFENDER
9 JULY 1864**

Here the *Call* reporter, the same who unmercifully blasted children in Washoe, hints at his true affection for the tribe. It may be detected in the details used to describe Amelia, or the infant in "Lost Child" (Item 93). San Francisco's Industrial School had ninety children enrolled. It was supported by appropriations from the City and County General Fund and from the state.

While we were lounging in the City Jail yesterday afternoon, Officer Cook brought in a little girl, not more than seven or eight years old, whom he had arrested for stealing twenty-five dollars from a man in an auction-room the day before. She gave her name as Amelia Brown Wascus, and seemed to be a half-breed Indian or negro—probably the latter, if one may judge by the kind of taste she displayed in laying out the stolen money, for she had spent a portion of it in the purchase of a toy hand organ with limited accomplishments, and those of a marked contraband tint—the same being indexed on the back of the plaything as "Buffalo Gals," and "My Pretty Yaller Gals." She had expended about fifteen dollars for various trinkets, and the balance of the money had been recovered by Officer Cook from the child's mother. Amelia cried bitterly all the time she was in the station-house, but she said nothing, and appealed for no compassion save in the pleading eloquence of her tears. She was taken to the Industrial School, and her accomplice—for it seems she had one of about her own age and sex—will follow her if she can be found.

"WE FEEL FOR HIM AS A MAN OF NOBLE LITERARY INSTINCTS"

91

THE "COMING MAN" HAS ARRIVED
16 JULY 1864

And he fetched his things with him.—John Smith was brought into the city prison last night, by Officers Conway and Minson, so limbered up with whiskey that you might have hung him on a fence like a wet shirt. His battered slouch-hat was jammed down over his eyes like an extinguisher; his shirt-bosom (which was not clean, at all,) was spread open, displaying his hair trunk beneath; his coat was old, and short-waisted, and fringed at the edges, and exploded at the elbows like a blooming cotton-boll, and its collar was turned up, so that one could see by the darker color it exposed, that the garment had known better days, when it was not so yellow, and sun-burnt, and freckled with grease-spots, as it was now; it might have hung about its owner symmetrically and gracefully, too, in those days, but now it had a general hitch upward, in the back, as if it were climbing him; his pantaloons were of coarse duck, very much soiled, and as full of wrinkles as if they had been made of pickled tripe; his boots were not blacked, and they probably never had been; the subject's face was that of a man of forty, with the sun of an invincible good nature shining dimly through the cloud of dirt that enveloped it. The officers held John up in a warped and tangled attitude, like a pair of tongs struck by lightning, and searched him, and the result was as follows: Two slabs of old cheese; a double handful of various kinds of crackers; seven peaches; a box of lip-salve, bearing marks of great age; an onion; two dollars and sixty-five cents, in two purses, (the odd money being considered as circumstantial evidence that the defendant had been drinking beer at a five-cent house;) a soiled handkerchief; a fine-tooth comb; also one of coarser pattern; a cucumber pickle, in an imperfect state of preservation; a leather string; an eye-glass, such as prospectors use; one buckskin glove; a printed ballad, "Call me pet names;" an apple; part of a dried herring; a copy of the Boston Weekly Journal, and copies of several San Francisco papers; and in each and every pocket he had two or three chunks of tobacco, and also one in his mouth of such remarkable size as to render his articulation confused and uncertain. We have purposely given this prisoner a fictitious name, out of the consideration we feel for him as a man of noble literary instincts, suffering under temporary misfortune. He said he always read the papers before he got drunk; go thou and do likewise. Our literary friend gathered up his grocery store and staggered contentedly into a cell; but if there is any virtue in the boasted power of the press, he shall stagger out again to-day, a free man.

"HE WANTS TO GO AND STAY A WHILE WITH SOME PRIEST"

INDEPENDENT CANDIDATE FOR STOCKTON
17 JULY 1864

Officer Forner arrested and brought into the City Prison, at noon yesterday, a wanderer named Patrick O'Hara, who had been sleeping in the sand-hills all night and tramping dreamily about the wharves all day, with a bag containing nearly seven hundred dollars in gold sticking suggestively out of his coat pocket. He looked a little wild out of his eyes, and did not talk or act as if he knew exactly what he was about. He objected to staying in the Jail, and he was averse to leaving it without his money, and so he was locked up for the present safety and well-being of both. He begged hard for his worshipped treasure, and there were pathos and moving eloquence in the poor fellow's story of the weary months of toil and privation it had cost him to gather it together. He said he had been working for a Mr. Woodworth on a ranch near Petaluma, and they set two men to watching him, and when he found it out he wouldn't stay there any longer, but packed up and came down here on the boat night before last. He also said they had given him an order on Mr. Woodworth here for forty dollars, for a month's work, but when he got on the boat he found it was dated "1833," and he threw it overboard. He brought a carpet-sack with him, and left it at some hotel, but he can't find the place again. He says he wants to go and stay a while with some priest— and if he can get a chance of that kind, he had better take it and keep away from the wharves and the sand-hills; otherwise somebody will "go through him" the first thing he knows.

"CALLED FOR, COLLECTED AND CARRIED AWAY BY ITS FATHER"

LOST CHILD
2 SEPTEMBER 1864

A fat, chubby infant, about two years old, was found by the police yesterday evening, lying fast asleep in the middle of Folsom street, between Sixth and Seventh, and in dangerous proximity to the railroad track. We saw the cheerful youngster in the city jail last night, sitting contentedly in the arms of a negro man who is employed about the establishment. He had been taking another sleep by the stove in the jail kitchen. Possibly the following description of the waif may be recognized by some distressed mother who did not rest well last night: A fat face, serious countenance; considerable dignity of bearing; flaxen hair; eyes dark bluish gray, (by gaslight, at least;) a little soiled red jacket; brown frock, with pinkish squares on it half an inch across; kid gaiter shoes and red-striped stockings; evidently admires his legs, and answers "Dah-dah" to each and all questions, with strict impartiality. Any one having lost an offspring of the above description can get it again by proving property and paying for this advertisement.

THE LOST CHILD RECLAIMED
3 SEPTEMBER 1864

The child which we mentioned yesterday as having been found asleep in the middle of Folsom street by the Police, and taken to the City Jail, has been called for, collected and carried away by its father. It knew its father in a moment, and we believe that is considered to be a severe test of smartness in a child.

C. WOULD-BE SUICIDES

"HE WAS THROWN OUT OF EMPLOYMENT, AND IT WEIGHED UPON HIS SPIRITS"

95

ATTEMPTED SUICIDE
3 AUGUST 1864

When Clemens found an absurdity to expose or a cause to plug in his reports, the writing often picked up. Thus the first piece below was neutral and colorless. But a day later he was getting mean about Ira P. Rankin, the wealthy owner of the Pacific Iron Works, and the writing began to crackle. But the drama ended in farce as the reporter somewhat wickedly told of the disagreement between Dr. F. DeCastro and Dr. Thomas Elliott. Poor Ferguson, the patient, "emeticized, purged and pumped," was forgotten, merely a minor character along with the druggist Calvin Riley and the pharmaceutical chemist George Dickey, both of Howard Street.

Last night, a young man by the name of John Ferguson went to the drug store of Mr. Riley, on the corner of Mission and Second streets, and asked for strychnine, as he said, to kill a dog. He got ten grains. He went into Mission street, took the poison, and was soon met by a friend, to whom he said that he was sick, had taken poison, and was dying. A doctor was called at once, who administered mustard and warm water, which caused nausea and vomiting, which relieved him by freeing the stomach of the poison. Hopes are entertained of his recovery. The cause of this attempt upon his own life is said to be depression from loss of employment and pecuniary difficulties.

RECOVERED
4 AUGUST 1864

The young man, John Ferguson, whose attempt to poison himself by strychnine we recorded in yesterday morning's CALL, is beyond danger. This gratifying result is due to the exertions of Dr. De Castro, who was summoned after the first-called physician had abandoned the case and declared recovery impossible. The Doctor remained with the patient until the effects of the poison had been completely subdued. Ferguson, we understand, is a moulder by trade, and was lately in the employ of Ira P. Rankin. He lost his situation through no fault of his own;

but simply because, with others of his craft, he asked an advance of fifty cents per day on his wages to meet increased expenses of living. For this presumption he was thrown out of employment, and it weighed upon his spirits to the extent of suicide. With some money-getters fifty cents have more importance than many lives.

ROW AMONG THE DOCTORS
7 AUGUST 1864

There is a nice little breeze between the practitioners who were called on in the case of Ferguson, said to have taken strychnia, lately, to end his life, but was prevented by Dr. De Castro. Dr. Elliott, as a cloud of witnesses state, was first called, and gave up the case, saying "he (the patient) was a dead boy;" in other words, recovery was hopeless. De Castro was then called, and as the same witnesses state, found the unhappy Ferguson in the throes of death. He emeticized, purged and pumped him, till the poison had no show, and felt a little justifiable pride at his success. Now, Dr. Elliott says he was not poisoned at all; that the druggist, when the patient applied for the noxious drug, "to kill a dog," suspected his design, and gave him some comparatively harmless preparation—piperine, or something of that sort—and that De Castro was humbugged. He furnishes an analysis from Chemist Dickey, of the drug said to be furnished by the apothecary, in proof. De Castro thinks the fact that the man was swollen fearfully, and almost lifeless when he saw him, and also the druggist Riley's statement that he *did* furnish the deadly article, and marked it "strychnia—poison, ten grains," proof more convincing on his side. Thus the matter stands. Who can decide when Doctors disagree?

"UNTO HIM THE DAY WAS DARK"

ATTEMPTED SUICIDE
7 AUGUST 1864

Clemens limbered up his burlesque style, mixing the mock-romantic with the mock-didactic, in writing of Manuel Lopez, misnamed Emanuel Lopus below. Dr. James Murphy was the surgeon almost done in by Lopez. The French Hospital, on Bryant between Fifth and Sixth streets, was sustained by the French Benevolent Society.

Yesterday at eleven o'clock in the forenoon, Emanuel Lopus, barber, of room No. 23, Mead House, wrote to the idol of his soul that he loved her better than all else beside; that unto him the day was dark, the sun seemed swathed in shadows, when she was not by; that he was going to take the life that God had given him, and enclosed she would please find one lock of hair, the same being his. He then took a teaspoonful of laudanum in a gallon of gin, and lay down to die. That is one version of it. Another is, that he really took an honest dose of laudanum, and was really anxious to put his light out; so much so, indeed, that after Dr. Murphy had come, resolved to pump the poison from his stomach or pump his heart out in the attempt, and after he had comfortably succeeded in the first mentioned proposition, this desperate French barber rose up and tried to whip the surgeon for saving his life, and defeating his fearful purpose, and wasting his laudanum. Another version is, that he went to his friend Jullien, in the barber shop under the Mead House, and told him to smash into his trunk after he had breathed his last and shed his immortal soul, and take from it his professional soap, and his lather-brush and his razors, and keep them forever to remember him by, for he was going this time without reserve. This was a touching allusion to his repeated asser-

tions, made at divers and sundry times during the past few years, that he was going off immediately and commit suicide. Jullien paid no attention to him, thinking he was only drunk, as usual, and that his better judgment would prompt him to substitute his regular gin at the last moment, instead of the deadlier poison. But on going to No. 23 an hour afterwards, he found the wretched Lopus in a heavy stupor, and all unconscious of the things of earth, and the junk-bottle and the laudanum phial on the bureau. We have endeavored to move the sympathy of the public in behalf of this poor Lopus, and we have done it from no selfish motive, and in no hope of reward, but only out of the commiseration we feel for one who has been suffering in solitude while the careless world around him was absorbed in the pursuit of life's foolish pleasures, heedless whether he lived or died. If we have succeeded —if we have caused one sympathetic tear to flow from the tender eye of pity, we desire no richer recompense. They took Lopus to the station-house yesterday afternoon, and from thence he was transferred to the French Hospital. We learn that he is getting along first-rate, now.

THE POLICE COURT

A. ASSAULT AND BATTERY

Acts of violence were a major cause of the "surcharge of human misery"[1] that Clemens observed in Judge Philip W. Shepheard's Police Court. He and his fellow reporters also regularly took notes from the Clerk of Court's minutes at City Hall to use in their daily summaries of court actions. An example is Clemens' summary of 20 July:

> Stephen Storer, for assault and battery, was sentenced to imprisonment for ten days, or to pay a fine of twenty-five dollars. Catherine Moran, whom we spoke of yesterday as having attempted to segregate Mrs. Markee with an axe, was sentenced to forty days' imprisonment, or to pay a fine of one hundred and fifty dollars—and served her right. Mr. Swartz was arraigned on some charge or other —petty larceny, perhaps—in trying to steal a kiss from the widow Ellen Niemeyer, while she was locked up in the City Prison—a delicate attention, which, considering the extremely mild stagger she makes of beauty, she ought to have regarded as a most reckless and desperate compliment, rather than as a crime. We did not remain to hear the result of the trial. Fourteen drunks, etc., were disposed of.[2]

Obviously Clemens liked to be partisan. His summaries often moralize and pass judgment; they condemn or praise, express compassion or disgust. Sometimes they are flippant, or casual to the point of seeming negligence. His effort to spice these reports suggests a need to create interest in his job. Thus he often handled the court proceedings metaphorically and comically. Judge Shepheard's court is a "school of discipline," a "reception," a "levee." The prisoners are the Judge's "little flock," "recruits," or "constituents." The court calendar is a "muster roll," a "record of unrighteousness," a tapestry woven from "the woof of human nature with the warp of whiskey."[3] Every local sometimes seasoned his items, but the *Call's* reporter, who could be as factual as the next man, often poured it on.

Like the other reporters Clemens wrote separate notices of the more interesting cases. A good many of these items are "live," showing that he had lingered to watch the courtroom action. Sometimes he reconstructed the crime, formed his opinion of what the punishment should be, and went on to try the case in the *Call*. This procedure satisfied the moralist in him. It also shows that long before the age of radio and television and modern yellow journalism, the local news columns served to feed a public appetite for the gory and the sensational. As Clemens put it, the crime reports reflected "the marsh-fires of pestilence" [4] burning in the Police Court. He saw many a person in the dock justify his aggression or vice, or flaunt his deceitfulness or cupidity—and all with a dreadful indifference. He saw incompetent lawyers and lying witnesses. He smelled rottenness in the entire system. Although most of the trials that he pictured in later writings were for more exalted crimes than head-splitting or shoplifting, his courtroom experience in San Francisco taught him

Philip W. Shepheard, judge of the city Police Court
(*redrawn from a lithograph, Bancroft Library*).

much about the procedure and the drama of trials. It also helped to fix his attitudes toward "poor human nature."

In the person of Judge Philip W. Shepheard, the Police Court gave Clemens an image of the just man, one combining wisdom, firmness in chastising evildoers, and mercy toward the young and reclaimable; in short, a kindhearted person with a conservative and stoutly held moral code. In 1826, as a boy of fourteen, Shepheard had come to America from Plymouth, England, shipped as a common seaman on a merchantman and had his own ship before he was twenty-one. In 1849 he brought his family and a shipload of gold-seekers to California and remained in San Francisco when his ship the *Arkansas,* anchored in the stream, was badly battered by a storm. Shepheard served several terms as Justice of the Peace of the Second Township, studied law, and was admitted to the bar in 1856. Five years later he was elected Assistant District Attorney and handled most of the cases before Police Judge Cowles, whom he succeeded on the bench early in 1864. Widely respected, Shepheard died 16 December 1865. Clemens regarded him highly.

In a moment of gruesome humor Mark Twain once attributed Judge Shepheard's death to the "deadly miasma" in the police courtroom. The theme of his 1865 write-up of that "horrible hole" is the "fearful combination of miraculous stenches that infect its atmosphere." [5] The following passage is the more factual, less odorous, part of that description. It gives the setting for the selections below:

> The room is about 24 × 40 feet in size, I suppose, and is blocked in on all sides by massive brick walls; it has three or four doors, but they are never opened—and if they were they only open into airless courts and closets anyhow; it has but one window, and now that is blocked up . . . there is not a solitary air-hole as big as your nostril about the whole place. Very well; down two sides of the room, drunken filthy loafers, thieves, prostitutes, China chicken-stealers, witnesses, and slimy guttersnipes who come to see, and belch and issue deadly smells, are banked and packed, four ranks deep—a solid mass of rotting, steaming corruption. In the centre of the room are Dan Murphy, Zabriskie, the Citizen Sam Platt, Prosecuting Attorney Louderback, and other lawyers, either of whom would do for a censer to swing before the high altar of hell. Then, near the Judge are a crowd of reporters—a kind of cattle that did never smell good in any land. The house is full—so full that you have to actually squirm and shoulder your way from one part of it to another—and not a single crack or crevice in the walls to let in one poor breath of God's pure air!

99

ANOTHER CHAPTER IN THE MARKS FAMILY HISTORY
11 JUNE 1864

Henry Wood and Samuel Marks were rival Washington Street tailors. Judge Shepheard fined Wood $20 for striking Marks.

Samuel Marks had Dora Marks and Henry Wood before the Police Court yesterday, charged with assault and battery. The plaintiff said that Dora and Henry came into his shop, on Washington street, last Tuesday, and, without saying a word as to how they came there, knocked him into a senseless condition by blows on his head. Henry testified that he saw the fair Dora enter Samuel's shop, and shortly after he heard a clatter as if heaven and earth were bumping together, and running down to Samuel's doorway, and standing by the door-sill because he had no right to enter the premises, he saw Samuel hit the lamb-like Dora a slap on the sconce with a tailor's press board, and instantly after a huge pair of shears came flying at him. Before he could dodge them, they partially scalped his cranium, causing a plentiful flow of the ruby, and he thought that he had better prospect in other diggings, not so dangerous, and left. The meek and war-worn Dora sat like a penitent Magdalen, and had nary word to say, and the austere decision of the Judge was that the respective defendants, Henry and Dora, do appear in that Court this day, and receive sentence for their crimes.

100

A MOVEMENT IN BUCKEYE
3 AUGUST 1864

Alleck P. Green and Louis Jaszynsky were well known brokers.

"How's stocks this morning?" "Movement in 'Buckeye.'" This little characteristic salutation, a few days since, prefaced a breach of the peace on Montgomery street, thus: Mr. Green, who is learned in the matter of stocks, was authorized to purchase fifty shares of "Buckeye" at four dollars and a half. Mr. Jazinski, also talented in the same line, had a quantity for sale at five dollars, the same having previously been purchased by his principal at twenty-one dollars, showing conclusively that stocks are sometimes up and at other times very much down. Mr. G., the author of the second remark in the above brief dialogue, said he would see whether his principal would give five dollars, and departed for that purpose. Mr. J. waited expectantly for a long time, say a matter of several hours, but in the interval saw G. a number of times and was by him informed that the person who wanted the stock was for the time being distinctly invisible to the naked eye. During this invisibility, "Buckeye" depreciates, and the seller becoming impatient, at last insists that Mr. Green should take the stock at five dollars, himself, without reference to his principal, laying down the proposition that the latter gentleman had inaugurated the transaction in the character of principal himself, and that he held him for it. Mr. Green took issue on this point, and declared that there had been no purchase. Mr. J. said there had—Mr. G. said there hadn't. The mutual contradiction grew positive, with expletives and profane adjectives, amounting to a mutual impeachment of veracity, upon which Mr. Green smote the countenance of the other broker, thereby breaking up the negotiations and breaking the peace at the same time. A blow at sea may be a breeze, a gale or a tempest, but a blow on land is very likely to be an assault and battery. Of this latter kind was the blow given by Mr. Green, and in consequence thereof he was yesterday ordered by Judge Shepheard to appear this morning for sentence.

" 'I'M NOT YOUR AUNTY,' SHE ROARED. 'I'M MRS. HAMMOND' "

101

A DARK TRANSACTION
24 AUGUST 1864

Describing physical violence did not always bring out the best in Clemens' prose. It encouraged hasty writing and reliance on puns or jargon or comic circumlocution. But the brief sketch of Mrs. Hammond has merit. Bearing a double burden of race and weight, she insists on her right to be treated as a person. Her dignity rises above the murky racial condescension shared by the courtroom onlookers and the eccentric, witty lawyer Samuel Platt—and to a certain extent, it seems, by the reporter.

A gloom pervaded the Police Court, as the sable visages of Mary Wilkinson and Maria Brooks, with their cloud of witnesses, entered within its consecrated walls, each to prosecute and defend respectively in counter charges of assault and battery. The cases were consolidated, and crimination and recrimination ruled the hour. Mary said she was a meek-hearted Christian, who loved her enemies, including Maria, and had prayed for her on the very morning of the day when the latter threw a pail of water and a rock against her. Maria said she didn't throw; that she wasn't a Christian herself, and that Mary had the very devil in her. The case would always have remained in doubt, but Mrs. Hammond overshadowed the Court, and flashed defiance at counsel, from her eyes, while indignation and eloquence burst from her heaving bosom, like the long pent up fires of a volcano, whenever any one presumed to intimate that her statement might be improved in point of credibility, by a slight explanation. Even the gravity of the Court was somewhat disturbed when three hundred weight of black majesty, hauteur, and conscious virtue, rolled on to the witness stand, like the fore quarter of a sunburnt whale, a living embodiment of Desdemona, Othello, Jupiter, Josh, and Jewhilikens. She appeared as counsel for Maria Brooks, and scornfully repudiated the relationship, when citizen Sam Platt, Esq. prefaced his interrogation with the endearing, "Aunty." "I'm not your Aunty," she roared. "I'm Mrs. Hammond," upon which the citizen S. P., Esq., repeated his assurances of distinguished regard, and caved a little. Mrs. Hammond rolled off the stand, and out of the Court room, like the fragment of a thunder cloud, leaving the "congregation," as she called it, in convulsions. Mary Brooks and Maria Wilkinson were both convicted of assault and battery, and ordered to appear for sentence.

"THIS PRODIGY OF PHYSICAL AND MORAL FIRMNESS"

102

STRONG AS SAMPSON AND MEEK AS MOSES
31 AUGUST 1864

Dr. Foster lost his case.

Ellen Clark and Peter Connarty were up yesterday, charged with an assault and battery committed on Dr. S. S. Foster, gymnast and athlete, at Callahan's building, on Dupont street. The Doctor says he was assailed by these persons without any provocation on his part, and suffered at their hands divers indignities and abuses, but being under a vow made some years since never to strike any one thereafter, no matter what might be the aggravation, he quietly dropped his cane, folded his hands, and submitted. King Solomon says, "It is the glory of a man to pass by an offence." Behold what a glorious fellow Dr. Foster must be; he declared that although no three men in the profession can handle him, yet if a person were to spit in his face he would not resent it. That's a high order of Christian meekness and forbearance—a sublime instance. Other witnesses, however, tell a story less creditable to this prodigy of physical and moral firmness, and as they were about equally balanced in the weight of their testimony, the Doctor was allowed time to procure some preponderating evidence. So the case was held over until to-day.

"IN ORDER TO MAKE UP THE DEFICIT OF FUN"

103

**PEEPING TOM OF COVENTRY
6 SEPTEMBER 1864**

An amorous old sinner, named John Fine, went to the North Beach bath-house on Sunday for a swim. Owing to the number of pounds he weighed, he was forced to wade—his weight being considerably over several stone he couldn't swim, for who ever heard of stones swimming. In order to make up the deficit of fun, he went to the partition that screens the ladies' department, and peeped through a crevice. Mr. Ills, the proprietor of the establishment, witnessed the untoward scrutiny, and ordered him away; but life's charms riveted Fine to the spot, and he heeded not the Ills, when his person suffered under the weight of another stone. The proprietor sent a projectile which struck him in the face, near the left eye. Astronomically speaking, Fine saw stars, but didn't think it a fine sight. He left at once and prosecuted Ills. Yesterday Mr. Ills was fined five dollars for assault and battery.

"THE WEAPON USED WAS A BUTCHER-KNIFE"

104

**A TERRIBLE WEAPON
21 SEPTEMBER 1864**

After the local's interest turns from the violence of the butchers' quarrel to the ancient customs they observed, his reporting betrays that tone of enthusiastic interest in the strange and unusual often found in Mark Twain's travel writing.

A charge of assault with a deadly weapon, preferred in the Police Court yesterday, against Jacob Friedberg, was dismissed, at the request of all parties concerned, because of the scandal it would occasion to the Jewish Church to let the trial proceed, both the assaulted man and the man committing the assault being consecrated servants of that Church. The weapon used was a butcher-knife, with a blade more than two feet long, and as keen as a razor. The men were butchers, appointed by dignitaries of the Jewish Church to slaughter and inspect all beef intended for sale to their brethren, and in a dispute some time ago, one of them partly split the other's head open, from the top of the forehead to the end of his nose, with the sacred knife, and also slashed one of his hands. From these wounds the sufferer has only just recovered. The Jewish butcher is not appointed to his office in this country, but is chosen abroad by a college of Rabbis and sent hither. He kills beeves designed for consumption by Israelites, (or any one else, if they choose to buy), and after careful examination, if he finds that the animal is in any way diseased, it is condemned and discarded; if the contrary, the seal of the Church is placed upon it, and it is permitted to be sent into the market—a custom that might be adopted with profit by all sects and creeds. It is said that the official butcher always assures himself that the sacred knife is perfectly sharp and without a wire edge, before he cuts a bullock's throat; he then draws it with a single lightning stroke (and at any rate not more than two strokes are admissible,) and if the knife is still without a wire edge after the killing, the job has been properly done; but if the contrary is the case, it is adjudged that a bone has been touched and pain inflicted upon the animal, and consequently the meat cannot receive the seal of approval and must be thrown aside. It is a quaint custom of the ancient Church, and sounds strangely enough to modern ears. Considering that the dignity of the Church was in some sense involved in the misconduct of its two servants, the dismissal of the case without a hearing was asked and granted.

"HE CARRIES AN ARMAMENT BETTER SUITED TO A FORTRESS"

During the presidential campaign of 1864 McClellan supporters organized Broom Ranger clubs. Shouldering brooms and marching in formation, members were likely to appear at both Union and Democratic rallies. Newspapers endorsing Lincoln often criticized them for heckling and for drunken disorderliness. Judge Shepheard gave Roderick a choice of ninety-five days or a fine of $250.

In the second item on Roderick below, Clemens exploded his opinions and judgments with unusual force to achieve his comic effect.

A ROUGH CUSTOMER
8 OCTOBER 1864

Benjamin Roderick has been arrested on charges of malicious mischief, carrying a concealed weapon, and assault with a deadly weapon with intent to kill. Yesterday morning, shortly after midnight, he went to the house of Mary Roberts and got into a quarrel with her, and drawing a Bowie-knife, threatened to take her life; he went away, and afterwards returned, renewed his threats, and proceeded to smash up all the furniture in her house; he created havoc and destruction on all sides, and ended by breaking the windows with large stones. At last the cries of the woman attracted the attention of Special Officer Forner, and he was about to arrest Roderick when the latter broke away and ran. Forner fired his pistol in the air, which frightened the fugitive, and he stopped and gave himself up. Be- sides his Bowie-knife, he carried on his person a murderous weapon in the shape of a short-handled hatchet —an equipment calculated to make him rather formidable at short range. Roderick had been marching with the Broom Rangers, and the woman says he was drunk when he entered her house.

106

THE RODERICK CASE
9 OCTOBER 1864

The would-be desperado, Roderick, who threatened the life of Mary Roberts, in a house in Broadway, on Thursday night, was tried and convicted in the Police Court, yesterday morning, on three separate charges. The first charge was carrying a concealed deadly weapon; he had a pocket full of them—a Bowie-knife, a short-handled hatchet, and a hat-full of bed-rock, with a trace of quartz in it. The second charge, of assault with a deadly weapon, was sustained by the testimony of the complaining witness, Mary Roberts, who swore that Roderick seized her and aimed a blow at her with his Bowie-knife, when Providence provided her with invisible wings. She said she knew she had wings at that moment of her utmost need, although they were not palpable to her imperfect mortal vision, and she flew away—she gently soared down stairs. Judging by the woman's general appearance, and her known character and antecedents, this interference of Providence in her behalf was remarkable, to say the least, and must have been quite a surprise to her. The third charge was of malicious mischief. It was shown in evidence that he wantonly destroyed furniture belonging to the woman, worth one hundred dollars. The prisoner was ordered to appear for sentence on all three of the charges, to-morrow morning. Roderick killed a man once. He is rather a bad looking man, but probably not nearly so dangerous as one might suppose from his lawless conduct. He has bad habits, similar to those of many a professedly better man, and he carries an armament better suited to a fortress than a well-meaning private citizen. All these things are against him, and he deserves to be punished for having them against him, and for breaking furniture that did not belong to him. He was not anxious to kill the woman, though, or even do her a bodily injury, as his opportunities for doing so were ample, and he threw them away. He might have made a good sensation item for the newspapers, and he carelessly threw that opportunity away also. Roderick is a useless incumbrance, any way you take him.

B. SWINDLING AND USURY

**"THIS WAS HIS FIRST OFFENCE IN BEING SO
CRIMINALLY GREEN"**

107

**THE OLD THING
1 JULY 1864**

Prosecutions in the Police Court for fraudulent business deals and for
fleecing innocent strangers were not uncommon. In a letter which appeared in the *Territorial Enterprise* early in 1866, Mark Twain revealed
that Wellington had turned stool pigeon for Police Captain Isaiah Lees,
and "secret detective" for the Police Commissioners, only to use his
favored positions as stepping-stones to other crimes.[6]

We conversed yesterday with a stranger, who had suffered from a game familiar to some San Franciscans, but unknown in his section of the country. He was going home late at night, when a sociable young man, standing alone on the sidewalk, bade him good evening in a friendly way, and asked him to take a drink, with a fascination of manner which he could not resist. They went into Johnson's saloon, on Pike street, but instead of paying promptly for the drinks, the sociable young man proposed to throw the dice for them, which was done, and the stranger who was a merchant, from the country, lost. Euchre was then proposed, and two disinterested spectators, entirely unknown to the sociable young man—as he said—were invited to join the game, and did so. Shortly afterwards, good hands were discovered to be plenty around the board, and it was proposed to bet on them, and turn the game into poker. The merchant held four kings, and he called a ten dollar bet; but the luck that sociable young man had was astonishing—he held four aces!

This made the merchant suspicious —he says—and it was a pity his sagacity was not still more extraordinary—it was a pity it did not warn him that it was time to quit that crowd. But it had no such effect; the sociable man showed him a check on Wells, Fargo & Co., and he thought it was safe to "stake" him; therefore he staked his friend, and continued to stake him, and his friend played and lost, and continued to play and lose, until one hundred and ninety dollars were gone, and he nothing more left wherewith to stake him. The merchant complained to the Police, yesterday, and officer McCormick hunted up the destroyer of his peace and the buster of his fortune, and arrested him. He gave his name as Wellington, but the Police have known him well heretofore as "Injun Ned;" he told the merchant his name was J. G. Whittaker. Wellington Whittaker deserves to be severely punished, but perhaps the merchant ought to be allowed to go free, as this was his first offence in being so criminally green.

"THEY DO NOT LOVE HIM SO MUCH NOW"

108

FRUIT SWINDLING
4 AUGUST 1864

No one named Cornwall is listed as a justice of the peace in 1864. Probably Clemens meant to indicate C. Cornell, Justice of the Sixth District Court.

Last Saturday morning, a man named Cheesman, proprietor of a fruit store at the corner of Market and Second streets, purchased quantities of fruit from different dealers, and in the afternoon, after taking an inventory of his wares, sold out his whole establishment for one thousand dollars. In order to avert suspicion, he paid a month's advance on his room rent on Friday, and conducted himself in all respects as if he had made up his mind to remain in San Francisco a century. However, notwithstanding his subtle diplomacy, his creditors began to suspect him of an intention to defraud them, and when the places which knew him once got to knowing him no more, shortly they grew alarmed and fell to searching for him. They sought him from Saturday night until Tuesday, and finally found him. He began to play himself for an honest man, at once, and declared his willingness to pay his debts. They took him to Justice Cornwall's office, and made him disgorge the money he had with him, seven hundred and fifty dollars, after which, by authority of a writ served for that purpose, they submitted him to a rigid examination. The seven hundred and fifty dollars was deposited in Court; he went there yesterday morning, with his lawyer, and tried to substitute green-backs for the amount, but the Judge refused to permit it, and said it must remain as it was, for distribution among the creditors. Suits have been commenced against Cheesman by those who loved him and trusted him, and got burnt at it. They do not love him so much now. He owes about twelve hundred dollars for fruit, and six hundred dollars borrowed money. His indebtedness for fruit is distributed among a large number of dealers, in bills ranging from three dollars up to two hundred and thirty dollars.

"A DOUBT IN LAW, BUT NOWHERE ELSE"

109

LOOKS LIKE SHARP PRACTICE
4 SEPTEMBER 1864

The tricky Simon Lewis was a pawnbroker on Kearny Street, who had been in court before. Adolph Warner, his victim, was a dealer in stoves and tinware.

The examination of Simon Lewis, the pawnbroker, charged with exacting usurious interest, was concluded yesterday, in the Police Court. The testimony for the prosecution presents this state of facts: Adolph Warner took a watch, with chain attached, to the shop of the pawnbroker and pledged it for forty dollars, but did not receive the ticket which the law requires pawnbrokers to give in all cases to the person pledging an article, containing a description of the article, number of the pawn, and date of the transaction, signed by the broker. When Warner's wife discovered that he had left the watch with Lewis, without taking a ticket, she went herself for it, and received from the broker two tickets, one for the watch and one for the chain, purporting to evidence two separate loans of twenty dollars each, instead of one entire loan of forty dollars. The law prohibits pawnbrokers from taking a greater amount of interest than four per cent on sums over twenty dollars; but on sums of twenty dollars, and under, they are in the habit of charging ten per cent. The prosecution claims that his was but one loan, but that defendant had bifurcated the pledge so as to reduce the sums to within the limit upon which the high rates are charged, and thus compelled him to pay ten, instead of four per cent. The case looked badly for the pawnbroker; but when his own books were introduced in evidence, with his own clerk to explain them, of course Lewis would be exculpated, at least in the eye of the law; that is to say, he would—and he did—escape through a mere doubt—a doubt in law, but nowhere else. Lewis had the manufacturing of all the record and documentary evidence himself, and he would have been a more stupid knave than is generally to be found among pawnbrokers, if he had not made it to suit his side of the case in the event of a future controversy about it. From the contradictory character of the evidence, the Judge could not convict the defendant, but he delivered a short and pointed homily on the subject of honesty, as the best policy, and gave notice that he would be somewhat rigorous in future complaints of that sort.

"DR. RAYMOND HAD BEEN IN A STATE OF GREAT MENTAL DEPRESSION"

Charles H. Raymond, M.D., seems to have been the victim of malicious testimony, inefficient hospital management, and his own suicidal tendencies. An Ohioan in his late fifties, he had practiced in Cleveland and Buffalo before situating himself in New York City as visiting physician first at Bellevue Hospital and then at Blackwell's Island. He traveled to San Francisco as a ship's surgeon and in 1857 became resident physician at the City and County Hospital overlooking the shore of North Beach. Following his suicide his accounts were found to be in good order, and Clemens noted the irony that his dismissal from his job was "void and of no effect" because the Board of Supervisors had acted illegally in bypassing its own hospital committee. Earlier Clemens had implied that a September 15 article about the dismissal in the *Alta California* had triggered Dr. Raymond's suicide, but his own piece of that date is the sharper. Did he feel guilty about his handling of the doctor's dismissal and of Vogel's charges?

Mrs. Anna Weeks was the hospital matron, and Dr. S. Russell Gerry — twice spelled "Geary" in the *Call*—was the visiting physician. Others involved in the investigation into Dr. Raymond's death were the hospital apothecary M. B. Pond, Dr. Robert K. Nuttall, Dr. F. A. Holman of the City Hospital at Sutter and Montgomery streets, and the dead man's cousin I. W. Raymond, with the Central American Steamship Transit Company.

110

TURNED OUT OF OFFICE
6 SEPTEMBER 1864

Resident Physician Raymond, Visiting Physician Geary, and Matron Weeks, of the City and County Hospital, were all summarily bundled out of office, last night, by the Board of Supervisors, for alleged official neglect, indifference, indolence, and general "dry rot" produced by long continuance in office, and apparent security in the possession of their places. Notice was given of a motion to reconsider this action, and in the meantime the two doctors and the matron were, by resolution, to retain their offices until their successors were appointed.

111

COUNTY HOSPITAL DEVELOPMENTS
15 SEPTEMBER 1864

They do say that when rogues fall out, honest men get their dues. Messrs. Vogel and Isaacs, of the County Hospital, have fallen out. The seeming insinuation in the remark is the fruit solely of unworthy suspicion in the prejudiced mind of the reader. Isadore Isaacs, who for years has had the lucrative job of repairing all the windows that chanced to get broken in the Hospital, a day or two ago procured the arrest of Vogel, an employé of his, for using improper language to Mrs. Isaacs. Vogel said at the time, that if the charge against him was prosecuted, he would retaliate upon Isaacs and others connected with the Hospital by throwing open to the public gaze such a three years' history of corruption and swindling in that institution as would set San Francisco dizzy with amazement. To make his threat good, he went yesterday to Officer Lindheimer and Detective Officer Watkin, and complained that for the past three years his boss, Isaacs, had been in the constant habit of charging in his bills against the County, double and treble the amount of glass actually put into the Hospital windows by him, and that he did it with the Resident Physician, Dr. Raymond's, connivance and consent, and that when the Doctor heard of Vogel's threatened exposé he offered him twenty dollars to keep quiet. Vogel says that whenever Isaacs put in ten panes of glass, he always charged the City for thirty; for thirty panes, he charged seventy-five, or such a matter, in his bills, and so on and so forth; thus managing, by naturally quick talents and close attention to business, to make a good thing out of an unpromising contract, with no capital save a gift in the way of slinging a multiplication table which amounted almost to inspiration. Mr. Vogel says he will prove that in three years the officers of the Hospital paid Isaacs thirteen hundred dollars for repaired win-

dows, but he does not know how much the City and County paid to those officers in the same time for the same work—a remark of Mr. Vogel's which savors of an insinuation. According to a judgment of men and their manners under circumstances where crime and their direct or indirect implication in it is concerned, sharpened by his long experience as a detective, Officer Watkin is satisfied that Vogel knows a vast deal about the hidden mysteries of the conduct of the Hospital, but he seems in doubt about the policy of unveiling them all in a heap. Upon the complaint made by Vogel, Chief Burke had Isaacs arrested, and upon the examination of the case to-day, comprehensive developments may be looked for. Considering the important nature of the case, however, Judge Shepheard should not have allowed Isaacs his liberty on fifty or sixty dollars' worth of green-backs —one hundred and fifty dollars in shinplasters. Now, how much credence is to be given to the statements of Vogel, who is smarting under a sense of injury, we are not prepared to say; but at the same time, if there are two departments of service in the Hospital that are not the subject of suspicion in the minds of taxpayers, we do not know it.

112

SUICIDE OF DR. RAYMOND
16 SEPTEMBER 1864

We gather the following facts concerning this sad event from Chief Burke: At eight o'clock yesterday morning, the daily papers, as usual, were taken to the Doctor before he had risen from bed. After the lapse

of half an hour, he was found lying in an insensible condition from the effects of a heavy dose of morphine, which he had swallowed. He had been reading, apparently; the Alta, with his spectacles lying upon it, was on the bed. Antidotes were administered, and the stomach pump applied, and he rallied enough to show by the intelligence in his eyes that he recognized the persons who stood about him, but he was speechless. In spite of all efforts to expel the poison from his system and annul its effects, he gradually sank until a few minutes past one o'clock in the afternoon, when he died. Ever since his removal from the position of Resident Physician of the County Hospital, by the Board of Supervisors, on last Monday week, Dr. Raymond had been in a state of great mental depression and unhappiness, and during the three days preceding his death he had several times expressed fears that he was going to commit suicide. He told Dr. Nuttall that he was "possessed of a suicidal devil," and gave that gentleman his knife because of a desire he felt to use it upon himself. He refused the Doctor's request that he would remain with him at his house, however. Dr. Raymond also mentioned this yearning to commit suicide to Mr. Pond, at the Hospital, and said, "Keep an eye on me." Dr. Raymond occupied the post of Resident Physician of the City and County Hospital during the past six or seven years; he came here from St. Louis, about ten years ago, and those who knew him best speak highly of his character. He was about fifty years of age.

113

THE ALLEGED SWINDLING
16 SEPTEMBER 1864

The sworn statement, before the proper officer, of Vogel, that his employer, Isaacs, had received $1,300 in three years for repairs to the windows of the County Hospital, does not tally with the Auditor's books, which show bills paid to Dr. Raymond for this purpose amounting to only $80.87. If Vogel really knows of any criminality in the management of the affairs of the Hospital, it should be wrung from him, upon Isaacs' trial, so that if any be guilty, they may be punished, and in order that if he has made false charges, suspicion may be removed from the parties wronged. If his statements are invented simply to gratify a thirst for revenge, the fact should be ferreted out and a stool of repentence provided for him in the State Prison.

114

DR. RAYMOND NOT REMOVED
17 SEPTEMBER 1864

We are informed by a member of the Board of Supervisors that the removal of the late Dr. Raymond from the post of Resident Physician of the County Hospital, and which action so preyed upon his mind, was not valid and binding, but on the contrary was void and of no effect, because it was not recommended by the Hospital Committee, from which, according to an unrepealed resolution of the Board, all such motions for removal must emanate.

115

THE LATE SUICIDE—CORONER'S INQUEST 17 SEPTEMBER 1864

An inquest was held last evening at the County Hospital, to inquire into the recent suicide of Dr. Raymond, late Resident Physician of that institution. R. G. Tobin, Esq., Justice of the First Township, officiated as Coroner. A number of witnesses were examined, who entered into a minute detail of everything that had transpired for several days previous to the death of the Doctor, having the slightest bearing on the matter, as showing the causes that led to the commission of the rash act. The testimony fully establishes the fact that the Doctor, at the time and for some time previous, was laboring under a temporary aberration of mind. Our limited space precludes the possibility of giving more than a faithful epitome of the witnesses' statements. Dr. Holman, on the morning of the 10th, received a note informing him that Dr. Raymond was ill, and leaving a message to that effect for Dr. Nuttall, he repaired at once to the Hospital, where he found deceased insensible, and evidently under the effect of morphine. He found it impossible to arouse him. The electro galvanic battery was applied by Dr. Gerry; an emetic of the sulphate of zinc was administered by Mr. Pond, the apothecary of the Hospital, previous to the arrival of the physician, and an injection was given. Every remedy was used that medical skill could summon, without even appearing to rally him from the comatose condition in which he was at first discovered. The only sign of sensibility seemed to have been indicated when Mr. Pond applied his mouth close to the Doctor's ear, and called him in a loud voice. Dr. R. opened his eyes for a moment, and fixed them on Mr. Pond, but did not speak. From the first the sufferer exhibited all the effects of narcotic poison or apoplexy. His features were rigid, and his jaws so firmly set that it was only with the greatest difficulty that the tube of the stomach-pump could be introduced into his stomach. In an adjoining room, on a table, was a drachm vial of morphine, partly empty, and close by it a tumbler of water with morphine dissolved in it, from which he had evidently taken the fatal draught. On the bed in which the Doctor was lying was the Morning Alta, as Dr. Gerry positively states, and by it his spectacles. The witnesses differed some in their impressions concerning the effect on the mind of deceased of certain newspaper articles of that morning. Dr. Nuttall felt sure that the rash act was hastened from having read certain articles reflecting on his character, while Dr. Gerry and Mr. Pond both agree in their impressions, from the appearance of things, that the fatal dose was taken a considerable length of time before he got the paper, and that he had not even so much as seen the article in the paper that morning, as it was lying on his bed, having the appearance of not having been unfolded. Witnesses state that there was no other paper in the room. Deceased has recently spoken of suicidal propensities that possessed him at times, and made him apprehensive that he would make an attempt at self destruction. He spoke calmly about it, and said that at times it was almost irresistible. At such times he seemed extremely dejected; told Dr. Nuttall, a day or two before his death, that his "evil genius was a suicidal devil," and gave the Doctor his knife, fearing he might attempt violence on himself with it. He placed himself under treatment of Dr. N. a short time since, for this mental disease, and after two days seemed much better. All the medical witnesses, Drs. Holman, Nuttall and Geary, agree in their belief that the suicide was committed during a temporary fit of insanity, aggravated doubtless by certain recent charges implicating him in frauds in the Hospital accounts and management. He spoke of the matter as if his sense of honor was wounded, though Dr.

Gerry testifies that he "saw Dr. Raymond previously with regard to the charges in the morning papers, and he appeared to regard them with the contempt which they merited." Dr. Raymond stated to Mr. Pond on Monday last, during a conversation with reference to his suicidal propensities, that he had twice before in his life been affected in the same manner, and he was fearful at times that he would do himself an injury. The day before he died he conversed very calmly with his cousin, Mr. I. W. Raymond, on this subject. Dr. Nuttall felt certain that the act was not one of his volition; that if deceased had been in a proper state of mind, his energies would have been directed against it. Deceased was in comfortable circumstances, suffered from no pecuniary embarrassments, had, he said, five thousand dollars in the Savings Bank, and about as much in United States Bonds, besides what he had in his pocket; said he was never better off in his life, and had plenty saved up for the time he was likely yet to live. Deceased was a native of New York, fifty-eight years of age. He has a step-mother and two brothers living—one in New York and one in Maryland. The jury returned a verdict in accordance with the above facts.

C. OBSCENITY AND SEDUCTION

Schoolgirl scandals rocked San Francisco about as often as earthquakes did. When Clemens wrote on this subject he respected the common social taboos. He fell back on cliché, as if by adhering to the conventional in imagination he could shore up a tottering sexual morality. The first report below is almost smothered in a chaste stodginess. From such central euphemisms as "their ruin was effected" the language spreads outward to report the "infamous association" of "scoundrels" who "had banded themselves together" to accomplish their "villanous transactions." In such a context of sustained conventional outrage, the reporter dutifully placed the argot of the "miscreants" within quotation marks.

Clemens' outrage also was genuine. He valued innocence, and besides, the debauchers seemed to him to be taking over then, in late July and early August. On the river and in Nevada he may have come across men like Lambertson, Powers, and several other "active propagandists of an equivocal school of morals" [7] which he reported on that summer, but hardly in such rapid-fire order as in San Francisco. Although Tom Sawyer's St. Petersburg sometimes emits an aura of innocence, Mark Twain knew very well that Hannibal, its original, was far from pristine; but could he ever even faintly have imagined San Francisco anywhere on his scale of innocence except near the bottom?

"THE ONLY REGRET IS THAT THE POWER OF THE JUDGE TO PUNISH IS LIMITED"

Mark Twain remembered the Lambertson-Doyle case and a contemporary trial of some dealers in obscene pictures when he wrote "Goldsmith's Friend Abroad Again" in 1870. In that narrative the immigrant Ah Song Hi is jailed for disturbing the peace, for he has tried to protect himself when some hoodlums set a dog on him. In his cell was "a boy of fourteen who had been watched for some time by officers and teachers, and repeatedly detected in enticing young girls from the public schools to the lodgings of gentlemen down town. He had been furnished with lures in the form of pictures and books of a peculiar kind, and these he had distributed among his clients." [8] Ah Song Hi learns that the boy has been sent to the House of Correction but that his employers have gone unpunished because the publicity would have hurt them socially. In "Goldsmith's Friend" the police judge who eventually sentenced Ah Song Hi is a weak tool of a corrupt system. Perhaps Mark Twain was distorting his memory of Judge Shepheard to add force to Ah Song Hi's indictment of American justice, or he may have had another judge in mind.

Some of the girls who were decoyed by—or who themselves seduced—manly little Doyle were from the Rincon School, and Mr. Pelton, their principal, was the man who worked with the police. The amount of time that he devoted to amassing evidence in the case eventually hurt him, for when the Board of Education later tried to remove Mr. Pelton from his job, it charged him with neglect of duty for having taken more time than had been authorized to round up the obscene publications.

116

DEMORALIZING YOUNG GIRLS
23 JULY 1864

Yesterday, in the Police Court, George Lambertson and Ralph Doyle, one a full-grown man and the other a boy of fourteen, pleaded guilty to the charge of exhibiting obscene pictures. Officers Lees, Evrard and Rose, some time since, got on the track of a regular system of prostituting young girls, which was being carried on by a number of men and boys who had banded themselves together for the purpose, and their efforts have resulted in the arrest of the two persons above named, and the unearthing of two more of the boys and two or three men, who are probably all captured by this time. The name of one of the men is Emile Buffandeau; two of the boys are Harry Fenton and George Ayres. The men made use of the boys to decoy the girls to their rooms, where their ruin was effected. These rooms were well stocked with obscene books and pictures. The officers say that the further they probe the matter the more astounding are the developments, and the more widespread the operations of this infamous association are discovered to be. The names of some fifteen of these debauched girls have already been ascertained, and others are suspected of properly belonging on the list. Some of them are members of families of high respectability, and the balance, as young Doyle phrases it, are "baldheaded," that is, unbonneted street girls. The ages of the lot vary from ten or twelve to fifteen. Ralph Doyle says that he and the other two boys, Ayres and Fen-ton, were "confidants," but that he knows of no "gang," nor confederation of men and boys together, in the wretched business. He is aware, however, that a large number of men and boys and young girls are in the habit of visiting each other's rooms, but on their own individual responsibility only, he thinks. He says the girls showed him the obscene pictures, instead of his being guilty of that sort of conduct with them, and he is further of the opinion that they have done the seducing in most of the other cases, as they did in his. He is a fine, handsome, manly little fellow, uses excellent language, and his bearing is quiet and perfectly well-bred. He tells his story the same way every time, and we believe he tells the truth. All his revelations, however, will not do to print. The boys concerned in this extraordinary affair will be sent to the Industrial School, as they are all very young, and it is to be hoped that the law will be stretched to its utmost tension for the punishment of the men. . . . Since the above was in type, we have learned that the terrible developments detailed above, were brought to light through the energy and industry of the master of one of the Schools. He had ascertained the names and addresses of a great number of men and boys not mentioned in this article, who were implicated in these villanous transactions, and was in a fair way of securing their apprehension, but the premature disclosure of the facts and their publication in the evening papers, it is feared, will put the scoundrels on their guard, and prevent their capture. Furthermore, according to our latest information, there are *thirty* names of debauched young girls on the list. The man Lambertson, by whom a poor orphan girl of fifteen has become *enceinte,* has made over to her, in the hope of escaping the penitentiary, such property as he owned in the city. We are also very glad to learn, from the best authority, that Ralph Doyle, so far from being a leader among the miscreants, as has been said of him, was the most innocent in the party, and that it is not in his nature to do an unworthy action when left to the guidance of his own good instincts.

117

A MERITED PENALTY
24 JULY 1864

We chronicle the usual visitations of justice upon those persons whose errors are venial, and the result of an unfortunate appetite, or temper, always with a feeling of regret that the well-being of society demands inflexibly a judgment "according to the law and the testimony." We can compassionate the man whose domestic troubles, or business reverses, drive him to drink frenzy from the bowl, or who, in a momentary heat, retaliates on wanton injury, or insult, or errs through ignorance; but there are instances where the only regret is that the power of the Judge to punish is limited to a penalty not at all commensurate with the magnitude of the offence. In the case of George Lambertson, who was arrested for infamous demoralizing practices with young school girls, and who pleaded guilty in the Police Court, Judge Shepheard inflicted upon the miscreant the heaviest penalty prescribed by the law for his crime. Lambertson receives a term of three months in the County Jail, and a fine of five hundred dollars, (which fine will extend the term of imprisonment until the full amount is served out, at the rate of two dollars per day, in addition to the three months aforesaid,) is a part of the penalty.

"HE WRITES CHATTY, FAMILIAR LETTERS TO YOUNG GIRLS IN THE CALIFORNIA SEMINARIES"

According to the *Alta California* George Powers wrote "songs of questionable purity for the singers of low melodeons." [9] The man with Powers when he escaped was Manuel T. Brocklebank, a real-estate agent. Officer James Hesse, who nailed Powers, proved to be a tricky detective, at least in trapping someone of Powers' mentality. But a little like Mark Twain's Pinkerton sleuths, he sometimes overlooked the obvious. It seems, he almost lost his man by failing to have an assistant at the Post Office to nab Powers as he picked up the decoy letter, while he himself was out to lunch. The city postmaster was Richard F. Perkins, himself under heavy public fire at that time for inefficiency.

Mayor Henry P. Coon, whose name already has cropped up several times in this book, arrived in San Francisco in 1852, a young physician trained at Williams College and the University of Pennsylvania. Running on the People's ticket in 1856, he was elected Police Judge and made a name for himself as a reformer and an efficient member of the Board of Police Commissioners. In 1860 he resumed his medical practice but was soon back in public office as the city's mayor for two terms. Later he farmed a large ranch at Menlo Park and became president and a major stockholder of the King Morse Canning Company. He died in 1884.

118

ANOTHER OBSCENE PICTURE KNAVE CAPTURED —HE SOLICITS THE CUSTOM OF SCHOOL GIRLS 6 AUGUST 1864

A scoundrel named George R. Powers has been detected in the obscene book trade and captured. He has been carrying on the trade after a fashion of his own. Over the signature of "Mrs. Amelia Barstow," he writes chatty, familiar letters to young girls in the California seminaries, soliciting patronage for his infamous books and pictures. He made a mistake, though, when he addressed the following epistle to a school girl of fourteen years of age, for her home teachings had not been of a character to enable her to appreciate it, and she sent it at once to her father. From him it passed to Judge Coon, who handed it to Chief Burke to be disposed of. The Chief took a lively enough interest in the matter to take officer Hess from his regular duties in the Police Court and keep him on the track of Mrs. Barstow for a week and a half, with Officer Pike to assist him. We suppress the name of the young lady and that of the school she belongs to, of course:

San Francisco July 21st, 1864.

MISS ——:—I have just received from New York a large number of the *most delightful books* you can imagine. To refined young ladies of an *amorous* temperament, they are "just the thing." For five dollars sent to me through the Post Office, in two separate enclosures of two dollars and a half each, I will forward you two different volumes, each containing *five tinted engravings.* Accompanying the package will also be a beautiful *life photograph,* entitled "* * * * * * *." The strictest secrecy will be observed, which may be heightened by your transmitting a fictitious address, in case you reply to

MRS. AMELIA BARSTOW.

(We suppress the title of dear Amelia's "life photograph," as being somewhat too suggestive.—REPORTER.)

Daily Morning

VOL. XVI. SAN FRANCISCO, SATURDAY MORNING, JULY

Dispatches by State Line.

[EXCLUSIVELY TO THE MORNING CALL.]

Earthquake Items—Sacramento Exempt.

SAN JOSE, July 22.—Four shocks of earthquake felt here last night—the second shock very severe. It occurred about 10:40.

SACRAMENTO, July 22.—No earthquake felt here last night.

STOCKTON, July 22.—Violent shock of earthquake felt at eight minutes of eleven o'clock last night.

LOS ANGELES, July 22.—Very slight shock of an earthquake felt here last night.

DEMORALIZING YOUNG GIRLS.—Yesterday, in the Police Court, George Lambertson and Ralph Doyle, one a full-grown man and the other a boy of fourteen, pleaded guilty to the charge of exhibiting obscene pictures. Officers Lees, Evrard and Rose, some time since, got on the track of a regular system of prostituting young girls, which was being carried on by a number of men and boys who had banded themselves together for the purpose, and their efforts have resulted in the arrest of the two persons above named, and the unearthing of two more of the boys and two or three men, who are probably all captured by this time. The name of one of the men is Emile Buffandeau; two of the boys are Harry Fenton and George Ayres. The men made use of the boys to decoy the girls to their rooms, where their ruin was effected. These rooms were well stocked with obscene books and pictures. The officers say that the further they probe the matter the more astounding are the developments, and the more wide-spread the operations of this infamous association are discovered to be. The names of some fifteen of these debauched girls have already been ascertained, and others are suspected of properly belonging on the list. Some of them are members of families of high respectability, and the balance, as young Doyle phrases it, are "baldheaded," that is, unbonneted street girls. The ages of the lot vary from ten or twelve to fifteen. Ralph Doyle says that he and the other two boys, Ayres and Fenton, were "confidantes," but that he knows of no "gang," nor confederation of men and boys together, in the wretched business. He is aware, however, that a large number of men and boys and young girls are in the habit of visiting each other's rooms, but on their own individual responsibility only, he thinks. He says the girls showed him the obscene pictures, instead of his being guilty of that sort of conduct with them, and he is further of the opinion that they have done the seducing in most of the other cases, as they did in his. He is a fine, handsome, manly little fellow, uses excellent language, and his bearing is quiet and perfectly well-bred. He tells his story the same way every time, and we believe he tells the truth. All his revelations, however, will not do to print. The boys concerned in this extraordinary affair will be sent to the Industrial School, as they are all very young, and it is to be hoped that the law will be stretched to its utmost tension for the punishment of the men.... Since the above was in type, we have learned that the terrible developments detailed above, were brought to light through the energy and industry of the master of one of the Schools. He had ascertained the names and addresses of a great number of men and boys not mentioned in this article, who were implicated in these villanous transactions, and was in a fair way of securing their apprehension, but the premature disclosure of the facts and their publication in the evening papers, it is feared, will put the scoundrels on their guard, and prevent their capture. Furthermore, according to our latest information, there are *thirty* names of debauched young girls on the list. The man Lambertson, by whom a poor orphan girl of fifteen has become *enceinte*, has made over to her, in the hope of escaping the penitentiary, such property as he owned in the city. We are also very glad to learn, from the best authority, that Ralph Doyle, so far from being a leader among the miscreants, as has been said of him, was the most innocent in the party, and that it is not in his nature to do an unworthy action when left to the guidance of his own good instincts.

STATE GUARD CADETS.—This organization will drill again this evening, at the armory of the State Guard, the exercises to

LETTER FROM THE BOISE REGION.

[From an Occasional Correspondent.]

IDAHO CITY, July 9th, 1864.

DULL TIMES—A GOLD CURRENCY.

Here we are, and judging from the dullness of the times, and the scarcity of "amalgam" and water, you would imagine that the bottom of this terrestial basin had fallen out, as every one appears to be skedaddling over the river, to regions unknown, taking with them all they can legally lay their hands on, and if they can't get it that way, "bound to have it anyhow." Four weeks since, goods were arriving, merchants had no time to make out their accounts, express clerks were kept for the purpose, and even at an eating house a man was kept to weigh out the dust, and the rush was so great to get a "square" that what in ordinary cases cost $1, invariably cost $1 25 to $1 50, caused by the anxiety of the weigher to give the "boys" a chance as speedily as possible, without any possibility of the "boss" coming out the wrong end of the horn; and I cannot help remarking for the benefit of such societies, who make a study of *mineralogy*, that there are certain unknown causes which deeply affect the "specific gravity" of precious metals in this country, for, on being paid any small sum of dust, you will be struck with the density in comparison to the bulk, whereas, on paying, you will be equally astonished at the bulk, and will leave the store with your head in a muddle wondering whether it is caused by the lightness of the atmosphere or the last glass of old Bourbon at Beadley's, (formerly Gilbert's,) his whiskey being addicted to getting one in the "potential mood;" but even now how changed. Instead of bustle, noise, dog fights, rows, (another word here for a spree,) political discussions on the street, prospecting parties, occasional capsising gambling tables, nothing remains but the dull monotony of every-day domestic life, commencing in the morning with regular hash, and winding up with "another before going to bed;" and then passes away a few hours only disturbed by a few harmonious sounds strikingly resembling a full chorus of "little pig, big pig, root hog or die," until to-morrow, and then—well, never mind, let me tell you now a little about the place, men, and last, not least, politics.

A RICH QUARTZ COUNTRY, BUT NO CAPITAL TO DEVELOP THE MINES.

Unless some rich quartz veins are struck, this basin must and will, of necessity, cave in, not from want of gold, but from want of water, as you cannot work the hill claims unless the water is brought in from the Payette, or the Boise River, and that brought from such a distance as will be of such height to use the hydraulic over the whole of the basin. This will not be less than forty to seventy miles, at least, and cannot be done under a cost of two hundred and fifty thousand dollars, which is more money than will ever be subscribed in this country for that purpose. In the next place, is there any probability of quartz being found in *paying* quantities? Evidences at present in the hands of reliable men here tend to show that this Territory is an *immense* gold-bearing quartz country, and the color that of the best description, "rose color." The Garrison Gamburnes Gold and Silver Mining Company have just incorporated, and have set to work in good earnest, viz: "Sent for a mill." The shareholders are substantial men, and you may rely on it, it will not be the public money, but the shareholders, which will develop it, and lose their money in case of failure. There are other equally good, if not better, locations, all biding their time. Owyhee has immense quartz leads, in the hands of many without means, who are trying to get capitalists to aid them, either with their money or their credit.

DEPRECIATION OF PROPERTY.

As regards the hill claims, they have long since, on Buena Vista Bar, been laid over till next year, for want of water, and on Moore's Creek the water is rapidly giving out, and is not in sufficient quantity to meet the requirements of miners generally. The gold here is of various kinds, averaging from ten to fourteen and one-half dollars per ounce, but I do not think any is worth, in actual value, eighteen dollars per ounce. The value of property here is on the decline, and houses that in the Spring were worth three thousand dollars cannot now bring two thousand, and next year will not bring—well, what is the use of speculating on next year? for if that great comet should arrive and strike the earth, we shall all be knocked into a cocked hat.

Rebel Views of our Nominations

DAVIS RELIES ON THE DEMOCRACY—THEIR INTEREST IS TO WEAKEN THE UNION ARMY AND BREAK DOWN THE FINANCES.

[From the Richmond Examiner, June 13.]

The Convention of Black Republicans in Baltimore have renominated for President of their country, Abraham Lincoln, the Illinois rail-splitter, and for Vice President, Andrew Johnson, known in the West as the Tennessee tailor, one of the meanest of that craft; whether they shall ever be elected or not depends upon the Confederate army altogether.

The people of the enemy's country have now two Black Republican "tickets" before them, and the Democrats are to come yet. All these several movements we are obliged to watch, and, if possible, understand—by reason of their possible effect upon the war, otherwise we have no earthly interest in the matter; and if we were now at peace with that nation, it would be altogether indifferent to us what ape, or hyena, or jackass, they set up to govern them.

The great army of contractors, then, and office-holders—in short, those who live by the war, and on the country—have succeeded, at least, in starting Lincoln fairly for another race. It amounts to a declaration that those conventioners desire to see four years more in all respects like unto the last four years. They want no change at all; to the present incumbents of power and profit, all works well enough as it is. They care little, perhaps, about the "Emancipation Proclamation," or the exact definition which may be applied to Lincoln, as an immediate, or essential, or contingent Abolitionist; care little indeed, about politics at all, or principles, or the destiny of their nation, or other "abstractions" of that sort; they are practical men; and what they know and feel in their inmost souls is, that four more years of revelling at will in treasure and plunder, will make them all rich enough, they and their descendants to the third and fourth generation.

It appears, also, that Lincoln and his friends have been lucky, so far, in the ill success of Grant and Butler, and in their precise measure of ill success. If either of those two had taken Richmond before the Convention, then Butler or Grant would have been nominated for President. If they had been already utterly and decisively defeated, and their armies cut to pieces, then neither Lincoln nor any other Black Republican would have had the slightest chance of election. So essential was it for the right guidance of the Convention in this matter that Grant should not take Richmond, nor be advancing in triumphant march toward it, that the New York Times, Lincoln's "organ," took care to publish at length a dismal account of the bloody defeat inflicted on the Federals on the 3d of June, and to express the opinion that it was a most disastrous affair. This was true; but the Times did not state it because it was true. The Times stated it, notwithstanding that it was true, in order to lower Grant's stock in the Convention, just in the nick of time—and succeeded. Our soldiers, who on the 3d, strewed the earth in front of their entrenchments with twelve thousand dead and wounded Yankees, then and there secured the nomination of Lincoln over Grant.

Lincoln, then, and his gang have been lucky, as we said, *so far*. But to win his election in November this indecisive work of the Federal armies, neither triumphantly victorious nor hopelessly cut to pieces—neither taking Richmond nor taken by Richmond—will not do at all. Grant and Butler are now at liberty to achieve the most brilliant success they can, and the New York Times will not tell the truth any more when it is unfavorable to them. In fact, the Lincoln party had been reconciled to the delay in capturing Richmond by this consideration, among others, that the Fourth of July approaches; and they are aware of the theory entertained by their old acquaintance, Pemberton, now in high favor at Richmond, and commanding the fortifications of the city, namely: that the Fourth of July is the very best day to surrender a place to the Yankee army, because, in the warmth of their gratification at celebrating their anniversary with a triumph, they give good terms. It is like approaching a *bon vivant* after dinner to ask him for a favor. And, accordingly, the Yankee nation is now holding itself prepared to put on its most gracious smiles, and accord to us the same tender consideration which has been shown to the citizens of Vicksburg. Let them only haul down our flag on that auspicious morning, and read their Declaration of Independence in our Capitol Square, and Lincoln is already elected President. In this stage of the business also, however, our army has a voice; and if it should continue to baffle,

Officer Hess suggested the policy of writing an answer to Amelia's note, and getting it sent through the Post Office to her, as coming from the young girl she had addressed. He framed the following note, putting in punctuation marks with great liberality where they did not belong, and leaving them out where they did, and mimicking school-girl simplicity of phraseology, and proneness to tautology, with great ingenuity. The Chief having approved of it, a lady copied it in the microscopic chirography of sweet fourteen, and it was ready for mailing, as set forth here below. We suppress the girl's name, and that of the Post Office:

* * * * *, July 27, 1864.

MRS. AMELIA BARSTOW—Dear Madame:—I received your letter which you sent on the 21st of this month and I am glad, for I have been wishing for something nice to read for a long time. Father has not given me much money this month and I cannot send this time the amount you say; but if you will send me *one* book by sending two dollars and a half, please write and tell me so, and by return mail I will send it. A number of the girls in my class wants some books also, and if you will send one book for two dollars and a half some four or five others will send for some also. Please direct to Charles Harris for if directed to a Miss or Mrs. some of the teachers may get the letter.

Yours truly, * * *   * * *

The letter was put into the hands of Postmaster Perkins, who at once entered into the work of entrapping the miserable Mrs. Barstow with as much alacrity and earnestness as if the insulted girl had been his own child. He enclosed the decoy letter in a department envelop to the Postmaster of _____, with instructions to postmark and send it back through the mail to Mrs. Amelia Barstow at once. He also instructed the Post Office clerks to give Officer Hess and his assistant every facility for corralling the masculine miscreant who was doubtless passing himself for a woman in his nefarious correspondence; (no female had ever applied for letters under the name of Mrs. Amelia Barstow.) The decoy letter came back in due time, and was taken out by Mr. Powers while Mr. Hess was absent at lunch, but the clerk who officiates in the ladies' department at the Post Office took such a minute mental photograph of him, that the officer had no difficulty in following after and detecting his man in the street, from the description given of him. After walking around town for some time, Powers finally opened the letter, read it, and replaced it in his pocket. Hess entered into conversation with him, and in answer to certain questions, the fellow said he had no appointment to meet Mrs. Barstow at any particular place—expected to stumble on her in the street; said he had no particular occupation; was in the habit of taking her letters from the

A close-up of the *Call's* July 23 front page (*opposite*) shows Clemens' story "Demoralizing Young Girls" (*Bancroft Library*).

Post Office for her. It took him but a short time to discover that he was in the hands of an officer, and then his replies became decidedly non-committal. Hess asked him if he wrote the letter signed "Mrs. Aurelia Barstow." Powers said, "If I were to say I did, what would be done with me? what could you make out of it?" When asked if Mrs. Barstow would come and clear him of suspicion if she knew he was about to suffer for an offence committed by her, he caught at the idea, and said she would; the thoughtless numskull even eagerly wrote her a note, which the officer was to deliver to her after accomplishing the hopeless task of finding her. That act furnished the officer all the information he lacked, and enabled him to "rest his case," but it ruined the unthinking Powers —for behold, the first words of the note, "MRS. AMELIA BARSTOW," were a perfect fac-simile of the name signed to the letter to the school-girl, and fully convicted him of being the writer of it. Powers will be tried this morning for offering to sell obscene pictures, and perhaps for opening other people's letters, and the chances are that he will be severely dealt with. He deserves it, for any one acquainted with the impressible nature of young girls, shut out from the world and doomed to irksome and monotonous school-life, knows the heightened charm and excitement they find in amusements that are contraband and have to be secured by risky evasions of the rules, and is also aware that a whole school might be corrupted by the circulation among them of a single volume of the lecherous trash dealt in by Mr. Powers.

119

ESCAPED
9 AUGUST 1864

Mr. Powers, who was arrested the other day for writing to young girls in the seminaries over the signature of "Mrs. Amelia Barstow," and soliciting their custom in the obscene picture line, has escaped and gone into hiding. He went in charge of officer Bowen to confer with his "attorney" (or his confederate?) and while closeted with that individual, jumped out of a second-story window—so much so that when Bowen went after him to take him back, he was nowhere visible to the naked eye. Mr. Powers tried the same game on officer Hesse, when he was first arrested, but it failed; Hesse preferred that all private interviews should be held in his presence. Playing the extreme confidence game with officers is very old, and very well understood by most of them. Count Bowen among the latter class hereafter. The aforesaid "counsel" will be arrested to-day for complicity in the escape of the prisoner.

D. LARCENY AND BURGLARY

Trials for burglary and theft were frequent and often routine. In effect they challenged the reporter to write fresh, interesting copy, and at times Clemens met that challenge with considerable imagination and dramatic impact. His gift for felicitous and penetrating phrases also reminds us that a century ago local reporters, like today's disc jockeys, helped to satisfy the public craving for bright cracks and sharp jabs.

"WHEN LO! A ROSE BLOOMED
BEFORE HIS EYES"

120

BURGLAR ARRESTED
7 JUNE 1864

Detective George W. Rose, who is mentioned in several reports below, was a comic but genuine hero to Clemens. Time and again the local noted Rose's success in "fastening his infallible claws" [10] on his man, and in September he reported James Mortimer's murderous assault on the plucky little detective (Item 146). Rose was still good copy for Clemens late in 1865: "Detective Rose can pick up a chicken's tail feather in Montgomery street and tell in a moment what roost it came from at the Mission; and if the theft is recent, he can go out there and take a smell of the premises and tell which block in Sacramento street the Chinaman lives in who committed it, by some exquisite difference in the stink left" [11] —a bloodhound almost as accomplished as Archy Stillman in "A Double-Barrelled Detective Story."

John Richardson, whose taste for a cigar must be inordinate, gratified it on Saturday night last by forcing his way into a tobacconist's on Broadway, near Kearny street, and helping himself to fourteen hundred "smokes." In his hurry, however, he did not select the best, as the stolen tobacco was only valued at fifty dollars. He was congratulating himself last evening in a saloon on Dupont street, in having secured weeds for himself and all his friends, when lo! a Rose bloomed before his eyes, and he wilted. The scent of that flower of detectives was too strong even for the aroma of the stolen cigars. Richardson was conveyed to the station-house, where a kit of neat burglar's tools was found on his person. He is now reposing his limbs on an asphaltum floor—a bed hard as the ways of unrighteousness.

"HE FOLLOWS PEOPLE BY THE FOOT-PRINTS THEY MAKE ON THE BRICK PAVEMENTS"

121

DETECTIVE ROSE AGAIN
21 JULY 1864

As foolish a thing as a man can do is to steal anything while officer Rose is in town. A Mrs. Ashley, who lives in Bush between Powell and Mason streets, was robbed of a gold belt-buckle, some silver spoons, etc., on Saturday, the 9th, and yesterday she laid the matter before one of our Police officers, who told her to find officer Rose and give him charge of the matter. She found him, but she was too late for her information to be of any use—he had already recovered the stolen property and tracked the thief to his den also. It is said he follows people by the foot-prints they make on the brick pavements.

"KAHN WAS ABSENT AND SO WERE THE CIGARS"

122

FALSE PRETENCES
23 JULY 1864

A few days ago, L. Kahn bought ten thousand cigars from a man named Cohen, promising to pay twenty dollars per thousand in gold for them on delivery. He had them taken and left in a cellar, and told the plaintiff to call in an hour or so afterwards and get his money. When the man called, according to appointment, Kahn was absent and so were the cigars; and finally, when he did succeed in corralling his debtor, the fellow tendered green-backs in payment of his bill. The result was a charge preferred in the Police Court against Kahn, for obtaining goods under false pretences. After a patient hearing of the case, Judge Shepheard said he would send it up to the County Court, (placing defendant under one thousand dollars' bonds,) and if they felt there as he did, Kahn would certainly be punished for the crime he had been charged with, or perhaps even for grand larceny, which was the real spirit of the offence. He said Kahn's conduct was based in fraud, and carried out in fraud; there was fraud in its conception and fraud in its execution; and he considered the man as guilty as the occupant of any jail in the country. The counsel for defendant said if there was any fraud in the matter, it probably lay in the issuance of the green-backs in the first place. Judge Shepheard said, "I am aware that you are a Union man, Sir, but notwithstanding that, I will permit no more such language as that to be used in this Court; and I will punish any man who repeats the offence here, for contempt, or imprison him for treason, for I regard it as nothing more nor less than treason. It is your duty and mine, Sir, to uphold the Government and forbear to question the righteousness of its acts." The lawyer protested his innocence of any intention to commit the chiefest among crimes, and quiet was restored again.

"THE IMBECILE CLOCK"

123

BURGLARY
31 JULY 1864

On Friday morning, Catherine Leary, who lives in Waverley Place, got up and found all the doors in her house open, and a silk dress worth seventy-five dollars missing, and also an alarm clock, said to be worth ten dollars; but we beg to be left unmolested in the opinion that it isn't worth six bits, if it didn't know enough to give the alarm when the house was full of thieves. Officer Rose, of the Detective Police, recovered the silk dress yesterday, and the imbecile clock, and also the Chinaman who is supposed to have committed the burglary. Hoping the accused may prove innocent, we prefer not to blast his reputation by publishing his name yet, which is Ah Chum.

"ALL TEARS AND LAMENTATIONS IN A MOMENT"

124

SHOP-LIFTING
7 AUGUST 1864

Lucy Adler was arrested and locked up in the city prison last night, for petty larceny—stealing shoes, ribbons, and small traps of all kinds exposed for sale in shops. She brought her weeping boy with her —a lad of nine years, perhaps—and they were followed by a large concourse of men and boys, whose curiosity was excited to the highest pitch to know "what was up with the old woman," as they expressed it. The officers, and also the merchants, say this woman will travel through a dozen small stores during the afternoon, and go home and "clean up" a perfect junk-shop as a result of her labors. She cabbages every light article of merchandise she can get her claws on. She always has her small boy with her, and if she is caught in a theft, the boy comes the sympathy dodge, and pumps tears and jerks sobs until the pity of the shopman is moved, and his parent released. The boy is always on hand, and if an officer snatches the woman she pulls the metaphorical string that turns on the boy's sympathetic shower-bath, and he is all tears and lamentations in a moment. At any rate, this is what they say of the cunning pair.

"THE HEART OF MAN IS DESPERATELY WICKED"

125

INGRATITUDE
24 AUGUST 1864

George Johnson yesterday had his room-mate, M. Fink, arrested for stealing one hundred and fourteen dollars from him. Johnson says Fink is an old friend of his, and came to him three months ago and said he had no money, could get no work to do, and had no place to sleep; he had previously been tending bar at the Mazurka Saloon. Johnson has shared his bed with him, and paid his washing and board bills from that time until a few weeks ago, when the fellow got a situation of some kind on one of the steamers. He still continued to share Johnson's room, in the Wells Building, corner of Clay and Montgomery streets, however, when in port. Johnson left him in bed yesterday morning, early, and when he returned, he missed his money and his friend—the former from the bureau drawer and the latter from the bed. We consider that this only confirms what we have always said—namely, that the heart of man is desperately wicked.

"JOHN TOOK AN INVENTORY"

126

STRATEGY, MY BOY
1 SEPTEMBER 1864

One of our new policemen was lying exceedingly low in a Chinese alley the other night, for the purpose of surprising a loafer who was in the habit of stealing the bread of a butcher, the butcher thinking it was not meet that he should do so. While lying prone on the ground, the officer was discovered by a vigilant Chinaman, Ah Wah. The former feigned obliviousness. The benevolent Chinaman shook the prostrate form, but meeting with no response, decided that the ghost of the policeman had gone to another beat, and concluded to administer on his estate. John took an inventory. Item, one pistol, when suddenly the officer sprung to his feet and took John. He was brought before Judge Shepheard yesterday morning, charged with petty larceny. His counsel, Mr. Zabriskie, said that any innocent person might go through a man's pockets under similar circumstances. The argument was overpowering, and Ah Wah was discharged.

"LET THE HOARY HEADED SINNERS GO . . . BUT LOOK SHARPLY AFTER THE YOUNG CROP"

127

A TERRIBLE MONSTER CAGED
4 SEPTEMBER 1864

When Clemens wrote this item he had in mind the recent collision between the two steamers, the *Yosemite* and the *Washoe*. Seemingly he shared a popular belief that Captain Edward A. Poole had rammed the crowded *Washoe* deliberately. The captain still walked the streets a free man. Yet when an orphan picked up wood scraps from Dr. H. H. Toland's building then under construction, the "force conservatorial" sprang into action and seized the terrified boy. The reporter's imagination quickly transformed the orphan, who in reality lived with a "respectable family," into a "little ragged shaver . . . unkempt and uncared for, who flits from corner to corner, and from hole to hole . . ." There in miniature we see a motif repeated in *Huckleberry Finn:* the established order against unmoored, vulnerable youth.

A most wretched criminal was brought into the Police Court yesterday morning, on a charge of petty larceny. He stands between three and four feet in his shoes, and has arrived at the age of ten years. His name does not appear on the register, so the world must remain in ignorance of that. He is an orphan who has been provided with a home in a respectable family of this city, and is charged with having taken some chips and sticks from about Dr. Toland's fine new building, which it is supposed he uses in kindling the fires for the family he lives with. The person whose vigilance discovered grounds for suspecting this fatherless and motherless boy of the horrible crime, is a carpenter who works at the building. The county is indebted to him. The little fellow came into Court under a strong guard. He was terrified almost out of his senses, and looked as if he expected the Judge to order his head to be chopped off at once. The matter, if entertained at all, will be heard on Monday, and in the meantime the little boy will anticipate worlds of misery. It is a matter of wonder to some that a deliberate attempt to send an indefinite number of souls to Davy Jones' locker, by one who occupies a prominent position, escapes Judicial scrutiny, while the whole force conservatorial is hot foot in the chase after some little ragged shaver, some fledgling of St. Giles, unkempt and uncared for, who flits from corner to corner, and from hole to hole, as if fleeing from his own shadow. But such persons don't understand conservatorial policy. Let the hoary headed sinners go, they can get no worse, and soon will die off, but look sharply after the young crop. The old trunk will decay after a while and fall before the tempest, but the sapling must be hewn down.

128

**ROBBERY
30 SEPTEMBER 1864**

John Bassett, who had a crowd of witnesses to prove that his honesty was almost miraculous, and that his character was a holy hash of all the Christian virtues, and who stood through it all, in the prisoners' dock, stunned to learn it for the first time in his life, no doubt, was ordered to appear before the County Court and answer to a charge of highway robbery, committed lately on Pacific street, when he knocked a man down and took twenty-six dollars away from him. We have seen many a nice lot of witnesses in the Police Court, but those for the defence in this case could about discount the best of them in the matter of clean, straightforward swearing to doubtful propositions.

E. BIGAMY, RAPE, AND MISCEGENATION

"HE WANTS TO MARRY TOO MANY PEOPLE"

Hinzman was the correct name of the bigamist called Hingman below —perhaps the reporter's attention was riveted on the man's spectacular juggling act to the exclusion of all else. Clemens seems to have enjoyed reporting the case, perhaps because he could act the savagely comic moralist while stringing together his suggestive metaphors depicting the "old original Auburn wife" and the "ephemeral lager-beer wife" as two worked-over mines. Hinzman got off with a ten dollar fine for assault and battery against his second wife, but in September Judge Shepheard fined him forty dollars for a second offense.

129

**ARRESTED FOR BIGAMY
8 JULY 1864**

Isaac Hingman has been bigamized. He was arrested for it yesterday, by Officer W. P. Brown, on a complaint sworn to by his most recent wife, that he has a much more former wife now living in another part of the State. The wife that makes the complaint, and who drew a blank, in the eye of the law, in the husband lottery, married the prisoner on the 24th of June, in this city. A man is not allowed to have a wife lying around loose in every county of California, as Isaac may possibly find to his cost before he gets through with this case. He might as well make up his mind to shed one of these women.

130

THE BIGAMIST
8 JULY 1864

We have mentioned elsewhere in our present issue the arrest of Isaac Hingman, on a charge of bigamy. The woman he married last, went to the station-house last night to see him. She says she worked for two years in lager beer cellars here, and, during that time, had saved six hundred and fifty dollars. Hingman got this from her. He said he was going down on the Colorado to open a saloon, and she was to go with him. They were to leave to-day on a schooner, and he took her stove, her beds and bedding, and all her clothing, and put them on board the vessel. He told her he had been living with a woman at Auburn, and he would have to send her some money in order to get rid of her and her three children. The new wife gave him one hundred and thirty dollars for this purpose, and he went off and telegraphed his Auburn family to come down and go to the Colorado with him instead. The duped beer-girl got the answering dispatch sent by the Auburn wife, in which she acceded to the proposal, and said she would arrive by the boat last night. Sergeant Evrard, of the Police, saw the dispatch. The woman said Hingman told her, in the station-house, that the lucky Auburn woman was his lawful wife. Officer Evrard sent a policeman, disguised, to wait for the up-country wife at the Sheba Saloon, last night, and find out what he could from her affecting the case. The story of the illegal wife is plausible, and if it is true, Mr. Hingman ought to be severely dealt with. But not too severely—we go in for moderation in all things, and, considering all the circumstances of this case, it might be a questionable application of power to do more than hang him. To hang him a little while —say thirty or forty minutes— ought to be about the fair thing, though. He wants to marry too many people; and he needs treatment that will tend to check this propensity.

131

THE BIGAMIST
10 JULY 1864

The old original Auburn wife of the bigamist Hingman, arrived by the boat night before last, but her whereabouts were not discovered until last night, when she was found in one of the up-town hotels, with her three children, and subpoenaed to appear as a witness in the impending trial of her husband for bigamy.

$$\mathscr{132}$$

**THE BIGAMY CASE
12 JULY 1864**

The bigamy case came up in the Police Court yesterday morning, and Judge Shepheard dismissed it, because the charge could not be substantiated, inasmuch as the only witnesses to be had were the two alleged wives of the defendant—or rather, only one, the ephemeral lager-beer wife, as the old original wife, the first location, or the discovery claim on the matrimonial lead, could not be compelled to testify against her husband, and thereby also knock the props from under her own good name and her eternal piece of mind. The injured and deserted relocation now proposes to have Hingman arrested again and tried on a charge of assault and battery. This unfortunate woman seems to have been very badly treated, and it is to be hoped she may get some little soothing satisfaction out of her assault and battery charge to reconcile her to her failure in the bigamy matter.

"TRUE, THE LADY . . . HAD A NOTION TO HALLOO"

The appointed function of officer Bernard S. Blitz was to make erring hackmen observe the law, and he proved as vigilant in that role as Detective Rose was in his. Clemens put it this way more than a year after he had left the *Call:* "Detective Blitz can hunt down a transgressing hack-driver by some peculiarity in the style of his blasphemy." [12] As *Call* local, too, Clemens praised the able Blitz. Very probably he had his private reasons for disliking hackmen. He gloatingly recorded the conviction of a "rascally hackman" named Ambrose Kelly by Judge Shepheard, who acted "with neatness and dispatch, somewhat after the summary style of the old Caliphs," and he referred to hackmen under such headings as "Beasts in the Semblance of Men" and "The Sacrilegious Hack-Driver." If we credit his reports, hackmen drove recklessly, broke up funeral processions, and disregarded the preliminary agreements with their fares. These peccadilloes must have added excitement to hack rides and so may be partly excused. Still, it seems that some drivers expected overgenerous gratuities from their women fares. The Gillan case, coming not long after a rape charge against another driver, spurred Blitz on. As he "gobbled" hackmen right and left for not wearing their badges or not carrying their licenses or not lighting their lamps, the recording angel of the *Call* kept tabs in his columns.

A "card" published 14 August in the *Call* by a group of drivers protested "the course lately pursued by the press of the city towards drivers of hacks." Four days later the paper's local rather huffily told of "a gentleman" who was insulted and threatened, for no apparent reason, by a hackman who bellowed: "B-a-h; go to h- -l, you d- - -d hog!" This happened about a block from the *Call* building at 12:30 A.M. as the gentleman, his day's work just completed, was returning from his office to his room. The reporter concluded: "the gentleman naturally thought it very strange, and made a statement of the matter to a police officer not far distant, who, however, paid no attention to it. A number of hackmen, in a card published a few days since in several of the city papers, vindicated the respectable character of their fraternity, stating that newspaper reporters took every occasion to heap opprobrium upon them. If this is a feature of their respectability, they cannot find fault with members of the press and others for speaking of them only as ruffians and bullies." The bellicose tone is familiar, as is the complaint against do-nothing police. The gentleman, of course, could well have been Clemens—recognized by the driver as a hostile reporter—returning home late at night, his last item written.

Although Barney Gillan was acquitted of the rape charge, he was in court again the following November for robbing a discharged soldier.[13] Supervisor Alfred H. Cummings was the local freight agent for the San Francisco and San José Railroad.

133

RAPE
23 JULY 1864

Night before last, Miss Margaret McQuinn complained to Captain Lees that she had been raped by the driver of hack No. 28, and officer Blitz, whose duty it is to attend to the followers of that occupation, was deputed to ferret out the criminal and arrest him, which he did. The man's name is Barney Gillan. The woman is large and strongly built, and about thirty years of age. From her story—all of which it is not by any means necessary to publish—it would seem that she is supernaturally green. She says she arrived here from Manchester, New Hampshire, last Monday, in the Constitution, and since then three different hackmen have endeavored to entrap her. Day before yesterday, Gillan, under pretence of hunting a situation as a servant for her among some respectable families in the country with whom he represented himself as being very popular, took her to some out-of-the-way den kept by a Frenchman, near the Mission, and ruined her by force, as above stated. She returned to town with him, and then excused herself and went and laid the matter before the detective department. There is a charge of this kind brought against some hackman or other about once every five or six months, and it is fully time an example were made that would forever put a stop to such villany on their part. Gillan has been admitted to bail in the sum of one thousand dollars.

CONCERNING HACKMEN
26 JULY 1864

At the next meeting of the Board of Supervisors, Mr. Cummings, member from the Tenth District, will introduce an ordinance requiring all drivers of hacks, as well as hack-owners, to take out license, to the end that the eternal dodging of responsibility by that class of the community may be checkmated. One plan of extorting money from passengers, which is followed by hackmen under the present loose system, might be frustrated, perhaps, by Mr. Cummings' proposed bill. The plan we refer to is this: A stranger takes a hack at the steamboat landing, and makes a bargain for his transportation to a hotel; on the road, the driver's confederate takes the reins, delivers the passenger at the hotel, and charges him double, swearing he knows nothing of the previous contract. We were under the impression that the owner of the hack was responsible in cases of illegal charging, but those whose business it is to know, tell us it is not so. It ought to be, at any rate. It doesn't even require horse-sense to know that much. And while the subject is before the Board, an ordinance is to be framed requiring the hackmen around Portsmouth Square to stay where they belong, and not collect in squads, obstructing the sidewalks, and making a general nuisance of themselves. So far, Signor Blitz, and the Police Court, and the Board of Supervisors, all put together, have not been able to keep the hackmen straight. One of the fraternity, Barney Gillan, is up to-day for committing a rape on a defenceless young woman, thirty-five years of age, and they will probably make him sweat for it.

END OF THE RAPE CASE
30 JULY 1864

Barney Gillan, the hackman against whom a charge of rape was preferred some days since, had an examination yesterday before Judge

Shepheard. At first the tears and apparent distress of the victim of the alleged outrage, while occupying the witness's stand, were calculated to move the hearts of those present and unacquainted with the facts; but as the examination progressed the matter began to assume a very questionable phase, and it was soon apparent that if there had been any rape committed at all, it was of a very modified type. True, the lady did enter her protest, and had a notion to hal-loo, when Gillan was about taking undue liberties with her; but she sought a refuge and assuaged her grief that night at the Portsmouth Hotel, in the embraces of a benevolent person with whom she had met for the first time that day. He protected her injured innocence until seven o'clock the next morning, when she sallied forth to seek another protector. The case was discharged.

"SHE HAS HAD FOUR CHILDREN BY HER CHINAMAN"

136

MISCEGENATION
9 OCTOBER 1864

Reports of mixed marriages or of trouble arising from them were rare in the *Call*. "Miscegenation" suggests the kind of fascinated horror such "infernal" cases aroused.

A case of the most infernal description of miscegenation has come to light in this city—a mixture of white and Chinese. A Chinaman married a white woman in New York ten years ago, has had children by her, and has been living with her here in Sacramento street. Latterly, for some cause or other, he has become abusive toward her, and has several times beaten her. Finally, influenced by white friends, and by another beating at the hands of her pagan husband, on Thursday evening she left him, and applied to Chief Burke for protection, bringing two mixed children with her. A Special Officer tried to rescue her from this last assault, and succeeded in diverting the bulk of it to himself, receiving several powerful blows to his share, and giving several in return; the main Chinaman escaped from him, but he captured an accessory and brought him to the station-house. Officer Evatt accompanied the woman back to the place to protect her while she got possession of her clothing, and she is now living with some friends in Hinckley street. She is quite handsome, and of prepossessing appearance and address; one of her children is a very pretty little girl; she has had four children by her Chinaman. Late last evening, news came that the husband had been captured and confined by the mate of the ship Smyrniote, for stealing, and Officer Evatt went down to take charge of him.

OTHER COURTS

Proceedings in the higher courts were fewer and lengthier and usually more technical than those in the Police Court. Most of them lacked the raw violence and sexual titillation of the wife-beating cases. It is easy to understand why the *Call* management, intent on boosting circulation, featured juicy tidbits from the Police Court and why Judge Shepheard's "levee" commanded more lines than the other courts combined. Nevertheless the *Call* did not ignore the higher courts housed in City Hall and in the United States Court building at Jackson and Montgomery streets. These were the United States Circuit Court, the United States District Court, courts for the fourth, twelfth, and fifteenth state judicial districts, the County Court, and the Probate Court, not to speak of the courts run by justices of the peace which were scattered about in the city's six townships. Sometimes, but not always, Clemens covered the higher courts for the *Call;* another staff member, maybe Frank Soulé, helped out here. Certainly Clemens had enough to do already, and George Barnes may have felt that his local's distinctive manner was particularly suited to Police Court cases. However the labor may have been divided, it is safe to say that Clemens was no stranger to the other courts.

"HE WATCHED THE DISAPPEARING SHIP WITH HIS DESPAIRING EYES"

Captain Josiah Nickerson Knowles was acquitted by a jury that deliberated five minutes. The drowned sailor was John P. Swanson, and Captain Knowles had been indicted for not having rescued him, after his ship arrived in San Francisco from Boston on 16 May. A native of Brewster, Maine, Knowles had some fame as former captain of the *Wild Wave.* When that clipper had foundered on a coral reef at Oeno Island in the Pacific, he and his men had made their hazardous way to Pitcairn's Island and, then to Nukahiva, where they were rescued.[1] Knowles was defended in court by the quick-thinking Hall McAllister of Georgia, a successful San Francisco lawyer for forty years and the son of Matthew Hall McAllister, the first United States Circuit Judge of California. Nathan Porter was the District Attorney.

Stephen J. Field, recently appointed to the Supreme Court by President Lincoln, was still judge of the United States Circuit Court for the District of California. Clemens was to use Field's influence a few years later when he tried to get appointed as San Francisco Postmaster. Judge Ogden Hoffman was acting as Associate Judge on the United States Circuit Court. For forty years, beginning in 1851, he was judge of the United States District Court for the Northern District of California.

137

UNITED STATES CIRCUIT COURT
9 JULY 1864

Judges Field and Hoffman were occupied all day yesterday in hearing evidence in the case of Captain Josiah N. Knowles, of the ship Charger, indicted for manslaughter, in not stopping to pick up a sailor named Swansea, who fell from the royal yard arm of that ship, on the 1st of last April, during a voyage from Boston to San Francisco. From the testimony, it would appear that there was a heavy sea on at the time, and a stiff breeze blowing, and consequently it would not have been safe to send a boat after the man, while at the same time it would have been useless to shorten sail and put the ship about, because of the great length of time that would necessarily be consumed in the operation. Swansea fell one hundred and twenty feet, and one witness—the second officer of the ship—thought he struck the "main channels" in his descent, and was a dead man when he reached the water. The Charger was on a quick trip, and was making over ten knots an hour at the time of the accident. The evidence was almost completed yesterday, and the arguments of counsel will be commenced to-day.

138

UNITED STATES CIRCUIT COURT
12 JULY 1864

The case of Captain Knowles, late of the ship Charger, indicted for manslaughter, in not attempting to rescue a sailor, named Swansea, who had fallen overboard, was ably argued by Messrs. Hall McAllister and the District Attorney, yesterday, and a verdict returned by the jury of "Not guilty as charged in the indictment." The jury were charged that if they had any doubt of the man's having been alive after he struck the water, to give the prisoner the benefit of the doubt. That little doubt saved Captain Knowles, as, in the opinion of at least one member of the jury, he was guilty of a criminal indifference as to the fate of his lost sailor. He seized the wheel after the steersman had begun to put the ship about, put her on her course again, and then coolly marched down to finish his breakfast. He did not even throw over a chicken-coop for the poor fellow to rest upon while he watched the disappearing ship with his despairing eyes. The prisoner has been discharged from custody, and the witnesses also, who have been drearily awaiting the trial of the case, in prison, for the past two months.

"MOTHERS APPEAR TO GO MORE BY INSTINCT THAN POLITICAL ECONOMY"

139

**ASSAULT
19 JULY 1864**

Mrs. Moran's axe-swinging was more murderous than most offenses which ended up in the Police Court, and she appeared before County Judge Cowles who had jurisdiction on appeal in criminal cases and on cases from the courts of justices of the peace. In writing up her trial, Clemens used his familiar King Herod child-hating pose and that repetitious deadpan manner of the simpleton who comically understates what is important: "She asked the defendant not to split her Johnny." We notice here and also in the preceding report of Captain Knowles' trial the reporter's powers of quick dramatization, whether the action described is in the courtroom or in the cold sea as the lost sailor "watched the disappearing ship with his despairing eyes." Mrs. Moran was fined $150 with the alternative of forty days in the county prison for her bloodletting.

Mrs. Catherine Moran was arraigned before Judge Cowles yesterday, on a charge of assault with an axe upon Mrs. Eliza Markee, with intent to do bodily injury. A physician testified that there were contused wounds on plaintiff's head, and also a cut through the scalp, which bled profusely. The fuss was all about a child, and that is the strangest part about it—as if, in a city so crowded with them as San Francisco, it were worth while to be particular as to the fate of a child or two. However, mothers appear to go more by instinct than political economy in matters of this kind. Mrs. Markee testified that she heard war going on among the children, and she rushed down into the yard and found her Johnny sitting on the stoop, building a toy wagon, and Mrs. Moran standing over him with an axe, threatening to split his head open. She asked the defendant not to split her Johnny. The defendant at once turned upon her, threatening to kill her, and struck her two or three times with the axe, when she, the plaintiff, grabbed the defendant by the arms and prevented her from scalping her entirely. Blood was flowing profusely. Mr. Killdig described the fight pretty much as the plaintiff had done, and said he parted, or tried to part the combatants, and that he called upon Mr. Moran to assist him, but that neutral power said the women had been sour a good while—let them fight it out. Another witness substantiated the main features of the foregoing testimony, and said the warriors were all covered with blood, and the children of both, to the number of many dozens, had fled in disorder and taken refuge under the house, crying, and saying their mothers were killing each other. Mrs. Murphy, for the defence, testified as follows: "I was coomun along, an' Misses Moran says to me, says she, this is the redwood stick she tried to take me life wid, or wan o' thim other sticks, Missis Murphy, dear, an' says I, Missis Moran, dairlin',"— Here she was shut off, merely because the Court did not care about knowing what Mrs. Moran told her about the fight, and consequently we have nothing further of this important witness's testimony to offer. The case was continued. Seriously, instead of a mere ordinary she-fight, this is a fuss of some consequence, and should not be lightly dealt with. It was an earnest attempt at manslaughter—or woman-slaughter, at any rate, which is nearly as bad.

"IT WOULD BE A HARD THING SHOULD A CAPTAIN BE PUNISHED FOR MERELY KILLING A SAILOR OR TWO"

140

**MORE ABUSE OF SAILORS
20 AUGUST 1864**

Clemens' ready disposition at this time to attack men in positions of power for treating others unjustly is again evident in his remarks on Captain Luther Hopkins.

Yesterday afternoon a Commission was engaged in the United States District Court room, taking testimony in the criminal proceedings instituted against Luther Hopkins, Master of the American ship Carlisle, for brutally treating Andrew Anderson, one of the ship's crew. The affidavit of the prosecuting witness states that on the 2d April, 1864, Captain Hopkins cruelly beat him with a belaying pin, while he was sick, inflicting serious injuries on him; and also, on the 27th April, Anderson being still sick, Hopkins, the defendant, beat him on the head with a belaying pin; and again, on the 27th June, still being an invalid, he was beaten with a heavy, knotted rope, more than twenty blows, by the Captain of the vessel, who also caused him to be bitten by a dog. Poor Jack seeks redress and protection in a United States Court. When the Captain marshals his subordinates, from first officer down to forty-ninth cook, all dependent on him for the tenure of their dignities, they will with one voice swear they never saw the Captain do any such thing—blind as bats—while the poor victim felt it sensibly, and his quaking comrades in the forecastle saw it distinctly enough. It *would* be a hard thing should a Captain be punished for merely killing a sailor or two, as a matter of pastime.

"LET THEM ADHERE TO THE LATIN, OR FEJEE, IF THEY CHOOSE"

141

**DAMAGES AWARDED
1 OCTOBER 1864**

The "abominable scrawl" doctors used in writing prescriptions still bothered Clemens as late as 1892 when he was composing "Those Extraordinary Twins" in which Dr. Claypool "wrote a doctor's hand—the hand which from the beginning of time has been so disastrous to the apothecary and so profitable to the undertaker . . ." [2] The apothecary in "Damages Awarded" was C. French Richards, whose shop was on the corner of Sansom and Clay streets. The man who sued him probably was the William Galloway listed at that time in the directory as the agent for the tug *Goliah*.

The case of Wm. Galloway against C. F. Richards et al., in the Fourth District Court, was brought to a close yesterday evening, the jury, after two hours' absence, returning a verdict for four hundred dollars in favor of the plaintiff. The action was brought to recover damages laid at two thousand five hundred dollars, from defendants, who are druggists, for putting up a prescription in a wrongful manner, thereby causing a temporary injury to plaintiff's health. The verdict took some, who had heard the evidence throughout, by surprise; and a motion will be made on behalf of defendants for a new trial. The truth of the matter is, that in ninety-nine cases out of a hundred of these mistakes in putting up prescriptions, the whole blame lies with the prescribing physicians, who, like a majority of lawyers, and many preachers, write a most abominable scrawl, which might be deciphered by a dozen experts as many different ways, and each one sustain his version by the manuscript. When a physician writes the abbreviation of "pulverized cinchona" in such a manner that nine out of ten among experienced pharmacists would, without hesitancy, read it "pulverized cantharides," and damage results from it, if the apothecary is culpable at all, the physician certainly ought to come in for a share of blame. It would be a good thing for the world at large, however unprofessional it might be, if medical men were required by law to write out in full the ingredients named in their prescriptions. Let them adhere to the Latin, or Fejee, if they choose, but discard abbreviations, and form their letters as if they had been to school one day in their lives, so as to avoid the possibility of mistakes on that account.

SENSATION ITEMS: MURDER AND ATTEMPTED MURDER

"Nothing in the world affords a newspaper reporter so much satisfaction as gathering up the details of a bloody and mysterious murder, and writing them up with aggravated circumstantiality. He takes a living delight in this labor of love . . ." So begins "The Killing of Julius Caesar 'Localized,' " published a month after Clemens and the *Call* had parted ways. The ex-local regretted that he had not been present to report Caesar's death. "In imagination I have seen myself skirmishing around old Rome, button-holing soldiers, senators and citizens by turns, and transferring 'all the particulars' from them to my note-book . . . I would have written up that item gloatingly, and spiced it with a little moralizing here and plenty of blood there; and some dark, shuddering mystery; and praise and pity for some, and misrepresentation and abuse for others, (who didn't patronize the paper,) and gory gashes, and notes of warning as to the tendency of the times, and extravagant descriptions of the excitement in the . . . street, and all that sort of thing." [1]

Clemens published a number of these "sensation items"—to use a phrase he liked—in the *Call*. Often featured on page one, they are long reports of the latest bloody crime, and in most respects they follow his formula in "Julius Caesar 'Localized.' " Sometimes they have a breathless air as though hurriedly composed, and sometimes they bear signs of his "skirmishing around" old San Francisco to get the facts. Perhaps he whipped them together hastily to meet the press deadline. He put in the "circumstantiality" too, even including such irrelevant details as Simon Kennedy having swum the Mississippi where it was more than one and a half miles wide. To get a sense of drama he paraphrased testimony and vividly recreated action. Characteristically he adopted an assured manner in stating facts, even though he often could not be sure. He commented and moralized so insistently that the editor feels the reporter's sympathies and condemnations were more heartfelt than his formula implies. To take sides, to become emotionally entangled in the human conflicts he reported, was a way of giving significance to his job and to his life.

"KENNEDY WAS GENERALLY CONSIDERED A SENSIBLE AND HARMLESS MAN"

The deranged Simon Kennedy was turned over to military authorities for trial, contrary to the reporter's assurances. Kennedy's outfit was the Third U.S. Artillery, recently transferred from Alcatraz to new fortifications at Black Point. His commanding officer was Captain William A. Winder. Other army officers Clemens mentioned were Major General Irvin McDowell, Commander of the Department of the Pacific; Major James Van Voast of the Eighteenth Infantry and the Provost Marshal; and Captain Frederick Mears of the Ninth U.S. Infantry stationed at San José Point. The priest to whom Kennedy turned was Father James S. Cotter, of St. Francis Church on Vallejo Street, the earliest Roman Catholic church in the city. Justice of the Peace Robert J. Tobin stood in for Coroner Benjamin A. Sheldon at the inquest.

142

SOLDIER MURDERED BY A MONOMANIAC
ESCAPE AND SUBSEQUENT ARREST OF THE MURDERER
5 AUGUST 1864

Just before three o'clock yesterday morning, a soldier named Simon Kennedy, while under the influence of a temporary hallucination, killed a fellow-soldier named Fitzgerald, who was confined in the guard-house with him, at Black Point, by stabbing the unfortunate man twelve or fifteen times with a bayonet. The shrieks of the struggling victim attracted the attention of the sentinel, who opened the door, when the murderer rushed out and escaped in the darkness, followed by three or four terrified prisoners. Captain Winder turned out his whole force to pursue Kennedy, but they found neither him nor any trace of him, save a bloody towel under the bank near the Bensley Water Works, where he had evidently washed the blood from his clothing. About seven o'clock a soldier arrived here with a message from Capt. Winder to Chief Burke, announcing the murder, and the latter left at once for Black Point, after giving orders for half a dozen members of the Police force to mount and follow him. He also requested Captain Van Vost, of the Provost Department, to detail an equal number of mounted men, to aid in the search for Kennedy, which request was promptly complied with. Arrived at Black Point, the Chief procured a description of Kennedy, and acquainted himself with his habits and antecedents. He was told that the man was a lunatic, but from the fact of his having wit enough about him to guard against detection by washing himself, it was evident that he was not stupidly mad, at any rate. Further inquiries elicited the information that Kennedy had requested several times, lately, to be taken to Father Cotter, in Vallejo street, and had once been there, a day or two ago, in charge of a soldier. The Chief thought it possible that he might have gone there after his escape, and sent officers Clark and Hoyt to ascertain if such were the case. The surmise proved correct, and Father Cotter was at once relieved of his dangerous guest —and dangerous enough he was, too, as he still had his bayonet with him, bloody and bent by the murderous thrusts inflicted with it upon the body of Fitzgerald. The best information concerning this tragedy goes to show that Kennedy is a sane man upon all subjects except one—that of hanging. He is quiet and sensible enough until halters and scaffolds are mentioned, and then he becomes a madman. Some of the causes of this are recent, and some date far back in the past. He is an extraordinary swimmer, and it is said he once swam the Mississippi at a point where it was more than a mile and a half wide, and his bare head being exposed so long to the burning rays of the sun, the strength and vigor of his brain were impaired by it, and at intervals since then he has seemed a little flighty. He enlisted in Davis street, here, and was sent with his company to Alcatraz, where they remained some time, and were finally transferred to Black Point. While at Alcatraz, Kennedy was swimming in the Bay with a comrade, upon one occasion, when the latter was seized with cramps and was drowned. The men used to tell Kennedy he murdered his comrade, and that he would be hanged for it; they kept it up until finally the poor wretch got to brooding over the fate predicted for him until he began to suspect his brother soldiers of an intention to hang him. He went twice to his Cap-

tain for protection against them. A day or two ago, at Black Point, the soldiers pestered him again about his chances of being hanged, and he says the Captain put him in the guard-house for safe keeping. The supposition is that during the night the horrors came upon him that his fellow-prisoners were going to hang him, and he seized the bayonet and fought desperately to save himself. Kennedy told us what he knew about the murder, but his statements were confused, and he said he did not recollect much about it. He only knew that three or four men came in the guard-house to hang him, and said they were going to do it at once; one of them seized and tried to choke him, and he snatched a bayonet from the wall, where it was hanging above a dark-colored cap, and struck out wildly with it in self-defence. He was not certain whether he hit anybody, but he thought he did. Afterward, he said it was likely he took the bayonet away from the man who was trying to choke him—and then he showed wounds on his hands, as if he had a vague notion that they were evidence of how he came into possession of the weapon. His person and his clothing were as black as a coal heaver's; he said he changed his clothes on his way to town, and left his uniform lying in the road. If he did, the latter was not found. When speaking of the murder, Kennedy gazes upon the visitor with a fixed, vacant stare, and looks like a man who is absorbed in trying to recollect something. The body of Fitzgerald lay at the Coroner's office yesterday; the breast, shoulders, stomach, hip and arms were covered with little triangular red spots, where the bayonet had entered. The inquest will be held to-day, so we were informed. The murderer and his victim were both members of Company D, Third Artillery. Fitzgerald was a married man; his widow resides in this city. Since the above was written, a soldier in the regular army has informed us how the bayonet happened to be in the guard-house within reach of a prisoner popularly considered to be insane. He says Captain Mears makes his prisoners do guard duty, and after they are relieved, their instructions are to take their muskets to the guard-room and clean them during confinement. He further says the members of Fitzgerald's Company are incensed at this conduct of permitting deadly weapons to be carried within reach of the lunatic imprisoned with their comrade. He says that when a prisoner does guard duty, it is usual for a non-commissioned officer to go with him and see that he cleans his musket at the quarters, and leaves it there, and then takes him back to be locked into the guard-house, unarmed. The soldier says Kennedy first attacked a man named McDonald, with the bayonet, and then assaulted Fitzgerald, who was asleep at the time. When he attacked McDonald, he first put his hand on his breast and asked him if he had a heart, and where it was situated, and then, without waiting for the desired information, made a stab at him. It was a wretched piece of business to let a deadly weapon be taken into a guard room where a man in Kennedy's condition was confined, and unmilitary people yesterday were wondering that weapons should be placed within reach of prisoners under any circumstances.

143

THE FITZGERALD INQUEST
6 AUGUST 1864

Last evening, in the absence of Coroner Sheldon, Justice Tobin held an inquest at the office of the Coroner, to inquire into the facts connected with the death of James Fitzgerald, private in Company D, Third Artillery, who was killed by a fellow-soldier named Kennedy, at Black Point, early on the morning of Thursday, the 3d instant. Three witnesses were examined who were on the spot at the time. The facts were substantially as stated in yesterday's *Call*, except that not so much was said about his insanity. A simple statement of the facts adduced on the inquest would be about as follows: About half-past one o'clock on Thursday morning, Fitzgerald was placed in the guard-house, Kennedy having been there for some time previous. Fitzgerald being without his blankets, Kennedy told him to come and share his. Deceased, however, went and laid down on the floor. The room was almost perfectly dark. About two o'clock in the morning, Fitzgerald got up and went to where one Michael Condol (also under guard) was lying, and whispered in his ear, telling him to turn over, he wanted to feel him; at the same time, he drew his hand across Condol's throat. Condol told him to go to his own bunk. Kennedy then placed his hand on Condol's breast, and raised something over him which in the darkness Condol took to be a dagger; he seized it and discovered that it was a bayonet. A struggle commenced, in which Kennedy succeeded in planting a thrust into Condol's arm. He cried out that he was stabbed, and called for a light, but the inmates of the room had become panic-stricken and crowded off to the corners. In the struggle with Kennedy, Condol kicked him, forcing him over towards the wall. He fell on Fitzgerald (deceased) and commenced stabbing him. Deceased cried out, "I'm murdered." The corporal outside hearing the noise, rushed to the guard-room, and as he opened the door, Kennedy and two other prisoners forced their way out, throwing him down on the ground. He went in with a light and saw deceased lying on the floor in a dying condition. He had twelve wounds on the body and four on the head. Of four of those on the body, penetrating the heart, lungs, liver, stomach, and large and small intes-

tines, either one would have produced death; the rest were flesh wounds. One of the fatal wounds was made on the thigh, severing the femoral artery. Kennedy was generally considered a sensible and harmless man, though he seemed rather disposed to shun his comrades. On one occasion, about a month since, while at Alcatraz, he expressed an apprehension that he was going to be hanged. On one or two other occasions he made "curious remarks." The day prior to the killing he broke out of the guard-house and ran down to Captain Winder's quarters. He said he wanted to see a clergyman, and must go to town. He was not generally considered insane, though he had curious ways, and the Corporal said he did not think he was altogether right. It was about half past three o'clock in the morning when Fitzgerald died. Deceased was a native of Limerick, Ireland, and aged about thirty-six years.

The jury returned a verdict in accordance with the facts.

144

THE MURDERER KENNEDY—A QUESTION OF JURISDICTION
10 AUGUST 1864

Judge Shepheard said yesterday, with reference to the case of Kennedy, the soldier who killed a fellow soldier at Black Point on Thursday last, that he would hold over the examination for three days, to give the military authorities an opportunity of making a formal demand of the prisoner, to be tried by a Court Martial, a claim to the exclusive jurisdiction over the case having been heretofore signified by them. We are

assured, however, that the military authorities do not desire to take the case out of the hands of the civil authorities; that both General McDowell and Captain Winder have so expressed themselves. And besides, two serious obstacles might be interposed as against such a jurisdiction. In the first place the prisoner is evidently insane, and was so at the time the murder was committed; Fitzgerald being, it is reported, the third victim to his terrible fits; and there is no provision of our laws, authorizing a Military Court to act as a *commission de inquirendo*. And in the next place, there is a question about the title of the United States Government to the property at Black Point, the title to which is now being litigated, which fact might so affect it as a military reservation as to throw a strong shade of doubt over the supremacy of the military law within those particular limits.

"AN AFFAIR LIKE THIS MAKES HURRYING TIMES IN THE POLICE DEPARTMENT"

145

DARING ATTEMPT TO ASSASSINATE A PAWNBROKER IN BROAD DAYLIGHT!
18 AUGUST 1864

Harris Myers' pawnshop was a door or two from the *Call* building, and Clemens arrived on scene a few minutes after Henry Myers had been slugged. The unsolved robbery and assault stayed in Clemens' memory a long time, perhaps because for two weeks he wrote frequent progress reports on Henry's condition.[2] Fifteen months later he referred to the criminal "who knocked young Myers in the head with a slung-shot a year ago and robbed his father's pawnbroker shop of some brass jewelry and crippled revolvers, in broad daylight . . ."[3] When he wrote that, he was after the scalps of Fitz Smythe and Chief of Police Burke, but his *Call* stories on the Myers case are rather favorable to the chief. They also show the way Burke thought and worked. As the initial excitement over the crime died down, the *Call* local's writing became livelier: "If anybody wants a spry, intelligent thief or two, the same may be obtained at Chief Burke's hotel, as all the thieves in the city were arrested on Wednesday night, in the hope of finding among them the robber of the pawnbroker."[4] Still later Clemens praised Dr. James Murphy for having Henry up and around by early September, but Henry could remember nothing about the crime.

Chief Martin J. Burke graduated from the London College of Surgeons and practiced medicine for several years in Milwaukee before going to San Francisco in 1850. There he opened two drugstores and began a stereotype and electrotype foundry. When James King of William was shot, Burke assisted in forming the Vigilance Committee of 1856 and became one of its executive heads as well as chairman of its police committee. As the People's party candidate he was elected police chief in

1858 and served eight years. Known as a man who would use tough methods when he believed it necessary, he seems to have gained general public approval in his work as chief. He became a real-estate agent in 1866. Later, at the time of the Kearney excitement of 1877, he reluctantly agreed to help direct the Committee of Public Safety that helped the police subdue anti-Chinese rioters.

THE WOUNDS PROBABLY FATAL!—EIGHT THOUSAND DOLLARS' WORTH OF DIAMONDS AND WATCHES STOLEN!

Yesterday afternoon about half-past two o'clock, a pawnbroker named Meyer, whose establishment is in Commercial street, below Kearny, went out and left his son Henry, a youth of eighteen or twenty, perhaps, to attend to the business during his absence. Upon returning, half an hour later, he found pools of blood here and there, a knife and double-barrelled shotgun on the floor—the latter weapon parted from its stock—several trays of watches, diamonds and various kinds of jewelry gone, the doors of the safe open, its drawers pulled out and despoiled of their contents—disorder visible everywhere, but his son nowhere to be seen! Hearing a faint groan, he ran into the back room, and there in the gloom he discerned his boy, lying on the floor and weltering in blood. Now, after reading the above, the public will know exactly as much about this ghastly mystery as the Police know—as anybody knows, except the murderer himself. So far as heard from, nobody was seen to enter the store during Mr. Meyer's absence, and nobody was seen to leave. The assassin did his work between half-past two and three o'clock in the afternoon, in the busiest portion of one of the busiest thoroughfares of the city, and departed unseen, and left no sign by which his identity may hereafter be established. Up to the present writing the boy has only groaned in pain and is speechless. We reached the spot a few minutes after the tragedy was discovered, and found the street in front blockaded by a crowd of men staring at the premises in blank fascination, and entering, found another crowd composed of policemen, doctors, detectives, and reporters, engaged as such people are usually engaged upon such occasions. The boy's body and his bunk were deluged in blood, and efforts were being made to relieve his sufferings. There was apparently but one wound upon him, and that had been inflicted on the back of his head, behind his right ear. The skull was indented as if by a slung-shot. Probably neither the knife nor the gun found upon the floor were used in the assault. Near one of the windows in the front office—closely curtained against observation from the street —was a pool of gouted blood, as large as a chair-seat; and the blow was given there, no doubt, for from that spot a roadway was marked in the dust of the floor to the extreme end of the back room where the body was found, showing that after he was knocked senseless, the robbers must have dragged him to that spot, to guard against his attracting attention by making an outcry. Mr. Meyer says the valuables carried off by the daring perpetrators of the outrage, are worth about eight thousand dollars. A man came in while we were present, and told Capt. Lees that about the time he saw the crowd running toward Commercial street, he met a man in Kearny street, running as if destruction were at his heels; that he broke frantically through a blockade of wagons, carriages, and a funeral procession, sped on his way and was out of sight in a moment; that he was thick set, about five feet seven or eight inches in stature, wore dark clothing, a black slouch hat, and had a sort of narrow goatee; that he had improvised a sack out of an old calico dress, the neck of which sack he grasped in his hand, and had the surplus calico wrapped round his arm; the appearance of the said sack was as if it might have a hat-full of eggs in it—two dozen, or thereabouts, you might say. Five minutes after the conclusion of the narrative, we observed the man who saw all this, speeding up town in a buggy with a detective. At the Chief's office, fifteen minutes after the discovery of the bloody catastrophe, Mr. Burke's campaign commenced, and he was dictating orders to a small army of Policemen, with a decision and rapidity commensurate with the urgency of the occasion: "You, and you, and you, go to the Stockton and Sacramento boats and arrest every Chinaman and every suspicious white man that tries to go on board; you, and you, go to the San José Railroad—same order; you go to the stable and order two fleet horses to be saddled and sent here instantly; you, and you, and you, go to the heads of the Chinese Companies and tell them to detain every suspicious Chinaman they see, and send me word; I'll be responsible."

And so on, and so forth, until squads of Policemen were scattering abroad through every portion of the city, and closing every prominent avenue of escape from it. An affair like this makes hurrying times in the Police Department. After all, the wonder is that an enterprise like this robbery and attempted assassination has not previously been essayed in Mr. Meyer's and other pawnbroking establishments. They are not frequented by customers in the day-time, and the glass doors and windows are rendered untransparent by thick coats of paint, and also by curtains that are always closed, so that nothing that transpires within can be seen from the street. One or two active men could enter such a place at night, gag the occupants, turn the gas nearly out, and take their own time about robbing the concern, for customers would not be apt to molest an establishment through whose shaded windows no light appeared.

———

Up to eleven o'clock last night, young Meyer was still irrational, although he had spoken incoherently several times of matters foreign to the misfortune that had befallen him. We have this from Dr. Murphy, his physician, who saw him at that hour. The Doctor says the wound was evidently inflicted with a slung-shot. Its form is an egg-shaped indentation at the base of the brain. There are also the distinct marks of four fingers and a thumb on the throat, made by the left hand of the man who assaulted him. (Whose left hand among ye will fit those marks?) The patient can only swallow with great difficulty, on account of the fearful choking he received, and the consequent swelling and soreness of the glands of the throat.

He suffers chiefly, however, from the pressing of the indented skull upon the brain. His condition improves a little all the time, and, although the chances are nearly all against his recovery, still that result is regarded as comfortably within the margin of possibility. Unless he comes to his senses, it will be next to impossible ever to establish the guilt of any man suspected of this crime. An ordinary deed of blood excites only a passing interest in San Francisco, but to show how much a little mystery enhances the importance of such an occurrence, we will mention that at no time, from three o'clock in the afternoon, yesterday, until midnight, was there a moment when there was not a crowd in front of Meyer's store, gazing at its darkened windows and closed and guarded doors. During the afternoon and night, several white men were arrested about town on suspicion, and seventy-two Chinamen were detained from leaving on the boats until after the hour for sailing. The right man is doubtless at large yet, however.

"A MAN OF HIS NERVE AND RESOLUTION REQUIRES MORE THAN ONE FATAL WOUND TO KILL HIM"

James Mortimer's attack on officer George Rose made sensational copy, and Clemens used the occasion to praise his favorite detective and to criticize the leniency of the courts. Well over a year later he remembered this case, too.[5] Rose first arrested Mortimer as a pickpocket in April 1864. Later Mortimer burglarized the home of Charles Wiggins, clerk to Mayor Coon. It was for this crime that Rose arrested Mortimer near the town of Belmont, but he was maimed by his prisoner, who escaped again. Although Rose's search for Mortimer proved fruitless for a long time, he nevertheless caught up with him in March 1865. Having been convicted of burglary in Yreka, Mortimer was in transit to San Quentin when Rose happened to see him in the city jail—an ironic confrontation for the detective so skillful he could "follow footprints on pavement." In his story of Mortimer's attack, below, Clemens also bows to his friend Michael Nolan, the railroad conductor.

ATTEMPTED ASSASSINATION OF A DETECTIVE OFFICER 11 SEPTEMBER 1864

Officer Rose, one of the coolest, shrewdest members of the detective force, was dispatched to Belmont, on the San José Railroad, by Chief Burke, on Friday morning, to arrest a suspected criminal named James

Charles Mortimer, reported to be in hiding there; he was to find satisfactory proofs of the man's guilt, first, and then make the arrest; (his crime is to be kept a secret, as yet.) Arrived at Belmont, Rose got the proofs that he wanted, from a woman with whom Mortimer had been living, and from her he also obtained a clue of his hiding place, and captured his man. He then went to Santa Clara with his prisoner, in search of further evidence, and the two repaired to a secluded spot a mile and a half from the town, at nine o'clock on Friday night, to get some stolen property which Mortimer said he had buried there. The prisoner watched his opportunity while the officer's back was turned for a moment, or while he was digging for the hidden treasure, and knocked him down by striking him in the back of the head with a stone; he then took the officer's knife from his pocket and cut his throat with it, severing the windpipe half in two; next he thrust the blade into his throat and twisted it round; then, to make the murder sure, he took Rose's revolver and struck him across the forehead with it, inflicting a ghastly wound. Considering his victim finished by this time, he returned to Santa Clara, rifled the officer's valise, paid for a check through to San Francisco on the freight train, but jumped off the cars near Belmont Station, while they were running slowly, and has not since been heard of. Rose lay insensible for some time, but woke up at last, stunned and confused by the blows he had received, and feeble from his loss of blood, and in this condition he crawled a long distance, and finally reached the house of a Mr. Trenneth, about midnight, where he was properly cared for, and from

whence he was removed to Santa Clara yesterday. It was at first supposed he could not survive his injuries, but he grew better rapidly and constantly, and now no fears are entertained that he will die. A man of his nerve and resolution requires more than one fatal wound to kill him. He was brought home to the city on the evening train yesterday. This man Mortimer (he has a dozen aliases,) half murdered a man named Conrad Pfister, in Dupont street, one night, and robbed him of nearly a thousand dollars, and for this highway robbery and attempted assassination our lenient Court of Assizes, as usual, only gave him a year in the State Prison. For the same offence, in the interior of the State, he would have got ten years at least, and been considered a favorite of Fortune at that. But you seldom find a longer sentence than one or two years on our Assize records. Mortimer is one of the worst men known to the Police. He paid his fare to San Mateo, in the morning train, about six weeks ago and then tried to slip by and go on to Belmont, but was detected by Mr. Nolan, the conductor, who put him ashore, and had a rough time accomplishing it. Mortimer swore he would remember the treatment he had received, and kill Nolan for it the first opportunity he got. Charles James Mortimer's photograph is No. 54 in the Rogue's Gallery at the office of the Chief of Police, and the countenance is not a prepossessing one. Accompanying the picture is this description of him, written some time ago: "Native of Maine; occupation, farmer; age, 23 years and 6 months; height, 5 feet 6 inches; weight, 160 pounds; hair, light; eyes, blue; complexion, light; full face, red cheeks, good looking;

has a crucifix, with lighted candles, three pierced with arrows, on his right fore arm, printed in red and black ink, and on his left arm the letters C. J. M.; also, on one arm, the name of Flinn." Captain Lees, and a posse of Policemen, were sent down to Belmont by special train, yesterday, and have scattered in different directions in search of the missing criminal. He will be captured, if it takes the department ten years to accomplish it.

Since the above was in type, Mr. Rose has made the following statement: He was walking along with Mortimer, half way between San José and Santa Clara, on the way to the buried property, when the prisoner suddenly jumped to one side, seized a stone and knocked him down with it, as above stated, and stabbed him in the neck, swearing he would "finish" him. Thinking him "finished," he went away, but returned in the course of ten minutes, to satisfy himself. Standing behind Rose, as he lay on the ground, he exclaimed, in a disguised voice, "Hallo, my friend, what are you doing there? Anything the matter? If you're ailing, my farm-house is close by." The stratagem was suc-

cessful; Rose was deceived, and raised his head, when the fellow remarked, "Oh, so you're not dead yet! I was afraid so; you've hunted me out, my man, and you can't live"— and he drew Rose's revolver and struck him three powerful blows, two back of the left ear, one on top of the head, and several about the forehead. Before taking his final farewell of his victim, Mortimer robbed him of his knife, revolver, and forty dollars in money. Chief Burke wishes us to extend his warmest thanks to the citizens living near the scene of the outrage, for the assistance rendered by them to Officer Rose, and especially to the members of Mr. Trenneth's family, who sat up with the wounded man all night, and did everything they could for his relief, and furnished him with blankets and bedding to use during his transportation on the cars; also, to Conductor Nolan and other officers of the Railroad, for their kindness in making every arrangement in their power for Mr. Rose's comfort, on his passage to the city. Rose was doing only tolerably well at last accounts, and was flighty at intervals.

147

OFFICER ROSE RECOVERING
16 SEPTEMBER 1864

Detective Officer Rose, who a few days ago was beaten and stabbed near Santa Clara, by a prisoner named Mortimer, whom he had arrested, is now entirely out of danger, and will be about the streets again shortly. We are glad it is so, for while rascality is so plenty herea-

bouts, the city could ill afford to lose so accomplished a detective. Officer Bovee, one of the men sent to track Mortimer through the southern country, has returned without having been able to obtain the slightest clue to his whereabouts.

148

MORTIMER AGAIN
25 SEPTEMBER 1864

Charles James Mortimer, who attempted to kill Detective Rose, a short time ago, has been seen in the coast range, between San Mateo and Spanishtown, within the past day or two. He was recognized by two men, and his capture attempted, but he shot one of his assailants in the hand, and the other in the foot, and escaped. These facts were ascertained by a telegram from Sheriff Keith, of San Mateo county, and Officer Chappel was at once sent down there to look after Mortimer. He telegraphed Captain Lees, yesterday, that no traces of the missing scoundrel could be found, and that it would be useless to send down a larger force to hunt for him. The country where he was seen is covered for miles with a dense growth of willows, and Mortimer can hide in them and elude pursuit as long as he wants to. He need not lack for animal food, for the district is full of fowls, pigs, sheep, and bullocks, from which he can take his choice at any time under cover of the night. The only sure method of catching him lies in burning the willows; but as this would probably result in the destruction of the crops thereabouts, the farmers will not permit it to be done.

149

AFTER MORTIMER
29 SEPTEMBER 1864

Detective Officer Rose is able to walk about the streets again, although the wounds he received at Mortimer's hands would have proved mortal to any but a petrified constitution. Rose's left hand is still in a badly crippled condition, and his little finger will have to be cut off. He says that when Mortimer struck him on the head with a stone, in the twilight of that eventful evening, the blow stunned him somewhat, but did not render him unconscious; he grappled with his man, but found that he was unable to cope with him, and when he was stabbed through the windpipe, he feigned death, and instead of spitting out the flowing blood that was threatening to choke him, he lay still and swallowed it. When Mortimer came back the second time and spoke to him, he did not answer, but the motion of his body, caused by breathing, betrayed him, and Mortimer commenced beating him over the head with the pistol. Rose counted the blows, down to the thump behind the ear that knocked him senseless. As we remarked above, Mr. Rose is now sufficiently recovered to be about again. He left yesterday to hunt for Mortimer, and has made up his mind to catch him.

Captain William C. Hinckley, a member of the city's Board of Supervisors (*Society of California Pioneers*).

San Francisco City Hall in Portsmouth Square (*collection of Roy D. Graves*).

The County Prison on Broadway above Kearny Street (*Society of California Pioneers*).

Chief of Police Martin J. Burke (*Bancroft Library*).

Davis Louderback, Jr., the assistant district attorney of San Francisco (*California Historical Society*).

Part Three

CRITIC AND POLITICAL REPORTER

THE JUDICIAL PROCESS

A. THE LITIGANT

Clemens believed in 1864 that the trouble with courtroom trials was the shoddy human material which went into them. He criticized litigants for their petty and malicious lawsuits, witnesses for their unreliable testimony, and lawyers for their incompetence—and by implication the public for putting up with the whole sorry mess. Perhaps because he witnessed few juries in action at this time, his *Call* reports had little to say, favorable or otherwise, about the jury system. On one occasion, it is true, he noted with no particular animus that a deadlocked jury ran up high food bills while one of its members with strong convictions was bringing the others around to his views. Wisdom from the bench offered some hope for salvaging justice in the courts, but, he seemed to ask, could it stand up under the flood of litigation?

"THEY MUST HAVE JUSTICE 'THOUGH THE HEAVENS FALL' "

150

PETTY POLICE COURT TRANSACTIONS
15 JUNE 1864

This item is an early record of disillusionment: behind the elaborate machinery of a trial, behind the profit-taking, lies "a lost spoon or a broken window . . ."

It is surprising to notice what trifling, picayune cases are frequently brought before the Police Judge by parties who conceive that their honor has been attacked, a gross outrage committed on their person or reputation, and they must have justice "though the heavens fall." *Distinguished* counsel are employed, witnesses are summoned and made to dance attendance to the successive steps of the complaints, and the patience of the Judge and Reporters is severely tested by the time occupied in their investigation which, after a close examination of witnesses, cross-questioning by the counsel, and perhaps some brilliant peroration at the close, with the especial injunction to the Court that it were better that ten guilty men should escape punishment rather than one innocent (one eye obliquely winking to their client) person should suffer; with a long breath of satisfaction that the agony is over about a hair-pulling case, a lost spoon or a broken window, the Judge dismisses the case, and, (if we *must* say it) the lawyers pocket their fees, and the client pockets his or her indignation that the defendant escaped the punishment which to their view was so richly deserved. Thus, yesterday, William Towerick, a deaf old man, complained that a woman struck him with a basket, on Mission street. The good looking German interpreter almost woke up the dead in his efforts to shout in the plaintiff's auricular appendage the respective questions propounded by counsel, but had eventually to give it up as a bad job and let the old lady the plaintiff's wife, try. Case dismissed. Then comes another complainant with a long chapter of grievances against one Rosa Bustamente, who didn't like her little poodle dog. Bad words from both parties and a flower pot thrown at somebody, bursting five panes of glass valued at twenty-five cents each. Court considered that plaintiff and defendant stood on nearly equal footing, and ordered the case dismissed.

"THIS MOST IMPORTANT TRIAL—
FREIGHTED . . . WITH MATTERS
OF THE LAST IMPORTANCE"

151

THE KAHN OF TARTARY
29 JUNE 1864

Perhaps "The Kahn of Tartary" is Clemens' most detailed exposure of the petty controversies he said San Franciscans loved (Item 152). The comedy of this "triangular row" cannot hide the unpleasant and discouraging facts of the case. Yet the publication of the story implicitly acknowledged the reporter's faith—never entirely lost—in the corrective power of ridicule and laughter.

Benjamin Oppenheim had a crockery store on Dupont Street. The combatants Frederika Kahn and Lena Oppenheim—Clemens mixes up the names some—were fined twenty dollars apiece for unprovoked assault, a decision that may have been as wise as it was illogical.

Lena Kahn, otherwise known as Mother Kahn, or the Kahn of Tartary, who is famous in this community for her infatuated partiality for the Police Court as a place of recrea-tion, was on hand there again yesterday morning. She was mixed up in a triangular row, the sides of the triangle being Mr. Oppenheim, Mrs. Oppenheim, and herself. It appeared from the evidence that she formed the base of the triangle—which is to say, she was at the bottom of the row, and struck the first blow. Moses Levi, being sworn, said he was in the neighborhood, and heard Mrs. Oppenheim scream; knew it was her by the vicious expression she always threw into her screams; saw the defendant (her husband) go into the Tartar's house and gobble up the partner of his bosom and his business, and rescue her from the jaws of destruction (meaning Mrs. Kahn,) and bring her forth to sport once more amid the ——. At this point the lawyer turned off Mr. Levi's gas, which seemed to be degenerating into poetry, and asked him what his occupation was? The Levite said he drove an express wagon. The lawyer—with that sensitiveness to the slightest infringement of the truth, which is so becoming to the profession—inquired severely if he did not sometimes drive the horse also! The wretched witness, thus detected before the multitude in his deep-laid and subtle prevarication, hung his head in silence. His evidence could no longer be respected, and he moved away from the stand with the consciousness written upon his countenance of how fearful a thing it is to trifle with the scruples of a lawyer. Mrs. Oppenheim next came forward and gave a portion of her testimony in damaged English, and the balance in dark and mysterious German. In the English glimpses of her story it was discernible that she had innocently trespassed upon the domain of the Khan, and had been rudely seized upon in such a manner as to make her arm turn blue, (she turned up her sleeve and showed the Judge,) and the bruise had grown worse since that day, until at last it was tinged with a ghastly green, (she turned up her sleeve again for impartial judicial inspection,) and instantly after receiving this affront, so humiliating to one of gentle blood, she had been set upon without cause or provocation, and thrown upon the floor and "licked." This last expression possessed a charm for Mrs. Oppenheim, that no persuasion of Judge or lawyers could induce her to forego, even for the sake of bringing her wrongs into a stronger light, so long as those wrongs, in such an event, must be portrayed in language less pleasant to her ear. She said the Khan had licked her, and she stuck to it and reiterated with unflinching firmness. Becoming confused by repeated assaults from the lawyers in the way of badgering questions, which her wavering senses could no longer comprehend, she relapsed at last into hopeless German again, and retired within the lines. Mr. Oppenheim then came forward and remained under fire for fifteen minutes, during which time he made it as plain as the disabled condition of his English would permit him to do, that he was not in anywise to blame, at any rate; that his wife went out after a warrant for the arrest of the Kahn; that she stopped to "make it up" with the Kahn, and the redoubtable Kahn tackled her; that he was dry-nursing the baby at the time, and when he heard his wife scream, he suspected, with a sagacity which did him credit, that she wouldn't have "hollered 'dout dere vas someding de matter;" therefore he piled the child up in a corner remote from danger, and moved upon the works of the Tartar; she had waltzed into the wife and finished her, and was already on picket duty, waiting for the husband, and when he came she smacked him over the head a couple of times with the deadly bludgeon she uses to elevate linen to the clothes-line with; and then, stimulated by this encouragement, he started to the Police Office to get out a warrant for the arrest of the victorious army, but the victorious army, always on the alert, was there ahead of him, and he now stood in the presence of the Court in the humiliating position of a man who had aspired to be plaintiff, but overcome by strategy, had sunk to the grade of defendant. At this point his mind wandered, his vivacious tongue grew thick with mushy German syllables, and the last of the Oppenheims sank to rest at the feet of justice. We had done less than our duty had we allowed this most important trial—

freighted, as it was, with matters of the last importance to every member of this community, and every conscientious, law-abiding man and woman upon whom the sun of civilization shines to-day—to be given to the world in the columns, with no more elaboration than the customary "Benjamin Oppenheim, assault and battery, dismissed; Lena Oppenheim and Fredrika Kahn, held to answer." We thought, at first, of starting in that way, under the head of "Police Court," but a second glance at the case showed us that it was one of a most serious and extraordinary nature, and ought to be put in such a shape that the public could give to it that grave and deliberate consideration which its magnitude entitled it to.

"A PROSECUTING PEOPLE WE ARE"

152

INTERESTING LITIGATION
15 SEPTEMBER 1864

By late summer Clemens had seen more than enough to make his forceful indictment of the typical litigant in the piece below.

San Francisco beats the world for novelties; but the inventive faculties of her people are exercised on a specialty. We don't care much about creating things other countries can supply us with. We have on hand a vast quantity of a certain kind of material and we must work it up, and we do work it up often to an alarming pitch. Controversy is our forte. Californians can raise more legal questions and do the wager of combat in more ways than have been eliminated from the arcana of civil and military jurisprudence since

Justinian wrote or Agamemnon fought. Suits—why we haven't names for half of them. A man has a spite at his neighbor—and what man or man's wife hasn't—and he forthwith prosecutes him in the Police Court, for having onions for breakfast, under some ordinance or statutory provision having about as much relation to the case as the title page of Webster's Dictionary. And then, there's an array of witnesses who are well posted in everything else except the matter in controversy. And indefatigable attorneys enlighten the Court by drawing from the witnesses the whole detailed history of the last century. And then again we are in doubt about some little matter of personal or public convenience, and slap goes somebody into Court under duress of a warrant. If we want to determine the age of a child who has grown out of our knowledge, we commence a prosecution at once against some one else with children, and elicit from witnesses enough chronological information to fill a whole encyclopedia, to prove that our child of a doubtful age was cotemporary with the children of defendant, and thus approximate to the period of nativity sought for. A settlement of mutual accounts is arrived at by a prosecution for obtaining goods or money under false pretenses. Partnership affairs are elucidated in a prosecution for grand larceny. A burglary simply indicates that a creditor called at the house of his debtor the night before market morning, to collect a small bill. We have nothing but a civil code. A portion of our laws are criminal in name only. We have no law for crime. Cut, slosh around with pistols and dirk knives as you will, and the worst that comes of it is a petty charge of carrying concealed weapons; and murder is but an aggravated assault and battery. We go into litigation instinctively, like a young duck goes into the water. A man can't dig a shovel full of sand out of a drift that threatens to overwhelm his property, nor put a fence around his lot that some person has once driven a wagon across, but what he is dragged before some tribunal to answer to a misdemeanor. Personal revenge, or petty jealousies and animosities, or else the pursuit of information under difficulties, keep up a heavy calendar, and the Judge of the Court spends three-fourths of his time listening to old women's quarrels, and tales that ought, in many cases, to consign the witnesses themselves to the prison cell, and dismissing prosecutions that are brought without probable cause, nor the shadow of it. A prosecuting people we are, and we are getting no better every day. The census of the city can almost be taken now from the Police Court calendar; and a month's attendance on that institution will give one a familiar acquaintance with more than half of our domestic establishments.

B. THE WITNESS

Clemens wrote his *Golden Era* satire "The Evidence in the Case of Smith Vs. Jones" soon after joining the *Call*. The reporter in the sketch sets down "the plain, unembellished statements of the witnesses as given under oath before his Honor Judge Shepherd, in the Police Court" during an assault and battery case. The result is a carnival of conflicting testimony. Some witnesses, comments the reporter, "swore that Smith was the aggressor, and others that Jones began the row; some said they fought with their fists, others that they fought with knives, others tomahawks, others revolvers, others clubs, others axes, others beer mugs and chairs, and others swore there had been no fight at all." The ironic reporter is serenely confident that the people's "judgment will be as righteous as it is final and impartial . . ." [1] Whether coming from litigants or from supporting witnesses, extravagant and contradictory testimony always riled the *Call's* local. The noble Dutchwoman's husband and the other "reckless swearers" below are among the first of many unreliable or corrupt witnesses in Clemens' writings.

"HE TRIED TO TURN THIS NOBLE DUTCHWOMAN INTO A CORPSE"

153

POLICE COURT TESTIMONY
12 JULY 1864

If there is anything more absurd than the general average of Police Court testimony, we do not know what it is. Witnesses stand up here, every day, and swear to the most extravagant propositions with an easy indifference to consequences in the next world that is altogether refreshing. Yesterday—under oath—a witness said that while he was holding the prisoner at the bar so that he could not break loose, the prisoner "pushed my wife with his hand —so—*tried to push her over and kill her!*" There was no evidence to show that the prisoner had anything against the woman, or was bothering himself about anything but his scuffle with her husband. Yet the witness surmised that he had the purpose hidden away in his mind somewhere to take her life, and he stood right up to the rack and swore to it; and swore also that he tried to turn this noble Dutchwoman into a corpse, by the simple act of pushing her over. That same woman might be pushed over the Yo Semite Falls without being killed by it, although it stands to reason that if she struck fair and bounced, it would probably shake her up some.

"THESE RECKLESS SWEARERS"

154

CROSS SWEARING
9 SEPTEMBER 1864

That a thing cannot be all black and all white at the same time, is as self evident as that two objects cannot occupy the same space at the same time, and when a man makes a statement under the solemn sanction of an oath, the implication is that what he utters is a fact, the verity of which is not to be questioned. Notwithstanding witnesses are so often warned of the nature of an oath, and the consequences of perjury, yet it is a daily occurrence in the Police Court for men and women to mount the witness stand and swear to statements diametrically opposite. Swearing positively—leaving mere impressions out of the question—on the one hand that the horse was as black as night, and on the other that he was white as the driven snow. Two men have a fight, and a prosecution for assault and battery ensues. Each party comes up prepared to prove respectively and positively the guilt and innocence of the party accused. A swears point blank that B chased him a square and knocked him down, and exhibits wounds and blood to corroborate his statements. B brings a witness or two who saw the whole affair, from probably a distant stand point, and he testifies that nothing connected with the fight could have escaped his observation, and that it was A who chased B a square and knocked him down, and between these two solemn statements the Court has to decide. How can he do it. It is an impossibility, and thus many a culprit escapes punishment. There was a case in point Tuesday morning. A German named Rosenbaum prosecuted another German named Levy, for running into his wagon and breaking an axletree. He swore that he kept as far over to the right hand side of the street as a hole in the planking would permit, stopped his wagon when he saw the impending colli-sion, and warned Levy off. Notwithstanding, Levy drove his vehicle against his wheel, breaking the axle, so as to require a new one which would cost twenty-five dollars. He stated also that Levy had been trying to injure him in that way for a long while. Levy brought a witness who swore that between Rosenbaum's wagon and the hole in the street, there was room for a wagon or two to pass; that Rosenbaum challenged the collision, and that it was unavoidable on the part of Levy; that instead of stopping his wagon, the prosecuting witness drove ahead at a trot until the wagons became entangled, and that no damage whatever was done to Rosenbaum. On the whole, that instead of Levy running into Rosenbaum's wagon, Rosenbaum intentionally brought about the collision for the purpose of recovering damages off of Levy. The case was stronger than we have stated it, and the Judge could do nothing but dismiss the matter. That there was perjury on one side, was apparent. Yet this is but the history of one-half the cases that are adjudicated in the Police Court. There should be examples made of some of these reckless swearers. It would probably have a wholesome effect.

"HE WOULD SWEAR A JACKASS WAS A CANARY, IF NECESSARY"

155

ACCOMMODATING WITNESS
25 SEPTEMBER 1864

A man was summoned to testify in the Police Court, yesterday, and simply because he said he would swear a jackass was a canary, if necessary, his services were declined. It was not generous to crush a liberal spirit like that.

C. THE PROSECUTOR

The prosecuting attorney was a key man in law enforcement. The following items clearly show that Clemens believed San Francisco's prosecutor, Davis Louderback, Jr., was incompetent.

Louderback was the Assistant District Attorney of the City and County of San Francisco. His job was to prepare criminal indictments and to prosecute in the Police Court, although a complainant was of course free to employ other counsel if he wished. A native of Philadelphia, Louderback was twenty-four in 1864, five years younger than Clemens. He had read law under Hall McAllister and had practiced briefly before being appointed prosecuting attorney early that year, succeeding Philip Shepheard who had moved to the bench. The inevitable comparison with Shepheard proved to be a cross for the younger man to bear. In the old days, wrote the local of the *Bulletin,* when stocks were up and money was plentiful to hire the best legal brains, everyone still wanted Prosecutor Shepheard to handle his grievance. "Very different is the case now. Nearly all who come into this court for protection and justice employ their own counsel. . . . It cannot be that the Prosecuting Attorney is utterly incompetent for his position?" [2]

Louderback was to have a notable career. He remained Prosecuting Attorney until 1872 and then served eight years as Police Judge, earning praise for his strict punishment of lawbreakers. That he may have been particularly hard on Chinese culprits is suggested by his statement that the Chinese were "a very immoral, mean, mendacious, thieving people as a general thing." [3] In 1880 he retired to a long and successful private practice. But in 1864 his inexperience told against him, and the city papers did not let him forget it. They charged him with laziness, ignorance, stupidity, and criminal carelessness. The local of the *Bulletin* wanted him banished from his well paid position: "there are too many old women and children who need the money more, and who are equally as competent," whereas, the paper contended, the "strong and hearty" Louderback was ideally suited for sawing wood. [4]

The *Call* reporter was not to be outdone in criticism. If we credit Clemens as a witness, Louderback prosecuted without grounds and—just as bad—permitted notorious thieves to go free because his indictments were insufficient. [5] His cross-examinations were repetitious and unrevealing, and his notion of what was sufficient evidence was ludicrous—like Bemis' in *Roughing It,* although less imaginative. The tattoo of criticism from Clemens kept up through the late summer and fall and continued through 1865. [6] During all that time Louderback's most unforgivable sin may have been dullness, although it should be said that once, without irony, Clemens praised a witticism he committed. [7]

156

**AN ILL-ADVISED PROSECUTION
16 AUGUST 1864**

Clemens first attacked Louderback in this item, memorable for its spirited defense of Rufus Temple and its tribute to Judge Shepheard. Alphonso F. Tilden, managing director of the Philadelphia Silver and Gold Mining Company, had commissioned Martin Vice to build the *Nina Tilden,* a small sternwheel steamer. By September the ship was carrying ore from the company's mine above La Paz on the Colorado River to the head of the Gulf of California for reshipment to San Francisco.

Yesterday morning, Rufus Temple was examined before Judge Shepheard on a charge of obtaining money under false pretenses, and acquitted. We are disposed to make a specific and more extended reference to this matter than its importance would seem to demand, from the fact that Mr. Temple is said to be an honest, industrious young man, who has been placed in an unfavorable light before the public by being arraigned in a Court of Justice on a criminal charge. The testimony, which signally failed to sustain the charge, went simply to show that the defendant, who follows the trade of a caulker, had been employed by Mr. Vice (the prosecuting witness) to do some extra work on the steamer Nina Tilden; that Temple presented a bill of thirty dollars to Mr. V. for this work, which was for some reason refused, upon which the bill was presented to Mr. Tilden, the owner or one of the owners of the vessel, who remarked, in substance, that he was not the proper person to pay such bills, but, as he did not wish any claims to stand against the vessel, he would pay it, which he did,

taking Mr. Temple's receipt therefor. Upon learning the fact of the payment, Mr. Vice saw the city prosecutor, and a verified complaint was made, embodying the averment that Temple had represented to Mr. Tilden that he was sent to him (Tilden) with a verbal order from affiant for the payment of the bill. Mr. Tilden, who was a witness for the prosecution, denied, on his oath, that Temple had made any such representation, and that fact being the gist of the offence, the prosecution was at once abandoned. We cannot but speak in terms of the strongest condemnation of the reprehensible manner in which parties very frequently come into the Police Court, under the sanction of the Prosecuting Attorney. With all of perjury except the technical animus, they seek to wield this tribunal as a mollifier of their personal feelings, as if it were instituted as a general dispenser of the lex talionis. It is indeed a fortunate thing for the community that we have just such a man as Judge Shepheard on the bench, where discrimination and decision are so much required.

"THE ATTORNEY HAD A PRECEDENT"

157

BOAT SALVAGE
27 SEPTEMBER 1864

The anecdote by John Phoenix cited by Clemens also is a precedent for a gag Mark Twain enjoyed pulling. For example, after describing a baby's prodigious feats, he wrote: "My report of this baby's performances is strictly true—and if any one doubts it, I can produce the child." [8]

One Pinkney, a 'longshoreman, had some of the crew of a French bark up before the Police Court, yesterday, for an assault and battery, alleged to have been committed upon him. The Frenchmen testified that a stray boat was drifting toward their vessel, and they received signals from a Bremen bark, to which it belonged, to catch it, which they prepared to do. Pinkney came out after it with his boat, and overtook it just as it touched the bow of the French bark; his mast got entangled in the vessel's chains, and fell over and struck him on the arm; five French sailors pushed off and took the stray boat away from Pinkney. Pinkney testified that he got the blow on his arm from an oar in the hands of one of the sailors, and when asked if he had any witnesses to prove that such was the case, he said "No;" that the District Attorney told him his arm would be sufficient evidence! The Attorney had a precedent. John Phoenix once told of a bull that pulled fifteen hundred logs at one time, and if any one doubted it, he could go and show him the bull. Pinkney's arm was not considered sufficient evidence of the assault, nor yet his whole anatomy together, and the case was dismissed.

"THE PROSECUTING ATTORNEY IS A
POWERFUL ENGINE, IN HIS WAY"

158

NUISANCE
27 SEPTEMBER 1864

Mrs. Hall entered complaint against a groggery at the corner of Post and Taylor streets, as a nuisance, yesterday, in the Police Court. The case was dismissed. It might not have been, if she had gone to the expense of procuring more legal assistance to prosecute it. The Prosecuting Attorney is a powerful engine, in his way, but he is not infallible. If parties would start him in and let him worm out of the witnesses all the facts that have no bearing upon the case, and no connection with it, and whether the offence was committed "In the City'n

County San Francisco" or not, and then have another talented lawyer to start in and find out all the facts that do bear upon the case and are really connected with it, what multitudes of rascals that now escape would suffer the just penalties of their transgressions. With his spectacles on, and his head tilted back at a proper angle, there is no question that the Prosecuting Attorney is an ornament to the Police Court; but whether he is particularly useful or not, or whether Government could worry along without him or not, or whether it is necessary that a Prosecuting Attorney should give all his time, or bend all his energies, or throw all his soul into the one thing of being strictly ornamental, or not, are matters which do not concern us, and which we have never once thought about. Sometimes he has some of his witnesses there, and isn't that sufficient?

"THE PROSECUTING ATTORNEY MAY MEAN WELL ENOUGH"

ADVICE TO WITNESSES
29 SEPTEMBER 1864

Witnesses in the Police Court, who expect to be questioned on the part of the prosecution, should always come prepared to answer the following questions: "Was you there, at the time?" "Did you see it done, and if you did, how do you know?" "City and County of San Francisco?" "Is your mother living, and if so, is she well?" "You say the defendant struck the plaintiff with a stick. Please state to the Court what kind of a stick it was?" "Did it have the bark on, and if so, what kind of bark did it have on?" "Do you consider that such a stick would be just as good with the bark on, as with it off, or vicy versy?" "Why?" "I think you said it occurred in the City and County of San Francisco?" "You say your mother has been dead seventeen years—native of what place, and why?" "You don't know anything about this assault and battery, do you?" "Did you ever study astronomy?—hard, isn't it?" "You have seen this defendant before, haven't you?" "Did you ever slide on a cellar door when you were a boy?" "Well—that's all." "Stay: did this occur in the City and County of San Francisco?" The Prosecuting Attorney may mean well enough, but meaning well and doing well are two very different things. His abilities are of the mildest description, and do not fit him for a position like the one he holds, where energy, industry, tact, shrewdness, and some little smattering of law, are indispensable to the proper fulfilment of its duties. Criminals leak through his fingers every day like water through a sieve. He does not even afford a cheerful amount of competition in business to the sharp lawyers over whose heads he was elected to be set up as an ornamental effigy in the Police Court. He affords a great deal less than no assistance to the Judge, who could convict sometimes if the District Attorney would remain silent, or if the law had not hired him at a salary of two hundred and fifty dollars a month to unearth the dark and ominous fact that the "offence was committed in the City and County of San Francisco." The man means well enough, but he don't know how; he makes of the proceedings in behalf of a sacred right and justice in the Police Court, a drivelling farce, and he ought to show his regard for the public welfare by resigning.

D. THE JUDGE

In a judge Clemens valued discriminating perception and firm decision, mercy toward the misguided or the young, and fearless punishment of the hardened evildoer. The bright spot in the system of law enforcement in San Francisco was the quality of individual judges like Philip Shepheard and Samuel Cowles.

"IT IS BETTER TO SAVE THAN TO DESTROY"

160

JUVENILE CRIMINALS
17 JULY 1864

Two children, a boy fourteen years old, and his sister, aged sixteen, were brought before the Police Court yesterday, charged with stealing, but the hearing of the case, although begun, was not finished. Judge Shepheard, whose official dealing with ancient criminals has not yet hardened his heart against the promptings of pity for misguided youth, said he would examine the prisoners at his chambers, to the end that he might only sentence them to the Industrial School if it were possible, and thus save them from the shame and the lasting stigma of imprisonment in a felon's cell for their crime. He said there was crime enough in the land, without driving children to its commission by heaping infamy and disgrace upon them for their first transgression of the law. He was right: it is better to save than to destroy, and that justice is most righteous which is tempered by mercy.

"TWO RARE JUDICIAL TRAITS"

161

ROUGH ON KEATING
22 JULY 1864

Judge Cowles was in his early forties when Clemens first knew him. He had settled in California in 1852 after graduating from Western Reserve

College and studying and practicing law in Cleveland. He became Deputy Clerk of the Supreme Court of California and was elected Police Judge in 1856, succeeding Henry P. Coon. He also succeeded Judge Coon in the position of County Judge in 1860 and held that office eight years. After leaving the bench, he practiced law and entered the banking business in San Francisco.

All of a sudden, we have imbibed a most extravagant respect for Grand Juries. Judge Cowles fined a man two hundred and fifty dollars, yesterday, and sentenced him to five days imprisonment in the County Jail, for cherishing a sentiment of the opposite character. Otto Keating was summoned before the Grand Jury for the May term, and refused to answer one or two of the questions asked him. Judge Cowles hauled him up for contempt, but let him go without punishment. He was again called for by the Grand Jury, when he answered the questions he had declined to answer before, but refused to answer some new ones that were asked him. The punishment we have mentioned was the result. The great popularity of Judge Cowles with the people of San Francisco rests upon two rare judicial traits, which are strongly developed in his character, viz: The quality of mercy, with the quality of discerning where it is proper to exercise it; and the quality of fearlessly administering red-hot penalties that make a transgressor fairly waltz, when he deserves it. An innocent man is safe enough in the County Court, but if he is guilty, he ought always to do what he honestly can to get a change of venue.

THE POLICE POWER

Clemens' journalism in the *Call* does not foreshadow his sharp criticism of Chief Martin J. Burke and the police force in 1865 and 1866. Years later, to be sure, he complained that George Barnes censored his indignant write-up of the brutal beating of a Chinese as an officer stood by and watched. But the available evidence suggests that only after leaving the *Call* did he develop strong personal reasons for disliking the police.[1] Although his local items criticize officials in other branches of public service, they do not indicate police corruption, laxity, or brutality. In fact, they suggest that he was on amiable terms with Chief Burke and his men. Only once, as below, did he protest a police action, and even then he spoke rather mildly and in the interest of his friend Lewis P. Ward.

"THE JUDGE REMARKED THAT OFFICERS MUST NOT GO BEYOND THE LAW"

162

CHARGE AGAINST A POLICE OFFICER
25 JUNE 1864

William H. Winans, presumably a lawyer, is not listed in the city directories, but he may have been part of the law firm of Joseph W. Winans and David Belknap. I assume that the charges made against Forner by Winans and by Lewis P. Ward (Item 163) grew out of a single incident: Forner's scuffle with two men and their subsequent arrest.

William H. Winans made a complaint in the Police Court, yesterday, against officer Forner, for assault and battery. From the testimony it appeared that Forner had had an arrest of two persons and then delivered them to the care of another officer. While the latter officer was taking the men to the Station house, the plaintiff went up to one of the prisoners to speak to him concerning his bail, when, as he alleges, Forner took him by the collar, pushed him away, and struck him. The Judge remarked that officers must not go beyond the law in the discharge of their duties. It was not unfrequently the case that they displayed abundant zeal concerning arrests that were wholly unjustifiable, alluding more particularly to their making arrests without a warrant, on the mere say-so of outside parties. They must either be an actual witness of the offence or make an arrest by a warrant specially issued for the purpose. After Forner had delivered his prisoners to another officer his control over them ceased, and he had no right to exercise the conduct alleged against him, and it should require him to appear to-day for sentence.

163

CHARGES AGAINST AN OFFICER
28 JUNE 1864

In 1864 Lewis P. Ward was a compositor for the *Alta California* and a well known gymnast. For a time he was Clemens' roommate and was often his companion.[2] Their mutual affection seems never to have dimmed. A quarter of a century after his *Call* days Mark Twain wrote to his old friend, and Ward's reply, tactful and sensitive, confessed to "lurking thoughts" that "wealth and greatness" had turned his former roommate "dignified and cold." But Clemens' letter, he continued, "dispelled all thoughts of the kind and proved to me that you were the same whole-souled, good fellow that you were when I last saw you, 24 years ago."[3] In October 1903 Mark Twain carefully wrote on the torn envelope of a letter mailed by Joe Goodman from Alameda: " 'Little Ward' is dead."[4] Their closeness in San Francisco is suggested by a notice in the *Alta California* in December 1865, a time when Clemens and Albert S. Evans were feuding in print—and when each man was using every advantage against the other. With heavy-handed insinuation Evans reported the theft of some shirts from Lewis P. Ward, "the printer," who "has applied to his old friends, the police—with whom he has always been on the most intimately friendly terms . . ."[5] The item plainly implied that Ward had had some run-ins with the police. Clemens lost no time in renewing his blasts at Fitz Smythe.[6]

Probably Ward was responsible for Clemens—never an enthusiast for physical exercise—having joined the San Francisco Olympic Club in 1864 (in a letter home Clemens joked with his mother about his membership), for Ward was a prominent member of that group. Excelling as a tumbler and trapeze artist, Ward also sometimes assisted Colonel T. H. Monstery in fencing exhibitions. He was a featured athlete in the club's public performances, and these with the dances that followed were regularly reported in the *Call*. The Olympic Club later sent him to give instruction in gymnastics to newly organized branch clubs in Nevada cities, where the papers described his feats in superlatives. For a time in 1878 he and Steve Gillis thought they had made their fortunes through speculation in mining stock. But in his letter to Clemens ten years later the old print acknowledged: "I am on the down-grade and must make the best of it." He still wrote on stationery of the Olympic Club.

The *Call* is the only city paper among those whose files for the period still exist to have reported Ward's charges and their outcome, and this was done without stating in so many words that Ward was one of the two citizens maltreated and arrested by Forner—an assumption I make. The Board of Police Commissioners was composed of Mayor Coon, Police Judge Shepheard, and Chief of Police Burke. On July 2 the *Call* local reported that the board, acting on Ward's final charge, had suspended Officer Forner from his pay for four days.

Lewis P. Ward prefers the following charges against Officer Forner, and Judge Shepheard has issued subpoenas for the witnesses: Using unnecessary violence in making an arrest; making the arrest without authority, (without a warrant and merely upon the say-so of an interested party); maltreating two private citizens where there was no call for such conduct on his part; and being off his beat and drinking in the "Flag" Saloon, when he should have been at his post. The Board of Police Commissioners will take the matter into consideration on Thursday afternoon at two o'clock. These charges are of a grave character, and will receive the strict examination to which their importance entitles them.

164

POLICE COMMISSIONERS
1 JULY 1864

The fine of five dollars imposed on Forner was for technical assault against William Winans. Clemens' restraint in his criticism of the Board of Police Commissioners may be gauged by his remarks in the *Territorial Enterprise* twenty months later:

Chief Burke's Star Chamber Board of Police Commissioners is the funniest institution extant . . . Now to see the Chief fly around and snatch up accuser and accused before the Commission when any policeman is charged with misconduct in the public prints, you would imagine that fearful Commission was really going to raise the very devil. But it is all humbug, display, fuss and feathers. The

Chief brings his policeman out as sinless as an angel, unless the testimony be heavy enough and strong enough, almost, to hang an ordinary culprit, in which case a penalty of four or five days' suspension is awarded. . . . And knowing that the father must share the disgrace if the son is found guilty, would you ever expect a conviction? Certainly not. . . . If Pontius Pilate was on the police he could crucify the Savior again with perfect impunity—but he would have to let Barrabbas and that other policeman alone, who were crucified along with him, formerly.[7]

Lewis P. Ward brought several charges against Policeman Forner, yesterday, before the Board of Police Commissioners. One was for maltreating two citizens who were not under arrest, and whom he had no business to lay his hands on anyhow. This charge was summarily dismissed; the offence involved being one of no consequence, as any one can see. Still, the Board might have thought the officer sufficiently punished for it already in the Police Court, where he was fined five dollars, which he paid in green-backs, if he is a loyal man. The second charge was for arresting a man without any authority for doing it. This was also dismissed—for good and sufficient reasons, maybe—but anyhow it was dismissed. The third charge against Officer Forner was for being off his beat when he should have been on it, instead of drinking in the "Flag" saloon. Several witnesses substantiated this charge, and we are informed that no evidence was produced against it. The Commissioners took it into consideration, and will render a decision in the matter shortly, perhaps.

THE BUREAUCRATIC MIND

Clemens' attack on authority in his *Call* journalism is often personal in motivation and tone and sometimes is explosive and bitter. His reporter's job in 1864 was a sorry comedown after his dreams of sudden wealth from mining and speculation in stocks; moreover, it could not have squared well with his sense of personal worth and power. Sometimes he must have felt that it led nowhere, and when inner pressures built up he lashed out irritably at persons or institutions that deprived him of money, news, respect, or a reputation for reliability. He felt, for instance, that many public servants and minor officials who had news to give out were too uppity. He accused them of being ignorant and uncooperative, even high-handed—especially when he could not extract an item or two from them. But when he thought of minor functionaries as overworked and underpaid drudges—like himself—he was ready to take out after their bosses.

Albert B. Paine believed that "A Small Piece of Spite" (Item 174) was the only one of Clemens' "several severe articles . . . criticizing officials and institutions" [1] not censored in the *Call* office. But Paine seems to have been mistaken, for Clemens had his say on the shortcomings of higher-ups in the mint, the custom house, the army, the boards of education and of supervisors, an employment bureau, mining companies and the Sanitary Commission. He was alert to official neglect of reporters' needs, and he carefully acknowledged rearrangements of municipal records and police records that made them more accessible to reporters. [2]

A. CIVIC IRRESPONSIBILITY

"THEIR CROP OF INFORMATION HAS FAILED THIS CENTURY"

165

MISSIONARIES WANTED FOR SAN FRANCISCO 28 JUNE 1864

After three weeks on the job, Clemens indicted "the conservators of public opinion" for sitting on the news and incidentally served notice that he was not permanently attached to local reporting.

We do not like it, as far as we have got. We shall probably not fall so deeply in love with reporting for a San Francisco paper as to make it impossible ever to wean us from it. There is a powerful saving-clause for us in the fact that the conservators of public information—the persons whose positions afford them opportunities not enjoyed by others to keep themselves posted concerning the important events of the city's daily life—do not appear to know anything. At the offices and places of business we have visited in search of information, we have got it in just the same shape every time, with a promptness and uniformity which is startling, perhaps, but not gratifying. They all answer and say unto you, "I don't know." We do not mind that, so much, but we do object to a man's parading his ignorance with an air of overbearing egotism which shows you that he is proud of it. True merit is modest, and why should not true ignorance be? In most cases, the head of the concern is not at home; but then why not pay better wages and leave men at the counter who would not be above knowing something? Judging by the frills they put on—the sad but infallible accompaniment of forty dollars a year and found—these fellows are satisfied they are not paid enough to make it an object to know what is going on around them, or to state that their crop of information has failed, this century, without doing it with an exaggeration of dignity altogether disproportioned to the importance of the thing. In Washoe, if a man don't know anything, he will at least go on and tell you what he don't know, so that you can publish it in case you do not stumble upon something of more vital interest to the community, in the course of the day. If a similar course were pursued here, we might always have something to write about—and occasionally a column or so left over for next day's issue, perhaps.

"THE TREATMENT OF THESE MEN IS NOT ONLY UNJUST BUT CRUEL"

Three men whom Clemens admired were his pipelines to the United States Branch Mint and to the Custom House. The superintendent of the mint, Robert B. Swain, had rented office space for himself and his secretary Frank B. Harte (as he was listed) in the *Call* building next door. The veteran journalist Frank Soulé who worked in the *Call* editorial room also was recording clerk of the Custom House. Not surprisingly, Clemens repeatedly voiced the grievances of the overworked federal employees in the mint and the Custom House who were compelled to accept their pay in greenbacks—when they could get it at all, bureaucratic snafus permitting. Clemens' past efforts to get plush office furnishing for Orion in Orion's official capacity as secretary to Governor Nye of Nevada Territory did not prevent his making a dig at Secretary of the Treasury Salmon P. Chase for *his* plush furnishings, and characteristically he delighted in the logical demonstration of how many months would be needed for the greenback-poor Custom House inspectors to pay their poll tax in coin. About the time that he presented the workers' case, Clemens wrote home: "You ask if I work for greenbacks? Hardly. What do you suppose I could do with greenbacks here?" [3]

Clemens did not care for David W. Cheesman who, as treasurer of the branch mint, was an Assistant United States Treasurer and the great champion of paper money on the West Coast. He was even more censorious in 1866 when Cheesman's brother-in-law William Macy, cashier of the mint, ran off after embezzling $39,000. At that time Clemens again referred to the division of authority between Cheesman and Swain and blamed Macy's theft for another delay in wage payments.[4] But Clemens was on rather intimate terms with Swain, whom he later described as a merchant prince of pure reputation.[5] For years Swain had been a respected commission merchant and insurance agent, doubling in his position at the mint from 1863 to 1869. Active in causes for social improvement, he was a prominent Unitarian and friendly with Dr. Bellows, as he had been also with Thomas Starr King. He died in 1872.

The poll tax collector probably was Charles R. Story, tax collector for the municipal government. J. Frank Miller was deputy collector and auditor of the Custom House, and J. Burke Phillips and E. Burke were deputy collectors.

**CUSTOM HOUSE RESIGNATIONS
31 JULY 1864**

Yesterday afternoon, the Deputy | Collector, Auditor, and fifteen other

Custom House officers sent in their resignations, assigning as a reason for doing so, that with green-backs at the present rates, (forty cents,) their wages were less than those received by day laborers, and being inadequate to defray the expense of living, they were compelled to resign. Custom House salaries are not very heavy, even when paid in gold. We are informed that the Collector telegraphed to Washington at once concerning the matter.

167

**REFUSED GREEN-BACKS
2 AUGUST 1864**

Last Saturday, eleven inspectors in the barge office of the Custom House received a call from the Poll-tax Collector, and they tendered their indebtedness in the kind of money their salaries are paid in—green-backs. The Collector said he was not allowed to take anything but coin, and the inspectors said they would suffer imprisonment before they would pay in anything but green-backs. The soundness of this position will be appreciated when you come to reflect that they only get four dollars a day, anyhow, and when that sum is mashed into green-backs at present rates, it only amounts to about a dollar and a half a day. Now, estimating their actual living expenses at a dollar and forty-five cents a day—and it cannot fall below that while they continue to eat anything—how long would it take one of those inspectors to pay this oppressive Poll-tax in coin out of the clear profits of his labor? Why, it would take two months and three weeks, as nearly as you could come at it; as the amount of the tax is four dollars.

168

**OTIUM CUM DIGNITATE
4 AUGUST 1864**

Secretary Chase's private offices at Washington are fitted with Axminster carpets, gilded ceilings, velvet furniture, and other luxurious surroundings which go to hedge about a Cabinet Minister with a dignity quite appalling to the unaccustomed outsider.

Five minutes after a Custom House clerk had read this item, and with the recollection of it still upon him, he was paid his monthly salary in green-backs, and the consequence was he lost his temper, and became profane to a degree approaching lunacy.

169

OUR U.S. BRANCH MINT
10 AUGUST 1864

When the Branch Mint was established in this city, it was upon the calculation that its annual coinage would amount to about five millions. Upon that supposition, its organization as to number of officials, accommodation, and the pay of the employés, was fixed. Although the coinage has about quadrupled what was calculated upon, neither accommodations, employés nor compensation have been increased. On the contrary, the pay is now in green-backs instead of gold, and the payment often delayed, as at present, for four months, through inefficiency on the part of some one in Washington. However, Congress made an appropriation at its last session for a new Mint here, and we hope that something may come of it different from the present miserable kennel called a Mint, and that something may also be done for the relief of the unpaid men and women who perform the labors of the institution. Herewith we give a synopsis of the business done by the Branch Mint in this city for the last twelve months. It will be seen that, instead of five, the coinage has been nearly twenty millions:

FISCAL YEAR 1863–4.

Gold	$19,068,400.00	
Silver	468,409.00	
		$19,536,809.00

FISCAL YEAR 1862–3.

Gold	$17,510,960.00	
Silver	1,040,638.68	
		$18,551,598.68

Gain of 1863–4 over 1862–3 .... $ 985,210.32
Loss of Silver, $572,229.68. Gain of Gold, $1,557,440.00.

170

THE MINT TROUBLES
25 SEPTEMBER 1864

A report is abroad that the Branch Mint is about to close—that the employés, being no longer able to support themselves and families on the mere prospect of getting the salaries due them paid some day or other, have given notice that unless their accounts are previously squared, they will quit work in a body on the 30th instant. These reports were not without foundation. We are glad to be able to state, however, that the Mint is not going to stop, nor the men be allowed to suffer much longer for the moneys due them. Within two weeks, or at farthest three, all cause of complaint will be removed, and the employés themselves have been satisfied of this fact. We get our information at headquarters.

171

THE LAST HITCH AT THE MINT
2 OCTOBER 1864

All of the officials in the Mint have, for the last six months, had a hard time of it, and some of them a very hard one. For six months they had received nothing until yesterday, although there has been money enough here to pay a portion of their demands. Some technical objection on the part of the Treasurer, Mr. Cheesman, is said to have been the cause. Latterly, Mr. Swain, the Superintendent, after long effort, succeeded in getting a positive order to use any money to the credit of the Mint in the payment of the officials. As Treasury Notes have fallen very much since a portion of their pay was due, Mr. Swain, having authority, allowed the pay-rolls to be made out in such amounts as would make up to the recipients an amount in gold at present prices of green-backs equal to what their pay would have been if received when due. This is strictly just. Most of the officials were thus paid three months' salaries of the six due. But two of the unfortunate clerks chance to be the appointees of the Treasurer, who objected to pay their salaries unless the additions mentioned were abated. Mr. Swain declined to thus make out their pay-rolls, knowing that if thus paid they would resign. They are faithful, honest, competent, and he cannot at once, if at all, supply their places. If they resign, the operations of the Mint must stop for a while, at least, and they cannot afford to remain for the pay insisted upon by Mr. Cheesman. The result yesterday was, that after waiting six months for their pay, they left the Mint, not having received a dollar. They are poor men, we hear, and greatly need their pay. If the operations of the Mint should cease to-morrow, we presume it will be because Mr. Cheesman desired to make capital with the Secretary at the expense of Mr. Swain, by showing that *his* appointees can be forced to submit to any loss which his own pertinacious technicalities have caused. The treatment of these men is not only unjust but cruel, and the effect upon the public will probably be great inconvenience and loss to all who have dealings with the Mint.

"BESIEGED BY FRANTIC CHAMBERMAIDS AND BLASPHEMOUS COOKS AND WOOD CHOPPERS"

172

INTELLIGENCE OFFICE ROW
10 AUGUST 1864

The names of those concerned in it are suppressed, and it is a matter of no consequence anyhow, but the foundation of the fight is of interest to some, as showing how the business of intelligence offices is sometimes conducted, in evasion of the law, but not in violation of it. The statute says that the keeper of the office must, in return for the money received from his customer, give him a receipt, in which the nature of the service rendered must be specified. This is done in this wise: "Received of John Doe, two dollars and fifty cents, for services rendered in procuring him a situation as stable-boy." That is according to law, and if John Doe goes to the stable and is refused the situation, he can make the intelligence man refund his money. But the latter takes no such chances. To the receipt he adds the following postscript, which blocks the game on the stable-boy, in spite of the statute: "If you are denied the situation, your money will be re- funded upon the presentation here of a *written statement* of the fact of the refusal *by the parties so refus- ing.*" The "parties" will not trouble themselves with writing communications for stable-boys and servant-girls to intelligence office keepers, and without the ceremonious "written statement," the noble dealer in occupations will not disgorge. He sticks to his contract. The result of this practice is, that every day the District Attorney is besieged by frantic chambermaids and blasphemous cooks and wood choppers, seeking redress for the wrongs they have suffered at the hands of the intelligence office keepers; but they go away without it. The law is a wonderful machine, and few there be that understand it; they say it does not cover the case we have spoken of, at all. This having been ascertained by a victim, yesterday, he went back to his chuckling spoiler and whaled him.

"WE DON'T MEAN IT ALL, NOR NEAR IT"

173

SCHOOL DIRECTOR POPE AND THE *CALL*
17 AUGUST 1864

On Wednesdays the San Francisco dailies published their reports of the regular Tuesday evening meetings of the Board of Education which were attended by the city's local reporters.[6] John F. Pope's criticism of Clemens generated less belligerence in the reporter than might have been expected. Pope was secretary of a mining company and representative on the Board of Education from the Second District. John C. Pelton of the Rincon School once described him as "an honest, intelligent gentleman, of fair education and average abilities," [7] whose main qualification for serving on the board was that he was the only member with a child in the public schools. The concert mentioned in Pope's resolution [8] was advertised in the *Call* 11 August as the "Grand Musical Concert by the Children of the Public Schools" to be given in Platt's Hall the next day at 2 P. M. in aid of the National Freedmen's Relief Association.

At the meeting of the Board of Education last evening, Mr. Pope complained that he had been misrepresented by the reporter for the *Call*, as well as by the Secretary of the Board in his minutes, in the statements of his resolution introduced at the last meeting, on the subject of the participation by the pupils of the different Schools in the exercises of the Freedman's Concert. Mr. Pope says that his resolution was not to require the Grammar class, that had declined to participate on that occasion, to do so against their will, but to inform the members of that class that if they did so decline, they would be required to continue their usual daily exercises in School. If this was Mr. Pope's statement, he may have the benefit of it, though the fact that both the reporter and the Secretary of the Board, who are both presumed to be, and really are close listeners to the proceedings of the body, should understand the Director exactly alike, and fall into the same identical error, is, to say the least, a very extraordinary coincidence. Whatever may have been the exact phraseology of the gentleman's motion, the evident intention of the measure and the disposition of more than one member of the Board was certainly expressed in our report and the Secretary's minutes. However, as we entertain no feelings of hostility toward any member of the Board, we, in our own individual reportorial capacity, will concede, retract or admit anything in the world, "for the sake of the argument," and to keep peace in the family. But understand we don't mean it all, nor near it.

"AS FERVENT A PRAYER AS EVER WELLED UP FROM THE BOTTOM OF OUR HEART"

174

A SMALL PIECE OF SPITE
6 SEPTEMBER 1864

Clemens relished "A Small Piece of Spite" as part of an imbroglio that —he believed—gave him a chance to pull down the mighty through his talent for intrigue and lobbying. The city's leading undertaker was Atkins Massey, who is said to have buried 16,000 San Franciscans by the time he followed them to the grave in 1892. Coroner Benjamin A. Sheldon kept a branch office in Massey's establishment at 651 Sacramento Street. There late in August "some witless joker" entered the false information in the coroner's books that a body had been seen floating off Meiggs wharf; Massey's employees, who kept the books, knew this to be a hoax. With the exception of the *Call's* man, who apparently did not make the rounds that day, the city's locals published the report, which they had to retract two days later. Their wrath led Massey or one of his men to deny them access to the records, whereupon the Black Avenger of the Petrified Man and the Terror of the Ladies of Carson City took command.

In a letter home he wrote: "I have triumphed. They refused me and other reporters some information at a branch of the Coroner's office . . . I published the wickedest article on them I ever wrote in my life, and you can rest assured we got all the information we wanted after that. It made Mr. Massey come to his milk, mighty quick." [9]

Coroner Sheldon died four days after "A Small Piece of Spite" appeared. He was only 39, had twice been elected coroner, and was one of the most popular men in San Francisco. On 19 September the Board of Supervisors selected Dr. Stephen R. Harris as the new coroner, which was noted without comment by the *Call*. Six days later Clemens wrote home: ". . . when they came to fill the vacancy I had a candidate pledged to take the lucrative job out of Massey's hands, & I went into the Board of Supervisors & button-holed every member & worked like a slave ⟨against⟩ for my man. When I began he hadn't a friend in the Board. He was elected just like a knife, & Mr. Massey is out in the cold." [10] He gloated a bit over his wire-pulling, just as a year before he had boasted about the bills that his influence either had killed or promoted successfully through the Nevada legislature. [11]

I do not know why Clemens favored Dr. Harris, unless he simply liked the doctor's distinguished record. Born in 1802, Harris was trained in New York and for six years was health commissioner of that state. He moved to San Francisco in 1849, lost everything he owned in disastrous fires, mined briefly, and in 1851 was elected the city's third mayor. Two years later he became City Comptroller and still later resumed his practice. During the Civil War he was a strong advocate of Lincoln and was president of the Union League, an influential organization solidly behind the Union party in California. He also served as president of the California Society of Pioneers. He died in 1879.

Massey, a Philadelphian born in 1819—an exact contemporary of Walt Whitman and just as bewhiskered—arrived in San Francisco a few months after Harris and with years of experience as a journeyman undertaker in the East, South, and Midwest. He quickly became the city's busiest undertaker and officiated at the funerals of such notables as Senator David C. Broderick and at the city's memorial funeral for Abraham Lincoln. This prominence in itself may have aroused Clemens' enmity, for undertakers usually upset him. Yet he could not leave them alone. As late as November 1865 when he worked for the *Dramatic Chronicle,* that paper began ridiculing Clemens' old enemy Albert S. Evans (Fitz Smythe), who had "gone into spasms of delight" in an *Alta* item about the new and elegantly sepulchral funeral car of Atkins Massey. Smythe, "this 'genius of abnormal tastes' . . . looks with a lecherous eye on this gorgeous star-spangled banner bone-wagon . . . This fellow must be cramped down a little. He would burst with ecstasy if he could clasp a real, sure-enough body-snatcher to his bosom once . . . He must be gagged." [12] Every partisan of Clemens will hope that he wrote those words, not wanting to deny him the intense pleasure of having yoked Massey and Fitz Smythe together for this double decapitation.

Some witless practical joker made a false entry, a few days ago, on a slate kept at the dead-house for the information of the public, concerning dead bodies found, deaths by accident, etc. The Alta, Bulletin, and Flag, administered a deserved rebuke to the Coroner's understrappers, for permitting the entry to remain there, and pass into the newspapers and mislead the public, and for this reason the slate has been removed from the office. Now it is too late in the day for such men as these to presume to deny to the public, information which belongs to them, and which they have a right to demand, merely to gratify a ridiculous spite against two or three reporters. It is a matter of no consequence to reporters whether the slate is kept there or not; but it *is* a matter of consequence to the public at large, who are the real injured parties when the newspapers are denied the opportunity of conveying it to them. If the Coroner permits his servants to close the door against reporters, many a man may lose a friend in the Bay, or by assassination, or suicide, and never hear of it, or know anything about it; in that case, the public and their servant, the Coroner, are the victims, not the reporter. Coroner Sheldon needs not to be told that he is a public officer; that his doings, and those of his underlings at the coffin-shop, belong to the people; that the public do not recognize his right or theirs to suppress the transactions of his department of the public service; and, finally, that the people will not see the propriety of the affairs of his office being hidden from them, in order that the small-potato malice of his employés against two or three newspaper reporters may be gratified. Those employés have *always* shown a strong disinclination to tell a reporter anything about their ghastly share in the Coroner's business, and it was easy to see that they longed for some excuse to abolish that slate. Their motive for such conduct did not concern reporters, but it might interest the public and the Coroner if they would explain it. Those official corpse-planters always put on as many airs as if the public and their master, the Coroner, belonged to them, and they had a right to do as they pleased with both. They told us yesterday that their Coronial affairs should henceforth be a sealed book, and they would give us *no* information. As if *they*—a lot of forty-dollar understrappers—had authority to proclaim that the affairs of a public office like the Coroner's should be kept secret from the people, whose minions they are! If the credit of that office suffers from their impertinence, who is the victim, Mr. Sheldon or the reporters? We cannot suffer greatly, for we never succeeded in getting any information out of one of those fellows yet. You see the dead-cart leaving the place, and ask one of them where it is bound, and without looking up from his newspaper, he grunts, lazily, and says, *"Stiff,"* meaning that it is going in quest of the corpse of some poor creature whose earthly troubles are over. You ask one of them a dozen questions calculated to throw more light upon a meagre entry in the slate, and he invariably answers, *"Don't know"*—as if the grand end and aim of his poor existence was not to know anything, and to come as near accomplishing his mission as his opportunities would permit. They would vote for General Jackson at the "Bodysnatchers' Retreat," but for the misfortune that they "don't know" such a person ever existed. What do you suppose the people would ever know about how their interests were being attended to if the employés in all public offices were such unmitigated ignoramuses as these? One of these fellows said to us yesterday, "We have taken away the slate; we are not going to give you any more information; the reporters have got too sharp—by George, they know more'n *we* do!" God help the reporter that don't! It is as fervent a prayer as ever welled up from the bottom of our heart. Now, a reporter can start any day, and travel through the whole of the long list of employés in the public offices in this city, and in not a solitary instance will he find any difficulty in getting any information which the public have a right to know, until he arrives at the inquest office of the Coroner. There all knowledge concerning the dead who die in mysterious ways and mysterious places, and who may have friends and relatives near at hand who would give the world and all its wealth for even the poor consolation of knowing their fate, is denied us. Who are the sufferers by this contemptible contumacy—we or the hundred thousand citizens of San Francisco? The responsibility of this state of things rests with the Coroner, and it is only right and just that he should amend it.

B. CORPORATE MISMANAGEMENT

"All the nabobs of '63 are pretty much ruined," [13] wrote Mark Twain to the *Territorial Enterprise* as 1866 got under way. The big financial panic had begun in 1864, and during the very season Clemens reported for the *Call* many small fry, who like him had "feet on the brain," lost all they owned. Just before Clemens moved to the coast the *Call* had asked: "Is it not time for our people to inoculate against this fearful disease, and if possible prevent the community from becoming a lazar-house of ruined and demented speculators?" [14] On 30 July the *Call* local stated that "The Gould & Curry gave a grand ball lately, at Virginia, and see what came of it": that same day a foot of G & C good for $6,000 in 1863 had sold for $900, and Real del Monte stock worth $510 late in 1863 had gone begging at $9. Already it was too late for many a speculator "to empty his pockets of their worthless certificates, ere they burst his pockets and his reason together." [15] In a glumly penitent mood the *Californian* declared: "All the while that we were priding ourselves on our gold and silver currency, a paper currency was actually in existence—the only difference being that we issued and circulated mining stock instead of greenbacks." [16]

As long as the market remained strong, no one looked twice at mine management. But early in 1864 the *Call* complained that stockholders in mining companies were being crushed by the cash assessments repeatedly levied upon them by company officials who, with the money thus collected, promptly indulged in "stupendous extravagance," whereas these same men rarely declared dividends from operational profits. "Montgomery street knows that one item in this vast expenditure is, say, thirty thousand dollars for the erection of a palatial residence for the housing of the superintendent; that another is a cool hundred thousand dollars for litigation; and that the balance has gone in improvements of the most magnificent and expensive character . . ." [17] Often the mine operators "could not manage their own affairs successfully," yet they "lived in the style of grand Moguls." [18] Merely "to say 'assessment,' " lamented the *Californian*, "is to touch almost any man on the 'raw,' and the entire community may be said to know the 'smart' of this blister which draws out their life and substance." [19] From all sides came the cry voiced by the Contra Costa *Gazette:* "Why keep on levying assessments and incurring expenses that might be so easily avoided by making the mine pay its own way?" [20]

Clemens understood the mining game better than most. In Nevada he had prospected and worked claims. He had labored in a quartz-mill. As a Virginia City reporter he had descended into the Ophir, the Spanish, and the Hale and Norcross mines on the Comstock Lode. He knew the risks of underground fires and cave-ins. He understood that mining stock values were peculiarly sensitive to unpredictable influences—even to rumors caused by a timely newspaper puff. In his Dutch Nick's newspaper hoax, "The Latest Sensation," scandalous "dividend-cooking" by a Nevada mining company led to the failure and insanity of the fictitious Philip

Hopkins. He knew these things, yet in mid-1863 he was so casually confident the boom would continue that he was not disturbed when he mislaid valuable certificates or forgot to sell them at a nice profit or neglected to pick up a proffered gift of "five feet of 'Overman'" soon to be worth $2,000.[21] But in San Francisco as the market fell, he was soon satirizing mining secretaries who "have nothing to do but advertise the assessments and collect them in carefully . . ."[22] In July he noted that the large stockholders in the Gould and Curry mine, anticipating the falling market, had got out from under.[23] By September he was straining every resource to pay a $50-a-foot assessment on his remaining Hale and Norcross stock, which at $425 was selling for about one-sixth of its value a year earlier.[24] Soon, like many other dabblers, he would be broke and in debt. But as he saw what was happening to the market—and to him—his reactions in the *Call* became increasingly sharp.

"A MINE SHOULD AT SOME PERIOD OF THE WORLD'S HISTORY BEGIN TO PAY ITS OWN EXPENSES"

175

REAL DEL MONTE
19 JULY 1864

In 1864 the Real del Monte mine of the Esmeralda district of Nevada Territory provided a notorious example of corrupt management. On 19 February dissatisfied stockholders set up a committee under James J. Robbins, a stockbroker living at the Occidental Hotel, to examine the mine's affairs thoroughly. The committee uncovered an intricate and classic fraud centering around Alexander Gamble, the mine president. "We then have the case of the President and Trustee of a corporation, in whose guardianship is placed the interests of the stockholders, first ascertaining that their stock is likely to depreciate in value, then selling them large quantities at exorbitant prices, he, in the same transaction, acting as seller for himself and buyer for his constituents."[25] The case went to court.

In the Fourth District Court, yesterday, an order was granted to the plaintiff in the suit of J. J. Robbins vs. Real del Monte Gold and Silver Mining Company et al., requiring the defendants to show cause why they should not be enjoined from selling stock for the collection of an assessment levied for the purpose of further improving their mine. It appears that stockholders are becoming dissatisfied with the management of the concern, and want to see the end of assessments for "further improvements." It is an idea entertained by some inconsiderate persons, that a mine should at some period of the world's history begin to pay its own expenses. Rolling into prosperity on the wheels of assessments may do for a while, but there's a time when dividends should relieve the drain on the individual's private resources, and he looks forward expectantly, but "hope deferred maketh the heart sick," etc.

"WHAT ACCOUNT OF STEWARDSHIP HAS BEEN RENDERED UNTO THE FLAYED STOCKHOLDER?"

176

WHAT GOES WITH THE MONEY?
19 AUGUST 1864

Clemens opened this attack on the operations of mining companies by referring to a famous legal battle which had been notoriously burdensome on the stockholders. The Chollar and the Grass Valley Mining Companies had ratified an agreement for the release of one-half of the Chollar's mining grounds to the Grass Valley in return for the latter's prosecution of a suit against the Potosi Gold and Silver Mining Company which claimed land that was claimed by both the other companies. When Clemens wrote his piece, litigation was under way, and the Grass Valley Company had levied numerous assessments. A large minority of stockholders refused to pay, and in June their stock was put up for sale as delinquent. They went to court to set aside the stock sale, which prompted the majority stockholders to sell out to the Chollar Company. The cases dragged on long after Clemens had left the *Call*.

Clemens' outburst here and in "It Is the Daniel Webster" (Item 177) is a tip-off that he was financially hard pressed and feeling frustrated. His rather bitter attack on the Hale and Norcross officers is understandable. He believed the mine still might turn out well with proper management, and he hoped that he and Orion, who was trying to pay off the debt on his new home in Carson City, could sell their H & N stock for a respectable sum.

Silver City lay south of Virginia City about halfway to Dayton, and Cedar Hill was west of Virginia City. Clemens knew all these Nevada cities well.

Since the recent extraordinary exposé of the concerns of the Grass Valley Silver Mining Company, by which stockholders discovered, to their grief and dismay, that figures *could* lie as to what became of some of their assessments, and could also be ominously reticent as to what went with the balance, people have begun to discuss the possibility of inventing a plan by which they may be advised, from time to time, of the manner in which their money is being expended by officers of mining companies, to the end that they may seasonably check any tendency towards undue extravagance or dishonest expenditures that may manifest itself, instead of being compelled to wait a year or two in ignorance and suspense, to find at last that they have been bankrupted to no purpose. And it is time their creative talents were at work in this direction. The longer they sleep the dread sleep of the Grass Valley, the more terrible will be the awakening from it. Money is being squandered with a recklessness that knows no limit—that had a beginning, but seemingly hath no end, save a beggarly minority of dividend-paying companies—and after these years of expectation and this waste of capital, what account of stewardship has been rendered unto the flayed stockholder? What does he know about the disposition that has been made of his money? What brighter promise has he now than in any by-gone time that he is not to go on hopelessly paying assessments and wondering what becomes of them, until Gabriel sounds his trumpet? The Hale & Norcross officers decide to sink a shaft. They levy forty thousand dollars. Next month they have a mighty good notion to go lower, and they levy a twenty thousand dollar assessment. Next month, the novelty of sinking the shaft has about worn off, and they think it would be nice to drift a while—

twenty thousand dollars. The following month it occurs to them it would be so funny to pump a little—and they buy a forty thousand dollar pump. Thus it goes on for months and months, but the Hale & Norcross sends us no bullion, though most of the time there is an encouraging rumor afloat that they are "right in the casing!" Take the Chollar Company, for instance. It seems easy on its children just now, but who does not remember its regular old monotonous assessment anthem? "Sixty dollars a foot! sixty dollars a foot! sixty dollars a foot!" month in and month out, till the persecuted stockholder howled again. The same way with the Best & Belcher, and the same way with three-fourths of the mines on the main lead, from Cedar Hill to Silver City. We could scarcely name them all in a single article, but we have given a specimen or so by which the balance may be measured. And what has gone with the money? We pause (a year or two) for a reply. Now, in some of the States, all banks are compelled to publish a monthly statement of their affairs. Why not make the big mining companies do the same thing? It would make some of them fearfully sick at first, but they would feel all the better for it in the long-run. The Legislature is not in session, and a law to this effect cannot now be passed; but if one company dare voluntarily to set the example, the balance would follow by pressure of circumstances. But that first bold company does not exist, perhaps; if it does, a grateful community will be glad to hear from it. Where is it? Let it come forward and offer itself as the sacrificial scape-goat to bear the sins of its fellows into the wilderness.

"CHICKEN-COCKS ON THE ROOF, WHICH ARE ABLE TO TELL HOW THE WIND BLOWS"

177

IT IS THE DANIEL WEBSTER
21 AUGUST 1864

The invitation to resign that Clemens issued wholesale to all mining company officials who would not open their books to public inspection was repeated soon to public prosecutor Davis Louderback, Jr. A few more exasperating months on the *Call,* and Clemens might have been after the scalps of all officials for hundreds of miles around.

The Devil's Gate District was in Gold Canyon near Silver City. The Coso District of California was a major mining area between Owens Lake and the Nevada line.

MINING COMPANIES' ACCOUNTS.—The *Morning Call* of yesterday has a lively article on Mining Companies, suggesting that Mining Trustees should publish quarterly statements of Expenditures and Receipts, concluding with:

"The Legislature is not in session, and a law to this effect cannot now be passed; but if one Company dare voluntarily to set the example, the balance would follow by pressure of circumstances. But that first bold Company does not exist, perhaps; if it does, a grateful community will be glad to hear from it. Where is it? Let it come forward and offer itself as the sacrificial scape-goat to bear the sins of its fellows into the wilderness."

In answer to this the officers of the Daniel Webster Mining Company, located in Devil's Gate District, Nevada Territory, have requested us to inform the shareholders and others who have purchased stock in this Company at high prices, that a complete exhibit of the Company's affairs will be made public in the Argus on Saturday next. This Company, in consequence of a couple of shareholders in Nevada Territory, (legal gentlemen at that,) paying their previous assessments in green-backs, has been the first to levy an assessment payable in currency. We believe, however, they will be the first "who dare" to make public their accounts. We hope the Coso will be the next to follow suit, as a correspondent of ours, in Sacramento, (whose letter appears under the appropriate heading,) seems anxious to learn what has become of the forty-three thousand two hundred dollars collected by this Company for assessments the last year.—(S. F. *Argus,* Saturday.)

So there *are* company officers who are bold enough, fair enough, true enough to the interests entrusted to their keeping, to let stockholders, as well as all who may chance to become so, know the character of their stewardship, and whose records are white enough to bear inspection. We had not believed it, and we are glad that a Mining Company worthy of the name of Daniel Webster existed to save to us the remnant of our faith in the uprightness of these dumb and inscrutable institutions. We have nothing to fear now; all that was wanting was some one to take the lead. Other Companies will see that this monthly or quarterly exhibit of their affairs is nothing but a simple act of justice to their stockholders and to others who may desire to become so. They will also see that it is *policy* to let the public know where invested money will be judiciously used and strictly accounted for; and, our word for it, Companies that *dare* to show their books, will soon fall into line and adopt the system of published periodical statements. In time it will become a *custom*, and custom is more binding, more impregnable, and more exacting than any law that was ever framed. In that day the Coso will be heard from; and so will Companies in Virginia, which sport vast and gorgeously-painted shaft and machinery houses, with costly and beautiful green chicken-cocks on the roof, which are able to tell how the wind blows, yet are savagely ignorant concerning dividends. So will other Companies come out and say what it cost to build their duck ponds; so will still others tell their stockholders why they paid sixty thousand dollars for machinery worth about half the money; another that we have in our eye will show what they did with an expensive lot of timbers, when they haven't got enough in their mine to shingle a chicken-coop with; and yet others will let us know if they are still "in the casing," and why they levy a forty-thousand-dollar assessment every six weeks to run a drift with. Secretaries, Superintendents, and Boards of Trustees, that don't like the prospect, had better resign. The public have got precious little confidence in the present lot, and the public will back this assertion we are making in its name. Stockholders are very tired of being at the mercy of omnipotent and invisible officers, and are ripe for the inauguration of a safer and more sensible state of things. And when it is inaugurated, mining property will thrive again, and not before. Confidence is the mainstay of every class of commercial enterprise.

C. MILITARY CENSORSHIP

"WE WOULD FURTHER ADVISE THE PUBLIC NOT TO GET IN A SWEAT ABOUT IT"

178

ARREST OF A SECESH BISHOP
22 JULY 1864

Hubbard H. Kavanaugh was born in 1802 near Winchester, Kentucky.

At twenty he became a Methodist minister. After filling several pulpits and acting as Kentucky's Superintendent of Public Education, he was elected a bishop of the Methodist Episcopal Church South in 1854. Ten years later his church conference sent him to California to ordain pastors in newly established churches; during his ten months in the state he gave 350 sermons. Notices of his ordination services appeared in California and Nevada papers. Presumably because of his southern connections, unknown accusers charged him with fomenting rebellion. By order of General Irvin McDowell, Commander of the Department of the Pacific, he was arrested, and at once he became a "cause" of the Democratic party organization in San Francisco. Some Union papers linked him with stage-robbers who claimed to be acting under commissions from Jefferson Davis. The Gold Hill *News* suggested he "may have brought the commissions out in a bundle of sermons, tracts, and hymn books. Hu nose?" [26] Bishop Kavanaugh and General McDowell soon reached agreement, and each released a statement to the papers. The bishop explained that "South" in the name of his church referred to church organization and not to political affiliation or loyalty. The general cleared the bishop of suspicion, although he still believed that the designation "South" should be changed because it gave rise to distrust.

At the time of the bishop's arrest, someone was likely to interpret almost anything as a rebel plot. It appears that Clemens' objection— made when nothing certain was known about the bishop's activities—was not to his arrest but to the military censorship that bottled up the news.

Brigadier General John S. Mason was Assistant Provost Marshal General of California, a veteran of Civil War battles. Colonel Richard C. Drum, later a Brigadier General, was Assistant Adjutant General and Chief of Staff at the Presidio, the original local military reservation. J. L. Van Bokkelen, Provost Marshal of Nevada Territory, was then staying at the Occidental Hotel. Clemens had known him in Carson City and, it is believed, alluded to him in *Roughing It*.[27] Keating, no doubt a friend of Clemens like Lewis Leland, probably was James M. Keating, owner of the Ivy Green Saloon at 624 Merchant Street, which Clemens had publicized before. Burke and Emperor Norton were, of course, well known to Clemens.

Rev. H. H. Kavanaugh, represented as a Bishop of the M. E. Church South, whose home until quite recently has been in Georgia, but who for some time past has been travelling around in this part of the State organizing Churches and preaching the Gospel as the M. E. Church South understand it, to many congregations of Rebel sympathizers, was on Monday arrested by Captain

Jackson, United States Marshal for the Southern District of this State. The arrest was made at Black's ranch, Salt Spring Valley, Calaveras county, whilst the Bishop was holding a camp-meeting. By the Reverend gentleman's request, he was granted his parole until he could preach a sermon, on promise to report himself at this city yesterday for passage on the San Francisco steamer, which he did accordingly. We cannot state the precise charges on which he was arrested.

Getting military information is about the slowest business we ever undertook. We clipped the above paragraph from the Stockton Independent at eleven o'clock yesterday morning, and went skirmishing among the "chief captains," as the Bible modestly terms Brigadier-Generals, in search of further information, from that time until half-past seven o'clock in the evening, before we got it. We will engage to find out who wrote the "Junius Letters" in less time than that, if we have a mind to turn our attention to it. We started to the Provost Marshal's office, but met another reporter, who said: "I suppose I know where you're going, but it's no use —just come from there—military etiquette and all that, you know— those fellows are mum—won't tell anything about it—damn!" We sought General McDowell, but he had gone to Oakland. In the course of the afternoon we visited all kinds of headquarters and places, and called on General Mason, Colonel Drum, General Van Bokkelen, Leland of the Occidental, Chief Burke, Keating, Emperor Norton, and everybody else that would be likely to know the Government's business, and knowing it, be willing to impart

the coveted information for a consideration such as the wealthy fraternity of reporters are always prepared to promise. We did finally get it, from a high official source, and without any charge whatever—but then the satisfaction of the thing was all sapped out of it by exquisite "touches on the raw"—which means, hints that military matters were not proper subjects to branch out on in the popular sensational way so palatable to the people, and mild but extremely forcible suggestions about the unhappy fate that has overtaken fellows who ventured to experiment on "contraband news." We shall not go beyond the proper limits, if we fully appreciate those suggestions, and we think we do. We were told that we might say the military authorities, hearing where the Bishop had come from, (and may be what he was about—we will just "chance" that notion for a "flyer,") did send Captain Jackson to simply ask the Bishop to come down to San Francisco; (he didn't arrest the Bishop, at all—but most anybody would have come on a nice little invitation like that, without waiting for the formal compliment of an arrest: another excessively smart suggestion of ours, and we *do hope* it isn't contraband;) the Captain only requested the Bishop to come down here and explain to the authorities what he was up to; and he did—he arrived here night before last—and explained it in writing, and that document and the Bishop have been taken under advisement, (and we think we were told a decision had been arrived at, and that it was not public property just yet—but we are not sure, and we had rather not take any chances on this part of the business.) We do know, however, that the Bishop and his document are still under advisement as far as the public are concerned, and we would further advise the public not to get in a sweat about it, but to hold their grip patiently until it is proper for them to know all about the matter.

This is all we know concerning the Bishop and his explanation, and if we have branched out too much and shed something that trenches upon that infernal "contraband" rule, we want to go home.

San Francisco Bay in the late nineteenth century, looking north from the city to Alcatraz Island and Mount Tamalpais.

ECHOES OF THE REBELLION

A. MILITARY PRECAUTIONS

Civic and military leaders in San Francisco began to petition the national government in 1861 for additional defenses to back up the guns of Fort Point and Alcatraz.[1] At stake was the security of the harbor—particularly the vulnerable inner harbor—the naval yard at Mare Island, and the Benicia military arsenal. As construction of new fortifications lagged, the newspapers kept the issue alive. Aware of the possible danger, the people were mildly susceptible to rumors and scares, to real or imagined crises that followed one after the other. An alleged secessionist plot to seize the powder magazine at Mare Island was exposed in 1862. In March 1863 the Confederate privateer *J. M. Chapman* was captured just in time to prevent a series of raids on treasure ships out of San Francisco. In February 1864 the papers rumored the approach of the "Anglo-Chinese Fleet,"[2] supposedly sold to the rebels, in company with the powerful raider *Alabama*. Other mild sensations that year were a "piratical vessel" lurking outside the harbor, the seizure by military authorities of a store of arms on land, and the seizure of the ship *Haze,* loaded with munitions, South of San Francisco in Halfmoon Bay.[3]

Early in 1864 a *Call* editorial gave the standard argument for more harbor defenses: Hostile ships could slip by Fort Point on a dark or foggy night:

> they would hug North Beach as closely as possible, so as to deter Alcatraz from shelling them and the city at the same time; proceeding then to an eligible location south of Rincon Point, they would send a flag of truce ashore requiring the city to dispatch immediately aboard of their fleet a number of the principal citizens as hostages. After Judge Coon, Michael Reese, John Parrott, Sam Brannan, Rev. T. Starr King, Louis R. McLean, etc., had been escorted on board the flag ship by Beriah Brown, information would be sent ashore that unless several millions of dollars were shelled out in a certain time, the city would be bombarded. Of course the money would be raised. In the meantime, many acts of destruction and spoliation would be committed, and when the fleet had completed its errand, it would sail past the forts, flying the Davis flag, unmolested; for no firing could be done as long as the hostages were on board.[4]

Brigadier General George Wright, who commanded the Department of the Pacific during the early 1860's, used the same argument with the War Department. On 1 July 1864 Major General Irvin McDowell replaced General Wright, and he too worked toward improvement of harbor defenses.

"ENOUGH TO KNOCK ANY FLEET THAT CAN EVER COME WITHIN REACH INTO SPLINTERS"

179

INSPECTION OF THE FORTIFICATIONS
14 JULY 1864

One of General McDowell's first acts as commander was to inspect the harbor fortifications, including new installations at Angel's Island. On 13 July he played host to the city's leaders and the press during an all-day tour of the harbor on the steam tug *Goliah*. This was a gesture to bolster public confidence, but it convinced General McDowell that the gun emplacements were poorly protected and that the overall defense set-up was insufficient to repulse enemy action. Clemens' account of the tour is unusually long for the *Call*, yet it is not as complete as the *Alta California* write-up. His distinctive manner is somewhat subdued here, perhaps because of the serious occasion. Still, there is a familiar ring to the writing: the respect for the general, the implicit sense of importance in hobnobbing with bigwigs, the eye for the picturesque, the unqualified and sometimes vivid expression of opinion, the casual handling of facts. We notice, too, the puff of his friend Lewis Leland of the Occidental Hotel and the image of reporters answering the call of popping corks. Mark Twain showed what he could do in that vein sixteen months later when he reported a very wet tour of San Francisco Bay with military officers and "gentlemen of note" on the trial run of the steamship *Rescue*.[5]

Among the tour guests named was Brigadier General John S. Mason, Provost Marshal General of California. Major James Van Voast was Provost Marshal of the Eighteenth Infantry. Commander Selim E. Woodworth was attached to the U.S.S. *Narragansett*. Benjamin B. Redding had been a newspaper editor and the mayor of Sacramento. Charles James was the Collector of the Port of San Francisco and the U.S. disbursing agent. Willard B. Farwell was a naval officer attached to the Custom House. John T. McLean was the Surveyor of the Port, and Richard Chenery was a U.S. Navy agent with offices on Montgomery Street. Others mentioned were Mayor Henry P. Coon, Postmaster Richard F. Perkins, the United States District Attorney Delos Lake, Major

General Lucius H. Allen of the California Militia, the San Francisco civic leader and merchant William T. Coleman, and Captain William A. Winder of the Third U.S. Artillery at Alcatraz. I have been unable to identify Mr. Benton and General Carpenter.

General McDowell was a controversial figure when he came to San Francisco. After the First Battle of Bull Run he had been succeeded by General McClellan as commander of the Army of the Potomac. Following the Second Battle of Bull Run he again was heavily criticized and was relieved of his divisional command, never to serve in the field again. Yet he was known as a good disciplinarian, and in 1864 some Unionist fire-eaters in San Francisco felt that he would stamp out "treasonable" activities on the West Coast more effectively than General Wright had. He was commander there until he was transferred to the Department of the East in 1868. In 1876 he returned to San Francisco, where he remained until his death in 1885.

Yesterday, General McDowell, accompanied by his Staff and many military officers, officials and civilians, made a tour of inspection of the harbor defences about the Bay of San Francisco. Many gentlemen had been invited to be of the party, and many answered by their presence. Besides Major General McDowell and Staff, were Brigadier General Wright and Staff, Brigadier-General Mason, Captain Van Vost, Provost Marshal, and other officers of the Army; Commander Woodworth of the Navy; Governor Low and suite; Mr. Redding, Secretary of State; Judges Field and Hoffman, of the U.S. Court; the Collector of the Port, Colonel James; Mr. Farwell, Naval officer; Dr. McLean, Surveyor of the Port; Captain Chenery, Navy Agent; Mayor Coon; Postmaster Perkins; Hon. Mr. Benton, Judge Lake, General Allen, General Carpenter, Wm. T. Coleman, and many other citizens whose names are not just now recollected, and several members of the Press, last but not least, always around where items are to be picked up, shells to be exploded, or corks to be drawn. A little after nine o'clock the "Goliah" left Broadway wharf with her precious freight. We could not help reflecting, should she blow up or sink, what a suit with bright buttons Neptune might wear, and how Army, Navy, Executive, Judiciary, Customs, Municipal and Civil services would suffer. Away went the pleasant company, steaming down the Bay towards Fort Point. The company—those not before acquainted—were introduced to General McDowell, and each and all seemed delighted with his frank and genial manner, his quietly social disposition, his soldierly appearance and bearing, and the facility with which he at once put every one at ease.

FORT POINT.—At the Fort he was received with his appropriate salute. The different parts of the fortifications were inspected by the General and his guests. To the eye of a civilian, the works and their warlike appliances appeared formidable and in excellent condition for service. There was but one exception. From the barbette, some shell practice was had, the target being on the opposite shore, at Lime Point. But the fuses proved imperfect, the shells exploding almost immediately upon starting on their journey. This of course will be at once remedied. After the shelling, the troops were drawn up within the Fort and were reviewed by General McDowell and Governor Low; the Band playing appropriate music. The officer of the day in command of the troops, is a gentleman who won his commission by meritorious service in eleven battles at the East. We regret that we have not his name. The party then returned to the steamer and started across the Bay towards that famous spot of which all have heard not a little for years past—

LIME POINT.—The steamer ran close along the northern shore for a considerable distance, allowing an excellent opportunity for judging of the superior qualities the formation affords for a strong fortification. It can readily be transformed into a second Gibraltar. The position is needed by Government, which should take it, and leave the consideration of pay to the future. Next the steamer was headed up the Bay, and the company invited below to partake of a lunch. That this interesting incident was all that could be desired will appear evident by saying that it was prepared at the "Occidental," and that Leland himself was present to see that chicken salad and champagne were properly dispensed. Soon the steamer reached the wharf at

ANGELS' ISLAND.—Here another salute greeted the General, who, with his guests, inspected the fortifications there fast growing into formidable proportions and condition. The little valley lying between the

Point at the entrance of Raccoon Straits, on which is a battery destined to guard that passage, and the high point to the south, where there is another new work, nearly ready for use, bears the appearance of a pleasant little village, with white houses and fixings, indicative of officers' families, soldiers' barracks, and domestic life. From this abode of the Angels the company proceeded through Raccoon Straits—beautiful sheet of water—around Angels' Island, and as they were passing the eastern end, all of a sudden found themselves saluted by scores of white handkerchiefs on shore, which was answered in kind, and with splendid music by the fine band of the Ninth infantry. A picnic party were on shore, and gave this very pleasing incident to the excursion. Passing the Point, the company had an opportunity to view the preparations for the battery there, apparently nearly ready for mounting its guns and then steamed across, and landed at

ALCATRACES, under a thundering salute from the southern batteries. A general examination of the whole Island and its defences followed; then a partaking of the hospitalities of Capt. Winder, Commandant of the Post, and shell practice from the northwestern battery. The shells here were in better condition, and the practice more satisfactory. The reported number of guns on the Island now, and to be, differs, ranging from ninety to one hundred and eighty. The exact number is not material. There are enough to knock any fleet that can ever come within reach into splinters. Leaving Alcatraces, after an inspection of the forces there, with another salute, the steamer's prow was pointed toward Yerba Buena Island—a look was had, while passing, at the positions yet to be fortified—and she passed up the Bay to the mouth of Mission Creek, past the Aquila—of which ship some of our readers have heard occasionally—and then back along the city front, the band playing national and other airs, to Broadway wharf, the place of starting. The General knows whether the inspection was satisfactory in a military light. We do not. But it may be said that the trip was exceedingly pleasant and satisfactory to all the guests of the gallant soldier to whose courtesy they were indebted for the delightful excursion.

"THE PUBLIC MAY REST EASY—WORK ON THE CAMANCHE IS STREAKING ALONG"

Early in the war the monitor *Camanche* was assigned to San Francisco harbor as a mobile fortress. This Ericsson-type ironclad of 1,875 tons was built in Jersey City by Secor and Company, then dismantled and shipped around the Horn on the *Aquila* in 1863. Two San Franciscans, Peter Donahue and James T. Ryan of the Union Iron Works, were responsible for reassembling the *Camanche* on the Coast. For months the city had anticipated the monitor's coming. But to the general consternation, no sooner had the *Aquila* docked at Hathaway's wharf, having braved privateers and ridden out storms, than it sank in gale winds on 16 November 1863. The *Camanche* with its weapons was entombed. Only after involved negotiations between contractors, underwriters, wharf owners, the city government, and the national government, was the monitor at last extracted piece by piece from the hold of the sunken *Aquila*. That unfortunate ship was successfully raised the second week of June—a few days after Clemens arrived in town.

The salvage of the *Camanche* led directly to Clemens' initiation as a San Franciscan. Hardly had he arrived in the city before he was drafted to deliver a speech before an audience gathered to bid farewell to Major Edward C. Perry, a Northern war hero and a popular marine engineer in the crew that had reclaimed the monitor. The selection of Clemens to do the honors suggests that community leaders had high regard for him as a man and a humorist as early as 1864. His skillfully fashioned speech reminds us too that he already was more accustomed to the platform than is usually recognized. The speech admirably suited the occasion, a stag farewell party less drenched in farewell tears than in liquor. To top the pleasure Clemens must have taken in it, his speech—loaded with phallic humor—received its only printing on the front page of the *Alta California*, in the city column of the high-minded but obtuse Albert S. Evans— Fitz Smythe himself.[6]

The *Camanche* very soon became a "regular" for Clemens, as it did for every other city reporter. Through the summer and fall the work of reassembly went on at Steamboat Point near the foot of Third Street and was nearly complete when Clemens left the *Call*. With great éclat the monitor was launched the morning of 14 November. The people felt more secure. But the ironclad was never to test her 15-inch Dahlgren guns in battle. After a long and slumberous career, she ended her service to the city as a coal barge and was junked in the 1920's.

180

**THE CAMANCHE
16 JULY 1864**

Steamboat Point, the place where Messrs. Donahue, Ryan & Secor are building the iron clad Camanche, looks brisker and very considerably brisker every day, in proportion as the progress of the work opens a larger field and affords more elbow-room for mechanics and laborers. Mr. Ryan commenced with ten men the first day, when everything was so mixed up and the yard so encumbered with trash, that a greater number could not work together without being in each other's way; afterwards men were added by the dozen, as use could be made of them, until now the number employed is fifty, and things begin to look shipshape about the premises. These enlistments will be constantly con-

Steamboat Point in 1865 (*from a photograph by T. E. Hecht, Bancroft Library*).

tinued until the yard swarms with workmen. About ninety feet of the keel had been laid and bolted together yesterday up to one o'clock in the afternoon, although the work in that department was only commenced yesterday morning; it will be finished this morning, and the construction of the "garboard streak" commenced. The Camanche will be one hundred and sixty feet long from stem to stern post, and two hundred feet on deck. Many of the materials are lost and others broken, and much hindrance is experienced from this source. The work is fairly under way now, and not a moment will be lost until the Camanche is completed and afloat.

181

THE CAMANCHE
31 JULY 1864

Work on the Camanche is progressing rapidly. The foreman observed yesterday, with the air of a man who is satisfied his listener is an uncommonly intelligent man, and knows all about things, that the "garboard streak" had been up some time. It is not possible to conceive the satisfaction we derived from that information. She must be all right now, isn't she? One of those gunboats is generally all right when she has her "garboard streak" up, perhaps. Such has been our experience. It is limited, but that is of no real consequence, probably. We looked around a little, and noticed that there was another streak up, also, running fore-and-aft, and several streaks running crossways, and enough old iron lying around to make as many more streaks as they want, if it holds out. It was excessively cheerful and gratifying. The public may rest easy—work on the Camanche is streaking along with extraordinary velocity.

182

CAMANCHE ITEMS—SANITARY CONTRIBUTIONS
23 AUGUST 1864

Business is progressing in lively style at the Monitor Yard. Some two hundred and seventy-five hands, including about fifty boys, swarm in and about the progressing hull, and all appear to work with a will, under the keen superintending eye of Mr. Ryan and his able assistants. On Saturday evening, after the men had struck work, they were invited to assist at a grand flag-raising. A tall tapering pole was planted, amid general enthusiasm, and a splendid American ensign hoisted to the truck, with cheers to its constellated glories and toasts for its ultimate triumph. Mr. J. W. Willard, the gentleman who attends to the contribution-box placed at the entrance gate, for aid to the Sanitary Commission Fund, informs us that visitors contribute their two bits with cheerfulness; in many instances coin of larger denomination are dropped, and change refused to be taken. On Sunday, a general visiting time, the amount contributed was two hundred and seventy-three dollars; and yesterday the box received from fifty to sixty dollars. The "Monitor Box" promises a good source.

183

THE CAMANCHE
13 SEPTEMBER 1864

The work at the Camanche goes vigorously on, and is being rapidly pushed towards completion. The scattering holes that were left in the bottom of the hull when the bulk of the riveting was done, have now all been reached by moving shores and supporting timbers. The outside tier of timbers running fore and aft, which is to receive the armor, is now put on from the bow back a distance of some forty or fifty feet on each side, and begins to give one a tolerable idea of her great strength and power of resisting the shots of an enemy. Much progress has also been made in the last few days in placing the machinery of the engine, and for turning the turret. The thorough manner in which all the work connected with the Camanche is done must be apparent to any one who makes frequent visits to it. The vigilant eyes of Mr. Ryan, one of the contractors, who is also the superintendent of the work, are every where and see every thing. The foremen of the different divisions of the work are indefatigable in their efforts to have the labor performed in the most perfect manner. The receipts at the gates, for the Sanitary Fund, for the week ending Saturday, will reach nearly five hundred dollars. A large number of our citizens visited the Camanche on Sunday.

184

THE CAMANCHE
9 OCTOBER 1864

The monitor Camanche is rapidly approaching completion. The side armor of wood is all on but about twenty feet at the stern, making nearly three and a half feet of solid wood on the sides of the monster, from stem to stern. The work of putting on the five inches of iron plating, outside of the wood, is being pushed rapidly forward, and already about seventy feet from the prow is completed. For the last two or three days, the workmen have been putting the iron plates on the deck, and about one thousand feet of the deck has been covered with the two plates of iron designed for it. Those who wish to see the monitor again before she is launched, and while they can witness the manner of securing the enormous weight of wood and iron with which the sides are covered, will do well to do so to-morrow, or within a few days, as she will soon be wholly encased with her impenetrable coat of mail.

B. THE SANITARY FUND

One way or another, the effort of the United States Sanitary Commission to help sick and wounded soldiers was always in the news. At the Mechanics' Institute Industrial Fair the exhibit of the great "Sanitary cheese" and the silver brick yielded a steady flow of money for the fund, which also received the quarters paid by thousands of citizens to view the reassembling of the *Camanche*. At the very time Clemens was preparing to leave Virginia City for the West Coast, his friend Ruel C. Gridley was auctioning the famous Sanitary Flour Sack at San Francisco's Metropolitan Theater on Montgomery Street. And all summer long from pulpit and platform came the pleas for donations. From first to last, California gave approximately $1,250,000 to the fund. This amount was five times greater than the combined contributions of all other areas of the Far West, and the lion's share of it came from San Francisco.

Clemens' Virginia City letters to the *Call* in 1863 enthusiastically reported the collection of $20,000 for the Sanitary Fund.[7] The following March the *Territorial Enterprise* praised the "large-souled and demonstrative"[8] Dr. Bellows to whom Nevada's 25,000 inhabitants had turned over $30,000 in bullion. In May Clemens joined Ruel Gridley, a brass band, and the "Army of the Lord"—which seems to have rolled along on lager beer kegs—as they escorted the Sanitary Flour Sack from Virginia City to Dayton, Nevada, and back, collecting pledges for the fund as they went. "We kept that Sanitary spree up for several days,"[9] he wrote Orion's wife, Mollie Clemens, but five days later he confessed to Orion: "I am mighty sick of that fund—it has caused me all my d—d troubles."[10] His troubles had arisen from two of his editorials in the *Territorial Enterprise*. The first charged that money raised by the ladies of Carson City for the fund had been sent to a Miscegenation Society in the East, and the second charged that the employees of the Virginia City *Daily Union* had not paid the money they had pledged to the fund. Beset from all sides by challengers, he left by stagecoach for San Francisco on May 29, and before leaving he bluntly advised Orion, who was to become president of the Ormsby County Sanitary Commission, not to stump for the fund. But once on the coast, Clemens again willingly publicized the Sanitary Fund.

"HIS PLANTATION . . . MAY BE REGARDED AS RATHER A 'DEADER THING' THAN GOULD & CURRY"

185

MORE SANITARY MOLASSES
30 JULY 1864

Mark Twain may have remembered this report when he wrote of Captain James Makee's Maui plantation in his correspondence from the Sandwich Islands in 1866.[11]

The bark Yankee arrived from Honolulu yesterday, bringing another hundred barrels of molasses to Rev. H. W. Bellows, contributed by Captain Makee, and to be sold for the benefit of the Sanitary Fund. We noticed a like donation from the same distant patriot a day or two ago, which was sold here and netted upwards of twelve hundred dollars to the fund. Captain Makee's sugar plantation, on one of the Hawaiian Islands, whence this molasses comes, is rather extensive. He has seven hundred acres of cane growing, and this area will be increased during the next few months to nine hundred or a thousand acres. There is no water on the plantation, and irrigation has to be resorted to. Even the water required for the steam engine and other purposes in the manufacture of sugar, has to be brought from a spring on a mountain, three miles distant, through iron pipes; yet, so rich is the land that *six tons of sugar* have been made on a single acre, and the average is about three tons. At his own mill, Captain Makee manufactures from eight thousand to ten thousand pounds of sugar a day. During the present year, his plantation has been very successful, and promises to produce the largest amount of sugar yet obtained from any one estate in the Hawaiian Islands. Its product will probably realize, at present rates, this year, over one hundred thousand dollars; and, altogether, its chances, in a business point of view, may be regarded as rather a "deader thing" than Gould & Curry. The estate is expected to yield over two million pounds of sugar next year. Captain Makee has invented a "molasses pan" and a "double cane cart," which are spoken of as great triumphs of Yankee genius.

"THIS . . . SPEAKS VOLUMES FOR THE LIBERALITY AND PATRIOTISM OF OUR POLICE"

186

POLICE CONTRIBUTIONS
24 AUGUST 1864

Clemens unwaveringly praised the generosity of Police Chief Burke and his men at this time. Frederick L. Post was the helpful clerk in the Police Department office; he was mentioned by Clemens in other *Call* items that summer. R. G. Sneath, treasurer of the Sanitary Commission's California branch, was an importer and wholesale grocer on Front Street.

Yesterday, F. L. Post, Property Clerk of the Police Department, paid over the fourth and fifth instalments of the monthly contributions of the Police force to the Sanitary Fund, amounting, in the aggregate, to a fraction under five hundred dollars. This makes a total of two thousand five hundred and sixty-four dollars, in gold, received by the Sanitary Commission from the same source since the beginning of the present year, and speaks volumes for the liberality and patriotism of our Police. Chief Burke contributes fifteen dollars monthly; officer Cook, twelve dollars and a half; officer Hesse, twelve dollars; Captains Lees and Baker, ten dollars each, and none of the members of the force less than five dollars. These donations are purely voluntary. While upon this subject, we would mention that R. G. Sneath, Treasurer of the Sanitary Committee, designs having a beautiful certificate engraved, suitable for framing as a parlor ornament, and one of these will be filled out and presented to each person who contributes ten dollars for the relief of the sick and wounded soldiers of the Union.

"TO HEAR DR. BELLOWS SPEAK, WAS WHAT THE PEOPLE THRONGED THE HALL FOR"

187

FAREWELL ADDRESS OF DR. BELLOWS
23 SEPTEMBER 1864

The Rev. Dr. Henry W. Bellows had preceded Clemens to San Francisco by one month, having arrived by steamer 30 April. Clemens apparently boasted of their friendship in a lost letter to his mother, for she retorted from St. Louis: "Sam tell Dr. B[ellows]. if he is a good friend of yours I wish he would give you good advice and I wish you would follow his advice." [12] Too late to reclaim him, her instructions were written at the end of September, when Dr. B. was five days at sea on his way to New York City. "Farewell Address of Dr. Bellows" is Clemens' respectful tribute to his departing friend, about whom he later wrote: "Bellows is an able, upright and eloquent man—a man of imperial intellect and matchless power—he is Christian in the truest sense of the term and is unquestionably a brick." [13] Bellows indeed had great energy and executive ability. During six months in the West he spoke and organized widely for the Sanitary Commission, while acting as Thomas Starr King's temporary replacement in the city's First Unitarian Church on Geary Street. Enlightened and witty, apparently he was a hearty "man's man" like Clemens' minister friend of later days, Joseph Twichell. His July Fourth oration in San Francisco on "The Three Johns" was a warm, intelligent plea for the underprivileged, including the Chinese and Indians.

Dr. David B. Cheney, who joined in the tribute to Dr. Bellows, had just been installed as the new pastor of the First Baptist Church on Washington Street near Stockton. He had traveled west with the Reverend Horatio Stebbins, formerly of Portland, Maine. Very possibly the "Farewell Address of Dr. Bellows" records Clemens' first sight of Stebbins, the new regular pastor of the First Unitarian Church. When Clemens knew him better, he wrote that they were "thick as thieves . . ." [14] That statement takes on considerable unconscious irony if a harsh interpretation is given to the poor character reference Stebbins later supplied for Clemens at the request of Jervis Langdon, when the success of Clemens' suit for Olivia Langdon's hand was hanging in the balance.

A fair idea of the estimation in which the Rev. Dr. Bellows is held by the people of this coast, and the impression he has made upon them in his patriotic and benevolent labors on behalf of our country and our country's defenders, might have been conceived from the attendance on the meeting last night at Platt's Hall appointed as an occasion for this great and good man to bid a final farewell to the people of California. The house was filled to its utmost capacity, yet not a sound of disorder was heard, nor a breath of disapprobation. The Presidio Band did its part, as usual, unexceptionably, the airs discoursed being somewhat of a solemn character, selected in adaptation to the occasion. The entrance of General McDowell was greeted with applause. Dr. Bellows was not present, when Governor Low, the President of the California Branch of the United States Sanitary Commission, opened the meeting with a short address, and consequently other speakers occupied the time until the Dr. entered. The Rev. Mr. Grot, of Marysville, made the opening prayer, and Rev. Dr. Cheney was presented to the audience. After speaking of the fame of Californians for their work in behalf of the Commission, their noble and generous contributions, referring feelingly to the death of Rev. Starr King, and stating the impressions he received during a recent visit of four months to the Eastern States, with regard to the strong current of feeling in favor of the Sanitary Commission, the substantial aid it receives from all quarters, the veneration the soldier has for the organization and its agents, and then referring to the pluck and the fortitude of the soldier, on the field, or wounded and maimed in the hospitals, he yielded the floor and was followed by Rev.

Mr. Stebbins, the successor of Dr. Bellows in the Pastorship of the Geary street Church, (late Starr King's.) Dr. Bellows arrived while Mr. Stebbins was speaking, and followed next in order. His appearance was the signal for prolonged applause. His speech was characterized by that animation of thought and fluency of expression that is peculiar to the Doctor. His devotion to the cause of the Commission of which he is the honored head, warmed up in him, and the relief of the suffering soldier and the support of the cause in which he is suffering usurped his every thought and lifted his soul above every other consideration. He paid an affectionate and mournful tribute to the memory of the late T. Starr King, and passed a glowing eulogy on the liberality of Californians to the cause of the Sanitary Commission; out of their impecuniosity they had contributed largely. He praised the people of this State for their fidelity to the Government; expressed his confidence in our civil and military heads; condoled with us in our present seeming adversity; and after exhorting the people to make the ballot box their paramount object, to which the cause of the Sanitary Commission must be held as secondary in importance, breathing his fervent loyalty to the Government, and declaring his thorough adhesion to the Administration, he invoked the blessings of Heaven on our people, and bade his audience an affectionate farewell. To hear Dr. Bellows speak, was what the people thronged the Hall for, and as soon as he closed his address, without waiting for a formal adjournment, they dismissed themselves and the meeting ended.

C. POLITICAL VIOLENCE

Tensions grew during the summer and fall of 1864 as the country moved toward the presidential election on 8 November. In San Francisco strong political feelings led to minor brawls and shootings. Arrests for treason and for the use of treasonable language increased. Mass meetings grew more raucous. Strongly pro-Lincoln, the major papers like the *Alta California*, the *Bulletin*, and the *Call* berated the Copperheads. Although they recognized the gulf between Union Democrats and professed rebel sympathizers, in general they thought that most Democrats were more apt to sacrifice principle in order to compromise with the Confederacy than to push on to a final military victory. The papers cautioned against shadowy conspiratorial organizations like The Golden Circle, The Loyal Leaguers, and The Knights of the Columbian Star—all of them supposedly waiting for the right moment to strike for the Confederacy in California—and a rash of stagecoach robberies in the countryside seemed to bear out popular fears of "secesh" (secessionist) plots.

"THE CLERK . . . HEARD A SUSPICIOUS NOISE AND RAISED THE CRY OF 'WATCH!' "

188

BURGLARY—THE BURGLAR CAUGHT IN THE ACT
9 JULY 1864

In this report Clemens shows a tendency to link city crimes to the countryside raids of secessionist guerrillas (see Items 189–191).

A bold robbery was attempted, last evening, in the second story of the premises owned by Janson, Bond & Co., corner of Battery and Pine streets, occupied as a fancy goods importing house, but which, owing to the vigilance of one of the clerks who slept in the store, and the promptitude of Special Officer Sweeney in answering his alarm, was frustrated. About half-past eleven, as the clerk was about retiring, he heard a suspicious noise and raised the cry of "Watch!" Officer Sweeney immediately ran in the direction, and met a man running hastily away. He asked him what the matter was, and he replied "Somebody has lost a watch round the corner." Sweeney ordered him to stop; in reply he made a desperate lunge at the officer with a bowie knife. Sweeney then struck him over the head with his night lantern and brought him to reason. He was then taken to the station-house, where, on being searched, four gold watches, three revolvers, a bowie knife, and two bunches of gold rings were found on his person. He stated his name as William Johnson, and further that he had accomplices, and the name of one was McCarty. Officers Minson and Greenwood then repaired to the scene of the attempted robbery and thoroughly searched the place. They found on the sidewalk, just under the window, where it had been let down by Johnson to his confederates, a bag containing fifteen pistols, five bowie-knives and two pairs of bullet moulds. Up to a late hour last evening, the accomplices of Johnson had not been captured. A box containing four hundred dollars in silver escaped the notice of the robbers. It is probable this gang is the same that were concerned in the recent attempted safe robberies. It is somewhat significant, taken in connection with matters transpiring in the interior of the State, that the purpose of these scoundrels seemed to be to get hold of all the arms they could, comparatively ignoring some valuable jewelry, and other articles, of which they might have possessed themselves.

"THE BAND WERE BOUND TO EACH OTHER BY HORRID OATHS"

On 30 June near Placerville six armed and masked men stopped the Pioneer stage from Virginia City. The bandits represented themselves as "southern gentlemen" [15] acting as Confederate guerrillas, and they made off with seven sacks of bullion and two thousand dollars in gold coin being shipped by Wells, Fargo & Company. Punctilious to the end, the guerrilla captain, a Missouri bushwhacker named John Ingraham or Ingram and also known as the Red Fox, gave a receipt for the stolen treasure. The money was to be used, he said, to recruit men for the Confederate service. On the next day officers surprised part of the gang at the Somers House in Placerville. Deputy Sheriff Joseph M. Staples was killed in the subsequent gunplay. Two weeks later a posse under Sheriff John Adams and Deputy Sheriff Van Eaton of El Dorado County surrounded gang members in a hideout on the New Almaden Road near San José. It was believed that these men intended to rob the stage carrying the payroll for the miners at the New Almaden quicksilver mine. Ingraham was captured and hanged; but coaches continued to be robbed, and other gangs were often being broken up.

Albert S. Evans (Fitz Smythe) writing in the Gold Hill *News* expressed the more hysterical fears aroused by the stagecoach robberies, saying there is "little doubt, none I might say, that we are threatened with civil war in California, and must be on our guard to put down with a strong hand the first demonstration made by the enemies of our country . . . or it will be upon us in all its horrors . . ." [16] A *Call* editorial also called for harsh measures, but recognized that "times are hard in Nevada as well as in California. There are the taxes, drouth, ruin by speculations, depreciation of mining stocks, discharge of hundreds of men from employment in the mines, from saloons and restaurants, and gambling shops, and the necessity of gaining a living somehow, to induce the unprincipled to acts of violence." [17] The threat was serious enough for General Wright, commander of the District of California, to give detailed orders on 11 July to Lieutenant W. L. Knight of the Second California Volunteer Cavalry to lead a special detachment for protection of the stage between Folsom and Carson City. And at least one Union party orator, noting that "Treason was gathered everywhere, in our mountains, in our valleys and in our cities," [18] used the stage robbers to whip up political sentiment for Lincoln and Johnson.

The Colonel Jackson (Item 190) who stocked up on ammunition probably was Captain A. Jones Jackson, Provost Marshal of the Southern District of California whose office was in San Francisco. Mr. and Mrs. R. F. Hall (Item 191) admitted that members of their stage-robbing "band were bound to each other by horrid oaths to revenge any punishment inflicted on them." Readers of *Huckleberry Finn* will recall that Tom Sawyer's oath bound his gang to take horrible revenge on anybody who "done anything to any boy in the band . . ." Tom insisted that his gang were robbers. He scorned mere burglary. "That ain't no sort of style. We are highwaymen. We stop stages and carriages on the road, with masks on, and kill the people and take their watches and money." [19]

189

A STAGE ROBBER AMONGST US
20 JULY 1864

Alman Glasby, (or Gillespie,) one of the Placerville stage-robbers, was brought up from San José yesterday by Sheriff Van Eaton, and lodged in the station house until the Sacramento boat left. He was captured at Hall's Tavern, between San José and the New Almaden mines, after a severe fight, on the night that the Sheriff's party killed his two comrades. He confesses that he belonged to an organized band of robbers, under the command of Ingram, who held a Captain's commission in the Confederate army, signed by Jeff. Davis, and says they were armed and equipped by Secessionists throughout the State, among whom he mentioned several who are well known in Santa Clara county, and two in this city. He says he is only nineteen years old; but to a disinterested spectator he looks older by two or three years.

190

MORE STAGE ROBBERS AND THEIR CONFEDERATES CAPTURED
3 AUGUST 1864

Under-Sheriff Hall, of Santa Clara county, and Messrs. Hume and Van Eaton, Under and Deputy Sheriffs of El Dorado county, arrived from San José by the cars, yesterday evening, with the following splendid haul of Placerville stage robbers, captured by them in the vicinity of San José, early yesterday morning: Henry Jarbo, George Cross, J. A. Robinson, Wallace Clendening, Joseph Gamble, Joseph Jordan, Thomas Freer, James Freer, John Ingraham, Gately and Hodges—eleven. Sheriff Hall also brought down another of the robber gang named Wilson, whom he caught a week ago. He has been upon the track of all these men, and has been "spotting" them for the past three months. The confession of young Glasby confirmed his suspicions concerning them. The prisoners are farmers, for the most part, and resided round about San José; they are all Constitutional Democrats. They are not all charged with having taken part in the stage robbery, but some of them did, and the others were members of the robber organization, and accessories to the robbery before and after the fact. The organization dates back to the first of May, and the process of forming it was under way a good while before that. Its object was to raise men for the Confederate service, and they were to furnish themselves with equipments and supplies by guerrilla practice on the highway. Its ramifications are supposed to be very extensive, and they are known to have received aid and comfort from many prominent citizens. Some of the men arrested are well-to-do farmers. We are told by a resident of Santa Clara county that the prisoner Robinson is a brother-in-law of the editor of the Stockton Democratic organ, the Beacon. It is not known whether the men recruited for the Confederate service were to do duty only in this State, or elsewhere. The headquarters of the gang were at the house of a man named Hodges, who lives in the mountains east of San José. The six who robbed Wells, Fargo and Co's stage, started from Hodges'. Under-Sheriff Hall arrested this man at the "Willows," near San José, early yesterday morning, where he had unsuspectingly come on business. Two of the prisoners in this new haul are believed to have taken a hand in the late robbery of Langton's Express. Grant, Baker, and Captain Ingram, of the gang, have escaped, and left for parts unknown. Baker and Ingram were kept in hiding for a day or two by one Green Duff at his house near San José, and the latter furnished Baker a horse to escape

on. Mr. Hall arrested a man at Duff's house, yesterday morning. The man is a good Constitutional Democrat. The rumor prevalent here yesterday, that there was a terrific fight in San José the night before, with the stage robbers, was groundless; there was no fight. Colonel Jackson telegraphed for one thousand rounds of ball cartridge yesterday morning—in order to be prepared for an emergency, perhaps, in case one should arise—and the militia of San José were called together the night before and provided with a signal for the same purpose; they went further than was required, and lay on their arms in anticipation of trouble. Out of these ominous circumstances the rumor we have spoken of probably grew. Sheriff Hall also brought up with him last night three State prisoners, viz: Henry Hoffman, Charles Buford and Antonio Leiva, all sentenced for one year for grand larceny; he will take them to San Quentin to-day, and the El Dorado officers will depart with the Secesh stage robbers on the Sacramento boat this evening. No blood was spilled in arresting the robber gang. One posse of men under Sheriff Hall, and another under officers Hume and Van Eaton, left San José before daylight yesterday morning, and travelled in different directions; the former made six of the arrests, and the latter five.

191

ARREST OF ANOTHER OF THE ROBBING GANG
27 AUGUST 1864

Sheriff Adams learned a few days | ago (says the San José Patriot, of the 24th,) that a man named R. F. Hall, a farmer and stock raiser living on the Salinas, fifteen miles south of San Juan, was an accessory before the fact in the robbing of the Los Angeles stages. That it was at his (Hall's) house the robbers were harbored, and that he lent them a gun and hatchet, with a full knowledge of their felonious purpose. These facts coming to the mind of the Sheriff, he dispatched Under Sheriff Hall last week to make the arrest, which he succeeded in doing without difficulty, on Friday last. The Under Sheriff found R. F. Hall at home, upon his ranch, took him to Monterey, and surrendered him to the authorities of that county. The Under Sheriff states that Hall is an intelligent man, and a well-to-do stock-raiser, having six hundred head of cattle, a wife and three children. We learn that after long conversations with both Hall and his wife, the Under Sheriff obtained a good deal of information in regard to the combination of robbing gangs, and finding the officer acquainted with Hall's complicity with the robbers, a confession of the facts was obtained from him. Hall, like all others engaged in these schemes of robbing, is a Secessionist, and both he and his wife admitted that all connected with the band were bound to each other by horrid oaths to revenge any punishment inflicted on them.

"AND SUCH ARE COPPERHEADS"

James F. Dolan, sometimes called Donlan in the *Call,* ultimately could convince neither Judge Shepheard nor Judge Cowles that "it wasn't him, but the whiskey in him that uttered the treason." [20] He was ordered to pay a fine of two hundred dollars or go to jail for thirty days. In this case Davis Louderback, Clemens' pet peeve, prevailed over the defense attorney E. A. Lawrence.

192

A "CONFEDERACY" CAGED
26 AUGUST 1864

"When wine is in, wit is out." So remarked Judge Shepheard yesterday morning, when J. F. Dolan offered intoxication as an excuse for belching treason—and by the way, speaking of Judge Shepheard, it is every day becoming more and more apparent that in his incumbency, the people have got the right man in the right place. The Judge further observed that when a man is under the influence of liquor, being too bold and independent for caution, he is very likely to let out his real sentiments, and that although this Dolan pretends to be a loyal man when sober, he had no confidence in the profession of loyalty in a man who, when intoxicated, would heap curses on every thing pertaining to the

Union cause, declare himself a strong Jeff. Davis man, wish for the destruction of the Union army, and that he was in the Southern army with a musket on his shoulder, as did Dolan. Mr. Riley, in whose saloon Dolan began his disloyal manifestation, and who is evidently a thorough-going Union man, created a sensation in the Court room while testifying, very decidedly in his favor, by giving forcible expression to his feelings on the subject. Dolan had gone up to his counter and called for a Jeff. Davis drink: he wanted none other than a Jeff. Davis drink. Mr. R. told him he'd be d—d if any body could get a Jeff. Davis drink in his house, and incontinently turned him out, telling him at the same time that but for the fact of his being drunk, he would give him a d—d thrashing. Dolan, notwithstanding his good loyalty when sober, was held in the sum of one thousand dollars to appear at the County Court. A little loyal when sober, and intensely disloyal when the tongue strings are loosened by liquor—and such are Copperheads.

193

GOOD FROM LOUDERBACK
26 AUGUST 1864

During the examination of Dolan, yesterday, for uttering treasonable language, when Mr. Lawrence, Dolan's counsel, proposed to offer evidence to prove that the defendant was not a disloyal man when sober, Mr. Louderback, the young Prosecuting Attorney of the Police Court, happily observed that it would be like proving a man's piety as an excuse in a prosecution for using profane and obscene language. The defence was squarely met, and waived the excuse.

194

OUT OF JAIL
21 SEPTEMBER 1864

James Donlan, who has been serving out a term of imprisonment in the County Jail, for uttering treasonable language, yesterday paid into the County Court one hundred and fifty dollars, the balance of his fine, after deducting the equivalent of seven and a half days confinement, and was released. Jail life must be very satisfactory, for those who have been compelled to spend a few days there come out of it completely satisfied. They don't want to go back, nor stay any longer than they can help, under the polite attentions of the man who carries the key.

D. THE ELECTION CAMPAIGN

Political fever in the city rose steadily as election day neared.[21] District clubs for the Union and Democratic parties formed early and the central committees organized. Late in August McClellan and Pendleton were nominated in Chicago to run against Lincoln and Johnson, and the two parties soon held state conventions to name candidates for presidential electors and Representatives to Congress. At mass meetings each party tried to outdo the other in attendance and noise, in the brilliance of bonfire and gaslight, and—it seems—in orations of stupefying length. By late summer the Union party obviously was drawing larger crowds. Sam Brannan was reported to be so sure of the outcome that he bet $10,000 against $500 that Lincoln would carry California by 20,000 votes—a shrewdly accurate guess.

The city was crowded. Crop failures and business depression had increased unemployment, and idle men collected on the corners. As election excitement grew and crowds became more demonstrative, Chief Burke made a point of publicly displaying his beefed-up police force. The excitable Albert S. Evans reported disorderly street crowds flinging insults at soldiers. "I infer," he added, "that it wants but a word to create a riot here at any moment." [22]

Among the more boisterous were the McClellan Broom Rangers, the backbone of Democratic "demon-strations," as the writer Occasia Owen put it. Shouldering brooms and flourishing torches, the Rangers paraded in giant formations, cheering for Little Mac and groaning at the mention of "Abe Linkum" and the bloody Abolitionists. On the night of 11 October almost 3,000 Rangers passed the corner of Clay and Montgomery streets, their procession lighted by bonfires and fireworks. The Union press linked them with Confederate highwaymen and self-righteously condemned them for disturbing Union meetings. The Democrats, in turn, disapproved of a large Union parade including five hundred discharged California volunteers, and when soldiers pointedly drilled in Platt's Hall the night of a Broom Ranger gathering, the McClellan press complained indignantly.

Clemens stepped into this excitement immediately. Already experienced in political reporting,[23] he helped cover the presidential campaigns. Following the outbreak of war, the *Call* had taken an early stand in support of the North, and in 1864 it backed the Lincoln-Johnson ticket. Clemens did not write the political editorials, most of which are rather stiffly formal—but forceful—pronouncements. They probably were the responsibility of George Barnes or Frank Soulé. Nor did Barnes often, if ever, assign Clemens to Union party rallies, which were reported prominently in the *Call* with enthusiastic thoroughness. He used his local man primarily to cover Democratic gatherings. Since his reports were likely to be satirical, perhaps it is not too much to say that in its campaign against the Copperheads the *Call* drew on Clemens' talent for wielding the hatchet.

Clemens' political reporting kept the personal touch common to much of his *Call* journalism, and in it he expressed himself in familiar ways. He fell back on favorite words and images: the allusion to a secret rebel organization as "this secret-steel trap which is to catch all infernal Abolitionists and send them to perdition without benefit of clergy"; the comparison of Copperheads to "mourners at a funeral"; the reference to "a chaste and reliable Copperhead"; the use of "gobbling up." There are the slangy thrusts ("he couldn't go Tod Robinson"; "He was bitter on the San Francisco boys"), the occasional biblical echo, the involved syntax that catches colloquial rhythms, the highlighting of political cliché in order to ridicule it. The disrespectful tone is familiar and evident in his use of the first name alone, in the parenthetical comments, and in the satirical paraphrasing of the speeches, especially Beriah Brown's "strong case." Also typical is the cavalier approach seen in the abrupt dismissal of speakers as of no consequence, and the bold interpretation given their remarks. The misspelled names, the omissions of fact, and the habit of leaving meetings early are implicit comments on his attitude toward Copperhead orators and toward his own job as well.

"THIS SECRET-STEEL TRAP . . . TO CATCH ALL INFERNAL ABOLITIONISTS"

195

DEMOCRATIC MEETING AT HAYES' PARK
3 AUGUST 1864

The Democratic rally reported below protested the arrest of Charles L. Weller in late July for disloyalty. Weller, a prominent San Franciscan, was the brother of California's former governor John B. Weller and was chairman of the Democratic State Central Committee. When he was reported to have advised an audience to arm against the anticipated military draft in California, General McDowell ordered his arrest and Weller was held at Alcatraz until 17 August. Military correspondence designated him as Lieutenant Governor General for California of the feared and secret rebel order The Knights of the Columbian Star.

California military leaders believed that Beriah Brown also was a top officer of the knights. In 1864 Brown edited the San Francisco *Democratic Press,* whose offices were to be sacked by a mob after Lincoln's assassination in 1865. Brown was widely known for his belligerence and such epithets for Lincoln as "the widow-maker" and "the old miscegenationist." At the Hayes Park meeting his resolutions, so wearily summarized by the *Call* reporter, echoed provisions in the Democratic state platform. A year later Mark Twain returned his attention to Brown, still a belligerent editor, in his "Answers to Correspondents." [24]

Colonel Abner Phelps, who chaired the meeting, was a West Point graduate and a lawyer. Dr. Oliver M. Wozencraft was a city physician commonly regarded as one of the more extreme Copperhead leaders. Zachariah Montgomery, a Kentuckian by origin and a former California state assemblyman, was a frequent and effective spokesman for the anti-war, Southern wing of the Democratic party. Tod Robinson arrived in Sacramento in 1850 from the deep South and served as judge of the Sixth Judicial District. In the early 1860's he moved to Virginia City where, known for his outspoken hatred of Lincoln, he became moderately prominent in Democratic politics; the *Call* item speaks knowingly of him.

The Democratic Indignation Meeting at Hayes' Park, last evening, amounted to a very short row of small potatoes, with few in the hill. The whole number present certainly did not exceed four hundred, of whom at least one-half were Union men, or supporters of the Administration, drawn thither by curiosity and the cars. The meeting was called to order by Col. Phelps. Vociferous calls for Beriah Brown brought him to the platform, and he delivered himself of a few remarks substantially as follows:

Gentlemen:—We have assembled here to-night as American citizens —(Great noise in the hall here, and the speaker's voice was inaudible for several moments.) We meet here to offer no opposition to the Government; but we meet here to discuss the question of our rights as citizens. We ask for no rights but what each individual is entitled to; to do as we would be done by under all circumstances—at the same time we do not propose to surrender our rights as American citizens. (Applause.) This, I understand, is the object of the meeting. The first business, gentlemen, is to hear the report of the Committee appointed to draft resolutions.

The following resolutions were then handed Mr. Brown, who had previously been appointed Chairman of the meeting, which were as follows. (We omit giving the preamble at length, as it all amounted simply to a renewal of fidelity to the Constitutions of the State and United States, and a declaration of intention to maintain the laws and yield a willing support to all just and legally constituted authorities in the administration thereof, etc.; and to the best of our ability to support whatever good citizens may rightfully do, to maintain domestic peace and promote general welfare. That they demand nothing but a uniform and faithful administration of the laws, and no privilege but what is clearly and indisputably guaranteed by the Constitutions of our Government. It also declared that where there is no law there is no freedom, and contained the usual declaiming against the abridgment of the freedom of speech and the press.)

Resolved, That we regard with alarm all exercise of power by the United States Government, or its agents, not specifically delegated to that Government, and in derogation of the reserved rights of States, and in abridgment of the constitutional guarantees to the people, as tending to central despotism and the subjugation of popular liberty.

Resolved, That, whenever through fear of spies or informers, or the power of military commanders to arrest and imprison American citizens, they shall be deterred from peaceably assembling together and freely expressing their approval or disapproval of measures of public policy, the point is reached beyond which submission merges the freeman into a slave.

Resolved, That the spotless reputation of Bishop Kavanaugh, and the well-known patriotism and devotion of Charles L. Weller, to the Constitution and the Union, justify the belief that the arrest of these gentlemen was procured by the perjury of mercenary spies and informers, or by persons actuated solely by personal malice, and we can but express the sentiments of all honorable men in denouncing the employment of those degraded wretches, an offence to civilization, and a disgrace to humanity.

After the passage of the resolutions, the band discoursed a National air.

Dr. Wozencraft was then introduced by the chairman. His speech was simply a rehash of all the whinings and hypocrisy of Copperheads since the conflict began. He had much to say about the imminence of our danger of becoming involved in scenes such as are now being witnessed in the Southern States, from a determination on the part of large numbers to resist with force the arbitrary and unconstitutional measures that were being inaugurated in our midst. "The record of the Democratic party is but a record of the Nation's power and glory; while that of the Abolition party is a record of her shame and disintegration." He said there are but two parties—the Democratic party, whose mission is to sustain the Union, and the Abolition party, which is seeking to destroy it. There is no hope for Union, peace and prosperity, only through a Conservative Democratic Administration. The North was unanimous in their opposition to the idea of Secession. To the support of the Government in suppressing the Rebellion, there was not a dissenting voice until the war was made one of subjugation, abolition and confiscation. Democrats were law-abiding and constitutional people, and the present supporters of the Administration are the Secessionists. Jeff. Davis and his followers are simply their allies in the work of destroying the Government. The speaker predicted that "so soon as we get control of the Federal Government, which by the help of God we hope to do at the coming election, they (the Republicans) will declare that the Pacific States will withdraw and form themselves into a separate Republic." Here he read an extract from a speech of Mr. Seward's, and continued for about twenty minutes in the usual strain of his ilk.

At the close of his speech the band made more music. After which, Zach. Montgomery, of Marysville, appeared on the stand. He commenced by saying that he would speak from the record, (thereby meaning that he would read his speech from a manuscript, which he did.) They had assembled there to consider how they should preserve the liberties of the people of California, and avert the horrors of civil war. Then followed the inevitable tirade against the measures of the Administration and its appointed agents, for suppressing treason and taking seditious persons into custody. He said that there is no use to try to disguise the fact that there is danger of civil war in this State, and intimated that a certain party, chafing under the discipline of Abraham Lincoln, was on the verge of outbreak, and the smothered volcano might burst out at any moment, and that we were nearer the scenes which our brethren in the older States were now witnessing than many might imagine. There were but two roads before us; the one leads to civil war, the other to peace. He declared in so many words that the Administration were determinedly pursuing the former road. Its acts were all in direct violation of the Constitution, and every blow struck at that instrument only drove us deeper into the danger of civil war and its attendant horrors. He spoke, as did Wozencraft, like a man who was in the secret of an organization existing in our midst, with the sole object of resisting by force and arms, all disciplinary, police or administrative measures which, in their estimation, might be deemed unconstitutional or oppressive; and

they are to be the judges. Like the other speakers, he also referred to them in terms which might, without much distortion, be construed into an approval of their patriotic purpose. The speaker dwelt at great length on this danger, hidden from unprivileged eyes, and ready to create a storm—a general disruption in our very midst—ere we were aware of the least danger. In a word, if General McDowell arrests any more noisy and treasonable babblers, or insidious enemies to the Government, why we may look out for guns and a fight.

Mr. Montgomery's enunciation was very impassioned, and he seemed extremely fearful that the infatuation of the Administration would yet inevitably, and at no distant period, transfer to our own California all the horrors of the Eastern battle-fields. In conclusion, he conjured all, both Republicans and Democrats, to respect and obey the Constitution and the laws under it, as the only means of averting the terrible catastrophe, to the brink of which we have been brought; the only pacificator of that secret element, that is now only resting in a temporary lull, while preparing for the great and sudden effort which is to follow the next persistent attempt of the administrative authorities to enforce an "arbitrary measure."

After a little music to soften down the lion which Montgomery had roused, (within himself,) Tod Robinson was presented, and with all the blandishments of an adept at honeyfugling, he proceeded to tell the people of the wrongs they were suffering at the hands of the present Administration. He also knows something of their hidden danger, this secret-steel trap which is to catch all infernal Abolitionists and send them to perdition without benefit of clergy. He prefaced his speech by stating the fact that he was born under the behests of freedom, and held no right nor privilege by the tenure of any man's will. A recapitulation of his speech would fall on the ear much like the repetition for the thousandth time of an old threadbare story. Every Californian knows Tod Robinson by heart, and nobody believes anything he says. We left while he was speaking, in company with a good Democrat, who said he wasn't "going to listen to such a d—d rascal as Tod Robinson." Though he rather favored some of the other speakers, he couldn't go Tod Robinson. So we all departed, and the meeting shortly after broke up, with the close of Robinson's speech.

"A CONFESSION THAT COPPERHEADS . . . LOOK SAD, LIKE MOURNERS AT A FUNERAL"

196

AN ACCUMULATION OF COPPERHEADS
11 AUGUST 1864

Lincoln supporters overflowed Platt's Hall the night of 10 August to hear the Rev. Henry Bellows and General George Wright at a meeting that Frank Soulé, who sometimes acted as secretary at Union gatherings, may have reported for the *Call*. While that rally was going on, the *Call* local covered the Second Ward Democratic Club meeting. His report thoroughly disposes of "the inevitable Beriah," then quickly polishes off a Mr. Kirtland, who seems to have been W. P. Kirkland, a janitor employed by the National Democratic Association and presumably put on the program to lend the common touch. James W. Towne and Jacob Bacon were printers, binders and engravers with offices on Clay Street. Their decision to hire only supporters of the Federal Union may have been calculated to cause trouble between the "war" or Union Democrats and the "peace" Democrats, who wanted conciliation and compromise.

CONSERVATIVE DEMOCRACY AND SECESSION AFFILIATIONS—THE SAME OLD TALK OF TYRANNY AND RESISTANCE

Last evening some fifty persons, perhaps, chiefly of the Copperhead persuasion, assembled in the "Democratic Club Room," on the corner of Stockton and Filbert streets, for the purpose of effervescing a little. "Conservative Democratic" imaginations pictured it a grand rally of persecuted and hunted down patriots. A rational person saw nothing there but aberrated beings, hugging the bugbear of martyrdom and iterating the formula laid down by the secret agents of Jeff. Davis' Government. We do not propose to give a detailed report of their proceedings; it wouldn't pay. One speech is a type of the whole. It is only Secession and Treason, modified in ex-

Atkins Massey, a San Francisco undertaker (*California Historical Society*).

Major General Irvin McDowell, Commander of the Department of the Pacific
(*California Historical Society*).

The sunken *Aquila* at Hathaway's Wharf (*San Francisco Maritime Museum*).

The reassembling of the monitor *Camanche* at Steamboat Point (*San Francisco Maritime Museum*).

The *Camanche* at the dock (*collection of Roy D. Graves*).

pression according to the rational caution and shrewdness of the speaker. Mr. Brown, the inevitable Beriah, was there, of course, and of course he spoke; but as he holds the leading string of "conservatism" in this vicinity, the practice of extreme caution has at length almost perfected the faculty of couching treason in loyal phrases, or at least evading, with consummate tact, the danger of crimination.

MR. BROWN'S SPEECH.—Mr. Brown said that he did not feel able to make, at that time, an effort proportioned to the importance of the occasion, for all his energies were spent in fighting their battles. He didn't go there to make a speech, but "to look into their (Copperhead) faces, to receive the assurance that Democracy was not dead." Upon which equivocal announcement of the party's vitality, there was a stamping of feet by several indiscreet persons. Discriminating ones saw therein a confession that Copperheads were sickly hereabouts, and look sad, like mourners at a funeral. The speaker proceeded, with faultless attitude and gesticulation and a countenance beaming with the light that is supposed to foreshadow posthumous glories of the immolated hero, to state that he couldn't argue with his opponents in the present conflict; there was no issue; if there was he couldn't see it; didn't know how to frame an argument. Doubtless Alcatraz frowning just in sight of his position, bothered his powers of composition. Syntax gives botheration, when the soul of the rhetoric is to be something that must not be expressed, for fear of disastrous consequences. All the old issues, he went on to say, were gone, the conditions that formerly divided the parties and kept up the bonfires of

party strife, and there was now but a single question; one which admitted of no argument; a question of brute force; whether we had a Government, or were the subjects of despotism. Then came in the inevitable stereotyped hobby of "inalienable rights," referring specifically to a number of the propositions of the Declaration of Independence. He pointed the "Conservative element" to their melancholy state of discomfiture, and told them there was but one thing left for them to do; that was to adhere to their principles, associate, organize and—protest. They could do nothing more; there was no argument. Then Beriah put a strong case. He asked them: What if they should get up some morning and find one of their number mysteriously missing; one whom they loved, and to whom they had been used to looking for counsel; and the next morning another should be gone in like manner; and another and another, and so on indefinitely, without warning, and no one knew whither or for what end they were taken away; they would feel badly, they would gather in groups, with pallor in their countenances, and bated breath, and bite their lips with vexation. They would want to know what had become of those loved ones. It would arouse the feelings and impulses of every Copperhead in the community. At this juncture Mr. Lincoln suffered at Beriah's hands a comparison which we have not room to give in full; said many things savoring strongly of what opens the gates of Alcatraz, and meekly observed that what he was then uttering might deprive him of his liberties; verifying the old adage of "A guilty conscience," etc. He said that the Administration asked them to surrender their liberties for a time, to preserve the Government; he wanted to know what a Government was worth without liberty, (Applause,) and more of the same sort. The people of the United States were then damagingly compared to Turks. Mr. Brown warned them to beware of surrendering their liberties. "Liberties once surrendered could only be recovered at a bloody sacrifice; the price of liberty won from tyranny is the blood of the patriot." As for his part, he didn't propose to surrender; their liberties should only be surrendered with their lives.

Beriah entertained his "small but appreciative" audience for about thirty minutes, in which he adroitly exhibited the virtues of resistance to the arbitrary measures of the Administration, all of whose measures were arbitrary; and yielded the floor.

A resolution was then adopted by the meeting, which as adopted, proposed to instruct the delegates from the Second District to the County Committee to take steps to have our citizens protected from military arrests, to apply to the Governor to give us the protection of the civil law of the State.

A second set of resolutions were then presented, which were somewhat rich. They conjured all good Democrats to withdraw their support and patronage from all newspapers that were inimical to their policy, and to exert their influence against the influence of such papers, generally; the Morning *Call, Alta,* and *Bulletin,* specifically. Then followed a resolution holding up Messrs. Towne & Bacon to the scorn and contempt of all good Copperheads, and advising them to steer clear of their printing establishment, as "adverse to Democratic money," because they, the said Towne & Bacon, had proscribed good "Union-loving Democrats."

We were in hopes that the resolutions would have passed in that shape, but the glare of inconsistency hurt Mr. Brown's eyes, and he hoped the adoption of those resolutions would be deferred until the phraseology could be altered so as to preserve the spirit and intent, but have the appearance of inconsistency hid in more subtle "verbiage." The idea did not at first penetrate the copper-coated intellects of the "Club," but Beriah must be right, so they assented, and hypocrisy is to be added to inconsistency, for their stomachs to receive.

The President of the Club then observed that some people had denied that there were any speakers among them—thereby intimating that so far the assertion had not been negatived, which made Beriah think that Copperheads were unappreciative and stupid, for hadn't he just sat down? And to prove the contrary, he called upon a man named Kirtland to give them a little more of the same he had favored them with before.

After a little hesitation, Kirtland stepped forth, and there was

A SECCESSIONIST edifying the Club with the same he had told them before. We did intend to report his speech, and took some notes, but, before proceeding far, he openly avowed himself a Southerner, with Southern feelings, and entertaining a Southern view of the question, and we paused. His speech was rampant, unmeaning, superficial rant not even worthy the name of sophistry. Had it emanated from a Northern man, who had any influence to fear, it would have consigned its author to Alcatraz. But, as it was only the impotent ravings of one who knew where a display of heroism would be safe, neither the speech nor the speaker challenge attention. This man was followed by a Mr. Farrel, whom we did not remain to hear.

"HE GAVE IT TO THEM HOT AND STRONG, AND ACCUSED THEM OF GOBBLING UP EVERYTHING"

197

DEMOCRATIC STATE CONVENTION
8 SEPTEMBER 1864

The Democratic State Convention met 7 and 8 September to nominate five presidential electors and three candidates for Congress. One of the delegates from Tuolumne County was Steve Gillis' brother Jim, who was to be Clemens' host at Jackass Hill within three months. Clemens' report of the first day's sessions is brief but tart. Obviously he enjoyed recording James W. Coffroth's skepticism about the reigning Democratic martyr, Charles Weller. Formerly an editor of the *Spirit of the Times,* Coffroth made a reputation as a poet in Sonora and later was a state senator from Tuolumne County before setting up law practice in Sacramento. The convention nominated him candidate for Congress from the Second District. In 1868 Mark Twain included Coffroth in his dream list of passengers for a pleasure excursion around the world and implied that he was a spirited, fun-loving person.[25]

John G. Downey, California's seventh governor (1860–1862), was nominated congressional candidate from the First District, but turned the honor down. McKewen, mentioned by Clemens, may have been E. J. C. Kewen of Los Angeles County who was nominated for elector. James W. Mandeville had been a state senator from Tuolumne County and the United States Surveyor-General for California. John D. Goodwin was a lawyer who later went to the state assembly from Plumas and Lassen counties and became judge of the Twenty-first Judicial District. Thomas L. Thompson was a veteran newspaperman who became a California congressman and then United States Minister to Brazil. Barclay Henley was a San Francisco attorney.

C. L. Weller, Chairman of the Democratic State Central Committee, called the Convention to order yesterday noon, at Turn-Verein Hall. He observed, in the opening speech, that it was the most important Democratic Convention which had met since the adoption of the Federal Constitution, inasmuch as upon it would devolve to decide whether our liberties were to be preserved or destroyed. Beriah Brown was chosen temporary Chairman, and temporary Secretaries and a Sergeant-at-Arms were also appointed. A Committee on Credentials was appointed, consisting of one Delegate from each county. A Committee on Permanent Organization was chosen in the same manner. The Convention then adjourned until three P.M.

Afternoon Session.—As soon as the Convention met, the work of forming the Committees on Credentials and Permanent Organization was begun, when the discovery was shortly made that Chas. L. Weller and Beriah Brown held proxies for the San Diego and Shasta delegations respectively. This riled Coffroth, of Sacramento, and expelled from his system a two hours' speech which had probably been festering there all day, on account of the evident disposition of the San Francisco delegation to rule the roost. He gave it to them hot and strong, and accused them of gobbling up everything else they could get their hands on. He was bitter on the San Francisco boys. Weller replied that he did not conceive himself guilty of any

very heinous crime, in being the recipient of a proxy, and reminded the Convention, in a general way, that he had always been a good and consistent Democrat, and had suffered martyrdom for the cause. Coffroth hit him back; said he was ready to bring flowers and lay them at the feet of any who had actually suffered martyrdom, and then ungenerously insinuated that he "didn't see it." He couldn't recognize a martyr in a man whose misfortunes were all aces in a deal for a Congressional nomination, perhaps. So the afternoon was wasted in wrangling, and actual work cannot begin in the Convention until to-day. Downey, Weller and McKewen are the most prominent aspirants for the nomination in this District, and Coffroth in the Middle District, as we are informed by a chaste and reliable Copperhead. The permanent officers of the Convention are as follows: Chairman, J. W. Mandeville, of Tuolumne; Secretaries, John D. Goodwin, of Plumas, T. L. Thompson, of Sonoma, and Barclay Henley, of San Francisco. A Committee on Resolutions, consisting of five members, was appointed. They are to report to-day.

"HE CONSIDERED HIMSELF BETTER THAN A NEGRO ANY DAY"

DEMOCRATIC RATIFICATION MEETING 9 SEPTEMBER 1864

As a climax to their state convention, the Democrats gathered around a gaslit platform in Portsmouth Square the night of 8 September to affirm the nomination of McClellan and Pendleton on the national ticket. Brass bands played beneath oversized portraits of the candidates. A huge bonfire burned on Brenham Place, and rockets and roman candles lighted up the sky before and between the speeches. The *Democratic Press* jubilantly asserted that 6,000 persons jammed the plaza.

Editorials supporting the Union party had observed with delight that the fire-eating faction of Democrats—those who condemned the idea of preserving the Union through complete military victory over the South —were uncomfortable in trying to square their separatist impulses with their support of the patriotic "war Democrat" McClellan. Sensitive on this point, most of the speakers at the ratification meeting stoutly asserted their loyalty to the Union. Only the lawyer J. Douglas Hambleton went overboard, he whom Clemens called Hamilton and advised to join Jeff Davis' cabinet. Speaking at the state convention the day before, Hambleton had vowed that the southern people never would "submit to the degrading terms offered by the present Lincoln Administration. When the last cartridge and the last cap were exhausted, they would dig up the bodies of their dead and hurl them at their hated foe." [26]

Among the other speakers, Joseph P. Hoge—misnamed Hayne by Clemens—W. D. Sawyer, and John T. Doyle all practiced law in the city. William T. Coleman was a distinguished San Francisco citizen and merchant. Henry P. Barber—not Barbour, as Clemens wrote it—was a cultured Englishman who had settled in Sonora.

Several hundred men and boys of all political colors, were gathered at the Plaza last evening to see the sky rockets, look at the pictures and hear the music and speeches. It was expected, of course, that all the apostles and prophets, saints and martyrs of the peace makers and the Constitution preservers would display themselves, no matter how diverse in their different shades of Democratic conservatism, as the exponents of the party that is now vaunting its determination to wreak a terrible retribution on the members and supporters of the present Administration, under the leadership of George B. McClellan. While the speakers were concentrating their thoughts for the grand effort before them, the lights were suddenly extinguished and darkness became visible. The accident was ominous. Soon, however, all was ablaze again, and the work of the evening begun. Colonel Hayne was chosen to preside over the meeting. A very moderate and carefully guarded inaugural embodied his appreciation of the honor thus conferred on him, and his views in regard to the conduct and results of the forthcoming campaign. He had always been a Democrat and a thorough Union man, opposed to dismemberment under any circumstances whatever. He defined the policy of the Democratic party, and expressed his belief that the salvation of the country lay through the Democratic party. Colonel H. was disposed to be charitable towards his opponents, and, on the whole, showed that parental solicitude and the good example of Republican politicians have not been entirely lost on him. After the Chairman had closed his remarks, the Hon. H. P. Barbour of Tuolumne was presented to the meeting. He spoke of the humiliation of the party, during the while past, but congratulated himself and his audience that the genius of civil liberty had rolled away the stone from the tomb, and the Democratic party had come forth. He abhorred the man whose argument is vituperation and epithets in a political discussion. He challenged an impeachment of his Unionism or his patriotism; deprecated this fratricidal war; arraigned the Administration for nullification and negro equality; pointed to a Democratic Administration as the only hope for the restoration of the unity of the nation and the Government; declared his confidence in the issue of the campaign, and exhorted the party to unity of action, asking no quarter, but to fight under the motto of "victory or death." He considered himself better than a negro any day.

Mr. Doyle, one of the Electors for the State at large, delivered a short address. His effort was rather feeble, characterized by moderation entirely unnatural to Democratic speakers. The whole substance of his speech was, that after trying Mr. Lincoln's Administration for three and a half years, the nation were satisfied that to continue it would only be to sink the country inextricably in ruin. A man is needed at the head of affairs who combines the elements of civilian and soldier; who knows exactly the right thing to do and the right time to do it in. McClellan is the man. The mind of the speaker lit for a moment on the Monroe Doctrine, and finally eliminated through his organs of speech in feeble tones, the expression of a desire to vote for a competent man.

Mr. Wm. T. Coleman responded to a call in a speech made up of a little glorification, followed by the usual expressions of confidence in the re-

sult of the party, vindicating his own loyalty, and pointing to McClellan as the man who is to restore our primal fraternity. Mr. C. said he was not a sycophantic Peace man—a clamorer for peace on any terms, whatever. He wanted to see a pacification between the States as speedily as possible, but one based only upon honorable terms.

After Mr. Coleman closed, a Mr. Hamilton was introduced, and was the first speaker of the evening to cross the bounds of moderation. Before he exhibited his positive sympathy for the South, we had begun to think that the discreet caution or sober temper of the declaimers would afford but such slight grounds for criticism, beyond their usual arrogations, and their reflections upon the war policy of the Administration. We have not space to give even an epitomized report of any of the speeches, but suffice it to say that Hamilton with the growing vehemence of his nervous temperament, declaimed immoderately against the Administration; asked the people if they were prepared to respond to its bloody mandates; declared that but for the fact that they saw relief in an approaching election day, the opponents of the Administration would have resisted with blood, and that those who attempted to carry out its measures would long ere this have been in their graves. The speaker grew more virulent as he progressed, and sounds of dissatisfaction were heard from different persons on the stand. His speech was not well received. Hamilton has certainly mistaken his party—he can't vote for McClellan; he'd better go and get a situation in Jeff. Davis' cabinet. His speech was the regular old stereotyped Radical Copperhead tirade—not even excepting the attack on ministers of the gospel.

In appropriate order, followed next C. L. Weller. His first remark was a fling at General McDowell, referring to Bull Run. He is troubled with Alcatraz on the brain. He inflicted upon his hearers that exaggerated woe of his morbid imagination, which he glories in parading on every possible occasion, and with which he ardently hopes to create a current of sympathy and devotion which will carry him irresistibly to high political preferment.

We left Mr. Weller alternating between General McDowell and the Chicago nominee. His chief idea in approving the nomination of General McClellan seemed to be that he could now rant, vituperate and administer such counsel as he saw fit, and yet vindicate his loyalty by drawing on General McClellan's well-known patriotism and constancy to the Union.

During one stage of the meeting, two speakers divided the attention of the crowd. W. D. Sawyer, Esq., had been called upon by some who were too remote to hear the speakers on the stand, and he addressed them from the west side of the Plaza.

Editor's note: The write-up of Barber's speech in the San Francisco *Alta California* throws a revealing light on Clemens' reporting and, it seems likely, on the profound incompatibility between Clemens' temperament and the demands of his job. According to the *Alta,* Barber criticized the administration for doing nothing to help Negroes. He made the point that when they were set free, they were "left without work, without food, without clothing, and they die by hundreds,"[27] untrained and unable to support themselves. Clemens wrote that Barber arraigned the administration for its policy of "negro equality," but he gave no indication that Barber supplied defining details or reasons. Then Clemens added: "He considered himself better than a negro any day"—suggesting that racial bias was the ground of Barber's criticism.

The speaker's exact words are irrecoverable, but the precision of the *Alta* report is convincing. It is possible, although not probable, that Clemens' version may be explained by faulty hearing or inadequate note-taking or momentary distraction or lack of space in the newspaper. But his sharp thrust at Barber very possibly may express a real insight into Barber's hidden feelings. Or it may express the intuition that Barber's real motive in his remarks was deviously political or it may express merely a shaky inference drawn from the Englishman's cultivated manner and voice. The anti-Copperhead *Call* had reason to value Clemens' ability to slant his political reports—within limits—in favor of the Union ticket. Judicious propaganda would help elect Lincoln. Yet in much of his *Call* writing, political or not, Clemens also deviated from usual journalistic norms because he was incurably "literary." Possessing exceptional sensitivity, he was likely to sacrifice fact and objectivity to the quick intuition or to the compelling emotion. He was impressionistic rather than thorough, and he made the imaginative stroke for the joy of it.

Aided by a century of hindsight, we can visualize a hypothetical and ironic situation, occurring—let's say—in September 1864. A puzzled George Barnes enters the *Call* newsroom from his office with some of Clemens' political copy in hand. He confronts his local reporter, whom he will gently fire in a few weeks. "Look here, Clemens," he says, "this is all well and good, but next time let's have more facts and less invention!" After all, how could George Barnes have known who it *really* was that he was talking to?

Reference Materials

Appendix A

MARK TWAIN ON HIS DAYS AS A *CALL* REPORTER

[From *Mark Twain in Eruption*, pp. 254–260 (Autobiographical dictation of 13 June 1906).]

About forty years ago—I was a reporter on the *Morning Call* of San Francisco. I was more than that—I was *the* reporter. There was no other. There was enough work for one and a little over, but not enough for two —according to Mr. Barnes's idea, and he was the proprietor and therefore better situated to know about it than other people.

By nine in the morning I had to be at the police court for an hour and make a brief history of the squabbles of the night before. They were usually between Irishmen and Irishmen, and Chinamen and Chinamen, with now and then a squabble between the two races for a change. Each day's evidence was substantially a duplicate of the evidence of the day before, therefore the daily performance was killingly monotonous and wearisome. So far as I could see, there was only one man connected with it who found anything like a compensating interest in it, and that was the court interpreter. He was an Englishman who was glibly familiar with fifty-six Chinese dialects. He had to change from one to another of them every ten minutes and this exercise was so energizing that it kept him always awake, which was not the case with the reporters. Next we visited the higher courts and made notes of the decisions which had been rendered the day before. All the courts came under the head of "regulars." They were sources of reportorial information which never failed. During the rest of the day we raked the town from end to end, gathering such material as we might, wherewith to fill our required column—and if there were no fires to report we started some.

At night we visited the six theaters, one after the other: seven nights in the week, three hundred and sixty-five nights in the year. We remained in each of those places five minutes, got the merest passing glimpse of play and opera, and with that for a text we "wrote up" those plays and operas, as the phrase goes, torturing our souls every night from the beginning of the year to the end of it in the effort to find something to say about those performances which we had not said a couple of hundred times before. There has never been a time from that day to this, forty years, that I have been able to look at even the outside of a theater without a spasm of the dry gripes, as "Uncle Remus" calls it—and as for the inside, I know next to nothing about that, for in all this time I have seldom had a sight of it nor ever had a desire in that regard which couldn't have been overcome by argument.

After having been hard at work from nine or ten in the morning until eleven at night scraping material together, I took the pen and spread this muck out in words and phrases and made it cover as much acreage as I could. It was fearful drudgery, soulless drudgery, and almost destitute of interest. It was an awful slavery for a lazy man, and I was born lazy. I am no lazier now than I was forty years ago, but that is because I reached the limit forty years ago. You can't go beyond possibility.

Finally there was an event. One Sunday afternoon I saw some hoodlums chasing and stoning a Chinaman who was heavily laden with the weekly wash of his Christian customers, and I noticed that a policeman was observing this performance with an amused interest—nothing more. He did not interfere. I wrote up the incident with considerable warmth and holy indignation. Usually I didn't want to read in the morning what I had written the night before; it had come from a torpid heart. But this item had come from a live one. There was fire in it and I believed it was literature—and so I sought for it in the paper next morning with eagerness. It wasn't there. It wasn't there the next morning, nor the next. I went up to the composing room and found it tucked away among condemned matter on the standing galley. I asked about it. The foreman said Mr. Barnes had found it in a galley proof and ordered its extinction. And Mr. Barnes furnished his reasons—either to me or to the foreman, I don't remember which; but they were commercially sound. He said that the *Call* was like the New York *Sun* of that day: it was the washerwoman's paper—that is, it was the paper of the poor; it was the only cheap paper. It gathered its livelihood from the poor and must respect their prejudices or perish. The Irish were the poor. They were the stay and support of the *Morning Call;* without them the *Morning Call* could not survive a month —and they hated the Chinamen. Such an assault as I had attempted could rouse the whole Irish hive, and seriously damage the paper. The *Call* could not afford to publish articles criticizing the hoodlums for stoning Chinamen.

I was lofty in those days. I have survived it. I was unwise, then. I am up-to-date now.

. . . .

But, as I was saying, I was loftier forty years ago than I am now, and I felt a deep shame in being situated as I was—slave of such a journal as the *Morning Call*. If I had been still loftier I would have thrown up my berth and gone out and starved, like any other hero. But I had never had any experience. I had *dreamed* heroism, like everybody, but I had had no practice and I didn't know how to begin. I couldn't bear to begin with starving. I had already come near to that once or twice in my life, and got no real enjoyment out of remembering about it. I knew I couldn't get another berth if I resigned. I knew it perfectly well. Therefore I swallowed my humiliation and stayed where I was. But whereas there had been little enough interest attaching to my industries, before, there was none at all now. I continued my work but I took not the least interest in it, and naturally there were results. I got to neglecting it. As I have said, there was too much of it for one man. The way I was conducting it now, there was apparently work enough in it for two or three. Even Barnes noticed that, and told me to get an assistant, on half wages.

There was a great hulking creature down in the counting room—good-natured, obliging, unintellectual—and he was getting little or nothing a week and boarding himself. A graceless boy of the counting-room force who had no reverence for anybody or anything was always making fun of this beachcomber, and he had a name for him which somehow seemed intensely apt and descriptive—I don't know why. He called him Smiggy McGlural. I offered the berth of assistant to Smiggy, and he accepted it with alacrity and gratitude. He went at his work with ten times the energy that was left in me. He was not intellectual but mentality was not required or needed in a *Morning Call* reporter, and so he conducted his office to perfection. I gradually got to leaving more and more of the work to McGlural. I grew lazier and lazier, and within thirty days he was doing almost the whole of it. It was also plain that he could accomplish the whole of it, and more, all by himself, and therefore had no real need of me.

It was at this crucial moment that that event happened which I mentioned a while ago. Mr. Barnes discharged me. It was the only time in my life that I have ever been discharged, and it hurts yet—although I am in my grave. He did not discharge me rudely. It was not in his nature to do that. He was a large, handsome man, with a kindly face and courteous ways, and was faultless in his dress. He could not have said a rude, ungentle thing to anybody. He took me privately aside and advised me to resign. It was like a father advising a son for his good, and I obeyed.

[From *Roughing It,* Definitive Edition, Vol. IV (1922), pp. 136–144.]

I fell in love with the most cordial and sociable city in the Union. After the sage-brush and alkali deserts of Washoe, San Francisco was Paradise to me.

.   .   .   .

What a gambling carnival it was! Gould & Curry soared to six thousand dollars a foot! And then—all of a sudden, out went the bottom and everything and everybody went to ruin and destruction! The wreck was complete. The bubble scarcely left a microscopic moisture behind it. I was an early beggar and a thorough one. My hoarded stocks were not worth the paper they were printed on. I threw them all away. I, the cheerful idiot that had been squandering money like water, and thought myself beyond the reach of misfortune, had not now as much as fifty dollars when I gathered together my various debts and paid them. I removed from the hotel to a very private boarding-house. I took a reporter's berth and went to work. I was not entirely broken in spirit, for I was building confidently on the sale of the silver-mine in the East. But I could not hear from Dan. My letters miscarried or were not answered.

One day I did not feel vigorous and remained away from the office. The next day I went down toward noon as usual, and found a note on my desk which had been there twenty-four hours. It was signed "Marshall"—the Virginia reporter—and contained a request that I should call at the hotel and see him and a friend or two that night, as they would sail for the East in the morning. A postscript added that their errand was a big mining speculation! I was hardly ever so sick in my life. I abused myself for leaving Virginia and intrusting to another man a matter I ought to have attended to myself; I abused myself for remaining away from the office on the one day of all the year that I should have been there. And thus berating myself I trotted a mile to the steamer wharf and arrived just in time to be too late. The ship was in the stream and under way.

I comforted myself with the thought that maybe the speculation would amount to nothing—poor comfort at best—and then went back to my slavery, resolved to put up with my thirty-five dollars a week and forget all about it.

.   .   .   .

By and by, in the due course of things, I picked up a copy of the *Enterprise* one day, and fell under this cruel blow:

NEVADA MINES IN NEW YORK.—G. M. Marshall, Sheba Hurst, and Amos H. Rose, who left San Francisco last July for New York City, with ores from mines in Pine Wood District, Humboldt

County, and on the Reese River range, have disposed of a mine containing six thousand feet and called the Pine Mountains Consolidated, for the sum of $3,000,000. The stamps on the deed, which is now on its way to Humboldt County, from New York, for record, amounted to $3,000, which is said to be the largest amount of stamps ever placed on one document. A working capital of $1,000,0000 has been paid into the treasury, and machinery has already been purchased for a large quartz-mill, which will be put up as soon as possible. The stock of this company is all full paid and entirely unassessable. The ores of the mines in this district somewhat resemble those of the Sheba mine in Humboldt. Sheba Hurst, the discoverer of the mines, with his friends corralled all the best leads and all the land and timber they desired before making public their whereabouts. Ores from there, assayed in this city, showed them to be exceedingly rich in silver and gold—silver predominating. There is an abundance of wood and water in the District. We are glad to know that New York capital has been enlisted in the development of the mines of this region. Having seen the ores and assays, we are satisfied that the mines of the District are very valuable—anything but wildcat.

Once more native imbecility had carried the day, and I had lost a million! It was the "blind lead" over again.

Let us not dwell on this miserable matter. If I were inventing these things, I could be wonderfully humorous over them; but they are too true to be talked of with hearty levity, even at this distant day.* Suffice it that I so lost heart, and so yielded myself up to repinings and sighings and foolish regrets, that I neglected my duties and became about worthless, as a reporter for a brisk newspaper. And at last one of the proprietors took me aside, with a charity I still remember with considerable respect, and gave me an opportunity to resign my berth and so save myself the disgrace of a dismissal.

* True, and yet not exactly as given in the above figures, possibly. I saw Marshall, months afterward, and although he had plenty of money he did not claim to have captured an entire *million*. In fact, I gathered that he had not then received $50,000. Beyond that figure his fortune appeared to consist of uncertain vast expectations, rather than prodigious certainties. However, when the above item appeared in print I put full faith in it, and incontinently wilted and went to seed under it.

Appendix B

DISPATCHES FROM MARK TWAIN IN THE 1863 *CALL*

Students of Mark Twain's western writing have long been familiar with the ten letters and two telegraphic dispatches that Twain, writing from Nevada, published in the *Call* in 1863. While going through the files of the *Call,* I found four additional dispatches that he sent from Virginia City in the autumn of 1863, and I have reproduced them below. They add to the record of Clemens' connection with the *Call* before he joined the staff of that paper in 1864. All four appeared on the paper's front page.

2 August 1863, p. 1
Dispatches by the State Line
(SPECIALLY TO THE DAILY MORNING CALL.)
Tom Fitch in a Duel—Officer Interposes.

VIRGINIA, AUGUST 1.—Thomas Fitch, editor of the Union, challenged J. T. Goodman, editor of the Enterprise. They went out to fight this morning, with navy revolvers, at fifteen paces. The police interfered and prevented the duel.

MARK TWAIN.

29 August 1863, p. 1
Dispatches by the State Line
Disastrous Fire at Virginia City—Seventy Buildings Burned.

VIRGINIA CITY, AUGUST 28—1:40 P.M.—Fire broke out in a wood-pile at the back of Pat Lynch's building, between Union and Sutton Avenue, at half-past eleven o'clock to-day. The fire extended from Lynch's, at the south of Taylor street, to the new Court House; thence up the hill, to Summit street; southerly to Taylor and South, burning some seventy residences and frame buildings. The fire is still raging, but will probably be kept from the business portion of the city. It is impossible to give particulars before night.

(Second Dispatch.)
(Specially to the Daily Morning Call.)
The Virginia City Fire—Firemen's Riot—One Man Shot Dead—
Incendiaries Arrested.

Virginia City, August 28—10 p.m.—Four blocks, frame buildings, burned to-day, between B and Howard streets and Taylor and Sutton Avenue—loss, three hundred thousand dollars.

A riot afterwards occurred between No. 1 and No. 2 engine companies; probably fifteen men slightly hurt, and half a dozen badly. John Cullen, of No. 2, shot Edward Richardson, a miner, through the lungs, killing him instantly. Cullen is under arrest. A. and L. A. Vorbe, arrested as incendiaries, were let out on five thousand dollars bail. All stores and liquor shops have been closed by order of the City Marshal. A dozen special Deputy Sheriffs have been appointed for to-night. All quiet at present.

MARK TWAIN.

3 September 1863, p. 1
Dispatches by the State Line
Important from Nevada Territory.
THE ELECTION IN VIRGINIA CITY, GOLD HILL, CARSON AND DAYTON, N.T., YESTERDAY—SPLENDID UNION TRIUMPH—SUICIDE OF A PIONEER—JACK MCNABB SHOOTING POLICEMEN—TALK OF A VIGILANCE COMMITTEE, ETC., ETC.

Virginia, September 2.—Virginia polled 2,737 votes; Gold Hill, 1,086. The straight Union ticket is elected by an overwhelming majority. Same in Dayton and Silver City.

James A. Rogers, one of the earliest pioneers, blew his brains out this evening. Cause, "discouraged." He had been very low with the mountain fever for some time.

We had fifty extra policemen on duty all day. They were kept busy.

This afternoon, Jack McNabb, a notorious desperado, shot at a negro. He was not arrested. Afterwards, he created a disturbance, and Officers Watson and Birdsall tried to arrest him, when he shot Birdsall in the breast, and a special officer, named Burns, in the arm. Birdsall is not expected to live till morning. The people wanted to hang McNabb, but were prevented by the officers. Gen. Van Bokkelen, Territorial Provost-Marshal, asserted his authority, guarded the jail, and closed the saloons and stores. The city is infested with thieves, assassins and incendiaries.

There is some little talk of a Vigilance Committee.

MARK TWAIN.

Appendix C

CHRONOLOGICAL LIST OF *CALL* WRITINGS ATTRIBUTED TO SAMUEL CLEMENS (7 JUNE-11 OCTOBER 1864)

The following list gives the titles of *Call* pieces that I attribute to Clemens and is intended to serve those who wish to pursue the subject of his *Call* journalism. It includes those pieces which are authenticated by external evidence and those which reveal, in my judgment, the most compelling internal evidence of his authorship. In drawing up this list I used the kinds of evidence enumerated in the introduction to this book.

A word about my selection process: The *Call* published approximately fifty-four hundred local items during the period Samuel Clemens served it as local reporter. Those items vary in quality from the thoroughly routine to the creatively original. They range from many one-sentence notices to a relatively few lengthy articles. My attempt to identify Clemens' *Call* reporting therefore required the scrutiny of a vast number of heterogeneous pieces which appeared to cluster in groups along a scale of authenticity upon which it was not possible to assign each piece a unique ranking. It seemed certain that a few items clearly were not written by Clemens. External, or biographical, evidence firmly established others as Clemens' writing, and various kinds of pronounced internal, or stylistic, evidence bespoke the genuineness of still others.

But what about the thousands of pieces falling into two remaining groups? First were items cloaked in seemingly impenetrable anonymity: Clemens must have written many of these if (as I believe) he was the *Call's* only local reporter for most of the four months in question. Then there were those troublesome pieces which were anonymous but which nevertheless emitted a teasing whiff of authenticity. Hundreds of these items were too short to reveal a telling structural pattern or stylistic tendency. Nevertheless, I made tentative attributions for some of the items in the second group.

The final result from three separate evaluations of the fifty-four hundred items is this list of four hundred seventy-one entries, a total of less than 10 per cent of the local items published in the *Call* from 7 June to 11 October 1864. I believe the pieces named below lay serious claim to legitimacy, but my choices, it goes without saying, are neither infallible nor necessarily exhaustive.

Items reprinted in this collection are identified by number, and those in the Moffett Scrapbooks are also indicated.

Title	Date	Page and Column
Burglar Arrested [Item 120]	6/7	3/2
Another Chapter in the Marks Family History [Item 99]	6/11	3/1
Beasts in the Semblance of Men	6/12	3/1
Petty Police Court Transactions [Item 150]	6/15	1/3
Short-Hand Law Reporter	6/21	2/1
Another of Them [Item 1]	6/23	2/1
A Trip to the Cliff House [Item 77]	6/25	1/2
Charge Against a Police Officer [Item 162]	6/25	3/2
Hackmen Arrested	6/28	1/1
Accessions to the Ranks of the Dashaways	6/28	2/1
Missionaries Wanted for San Francisco [Item 165]	6/28	2/1
Board of Supervisors	6/28	3/1
Charges Against an Officer [Item 163]	6/28	3/1
Swill Peddlers	6/28	3/1
The Kahn of Tartary [Item 151]	6/29	3/1
Police Court	6/29	3/1
Municipal Records	6/30	2/1
The Sacrilegious Hack-Driver	6/30	3/1
The Old Thing [Item 107]	7/1	1/3
House at Large [Item 11]	7/1	1/3
School Children's Rehearsal [Item 46]	7/1	3/1
Police Commissioners [Item 164]	7/1	3/1
More Steamship Suits Brewing	7/1	3/1
Policeman Suspended	7/2	1/4
The Swindle Case	7/2	3/1
Chance for the Hotels	7/2	3/1
Stole a Shirt	7/2	3/2
The Secesh Highwaymen	7/3	1/1
Theatrical Record. City	7/3	1/2

The Camanche [Item 180]	7/16	2/1
Remarkable Clock	7/16	3/1
Independent Candidate for Stockton [Item 92]	7/17	1/3
More Cigar Smoking	7/17	1/3
The County Prison [Item 84]	7/17	3/1
Progress of the Camanche—the Libel	7/17	3/1
Juvenile Criminals [Item 160]	7/17	3/1
Too Infernally Accommodating	7/17	3/1
Assault [Item 139]	7/19	1/1
Real del Monte [Item 175]	7/19	2/1
Camanche Matters	7/19	2/1
Police Court	7/19	3/1
State Prisoners	7/19	3/2
Lunatic	7/20	2/1
A Stage Robber Amongst Us [Item 189]	7/20	2/1
The Poetic Rabies	7/20	2/1
Police Court	7/20	3/1
Police Applicants	7/21	2/1
Amazonian Pastimes [Item 85]	7/21	3/1
More Young Thieves	7/21	3/1
Attempted Mayhem	7/21	3/2
Detective Rose Again [Item 121]	7/21	3/2
The Boss Earthquake [Item 2]	7/22	1/2
The Police Court Besieged	7/22	1/2
Good Effects of a High Tariff [Item 22]	7/22	1/2
Rough on Keating [Item 161]	7/22	1/2
A Scene at the Police Court—The Hostility of Color [Item 23]	7/22	2/1
First Regiment Election	7/22	2/1
Arrest of a Secesh Bishop [Item 178; Mof. Scr. 4, p. 8, part missing]	7/22	3/1
Astonishing Freak of Nature	7/22	3/1
Demoralizing Young Girls [Item 116]	7/23	1/2
Rape [Item 133]	7/23	1/2
The Nose-Biter	7/23	2/1
Oh! That Mine Enemy Would Make a Speech!	7/23	2/1
Discharged	7/23	3/1
False Pretenses [Item 122]	7/23	3/2
Startling!—The Latest General Order	7/24	2/1
Obscene-Picture Dealers	7/24	2/1
A Merited Penalty [Item 117]	7/24	3/1
The "Nina Tilden"	7/24	3/1

Out of the Frying Pan into the Fire	8/3	2/1
A Movement in Buckeye [Item 100]	8/3	3/1
Attempted Suicide [Item 95]	8/3	3/1
Otium Cum Dignitate [Item 168]	8/4	1/3
Recovered [Item 96]	8/4	2/1
A Long Fast for Poor Dame Partlet	8/4	2/1
The Tournament	8/4	2/1
Police Calendar	8/4	3/1
Fruit Swindling [Item 108]	8/4	3/2
Soldier Murdered by a Monomaniac [Item 142]	8/5	1/1
Misfortune Gobbleth the Lovely	8/5	1/1
Gentle Julia, Again	8/5	1/3
Gridley	8/5	1/3
Still Going	8/5	2/1
For Seal Rock and the Cliff House	8/5	2/1
Observing the Day	8/5	2/1
Almost an Item	8/5	2/1
For Gambling	8/5	3/1
Another Obscene Picture Knave Captured—He Solicits the Custom of School Girls [Item 118]	8/6	1/4
The Fitzgerald Inquest [Item 143]	8/6	1/5
Attention, Hackmen	8/6	2/1
Police Drill	8/6	3/1
Judicial Strategy	8/6	3/1
Arrested for Theft	8/6	3/1
Attempted Suicide [Item 98]	8/7	1/3
The Makee Molasses	8/7	2/1
The People's Excursion	8/7	2/1
To Be Mended	8/7	2/1
Forfeited Bail	8/7	3/1
Locked Up	8/7	3/1
Row Among the Doctors [Item 97]	8/7	3/2
A Dead Dog Case	8/7	3/2
Shop-Lifting [Item 124]	8/7	3/2
Distinguished Arrivals	8/9	1/1
Assault by a House [Item 15]	8/9	2/1
Escaped [Item 119]	8/9	2/1
Mysterious [Item 14]	8/9	2/1
Our U.S. Branch Mint [Item 169]	8/10	1/1
They Got Her Out	8/10	1/1
Intelligence Office Row [Item 172]	8/10	1/2

Fine Picture of Rev. Mr. King [Item 28; Mof. Scr. 4, p. 7]	9/1	3/1
Lost Child [Item 93]	9/2	1/3
The Camanche	9/2	1/3
The Art Gallery	9/2	1/4
Rewards of Merit	9/2	2/1
The Mechanics' Fair [Item 58]	9/2	3/1
The Roll of Fame	9/2	3/1
California Branch of the U.S. Sanitary Commission	9/3	1/1
Suicide out of Principle [Item 38]	9/3	1/3
Afloat Again	9/3	1/3
The Lost Child Reclaimed [Item 94; Mof. Scr. 5, p. 62]	9/3	2/1
A Wrecking Party in Luck	9/3	2/1
Marine Nondescript	9/3	3/2
Labyrinth Garden [Item 59; Mof. Scr. 5, p. 62]	9/3	3/2
Contempt of Court [Mof. Scr. 5, p. 62]	9/3	3/2
Another Pawnbroker in Trouble	9/3	3/2
Opening of the Fair	9/4	1/2
Looks Like Sharp Practice [Item 109]	9/4	1/4
A Terrible Monster Caged [Item 127]	9/4	1/4
The Hurdle-Race Yesterday [Item 48]	9/4	1/4
Domestic Silks [Item 60]	9/4	3/1
The Californian [Item 29]	9/4	3/1
Brutal	9/4	3/1
Criminal Calendar	9/4	3/2
Peeping Tom of Coventry [Item 103]	9/6	1/1
A Small Piece of Spite [Item 174]	9/6	1/2
A Promising Artist [Item 30]	9/6	1/4
Turned Out of Office [Item 110]	9/6	1/4
Mechanics' Fair	9/6	1/5
The Pound-Keeper Beheaded	9/6	1/5
A Long Fast	9/6	1/5
Conjugal Infelicity	9/6	3/2
Set for Wednesday	9/6	3/2
Terrible Calamity [Item 73]	9/7	1/3–4
Amende Honorable	9/7	2/1
Christian Fair [Item 57]	9/7	3/1
In Bad Company	9/7	3/1
Police Court Sentences	9/7	3/1
Come to Grief	9/7	3/2

Dr. Raymond Not Removed [Item 114]	9/17	2/1
The Late Suicide—Coroner's Inquest [Item 115]	9/17	3/1
Cruelty to Animals [Item 20]	9/18	1/1
Theatrical Record: Maguire's Opera House [Item 52]	9/18	1/2
The Election of Coroner	9/18	1/3
Take One!	9/18	1/3
Due Warning [Item 81]	9/18	3/1
Suffering for Opinion's Sake	9/18	3/1
Chinese Banquet	9/18	3/1
The "Board" and the Rincon School	9/20	1/1
Mayhem	9/20	1/2
The Chinese Banquet	9/20	1/3
Camanche Matters	9/20	1/4
Board of Supervisors	9/20	3/1
The Theatres, Etc.: Maguire's Opera House [Item 53]	9/20	3/2
The Theatres, Etc.: Wilson-Zoyara Circus [Item 54]	9/20	3/2
Street Obstructions	9/21	1/2
The New Poundkeeper	9/21	1/2
Stabbed [Item 39]	9/21	1/3
A Terrible Weapon [Item 104]	9/21	1/4
Judgments Against a Steamship Company	9/21	1/4
Earthquake	9/21	2/1
Out of Jail [Item 194]	9/21	2/1
Board of Education	9/21	3/1
Strike of the Steamer Employes [Item 32]	9/22	1/1
Very Foolish Policy	9/22	1/1
Weller's Bust	9/22	1/1
The Consequences of Indefiniteness	9/22	2/1
Queer Fish [Item 67]	9/22	2/1
Trial of a Hackman	9/22	3/1
Female Assault	9/22	3/1
Stabbing Case	9/22	3/1
Farewell Address of Dr. Bellows [Item 187]	9/23	1/4
Arrested for Riot	9/23	2/1
Dedication of Bush Street School [Item 33]	9/23	3/1
Ah Sow Discharged [Item 40]	9/24	1/4
Children at the Fair [Item 68]	9/24	2/1
Ellen French Fined	9/24	3/1
The Monitor's Progress	9/25	1/1
The Mint Troubles [Item 170]	9/25	1/1
The Fair at the Fair [Item 69]	9/25	1/2
Mortimer Again [Item 148]	9/25	1/2

NOTES

References to Mark Twain's writings are, unless otherwise indicated, to *The Writings of Mark Twain* (see DE, below). The following abbreviations are used in the notes:

Alta   San Francisco *Daily Morning Alta California*

Bull   San Francisco *Evening Bulletin*

Calif   *The Californian*

Call   San Francisco *Daily Morning Call*

DE   *The Writings of Mark Twain,* Definitive Edition. 37 vols. New York: Gabriel Wells, 1922–1925.

GE   *The Golden Era*

JC   Mrs. Jane Clemens

MC   Mrs. Orion (Mollie) Clemens

MTB   Albert B. Paine. *Mark Twain: A Biography,* Centenary Edition. 4 vols. in 2. New York: Harper & Brothers, 1935.

MTCor   *Mark Twain: San Francisco Correspondent,* ed. Henry Nash Smith and Frederick Anderson. San Francisco: Book Club of California, 1957.

MTE   *Mark Twain in Eruption,* ed. Bernard DeVoto. New York: Harper & Brothers, 1940.

MTEnt   *Mark Twain of the Enterprise,* ed. Henry Nash Smith with the assistance of Frederick Anderson. Berkeley and Los Angeles: University of California Press, 1957.

MTL   *Mark Twain's Letters,* ed. Albert B. Paine. 2 vols. New York: Harper & Brothers, c. 1917.

MTP   Mark Twain Papers, University of California Library, Berkeley.

MTWY   Ivan Benson. *Mark Twain's Western Years.* Stanford, California: Stanford University Press, c. 1938.

News   Gold Hill *Evening News.*

OC   Orion Clemens

PM   Mrs. Pamela Clemens Moffett

SLC   Samuel L. Clemens

SSix   Samuel L. Clemens and Bret Harte. *Sketches of the Sixties,* ed. John Howell. San Francisco: John Howell, 1927.

TE   Virginia City *Territorial Enterprise*

TS   Typescript

WG   *The Washoe Giant in San Francisco,* ed. Franklin Walker. San Francisco: George Fields, 1938.

YS   *Scrap Book of Newspaper Clippings of Twain's Articles from The Californian, the Nevada Enterprise, Etc.* [Yale Scrapbook], Beinecke Library, Yale University.

INTRODUCTION

1. *DE*, XXVI, 136.

2. *MTE*, pp. 254–259. For complete text, see Appendix A.

3. William Wright, "Reporting with Mark Twain," *California Illustrated Magazine*, IV (July 1893), 171.

4. "The Editor's Page," *Nevada Historical Society Quarterly*, V (Jan./Mar. 1962), inside back cover.

5. Wright, p. 170.

6. SLC to JC and PM, Steamboat Springs, 19 Aug. 1863, TS in MTP, reprinted with changes in *MTL*, I, 91–92.

7. "Blown Down," *MTEnt*, p. 43. This item is preserved as one of the many clippings from *TE* in the Moffett Scrapbooks. These valuable collections were kept mainly by Orion, were handed down to Anita Moffett, Mark Twain's grandniece, and are now among the Mark Twain Papers at Berkeley.

8. "Due Notice," *TE*, 10 Jan. 1863, p. 3; the *Nevada Historical Society Quarterly*, V (Jan./Mar. 1962) reprints this entire issue of *TE* in facsimile.

9. *DE*, IV, 8.

10. Wright, p. 171.

11. "'The Third House' and Other Burlesques," Virginia City *Daily Union*, 30 Jan. 1864, p. 2.

12. "Mark Twain," San Francisco *Illustrated Press*, I (Feb. 1873), [21–22].

13. "'Mark Twain,'" *Ohio State Journal*, 6 Jan. 1872, p. 1 (a lengthy report of Twain's lecture, including verbatim passages). In 1891 Mark Twain acknowledged the importance of his urban reporting: "I was a newspaper reporter four years in cities, and saw the inside of many things . . ." From a letter quoted in *MTB*, III, 915–916.

14. SLC to [JC and PM?], undated [1863?] fragment, MTP. Copyright © 1969 by The Mark Twain Company.

15. SLC to JC and PM, Virginia City, 16 Feb. 1863, *Mark Twain, Business Man,* ed. Samuel C. Webster (Boston, 1946), p. 77.

16. SLC to JC and PM, Lick House, San Francisco, 4 June 1863, MTP. Copyright © 1969 by The Mark Twain Company.

17. *WG*, p. 18.

18. SLC to JC and PM, Lick House, San Francisco, 4 June 1863, MTP; SLC to JC and PM, Virginia City, 5 Aug. [1863], TS in MTP. Copyright © 1969 by The Mark Twain Company.

19. *DE*, IV, 136.

20. SLC to JC and PM, Lick House, San Francisco, 1 June 1863, *MTL*, I, 90.

21. Ibid.

22. George E. Barnes, "Mark Twain. As He Was Known During His Stay on the Pacific Slope," *Call*, 17 Apr. 1887, p. 1.

23. "Those Blasted Children," *WG*, p. 18.

24. SLC to [JC and PM?], un-

dated fragment, MTP. Copyright © 1969 by The Mark Twain Company.

25. *Call,* 14 Dec. 1862, p. 1; *MTL,* II, 773. See also in the *Call* for 3 Dec. 1862, p. 1: "Newspapers 'Bulling' Washoe Stock," and "Nearly a Duel," both from *TE*.

26. " 'Mark Twain's' Letter," *Call,* 9 July 1863, p. 2. The ten letters in the series are reprinted in Arthur E. Hutcheson, "Mark's Letters to San Francisco *Call* from Virginia City, Nevada Territory, July 9th to November 19th, 1863," *Twainian,* XI (Jan./Feb. 1952–May/June 1952).

27. The three front-page dispatches appeared 2 and 29 Aug. and 3 Sept. 1863.

28. Barnes, "Mark Twain," p. 1.

29. SLC to JC and PM, Steamboat Springs, 19 Aug. 1863, *MTL,* I, 91–92.

30. PM to SLC, St. Louis, 6 Mar. 1864, TS in MTP. Copyright © 1969 by The Mark Twain Company.

31. "In the Metropolis," *WG,* p. 75.

32. "Washoe, Information Wanted," *WG,* p. 61, and "In the Metropolis," *WG,* pp. 74–75.

33. SLC to [JC and PM?], undated [Feb. 1864?] fragment, MTP. Copyright © 1969 by The Mark Twain Company. In "A Good-bye Article," *GE,* 22 Nov. 1863, p. 4, Ludlow wrote: "In funny literature, that Irresistible Washoe Giant, Mark Twain, takes quite a unique position. He makes me laugh more than any Californian since poor Derby died. He imitates nobody. He is a school by himself."

34. Wright, p. 176.

35. Untitled article, Unionville *Humboldt Register,* 11 June 1864, p. 3.

36. *DE,* IV, 117–118.

37. "Irreverence," *News,* 16 June 1864, p. 2; Lovejoy is quoted in the article cited in n. 35, above.

38. "Mark Twain in San Francisco," *Bookman,* XXXI (June 1910), 370.

39. Barnes, "Mark Twain," p. 1.

40. *DE,* IV, 114.

41. SLC to OC, Virginia City, 26 May 1864, *MTEnt,* p. 203.

42. "Our Sixteenth Volume," *Call,* 1 June 1864, p. 2.

43. "Our Present Municipal Government," *Call,* 19 Apr. 1864, p. 2.

44. "The Working Men Triumphant," *Call,* 19 May 1864, p. 2.

45. "Chinese Labor," *Call,* 30 Oct. 1864, p. 2.

46. "The Question of the Day," *Call,* 26 May 1864, p. 2.

47. See William Brief, "San Francisco Correspondence," Carson *Daily Appeal,* 24 May 1865, p. 1. Brief wrote of Peter Anderson of the *Elevator* (later of the *Pacific Appeal*), a Negro journalist who was shunned by his "brother editors": "There is one individual, however, in our midst in enviable connection with our city press who is encircling his brows with a chaplet of immortality. I refer to Mr. Twain . . . It thrilled me with delight to see Twain and Anderson the other day promenading Montgomery street arm in arm. Anderson really treated Twain with kindness and familiarity."

48. "The Town Crier," San Francisco *News Letter and Pacific Mining Journal,* XV (16 Sept. 1865), 9.

49. *MTE,* p. 256.

50. "Burglar Arrested," 7 June 1864, p. 3, is the first *Call* item I attribute to Clemens.

51. "Our Sixteenth Volume," 1 June 1864, p. 2.

52. *DE,* IV, 138; D. F. Verdenal, "In New York," San Francisco *Sunday Chronicle,* 10 Apr. 1887, p. 3;

Barnes, "Mark Twain," p. 1; *MTL*, I, 99–100; SLC to OC and MC, "Call Office" San Francisco, 28 [Sept. 1864], MTP.

53. As quoted in Will Clemens, *Mark Twain: His Life and Work* (San Francisco, 1892), pp. 56–57.

54. *MTE*, p. 255.

55. *DE*, VII, 193–197; originally "The Facts," *Calif*, 26 Aug. 1865, p. 5. The editorial office in this sketch is that of the *Calif*.

56. *MTE*, p. 255.

57. "Almost an Item," p. 2. The manufactured humor of this piece is reminiscent of some of Clemens' early apprentice writing. Clemens used the southern expression "no-rate" elsewhere. The punctuation within the parentheses follows his customary practice at this time.

58. *MTE*, p. 254.

59. "Inquirer, Sacramento" in "Answers to Correspondents," *Calif*, 8 July 1865, p. 5.

60. "Past and Present," *Call*, 10 Mar. 1878, p. 1. Every indication suggests that George E. Barnes wrote this unsigned article on the history of the *Call*.

61. Franklin Soulé took an advanced degree in journalism at Wesleyan University in Connecticut in 1841 and edited newspapers in Mississippi and New Orleans before moving to San Francisco in 1849. A prolific versifier and one of the authors of *The Annals of San Francisco* (1854), he held responsible positions on several city newspapers before joining the *Call* in 1864. Two years before Soulé's death in 1882, Mark Twain remembered him as "one of the sweetest and whitest & loveliest spirits that ever wandered into this world by mistake . . . I worked at his side in the Morning Call office . . ." (SLC to William Dean Howells, Quarry Farm [Elmira], 3 Sept. [1880], *Mark Twain-Howells Letters*, Cambridge, Mass., 1960, I, 325).

62. McGrew left the city for the East in November 1865, but some years later he showed up on the *Call* as legislative reporter. See Amigo [Albert S. Evans], "Our San Francisco Correspondence," *News*, 18 Nov. 1865, p. 2; "Past and Present," p. 1.

63. *MTE*, p. 259. "Smiggy McGuirrel" is the title of two song sheets published in the early 1860's by De Marsan and by Wrigley, the latter as sung by Charlie Gardner at the American Concert Hall on Broadway. A different version titled "Smiggy Maglooral" is in William W. Delaney, *Delaney's Irish Song Book: Number 3* (New York, 189?), p. 2. McGuirrel, evidently popular in minstrelsy, appears as Smiggy McGlural in "Smiggy McGlural's Speech.—A Bold Stroke for the Presidency," *GE*, 3 July 1864, p. 3 (a probable source for Mark Twain's knowledge of the name) and *Yankee Notions*, XIII (Sept. 1864), 290. Here Smiggy, running for President, is an Irish demagogue who promises all things to everybody; his campaign speech is larded with comic and chauvinistic tall talk.

64. "The Pavilion Concert and Ball," *Call*, 8 Oct. 1864, p. 1.

65. SLC to JC and PM [San Francisco], 25 Sept. 1864, *MTL*, I, 100.

66. Frank Soulé to SLC, San Francisco, 31 Mar. 1873, MTP; Barnes, "Mark Twain," p. 1.

67. SLC to William Wright, Occidental, San Francisco, 15 [July 1864], William Wright Collection, courtesy of the Bancroft Library, Berkeley; SLC to JC and PM [San Francisco], 25 Sept. 1864, *MTL*, I, 100; SLC to OC and MC, San Fran-

cisco, 12 Aug. [1864], MTP.

68. *Call,* 25 Sept. 1864, p. 3.

69. "Convicted," *Call,* 8 Oct. 1864, p. 3.

70. The references used for the paragraph are: *DE,* IV, 115; "The Facts," *SSix,* pp. 180–187; SLC to JC and PM [fragment c. Apr. 1863], TS in MTP; "Interviewing the Interviewer" (DeVoto No. 306, MTP); "The Back Number: a Monthly Magazine," TS in MTP c. 1893; "Mark Twain's Letters from Washington," No. IX, *TE,* 7 Mar. 1868, p. 1; "Mark Twain's Letter," Chicago *Republican,* 19 Feb. 1868; SLC to OC [19 Aug. 1869], *The Love Letters of Mark Twain,* ed. Dixon Wecter (New York, 1949), pp. 102–104; "Licence of the Press" (Paine No. 275, MTP), c. 1873; "School of Journalism" (Paine No. 70, MTP).

71. "Past and Present," p. 1; Barnes, "Mark Twain," p. 1. Barnes's comments were made when he was stung by publicity which incorrectly implied that he had grossly underpaid Clemens.

72. James J. Ayers, *Gold and Sunshine: Reminiscences of Early California* (Boston, 1922), pp. 223–224.

73. Barnes, "Mark Twain," p. 1.

74. *Call,* 28 Aug. 1864, p. 3.

75. "Police Court," *Call,* 19 July 1864, p. 3.

76. "Board of Supervisors," 30 Aug. 1864, p. 3; "The Pound-keeper Beheaded," *Call,* 6 Sept. 1864, p. 1; "The New Poundkeeper," *Call,* 21 Sept. 1864, p. 1.

77. "Caving In," *Call,* 30 July 1864, p. 2; "Still Going," *Call,* 5 Aug. 1864, p. 2.

78. *MTE,* p. 256.

79. *MTE,* p. 265.

80. In his column "Our San Francisco Correspondence" dated 13 October, Albert S. Evans wrote: "Mark had a brief and not very eventful career as a local in San Francisco" (*News,* 15 Oct. 1864, p. 3). "Had a Fit" (Item 21), published 11 October, is the latest item in the *Call* that I attribute to Clemens.

81. "Past and Present," p. 1.

82. *MTE,* pp. 259, 260, 304; *DE,* IV, 144; *Mark Twain's Autobiography,* ed. A. B. Paine (New York, 1924), I, 242.

83. SLC to Rollin Daggett, *TE,* 3 Feb. 1878, quoted from Francis Phelps Weisenburger, *Idol of the West* (Syracuse, New York, 1965), p. 58.

84. *From Sea to Sea,* II (New York, 1914), p. 181.

85. *DE,* IV, 144. In "Our San Francisco Correspondence," *News,* 15 Oct. 1864, p. 3, Albert S. Evans reported that Clemens "says he left the *Call* because 'They wanted me to w-o-r-k a-t n-i-g-h-t-s, and d-a-m-n m-e if I'll work n-i-g-h-t-s for any man a l-i-v-i-n-g!' " But Clemens had stopped night work more than a month earlier.

86. *MTE,* p. 256.

87. "Disgraceful Persecution of a Boy," *Galaxy,* IX (May 1870), 723, reprinted *Contributions to The Galaxy 1868–1871 by Mark Twain,* ed. Bruce R. McElderry, Jr. (Gainesville, Florida, 1961), p. 43. Three years later an anonymous writer who claimed to have worked with Clemens in Virginia City recorded in the San Francisco *Illustrated Press* that Clemens, as "local-items man on the *Call,*" had his items "sadly slashed, and clipped, and decapitated, until he became persuaded that 'what they wanted of him principally in the *Call* was his legs . . .' " —"Mark Twain," San Francisco *Illustrated Press,* I (Feb. 1873), [22].

88. *MTE,* p. 256.

89. Quarry Farm [Elmira], 3 Sept. [1880], *Mark Twain-Howells Letters*, I, 326.

90. For example, "Locked Up," *Call*, 7 Aug. 1864, p. 3: "A large pile of boys, ranging from ten to fifteen years of age, were locked up in a cell in the city prison, yesterday, to give them a modified conception of what they may expect if they continue to throw stones at Chinamen and engage in other evil pursuits." In reporting the many arrests of Chinese, the *Call*—and Clemens?—fairly often forced a joke at their expense, one way of flinging "bold brave mud," as in "Astonishing Freak of Nature," *Call*, 22 July 1864, p. 3: "Officers Lindheimer and Brant arrested Ah How and Ah Sow, for misdemeanor, yesterday. This latter cuss is an astonishing freak of nature, being unquestionably a male sow. We saw him. We have mentioned the circumstance because we thought it must necessarily be interesting to naturalists."

91. "Criminal Calendar," 4 Sept. 1864, p. 3.

92. "Discharged," 10 Sept. 1864, p. 3; "The Battered Chinaman Case," 11 Sept. 1864, p. 3.

93. "A Chance for Christian Missionaries," *Alta*, 4 Sept. 1864, p. 1.

94. "Pleasant Games for California Children," *Calif*, 9 Sept. 1865, p. 4. This piece also suggests setting dogs on Chinese carrying bundles, and it alludes to police indifference.

95. 12 Dec. 1865, p. 2.

96. *GE*, 21 Jan. 1866, p. 5, from *TE;* reprinted *WG*, pp. 97–99.

97. "The Treaty with China," New York *Tribune*, 4 Aug. 1868, p. 1.

98. "Our San Francisco Correspondence," *News*, 15 Oct. 1864, p. 3.

99. Barnes, "Mark Twain," p. 1.

100. "The Brummel-Arabella Fragment," *Mark Twain's Satires & Burlesques*, ed. Franklin R. Rogers (Berkeley, 1967), pp. 207–215.

101. See in the San Francisco *Dramatic Chronicle* for 1865: "Another Nabob," 26 Oct., p. 4; "Distressed," 27 Oct., p. 3; "Savage Little 'Call,'" 27 Oct., p. 4; "'Bummer' Not Dead," 3 Nov., p. 4; "'Call' Style of Criticism," 4 Nov., p. 2; "Cowardly Little 'Call,'" 11 Nov., p. 4; "How Dare You?," 19 Dec., p. 4.

102. "San Francisco Letter," dated 24 Jan. [1866], *YS*, p. 46.

103. "'Mark Twain's' Farewell," *Alta*, 15 Dec. 1866, p. 2.

104. "Our San Francisco Correspondence," *News*, 2 July 1864, p. 2; dated 30 June.

105. *MTB*, I, 257–258.

106. See the headnote to "The New Chinese Temple" (Item 44).

107. Clemens gave publicity to Orion, to his Nevada colleague Andrew J. Marsh, and to Jack Perry, marshal of Virginia City and a personal favorite. He noted that his friends Charley Bryan and Billy Claggett were stumping Nevada in opposition to the proposed state constitution, and he recorded the election of his old friend Ruel Gridley as president of the Austin Christian Association. He praised his billiard crony John B. Winters, president of the Yellow Jacket Silver Mining Company. He wrote up an embarrassing predicament of a former competitor, John B. Church, publisher of the Virginia City *Union*. He ridiculed the fiery Thomas Fitch, upon Fitch's nomination as Nevada's delegate to Congress. Clemens' outburst against Fitch, whom he had known well in Virginia City, came not long before he informed Orion by letter that Fitch was a two-faced dog who would blast his own mother's reputation to gain po-

litical advantage. And he poked fun at William M. Stewart (as he had in Nevada), soon to become Senator Stewart. Not long before Clemens left for the East, he still was working Stewart over ("Gas," San Francisco *Examiner*, 3 Nov. 1865, p. 3, from *TE*). For other published items referred to above, see in the 1864 *Call:* "Short-Hand Law Reporter," 21 June, p. 2; "Its Opponents," 13 July, p. 1; "Gridley," 5 Aug., p. 1; "Fair," 28 Aug., p. 1; "Great Seal of Nevada," 6 Oct., p. 2; "For the East," 16 Sept., p. 3; "Washoe Congressional Gossip," 18 Aug., p. 1; "A Virginia City Editor Imprisoned," 12 June, p. 1; "Insists on Its Correctness," 17 June, p. 3; "John Church," 8 July, p. 1; "Personal," 31 July, p. 1; "It Was True," 10 Aug., p. 1; "The Washoe Convention," 14 Aug., p. 2; "Dr. Bellows Safe," 31 July, p. 2.

108. I have found no evidence that Clemens' items were significantly edited by Barnes or another before being set in type, and my impression is that they were not. Clemens wrote many of his reports shortly before the late deadline. Moreover, he was an experienced writer with a reputation. According to Mark Twain, Barnes's censorship of his article attacking abuse of the Chinese came when he "found it in a galley proof and ordered its extinction" (*MTE*, p. 256). One wonders why the editor did not rephrase certain of Clemens' carelessly written *Call* items. Furthermore, the punctuation in the printed items generally follows Clemens' practice at that time.

109. 24 Dec. 1863, p. 1. The middle section on Margaret Johns's fall from her "respectable circle" is omitted.

110. "Biting His Nose," p. 3.

111. "Attempted Mayhem," 21 July 1864, p. 3.

112. *Call*, 22 July 1864, p. 1.

113. 22 July 1864, p. 5.

114. The *News* (16 Aug. 1864, p. 1) prefaced "What a Sky Rocket Did" (Item 79) with: "Mark Twain, now 'local' of the *Call*, thus describes the adventures and consequences of a Sky Rocket at San Francisco." The Unionville *Humboldt Register* (10 Sept. 1864, p. 2) published "Man Run Over" (Item 10) and headed it "One of Mark's Whoppers."

115. This collection reprints sixteen of the twenty-six *Call* pieces found in the Moffett Scrapbooks. In my judgment, twenty-two of the twenty-six are by Clemens, and these are documented in Appendix C. Two pieces, I believe, clearly are not by Clemens: the poem "The Volunteer's Vision" (4 Sept., p. 4) and an editorial titled "A Compromise Impossible" (6 Sept., p. 2); and one, "A Washoe Souvenir" (17 Aug., p. 1), probably is not. The twenty-sixth item, "The 'Republic' of Jones" (25 Aug., p. 1) consists almost entirely of a lengthy quotation from the Natchez *Courier* of 12 July.

116. I, 256.

PART ONE: THE LOCAL AT LARGE

"THE SUPERNATURAL BOOT-JACK" (pages 39–42)

1. "Earthquakes Yesterday," *Call*, 21 May 1864, p. 2.

2. "The Great Earthquake in San Francisco," New York *Weekly Review*, 25 Nov. 1865, p. 5, reprinted in Paul Carter, "Mark Twain Describes a San Francisco Earthquake," *PMLA*, LXXII (1957),

997–1004. See also: "The Cruel Earthquake," *News*, 13 Oct. 1865, p. 2, reprinted from *TE*; "Earthquake Almanac," San Francisco *Dramatic Chronicle*, 17 Oct. 1865, p. 3, and *GE*, 22 Oct. 1865, p. 1, the latter reprinted in *WG*, pp. 90–91; *DE*, IV, 138–143.

3. "San Francisco Correspondence," Napa County *Reporter*, 11 Nov. 1865, p. 2.

4. " 'Mark Twain' in the Metropolis," *GE*, 26 June 1864, p. 3, reprinted *WG*, pp. 74–76.

THE STREETS OF SAN FRANCISCO
(pages 43–53)

1. "Happenings of the Week," *Calif*, 8 Oct. 1864, p. 12.

2. For example, a few days after "Trot Her Along" appeared, he stated in a letter that his friend Dr. Bellows was "stuck after my local items," and forty years later he was still using the phrase with relish in "A Horse's Tale." SLC to OC and MC, San Francisco, 12 Aug. [1864], MTP. Copyright © 1969 by The Mark Twain Company; *DE*, XXVII, 167.

3. "Exit 'Bummer,' " reprinted from *TE* of 8 Nov. 1865 in *Calif*, 11 Nov., p. 12. Twain wrote that Bummer "died with friends around him to smooth his pillow and wipe the death-damps from his brow, and receive his last words of love," in contrast to the death Tom Sawyer later imagined for himself: "out in the cold world, with no shelter over his homeless head, no friendly hand to wipe the death-damps from his brow, no loving face to bend pityingly over him when the great agony came" (*DE*, VIII, 27).

On Bummer's death see: in the *Call*, "In Articulo Mortis," 2 Nov. 1865, p. 1, and "When 'Bummer' Died," 4 Nov. 1865, p. 2; "Exit

'Bummer,' " *Bull*, 2 Nov. 1865, p. 3; "Dead Indeed!," San Francisco *Examiner*, 4 Nov. 1865, p. 3; "Bummerians," *GE*, 5 Nov. 1865, p. 4. On Bummer's history, see "San Francisco Correspondence," by William Brief, Carson Daily *Appeal*, 28 May 1865, p. 1; Robert E. Cowan, Anne Bancroft, and Addie L. Ballou, *The Forgotten Characters of Old San Francisco* (Los Angeles, 1964), pp. 61–89.

4. " 'Mark Twain' on the Dog Question," *Call*, 9 Dec. 1866, p. 3.

5. "A New Business for Shiner No. 1," *Call*, 31 Jan. 1863, p. 1; "Playing it Sharp on Shiner No. 2," *Call*, 21 Jan. 1864, p. 3.

"WE RAKED THE TOWN FROM END TO END"
(pages 54–68)

1. "Accessions to the Ranks of the Dashaways," *Call*, 28 June 1864, p. 2.

2. *The Celebrated Jumping Frog of Calaveras County, and Other Sketches* (New York, 1867), pp. 58–59, reprinted from "Bearding the Fenian in His Lair" in "San Francisco Letter" dated 28 Jan. [1866], *TE*, clipping in *YS*, opposite p. 37.

3. SLC to JC and PM, [San Francisco], 25 Sept. 1864, *MTL*, I, 100; "Specie and Currency" in "San Francisco Letter" dated 15 Feb. [1866], *TE*, clipping in *YS*, p. 54.

4. Amigo (Albert S. Evans), "Our San Francisco Correspondence," *News*, 3 Sept. 1864, p. 2; "Opening of the 'Cosmopolitan,' " *Bull*, 1 Sept. 1864, p. 3.

5. "Letter from Mark Twain" dated Carson City, 12 Dec. 1863, *TE* n. d., reprinted *MTEnt*, pp. 96–100. Mark Twain wrote of Henning later in "San Francisco Letter" dated 6 Feb. [1866], *TE*, clipping in *YS*, opposite p. 41.

6. The charges against Pelton are detailed in *The Public Schools of San Francisco. John C. Pelton's Course in Regard to the Same Unmasked* (San Francisco, 1865). For the Pelton controversy, see in the 1864 *Call:* "The Agony Over," 29 June, p. 2; "Board of Education," 13 July, p. 3; 21 Sept., p. 3; 28 Sept., p. 3; "The 'Board' and the Rincon School," 20 Sept., p. 1; "The Board of Education's Fight against Pelton," 24 Sept., p. 1. Other contemporary accounts are: "San Francisco Dispatch," Esmeralda *Union,* 24 Sept. 1864, p. 2; "Versus Pelton," *GE,* 25 Sept. 1864, p. 4; "San Francisco Correspondence," *News,* 20 May 1865, p. 2.

7. J. C. Pelton to SLC, undated, MTP. Pelton may have remembered the warm defense of his cause by the *Call* reporter, very probably the outspoken and censorious Clemens, when Pelton came before the Board of Education 13 Sept.: "As a Committee of the Whole, the Board annulled the certificate of Mr. J. C. Pelton, Principal of the Rincon Grammar School, and one of the most efficient members of the Department. No cause was assigned for this measure . . . The Director of Mr. Pelton's District and Dr. Grover opposed the measure, and moved that it be laid over until the next meeting; but the Board was too anxious to get rid of a man whose good sense and perception made him capable of appreciating properly their unmitigated stupidity, and stood as a check to their tyranny" ("Secret Session" in "Board of Education," *Call,* 14 Sept. 1864, p. 3).

8. OC to the Reverend Thomas Starr King, Carson City, 26 Feb. 1864, MTP. The letter shows that Orion and Mollie Clemens were on good terms with the Kings.

9. "Podgers' Letter from New York," *Alta,* 10 Jan. 1866, p. 1. Clemens mentioned Ogden's purchase of *The Californian* in *DE,* IV, 145.

10. See in the 1864 *Call:* "Arrested for Riot," 23 Sept., p. 2; "The Rioters," 25 Sept., p. 3; "Trial of the Folsom Street Wharf Rioters," 6 Oct., p. 3.

11. "Past and Present," p. 1.

12. Some examples are: "Sanitary Fund," 12 Aug., p. 2; "Dr. Bellows' Address Last Evening," 13 Aug., p. 1; "Farewell Address of Dr. Bellows" (Item 187), 23 Sept., p. 1, all 1864.

13. "Dedication of the New School House," *Alta,* 23 Sept. 1864, p. 1.

SAN FRANCISCO'S CHINESE (pages 69–84)

1. "Goldsmith's Friend Abroad Again," *Galaxy,* X (Oct. 1870), 569–571; reprinted *Contributions to The Galaxy . . . ,* pp. 79–81.

2. "Chief of Police's Report," *San Francisco Municipal Reports, for the Fiscal Year 1864–5, Ending June 30, 1865* (San Francisco, 1865), p. 139.

3. "Around the World. Letter No. 7," Buffalo *Express,* 22 Jan. 1870, p. 2.

4. Ibid.

5. *DE,* IV, 105.

6. "The Treaty with China," New York *Tribune,* 4 Aug. 1868, pp. 1–2.

7. "Difficulty of Swearing Chinamen," *Call,* 25 Aug. 1864, p. 1.

8. *MTCor,* p. 81; Franklin R. Rogers, *Mark Twain's Burlesque Patterns* (Dallas, 1960), p. 78.

9. *DE,* IV, 108–109.

10. "Chinese Banquet," *Call,* 18 Sept. 1864, p. 3; "The Chinese Banquet," *Call,* 20 Sept. 1864, p. 1.

11. "Personal," *Alta,* 3 June 1864, p. 1.

12. For example, in "Right and Left" (*Alta*, 3 July 1864, p. 1) Evans wrote: " 'Was that money I sent you all right?' asked Jones of Stiggers, as he met the latter coming out of a doorway with ground glass numbers over it, at two o'clock in the morning. 'I (hic) sup(hic)pose so, as I (hic) haven't any *left*,' said Stiggers, ruefully shaking his empty pockets." The next day in the *Call* Clemens commented, "Dry as a squeezed orange must be the brain that moved the inditing of that paragraph" ("An 'Altagraph,' " p. 3). Evans usually would rise to such bait and, with ill-concealed irritation, lumberingly criticize Clemens' writing or, more usually, his appearance and personal habits: "the double-headed red man of the *Call*," the "aborigine from the land of sage brush and alkali, whose soubriquet was given him by his friends as indicative of his capacity for doing the drinking for two" ("That's What's the Matter," *Alta*, 24 Aug. 1864, p. 1).

13. SLC to Elisha Bliss, Buffalo, 29 Oct. 1870, TS in MTP.

TIME OFF (pages 85–115)

1. "Answers to Correspondents," *Calif*, 10 June 1865, p. 9, and 17 June 1865, pp. 4–5. Here Mark Twain referred to the song "Lily Dale" as a "lugubrious ditty," repeating his phrase from "School Children's Rehearsal."

2. "Meteoric," *Call*, 11 Aug. 1864, p. 2.

3. Letter from Mary Josephine Anthony to Mrs. Bishop, 1925, MTP.

4. See "First Annual Fair of the Washoe Agricultural, Mining and Mechanical Society" dated Carson City, 19 Oct. 1863, *MTEnt*, pp. 80–86. Under the standing title "Thirteenth Annual State Fair" the

Sacramento *Union* printed fair reports on 11, 12, 13, 14, 15, and 17 Sept. 1866. Clemens wrote on the races and stock exhibitions at the Union Park track, but he did not cover the exhibits and speeches at the Agricultural Pavilion. See Edgar M. Branch, "Mark Twain Reports the Races in Sacramento," *Huntington Library Quarterly*, XXXII (1969), 179–186.

5. Edgar M. Branch, " 'My Voice Is Still for Setchell': A Background Study of 'Jim Smiley and His Jumping Frog,' " *PMLA*, LXXXII (Dec. 1967), 591–601.

6. Clemens may have reviewed *The War of the Roses*, a comedy by Elizabeth Chamberlain Wright, a San Francisco writer of light sentimental verse (under the names Carrie Carlton and Topsy Turvy). On 6 August the *Call's* drama critic gave advance notice of the play's première at the Metropolitan Theater and, after summarizing part of the plot, called for a good turnout to help the "talented" author, "a lady of education . . . a mother with a family to support and educate by her unaided efforts" ("The Theatres, Etc.," p. 3). Three days later the reporter in effect excused his preperformance enthusiasm by dusting off the play in these words: "There is some merit in it; but as acted, it does not bear out the promise of the MS. Like most all the efforts of tyros in dramatic literature, it is badly jointed and has too much talk. Furthermore, the first scene may be called an advertising one, for the names of several business houses in this city are rather neatly 'rung' into the dialogue. Perhaps the authoress thought it was perfectly consistent with the character of the piece; perhaps, like the Directory, she got so much per name. If the

latter supposition be correct, we can give the lady credit for business shrewdness, if we cannot for literary excellence" ("The Theatres, Etc.," 9 Aug. 1864, p. 3).

7. "A Voice for Setchell," *Calif,* 27 May 1865, p. 9; "People and Things," Buffalo *Express,* 11 Sept. 1869, p. 2. Favorable notices and items about individual minstrel players and performances occurred frequently in the *Call* during Clemens' term of employment. See, for example, "Startling!—the Latest General Order" (24 July 1864, p. 2), "New Idea" (4 Aug. 1864, p. 2), or almost any theater column. Some of the minstrels praised in the *Call* were Ben Cotton, Billy Birch, Sam Wells, Dave Wambold, Charley Backus, A. J. Talbott, W. Bernard, Otto Burbank, Johnny De Angelis, George Winship, J. W. McAndrews, and Tommy Peel. In old age Mark Twain nostalgically recalled the art of the minstrel show, naming Billy Rice, Birch, Wambold, and Backus (*MTE,* pp. 110–118).

8. "Theatrical Record," *Call,* 28 Aug. 1864, p. 1.

9. "A Pioneer Abroad and at Home," *Alta,* 2 Sept. 1864, p. 1. Also see: "Dramatic and Musical," *GE,* 4 Sept. 1864, p. 5; "Musical and Dramatic," *Calif,* 3 Sept. 1864, p. 12.

10. "The Christian Commission," *Call,* 24 Aug. 1864, p. 1.

11. "Thoughts and Things," *GE,* 28 Aug. 1864, p. 3; "Happenings of the Week," *Calif,* 1 Oct. 1864, p. 12. Using newspaper reports in the *Alta* and *Bull,* Dorothy H. Huggins has given an account of the fair in "Women in War-Time, San Francisco, 1864," *California Historical Society Quarterly,* XXIV (Sept. 1945), 261–266.

12. "'Mark Twain's' Letter," *Call,* 23 July 1863, p. 1, reprinted *Twainian,* XI (Jan./Feb. 1952), 3–4.

13. "The Ladies' Fair," *Call,* 8 Sept. 1864, p. 1.

14. "Reflections on the Sabbath," *GE,* 18 Mar. 1866, p. 3, reprinted *WG,* pp. 115–116. Also see "Important Correspondence," *Calif,* 6 May 1865, p. 9, reprinted *SSix,* pp. 166–175.

15. "Still Further Concerning that Conundrum," *Calif,* 15 Oct. 1864, p. 1, reprinted *SSix,* pp. 131–135.

16. "The Art Gallery," *Call,* 2 Sept. 1864, p. 1.

17. "The Projected Fair of the Mechanics' Institute," *Call,* 14 Apr. 1864, p. 1.

18. "Curious Compounds," *Mining & Scientific Press,* IX (10 Sept. 1864), 170.

19. "Mark Twain's Interior Notes —No. 3," *Bull,* 7 Dec. 1866, p. 5, reprinted *MTWY,* pp. 208–210.

20. "California Branch of the U.S. Sanitary Commission," *Call,* 3 Sept. 1864, p. 1.

SUDDEN DEATH (pages 116–124)

1. "A Terrible Monster Caged" (Item 127), *Call,* 4 Sept. 1864, p. 1.

2. "The Lick House Ball," *GE,* 27 Sept. 1863, p. 4, reprinted *WG,* pp. 33–38.

3. SLC to JC and PM, [San Francisco] 25 Sept. 1864, TS in MTP, from a postscript omitted by Paine in *MTL,* I, 99–100. Copyright © 1969 by The Mark Twain Company.

4. Walter F. Frear, *Mark Twain and Hawaii* (Chicago, 1947), p. 338.

5. *DE,* III, 225.

FIVE SKETCHES (pages 125–135)

1. "The People's Excursion," *Call,* 7 Aug. 1864, p. 2.

2. *GE,* 3 July 1864, p. 4, reprinted *WG,* pp. 83–88.

3. *Pacific Monthly*, XI (July 1864), 753–754.

4. SLC to OC and MC, San Francisco, 12 Aug. [1864], TS in MTP.

5. "Board of Supervisors," *Bull*, 7 June 1864, p. 3.

6. "Board of Supervisors," *Call*, 28 June 1864, p. 3.

7. " 'Now and Then,' " *Alta*, 15 Aug. 1864, p. 1, describes a day's outing to San José and Warm Springs by a group of San Francisco men, one of whom was the reporter. From the context I assume that this was the trip Clemens described, and I have taken some of my information from the Alta report.

8. DW 1, untitled TS in MTP, addressed to "EDS. GOLDEN ERA" and copied from the MS in the Samuel C. Webster collection. Rice, whom Clemens knew well in Nevada, may have been one of the group.

9. "Unfortunate Thief," Stockton Daily *Independent*, 14 Jan. 1863, p. 1, reprinted in Paul Fatout, *Mark Twain in Virginia City* (Bloomington, 1964), p. 28.

PART TWO: CRIME AND COURT REPORTER

STATION HOUSE AND JAIL   (pages 139–152)

1. "Insane," *Call*, 8 July 1864, p. 3.

2. "The Christmas Fireside," *Calif*, 23 Dec. 1865, p. 4, reprinted *DE*, VII, pp. 44–48, as "The Story of the Bad Little Boy."

3. "A Revolutionary Patriot," *Call*, 20 Aug. 1864, p. 1.

4. "In the Station House," *Selected Shorter Writings of Mark Twain*, ed. Walter Blair (Boston, 1962), pp. 31–32.

5. "One Day for Reflection," *Call*, 31 July 1864, p. 3.

6. "Police Judge's Court," *San Francisco Municipal Reports for the Fiscal Year 1863/64* (San Francisco, 1864), pp. 137–139.

7. "The Roll of Honor," *Alta*, 2 Aug. 1864, p. 1.

8. "Goldsmith's Friend Abroad Again," *Galaxy*, X (Nov. 1870), 727–729, reprinted *Contributions to The Galaxy . . .* , pp. 91–93.

9. "They Got Her Out," *Call*, 10 Aug. 1864, p. 1.

THE POLICE COURT (pages 153–187)

1. "Plethoric," *Call*, 13 Sept. 1864, p. 3.

2. "Police Court," *Call*, 20 July 1864, p. 3.

3. For these and similar examples, see in the 1864 *Call:* "Police Court Doings," 24 July, p. 3; "Police Calendar," 4 Aug., p. 3; "Forfeited Bail," 7 Aug., p. 3; "Police Judge's Budget," 11 Aug., p. 2; "Growing," 12 Aug., p. 3; "Judge Shepheard's School of Discipline," 17 Aug., p. 3; "Sentenced Yesterday," 23 Aug., p. 3; "The Forlorn Hope," 27 Aug., p. 3; "Police Calendar," 30 Aug., p. 2; "Police Subjects," 1 Sept., p. 2; "The Roll of Fame," 2 Sept., p. 3; "Large," 11 Sept., p. 3.

4. "The Same Subject Continued," *Call*, 20 Aug. 1864, p. 1.

5. "The Black Hole of San Francisco," in "San Francisco Letter" dated 29 Dec. [1865], *TE*, reprinted *MTCor*, pp. 91–95.

6. "Gorgeous New Romance, by Fitz Smythe!" and "Another Romance" in "San Francisco Letter" dated 11 Jan. [1866], *TE*, reprinted *MTCor*, pp. 24–32.

7. "More of the Fine Arts and Polite Literature," *Call*, 13 Aug. 1864, p. 2.

8. "Goldsmith's Friend Abroad Again," *Galaxy*, X (Nov. 1870), 729,

reprinted *Contributions to* The Galaxy . . . , p. 93.

9. "An Infamous Villain Caged," *Alta*, 6 Aug. 1864, p. 1.

10. "Green-back Theft," *Call*, 10 July 1864, p. 3.

11. "San Francisco Letter" dated 19 Dec. [1865], *TE*, clipping in *YS*, opposite p. 43.

12. Ibid. Earlier Twain had written: "Blitz is a small man, but if there were eighteen more vacancies to fill in the police department, I think Blitz would come nearer filling the whole lot by himself and filling them well and doing justice to the position than any eighteen men in San Francisco. Blitz does an eternal sight of talking, but he does work enough for the city to cover the sin" ("Twainiana," San Francisco *Examiner*, 8 Nov. 1865, p. 3, from *TE*).

13. For the 1864 *Call* articles referred to in this and the two preceding paragraphs see: "Beasts in the Semblance of Men," 12 June, p. 3; "Hackmen Arrested," 28 June, p. 1; "The Sacrilegious Hack-Driver," 30 June, p. 3; "Attention, Hackmen," 6 Aug., p. 2; "Judicial Strategy," 6 Aug., p. 3; "After the Hackmen," 7 Aug., p. 3; "To the Public . . ." 14 Aug., p. 2; "Insolent Hackmen," 18 Aug., p. 3; "Hackmen at Work Again," 5 Nov., p. 3.

OTHER COURTS (pages 188–193)

1. E. E. Hale, *Stories of the Sea Told by Sailors* (Boston, 1919), pp. 195–225.

2. *DE*, XVI, 281.

SENSATION ITEMS: MURDER AND ATTEMPTED MURDER (pages 194–205)

1. "The Killing of Julius Caesar 'Localized,' " 12 Nov. 1864, p. 1, revised and reprinted *DE*, VII, 352–356.

2. See in the 1864 *Call:* "The Wounded Boy," 19 Aug., p. 2; "False Rumor," 21 Aug., p. 1; "Still Improving," 21 Aug., p. 2; "Henry Meyer," 25 Aug., p. 2; "Henry Meyer," 31 Aug., p. 1.

3. "The Old Thing," *Calif*, 25 Nov. 1865, p. 12, from *TE*, 18 Nov. 1865 and reprinted *MTWY*, pp. 195–196.

4. "Who Lost Them?," *Call*, 20 Aug. 1864, p. 1.

5. In "The Old Thing," *op. cit.*, Mark Twain refers to the man "who half-murdered detective officer Rose in a lonely spot below Santa Clara . . ."

PART THREE: CRITIC AND POLITICAL REPORTER

THE JUDICIAL PROCESS (pages 209–221)

1. "The Evidence in the Case of Smith Vs. Jones," *GE*, 26 June 1864, p. 4, reprinted, *WG*, pp. 77–83.

2. "Are the Times Really so Hard?," *Bull*, 13 Aug. 1864, p. 3.

3. Charles C. Dobie, *San Francisco's Chinatown* (New York, 1936), p. 129.

4. "Complaints against the Prosecuting Attorney," *Bull*, 27 Sept. 1864, p. 3. Also see "Court Proceedings," *Alta*, 1 Oct. 1864, p. 1, and 6 Oct. 1864, p. 1.

5. See "A Hotel Thief Arrested," *Call*, 14 Aug., p. 1, and "Mark Mayer Ahead on the Home Stretch," *Call*, 8 Sept. 1864, p. 3.

6. See, e.g., "Inspiration of Louderback" in "San Francisco Letter" dated 29 Dec. [1865], *TE*, reprinted *MTCor*, pp. 95–97.

7. "Good from Louderback"

(Item 193), *Call,* 26 Aug. 1864, p. 2.

8. "Young Mother" in "Answers to Correspondents," *Calif,* 24 June 1865, pp. 4–5.

THE POLICE POWER (pages 222–225)

1. I have found no record of Steve Gillis' arrest in the fall of 1864 or of any difficulty Clemens had at that time with the police, which is the reason Paine gives (*MTB,* I, 265–266) for Clemens' visit to Jackass Hill. Nor in 1864 had Clemens begun his *TE* letters attacking the police. Therefore it is not clear that Chief Burke either held a grudge against him in 1864, as Paine believed, or that he had reason to. Since Paine's chronology for this period is not always accurate, the Gillis arrest may have occurred after Clemens' return from Jackass Hill and before his attacks on the police, which began in 1865.

Clemens once admitted that he had spent a night in prison for drunkenness. Although this jailing happened in San Francisco, it came considerably later than autumn 1864. After his night in the lockup he appeared before Alfred Barstow, justice of the peace for the Second Township, who released him. Barstow had first been elected to the bench on 18 October 1865. In the column "Our San Francisco Correspondence" (*News,* 22 Jan. 1866, p. 2) Albert S. Evans (Amigo) compared the stench of the city slaughterhouses to the "horrible density . . . which prevails in the Police Court room when the Bohemian of the Sage-Brush is in the dock for being drunk over night"—an obvious hit at Mark Twain elaborated in Evans' column one week later. A good possibility is that the jailing occurred in January 1866 after Clemens had begun his attacks on the

force. See *Mark Twain's Notebook,* ed. Albert B. Paine (New York, 1935), pp. 399–400; "Death of Alfred Barstow," *Call,* 14 Mar. 1895, p. 14, available in the Byram Scrapbook No. I, p. 40, California Historical Society, San Francisco.

2. *MTB,* I, 253–254.

3. L. P. Ward to SLC, 23 Feb. 1889, MTP. Clemens' letter is not extant.

4. MTP. The envelope is postmarked 2 Oct. 1903 and addressed to Clemens in Elmira.

5. "Acting on Good Advice to the Letter," *Alta,* 2 Dec. 1865, p. 1.

6. "Delightful Romance," San Francisco *Dramatic Chronicle,* 5 Dec. 1865, p. 4.

7. "San Francisco Letter" dated 15 Feb. [1866], *TE,* clipping in *YS,* p. 53.

THE BUREAUCRATIC MIND (pages 226–245)

1. *MTB,* I, 258.

2. See in the 1864 *Call:* "Municipal Records," 30 June, p. 2; "Police Record," 24 Aug., p. 3; "Mechanics' Fair," 1 Sept., p. 2.

3. *MTL,* I, 100.

4. "San Francisco Letter" dated 8 Jan. [1866], *TE,* clipping in *YS,* p. 41.

5. SLC to Jervis Langdon, Cleveland, 29 Dec. [1868], *The Love Letters of Mark Twain,* pp. 36–40. In an undated letter, MTP, Swain cordially invited Clemens to dinner at his San Francisco home.

6. Other indications in addition to Item 173 suggest Clemens' presence at the weekly meetings. The *Call* local was familiar with the meeting room and requested spittoons for the reporters ("New Board Rooms," *Call,* 13 July 1864, p. 2). Unlike his fellow locals, Clemens sometimes punctuated his weekly reports with

sassy questions or comments labeled "Q" or "Rep.," as he had in reporting the Nevada legislature. For example, when the "lady teachers" complained of their meager pay raise, a board member replied that "they had overlooked the fact that they were going to be paid for a three weeks' vacation," whereupon the reporter inserted in brackets: "He forgot to state, though, that if the new wages won't pay board and lodging while the ladies are at work, it won't pay those expenses in vacation either" ("Board of Education," *Call*, 13 July 1864, p. 3). The board meetings left an impression on him which was recorded a year later. In speaking of a man whose "intellect is so dense that it would take the augur of common sense longer to bore into it than it would to bore through Mont Blanc with a boiled carrot," Mark Twain wrote: "I have found that man. And I have found him—not in Stockton—not in Congress—not even in the Board of Education . . ." ("Charming Simplicity" in "Answers to Correspondents," *Calif*, 17 June 1865, p. 4).

7. "The Personnel of the Board of Education," *Call*, 26 Apr. 1864, p. 1. Pelton later admitted writing this unsigned article. Because Clemens' sympathies lay with Pelton in his struggle with the Board of Education, it is worth noting that Pope voted with the majority of board members to dismiss Pelton as principal of Rincon School. Pope then chaired a committee that considered and denied a petition from 1,500 citizens requesting Pelton's reinstatement. For some time he had been chairman of a board committee on the history of the city schools. His report, discussed at the board meeting of 20 September, credited Colonel Thomas J. Nevins rather than

Pelton with founding the public school system. The *Call* reporter observed that the purpose of the discussion presumably was "to afford members of the Board an opportunity of saying something about Mr. Pelton" ("Board of Education," *Call*, 21 Sept. 1864, p. 3).

8. In "Board of Education," 10 Aug. 1864, p. 3, the *Call* local wrote: "It was stated that almost the whole of the Grammar Class of the Mason Street School had declined giving their participation in the exercises at the National Freedmen's Association's Concert, by the Public School children, at Platt's Hall, on Friday, August 12th.

"Mr. Pope suggested that the class referred to be informed that they will be required to come out and give their aid on that occasion. The subject gave rise to an inordinate amount of speech making, in which the words 'patriotism' and 'stigma' occurred frequently. The matter was referred to a Committee, to act."

9. SLC to JC and PM, 25 Sept. 1864, *MTL*, I, 100 and, for the last sentence, omitted by Paine, TS inserted in annotated MTP copy of *MTL*, I, opposite p. 101. Copyright © 1969 by The Mark Twain Company.

10. SLC to JC and PM, 25 Sept. 1864, TS inserted in annotated MTP copy of *MTL*, I, opposite p. 101, a passage Paine omitted. Copyright © 1969 by The Mark Twain Company. Given Clemens' active interest in the appointment of Dr. Harris, it seems likely that he wrote "The Election of Coroner" (*Call*, 18 Sept. 1864, p. 1) signed "Citizen." This piece appeared the day before the board met. It cautioned the members not to "thrust on the people old dilapidated characters" and stated, "There are eminent, qualified applicants to se-

lect from, who have been here for years, who are identified with the interests of the city, and who will confer honor on the position." Dr. Harris appears to have qualified in most or all of these respects.

11. SLC to JC and PM, Steamboat Springs, 19 Aug. [1863], TS in MTP, omitted from *MTL*, I, 93.

12. "In Ecstasies," San Francisco *Dramatic Chronicle*, 13 Nov. 1865, p. 4. "Cheerful Magnificence" (11 Nov., p. 3) began the attack.

13. "San Francisco Letter" dated 29 Dec. [1865], *TE*, clipping in *YS*, p. 57, reprinted *WG*, pp. 108–109, as "Busted, and Gone Abroad."

14. "The Mining Mania," *Call*, 22 May 1864, p. 2.

15. Ibid. In "Mining Review for 1864" the tri-monthly newspaper *Mercantile Gazette and Shipping Monthly* of 12 Jan. 1865 noted that in May stocks began to drop seriously and that "in the course of a few months they depreciated, with slight exceptions, more than one half, some of them falling even lower than this, and very many being wholly stripped of the imaginary value before attached to them. So general and rapid was this decline, that within four months from the time it set in[,] the nominal capital represented by these stocks had entirely disappeared, to the amount of many millions" (*Bancroft Scraps: Mining in California*, Vol. 51: 2, p. 460. Courtesy of the Bancroft Library). These four months correspond closely to the period Clemens was on the *Call*.

16. "Lost Riches," *Calif*, 13 Aug. 1864, p. 8.

17. "The Crisis," *Call*, 14 Jan. 1864, p. 2; "What's the Matter?," *Call*, 3 Feb. 1864, p. 2.

18. "Causes of the Panic in the Mining Stock Market, and the Rem-

edy," unidentified paper of 8 June 1864, *Bancroft Scraps*, Vol. 52: 1, pp. 35–36. Courtesy of the Bancroft Library.

19. "Mining Assessments," *Calif*, 10 Sept. 1864, p. 8.

20. As quoted in "Concerning the Monte Diablo Mines," *Call*, 26 June 1864, p. 3.

21. SLC to JC and PM, Virginia City, 18 July [1863], TS in MTP.

22. "The Evidence in the Case of Smith Vs. Jones," *GE*, 26 June 1864, p. 4. The narrator in *Roughing It* pays "oppressive" assessments and mentions a mining board that authorizes a tunnel 250 feet long under a hill twenty-five feet through because it was "living on the 'assessments'" (*DE*, III, 209, 243).

23. "The Sinking Ship Deserted," *Call*, 30 July 1864, p. 2.

24. Clemens regularly plugged the Hale & Norcross mine in his 1863 *Call* letters. In " 'Mark Twain's' Letter" published 13 Aug. 1863 he gave $2,600 as the price of H & N stock. See *Twainian*, XI (Mar./Apr. 1952), 3.

25. *Report of the Committee of Stockholders of the Real Del Monte Consolidated Gold and Silver Mining Co.* (San Francisco, 1864), p. 8.

26. "Arrest of Bishop Kavanagh [sic]," *News*, 22 July 1864, p. 2. Also see in the 1864 *Call*: "Bishop Kavanaugh at Liberty," 28 July, p. 1; "Bishop Kavanaugh's Statement," 13 Aug., p. 1. General McDowell's statement also may be found in *The War of the Rebellion*, Series I, Vol. L, Part II (Washington, 1897), p. 918.

27. The man who ate raw turnips, *DE*, III, 181–182. Mark Twain reported Van Bokkelen's measures to put down a lynch mob in Virginia City when it was "infested with thieves, assassins and incendiaries"

("Dispatches by the State Line," *Call*, 3 Sept. 1863, p. 1).

ECHOES OF THE REBELLION (pages 246–278)

1. Benjamin Franklin Gilbert, "San Francisco Harbor Defense During the Civil War," *California Historical Society Quarterly*, XXXIII (Sept. 1954), 229–240.

2. "The Anglo-Chinese Fleet," *Call*, 16 Feb. 1864, p. 2.

3. "A Supposed Pirate in the Offing—Great Sensation in the Harbor," *Call*, 12 May 1864, p. 2. See in the 1864 *Call:* "Chasing a Pirate," 13 May, p. 3; "Seizure of a Vessel Laden with Arms," 6 Aug., p. 1; "Contraband of War," 7 Aug., p. 1; "Why the Muskets were Seized," 9 Aug., p. 1; "Arms Taken in Charge by the Authorities," 21 Aug., p. 1. Also see "Another Seizure of Arms Destined for Mexico," *Alta*, 6 Aug., p. 1, and "Our San Francisco Correspondence," *News*, 19 Nov. 1864, p. 2.

4. "More About that Fleet," *Call*, 20 Feb. 1864, p. 1.

5. "Mark Twain's Trial Trip," *GE*, 19 Nov. 1865, p. 5, from *TE* and reprinted Lawrence E. Mobley, "Mark Twain and the *Golden Era*," *Papers of the Bibliographical Society of America*, LVIII (Jan./Mar. 1964), 8–23.

6. The speech is reprinted in Edgar M. Branch, "Major Perry and the Monitor *Camanche:* An Early Mark Twain Speech," *American Literature*, XXXIX (May 1967), 170–179.

7. See " 'Mark Twain's' Letter," 15 July, 23 July, 3 Sept., all p. 1, reprinted *Twainian*, XI (Jan./Feb., May/June 1952), 2–4, 1–2.

8. "Nevada's Bounty," *TE* [23 Mar. 1864?], Moffett Scrapbook 4, p. 15, MTP.

9. SLC to MC, Virginia City, 20 May 1864, *MTEnt*, pp. 190–191. Mark Twain used the phrase "Army of the Lord" in "Grand Austin Sanitary Flour-Sack Progress Through Storey and Lyon Counties!," *Bull*, 19 May 1864, p. 5, from *TE*, 17 May.

10. SLC to OC, Virginia City, 25 May 1864, *MTEnt*, pp. 201–202.

11. See Frear, *Mark Twain and Hawaii*, p. 399. As "Capt. McKee," Makee also is mentioned in Mark Twain's letter to the New York *Tribune*, 6 Jan. 1873 (Frear, p. 493). The earlier *Call* notice of Makee's gift is "Munificent Donation," 28 July 1864, p. 2.

12. JC to "my dear children," St. Louis, 28 Sept. [1864], Webster, *Mark Twain, Business Man*, p. 82.

13. SLC to JC and PM, San Francisco, 4 Dec. 1866, *MTL*, I, 122.

14. Ibid. Mark Twain poked friendly fun at Stebbins several times, perhaps too trustingly. For example, he wrote: "Rev. Mr. Stebbins . . . did precisely what I thought of doing myself at the time of the earthquake, but had no opportunity—he came down out of his pulpit and embraced a woman. Some say it was his wife" ("The Cruel Earthquake," *News*, 13 Oct. 1865, p. 2, from *TE*). The *Call* of 10 Oct. 1865 reported that when the quake brought down an organ pipe in the midst of the Sunday service, Stebbins made a "facile egress" from his church ("The Earthquake on Sunday," p. 1).

15. "Organized Gang of Robbers in the Interior," *Call*, 2 July 1864, p. 1: made up of dispatches to *Bull* of 1 July.

16. "Our San Francisco Correspondence," *News*, 22 July 1864, p. 2.

17. "Robbers and Guerrillas," *Call*, 2 July 1864, p. 1.

18. S. H. Parker in "Mass Meeting of the Union League," *Alta,* 9 Sept. 1864, p. 1.

19. *DE,* XIII, 10, 11.

20. "An Abolition Outrage," *Call,* 13 Sept. 1864, p. 1.

21. See Edgar M. Branch, "Samuel Clemens and the Copperheads of 1864," *Mad River Review,* II (Winter/Spring 1967), [3]–20.

22. "Our San Francisco Correspondence," *News,* 26 Sept. 1864, p. 2.

23. In Nevada Clemens had reported territorial politics for the *Enterprise* on several occasions. These assignments brought him into close touch with politicians and taught him much about party organization and political maneuvering. They exposed him to the rhythms and clichés of political oratory. Very likely his acquaintance with the politicians of Nevada did little to elevate his opinion of man or of politics. Thus in the early 1860's, while his political sympathies became increasingly "northern," his skepticism about politics itself deepened. The two developments are not incompatible when regarded as expressions of an engrained moralism. In 1876 he was to write Howells, "It seems odd to find myself interested in an election. I never was before. And I can't seem to get over my repugnance to reading or thinking about politics, yet" (SLC to William Dean Howells, [Hartford] 14 Sept. [1876], *Mark Twain–Howells Letters,* I, 151). His repugnance may have derived partly from his political experience in the West. He probably was not "interested" in the 1864 election if by that we mean either a disposition to identify closely with a party or a belief in politics as a saving activity.

24. In the section "Mary, Rincon School," *Calif,* 1 July 1865, pp. 4–5.

25. "Letter from 'Mark Twain,'" *Alta,* 8 Jan. 1868, p. 1. Among the three dozen ideal first-class passengers were Lewis Leland, John McComb, Frank Soulé, R. B. Swain, Emperor Norton, Sam Platt, Horatio Stebbins, and Charles Wadsworth. "Frank Bret Harte, George Barnes, Mark Twain and 300 other newspaper men" were consigned to the steerage.

26. "Democratic State Convention. Second Day's Proceedings," Weekly *Democratic Press,* 10 Sept. 1864, pp. 4–5.

27. "Copperhead Mass Meeting," *Alta,* 9 Sept. 1864, p. 1.

A SELECTED BIBLIOGRAPHY

The following list is limited to major commentaries and sources of information on the history of the San Francisco *Call* and on Clemens' connection with that newspaper.

Ayers, James J. *Gold and Sunshine: Reminiscences of Early California*. Boston, 1922.

Barnes, George E. "Mark Twain. As He Was Known During His Stay on the Pacific Slope," San Francisco *Morning Call*, 17 April 1887, p. 1.

Branch, Edgar M. " 'My Voice Is Still for Setchell': A Background Study of 'Jim Smiley and His Jumping Frog,' " *PMLA*, LXXXII (December 1967), 591–601.

———. "Samuel Clemens and the Copperheads of 1864," *Mad River Review*, II (Winter–Spring 1967), 3–20.

Brownell, George H. "About Mark Twain's Job on the San Francisco *Call*," *Twainian*, III (May 1944), 4–6.

Bruce, John Roberts. *Gaudy Century, the Story of San Francisco's Hundred Years of Robust Journalism*. New York, 1948.

Bunje, Emil T. H., F. J. Schmitz, and H. Penn, *Journals of the Golden Gate, 1846–1936*. Berkeley, 1936.

Clemens, Samuel L. "The Brummel-Arabella Fragment," *Mark Twain's Satires & Burlesques*, ed. Franklin R. Rogers. Berkeley and Los Angeles, 1967.

———. "Disgraceful Persecution of a Boy," *Galaxy*, IX (May 1870), 722–724. Reprinted in *Contributions to* The Galaxy *1868–1871 by Mark Twain*, ed. Bruce R. McElderry Jr. Gainesville, Florida, 1961.

———. *Mark Twain in Eruption*, ed. Bernard DeVoto. New York, c. 1940.

———. *Mark Twain's Letters*, ed. Albert B. Paine. 2 vols. New York and London, c. 1917.

———. *Roughing It*, Definitive Edition, Vols. III and IV. New York, 1922.

———. "Mark's Letters to San Francisco *Call* from Virginia City, Nevada Territory, July 9th to November 19th, 1863," ed. Austin E. Hutcheson.

Twainian, XI (January/February, March/April, May/June 1952), 1–4 each
number [Letters 1–10].

————. "Twain's Letters in San Francisco *Call* While a Reporter on the
Enterprise," ed. Austin E. Hutcheson, *Twainian,* VIII (September/October
1949), 1–2; IX (March/April 1950), 3–4 [Letters 1 and 2].

Clemens, Will M. *Mark Twain: His Life and Work.* San Francisco, 1892.

Cummins (Mighels), Ella Sterling. *The Story of the Files.* San Francisco, 1893.

Evans, Albert S. "Our San Francisco Correspondence," Gold Hill *Evening
News,* 2 July 1864, p. 2, and 15 October 1864, p. 3.

Fitch, George K. "Memorable Events in the History of the Call," San Francisco
Morning Call, 19 December 1897, p. 19.

Hart, Jerome A. *In Our Second Century.* San Francisco, 1931.

Kemble, Edward C. *A History of California Newspapers, 1846–1858,* ed. Helen
Harding Bretnor. Los Gatos, California, 1962.

Kipling, Rudyard. *From Sea to Sea.* New York, 1914.

Mark Twain Papers, University of California Library, Berkeley. Unpublished
correspondence between Clemens and his family, William Wright, Franklin
Soulé, Lewis P. Ward, John C. Pelton, *et alii.*

Millard, Bailey. "Mark Twain in San Francisco," *Bookman,* XXXI (June
1910), 369–373.

Paine, Albert Bigelow. *Mark Twain, A Biography.* 3 vols. New York, c. 1912.

"Past and Present," San Francisco *Morning Call,* 10 March 1878, pp. 1–2.

"The Story of the Call," San Francisco *Morning Call,* 19 December 1897, pp.
18–19.

Verdenal, D. F. "In New York," San Francisco *Sunday Chronicle,* 10 April
1887, p. 3.

Young, John P. *Journalism in California.* San Francisco, [1915].

INDEX

(Newspapers and periodicals are indexed under place of publication. For listings such as churches, schools, theaters, courts, museums, and saloons, San Francisco should be understood as the location when no other city is indicated. *Call* items and citations in the notes are not indexed, but Clemens' other writings mentioned in the text are listed under *Clemens, Samuel L., works of.* Names of persons included in Clemens' *Call* items are indexed when editorial commentary on them is provided.)

Esmeralda mining district (Nevada), 104, 238
Eureka Minstrel Hall, 8
Evans, Albert S. ("Fitz Smythe," "Amigo," "Altamonte," "Colonel Moustache") : *Call* local, 16; reporting characterized, 20–21, 30–31, 138; feud with Clemens, 33, 81–82, 199, 223, 235, 310 n12, 314 n1; on Clemens' occupation in 1864, 27; on Clemens' *Call* reporting, 29, 30; pseudonyms, 82; Armand Leonidas Stiggers (character), 30, 82–84 *passim*, 310 n12; printed Clemens' speech, 250; feared Confederate uprising, 260, 265; on Clemens' career, 305 n80; on Clemens' leaving *Call*, 305 n85; on Clemens in court, 314 n1

"Fair Rosamund" (Rosamund Clifford), 102
Farwell, Willard B., 247, 248
Female College of the Pacific, 113
Ferguson, George N., 92, 93
Field, Stephen J., 189, 248
First Baptist Church, 257
First Presbyterian Church, 66, 100
First Unitarian Church, 61, 257, 258
Fish, Benjamin, 92
Fitch, Thomas, 286, 306 n107
"Fitz Smythe." *See* Evans, Albert S.
Flag saloon, 224, 225
Flora Temple (horse), 92, 93
Folsom (California), 73, 260
Forner, Jacob B., 148, 161, 222–225
Forrest, Edwin, 96
Fort Point: Clemens at, 8, 248; mentioned, 246
Foster, Edward, 119, 120
Foster, John, 142, 143
Fourth District Court of California, 192, 238
Franklin, Benjamin, 126
Franks, Frederick, 40, 41
Freeport (California), 120
French Benevolent Society, 151
French Hospital, 151, 152

Galaxy, 24

Galloway, William, 192
Gamble, Alexander, 238
Gardner, Rowland B., 122–124 *passim*
George M. Patchen, Jr. (horse), 92
Gerry, Dr. S. Russell, 165–169 *passim*
Gibson, Mrs. Henrietta Molineux, 61, 62
Gilbert's Market Street Museum, 87, 90
Gilbert's Melodeon, 8
Gillan, Barney, 185, 186, 187
Gillis, James, 2, 273
Gillis, Stephen E., 10, 133, 134, 224, 273, 314 n1 "The Police . . ."
Gold Canyon (Nevada), 241
Golden Age (ship), 128
Golden Circle, The, 258
Golden City (ship), 64, 65, 124
Gold Hill (Nevada), Clemens in, 135
Gold Hill *Daily News*, 10, 33, 82, 243, 260
Goliah (ship), 192, 247, 248
Goodman, Joseph T., 1, 3, 6, 10, 19, 223, 286
Goodwin, John D., 273, 274
Goss and Lambard's Iron Works (Sacramento), 119, 121
Gould and Curry (mine), 109, 237, 238, 255, 284
Graben-Hoffmann, Gustav, 102
Grass Valley Mining Company, 239, 240
Grass Valley *National*, 74
Green, Alleck P., 156, 157
Gregg, John, 102
Grey, Lady Jane, 102
Gridley, Joseph C., 21
Gridley, Ruel C., 122, 254, 306 n107
Grissim, Wilson T., 92, 93
Gross, Frank W., 16, 82
Grotjan, Mrs. Louisa, 99, 101

Hale and Norcross (mine), 11, 19, 27, 237–240 *passim*, 316 n24
Halfmoon Bay, 246
Hall, Mrs. Eliza Jane, 108
Hall, R. F., 260, 263
Hambleton, J. Douglas, 275, 276

SAN FRANCISCO

DATE DUE

GAYLORD

PRINTED IN U.S.A.